American Wind Band Series
Series Editor: Raoul F. Camus

This series is devoted to research in all aspects of American wind band and wind music, including waits; hautboys; *Harmoniemusik*; Janissary music; brass, concert, marching, circus, military, and symphonic bands; symphonic wind ensembles; wind orchestras; and wind symphonies. Studies dealing with fifers, drummers, and buglers and their ensembles are also important aspects of American wind music not to be overlooked.

A History of the Trombone, by David M. Guion. 2010.

A History of the Trombone

David M. Guion

American Wind Band Series, No. 1

THE SCARECROW PRESS, INC.
Lanham • Toronto • Plymouth, UK
2010

Published by Scarecrow Press, Inc.
A wholly owned subsidiary of The Rowman & Littlefield Publishing Group, Inc.
4501 Forbes Boulevard, Suite 200, Lanham, Maryland 20706
http://www.scarecrowpress.com

Estover Road, Plymouth PL6 7PY, United Kingdom

British Library Cataloguing in Publication Information Available

Library of Congress Cataloging-in-Publication Data

Guion, David M., 1948–
    A history of the trombone / David M. Guion.
        p. cm. — (American wind band ; no. 1)
    Includes bibliographical references and index.
    ISBN 978-0-8108-7445-9 (cloth : alk. paper)
    1. Trombone—History. 2. Trombone. I. Title.
ML965.G83 2010
788.9'309—dc22   2010000846

Printed in the United States of America

For Pat, who has tolerated my disappearing to the library
and computer room for our whole married life.

Contents

Illustrations

Figures

Tables

Foreword

With the publication of David M. Guion's *A History of the Trombone*, Scarecrow Press launches a new series of scholarly works. The *American Wind Band* joins such other distinguished Scarecrow series as *American Folk Music and Musicians*, *Studies in Jazz*, *Film Score Guides*, and *Europea: Ethnomusicologies and Modernities*.

As the series title indicates, the emphasis is on American wind music, but since American music, or more correctly musics, have so many diverse roots and heritages, it is important to consider them as well. So it is with this history of the trombone: while chapters dealing with the instrument's early history are naturally European-based, American performers, performance styles, ensembles, social milieus, and the literature of a variety of musics are featured once the trombone comes into its own in the nineteenth century.

Guion's research is praiseworthily extensive; he has gleaned nuggets of information from a wide variety of sources, some common, but many unusual and esoteric, known only to the serious scholar. We believe this volume sets a very high standard for others to follow, and is a fitting inauguration to a new series.

Future volumes presently under contract include *The Tennessee Tech Tuba Ensemble and R. Winston Morris: A 40th Anniversary Retrospective* by Charles A. McAdams and Richard Perry and *Women's Military Bands during World War II* by Jill M. Sullivan.

Raoul F. Camus
Series Editor

Preface

About two and a quarter centuries ago, Charles Burney believed that he could compile enough primary source material to write a general history of music. Burney's travel diaries and comments on his writings make it clear that he frequently felt overwhelmed by the task he had taken on. As he labored over polishing his final draft, surely he realized that there was much more to be discovered, that he had only begun to scratch the surface of the history of music. But just as surely he felt great gratification when he held his publication in his hands for the first time and when, after all his hard work, he found that he had an appreciative readership.

Since the day that Burney rapturously gazed at what he had accomplished, there has been a veritable explosion of writing about music, with countless books, magazines, newspapers, patents, diaries, and whole other categories of source material. Today it requires monumental international cooperation to produce such tools as the *New Grove* or *Musik in Geschichte und Gegenwart*. Even the *Harvard Dictionary of Music* is no longer the work of a single individual.

Individual scholars still write books, of course, but even in such a narrow field as the history of the trombone it has become impossible for one person to have a complete command of even the secondary literature. Primary sources have come to encompass whole categories of material that Burney could not have imagined would hold any useful information, as well as others—such as recordings—that he could not have imagined at all. This is why any book on the subject must he understood as *a* history, not *the* history. On the other hand, fortunately, full-text electronic databases and modern communications technology mean that it is no longer necessary to travel under the difficult circumstances Burney faced for his research.

I was fortunate to find a publisher interested in my doctoral dissertation even before I finished writing it. Once the book appeared, I devoted my research efforts to journal articles on a variety of musical subjects, but always with the intention of eventually writing another book devoted to the entire history of the trombone. My most ambitious article, a study of Felippe Cioffi in *American Music*, took four years to get ready for publication. At that point, more than twelve years ago as I write this, I decided that if my objective was to write a book I had better get started. Subsequent journal articles resulted from research on the book, where I found much more information than could ever fit into a reasonably sized chapter.

In researching the history of the trombone, I wanted to trace the development of the instrument and its repertoire, but I also wanted to examine the people who played it and the conditions that shaped their world. When I was in college, I lost all patience with music- and art-history books that did not take the social, political, and economic context of the time into account, and with general social histories that did not consider music at all. It was immediately apparent when I started to consider a basic structure that I could not give my subject the treatment it deserved with a single chronological narrative.

After a general overview, the book is divided into two parts. The first traces the development of the instrument itself and examines the literature that was written about it. The second traces the history of performance on the trombone—the ensembles in which it participated, the kinds of occasions in which it took part, the people who played it, and the social, intellectual, political, economic, and technological forces that impinged on that history. The trombone has been active in so many different kinds of music during the last two hundred years that the last chapter itself requires multiple chronologies.

Acknowledgments

I am grateful to the staff and the wonderful collection at the Newberry Library in Chicago, where I drafted chapters two, three, five, six, and seven, and interlibrary loan librarians at numerous institutions where I have worked—especially Gaylor Callahan at the University of North Carolina at Greensboro.

Howard Weiner read and commented on every chapter and helped immeasurably with the German translations. He sent me copies of primary source documents by Cornette and Marx and a book with one of his articles, which contains other useful articles as well. No other individual has helped me in so many ways.

Dave Wilken read and commented on my discussion of jazz. Edmund A. Bowles, Dane Heuchemer, Stewart Carter, and Douglas Yeo each gave valuable advice on at least one chapter. Pierpaolo Polzonetti helped me with Italian translations and Mark Schumacher with

French. Wayne Shirley of the Library of Congress sent a photocopy of the third movement of Bristow's second symphony, which includes what are probably the first ever trombone solos in a symphony. Brian Thacker took my Finale files of musical examples and made them beautiful. I received a lot of interesting details via e-mail. Unfortunately, because of a server crash I can no longer identify who sent them, but if any reader recognizes sending me a particular detail, I am grateful to you even though I have no way to remember who you are!

I am also grateful to all the individuals and institutions who supplied me with illustrations and/or gave me permission to use them. They are identified in the captions to each figure. I need to make special mention of Tom Izzo, a freelance musician in the Chicago area who specializes in bass trombone but also plays a variety of other brass, woodwind, string, and percussion instruments. Tom owns more musical instruments, and in particular more trombones (at least twenty), than anyone else I have ever heard of. He graciously allowed me to come to his home to spend an entire morning photographing a selection of his trombones. Finally, I would like to thank Scarecrow's acquisitions editor, Renée Camus, and the series editor, Raoul Camus, for their hard work and encouragement.

CHAPTER ONE

Overview

What Is a Trombone?

Before considering the history of the trombone, it is necessary to know just what a trombone is. It is easy enough to find a definition in dictionaries, encyclopedias, or on the Web, and the instrument is well known by sight. Anyone remotely familiar with music (as it comes to us from Europe and the Americas) would recognize Fig. 1.1 as a trombone. The instrument in Fig. 1.2 has some extra tubing, but not enough to obscure the fact that it, too, is a trombone. Valve trombones like the one in Fig. 1.3 are easy enough to identify, but what about the ones in Fig. 1.4?

Once valves are applied to trombones, the traditional shape of the slide trombone is no longer necessary. All of these instruments, along with some other odd shapes, were manufactured and sold as trombones.

The trombone in Fig. 1.1 appears as one long tube that has been bent into the familiar shape, but it can be disassembled into a number of parts. The large end is called the bell. The other end has a detachable mouthpiece, into which the player blows air to produce the sound. The slide comes immediately after the mouthpiece. It moves back and forth, making the instrument longer or shorter and thus producing lower or higher notes. Sections of straight tubing are sometimes called *yards*, and sections of bent tubing *bows*.

The extra tubing in Fig. 1.2 is two valves, often called *triggers*, which act as adjuncts to the slide. Most often a trombone has only one trigger, operated with the left thumb; if there is a second trigger, it is usually operated with the left middle finger. The valves in Figs. 1.3 and 1.4 replace the slide. These instruments are fingered just like a trumpet.

Trombones are made in several different sizes. Figure 1.5 shows, from left to right, a contrabass trombone with a trigger, a bass trombone with two triggers, a large-bore tenor trombone with a trigger, a small-bore tenor trombone with no trigger, an alto trombone in E♭ with a trigger, an alto trombone in F, a soprano trombone, a sopranino trombone in E♭ and a piccolo trombone. These instruments, all in B♭ unless otherwise specified, comprise only a portion of Tom Izzo's remarkable collection.

Even the traditional shape has undergone some changes over the years. The older models are sometimes called sackbuts, but *sackbut* is only an obsolete English word for trombone. Several manufacturers make modern copies of sixteenth-century instruments. For sackbuts made in the sixteenth century, refer to Figs. 3.4 and 3.5 in chapter 3.

Trombone is actually an Italian word, first attested in 1439 in the archives of Ferrara. Trombones at that time looked nothing like any of the ones already pictured. The entire instrument moved along a single tube. Figure 1.6 shows a drawing of the goddess Luna and her children. Everything in it is connected with something that moves. The musician in the lower right-hand corner is teasing a dog by sliding his trombone toward it.[1] Today we would call this trombone a slide trumpet.

Clearly the word *trombone* has referred to a number of different instruments, designed according to different principles and playing different kinds of music. It would be difficult to find one definition that includes all of these different instruments. One task of a history of the trombone is to explain where the slide trumpet came from, how it became the familiar slide trombone, and how and why valve trombones were developed.

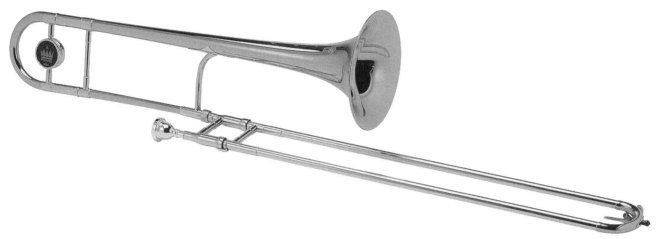

Fig. 1.1.   King 2102C tenor trombone. Courtesy of Conn/Selmer.

Fig. 1.2.   Conn 62H bass trombone. Courtesy of Conn/Selmer.

Fig. 1.3.   King 2166C valve trombone. Courtesy of Conn/Selmer.

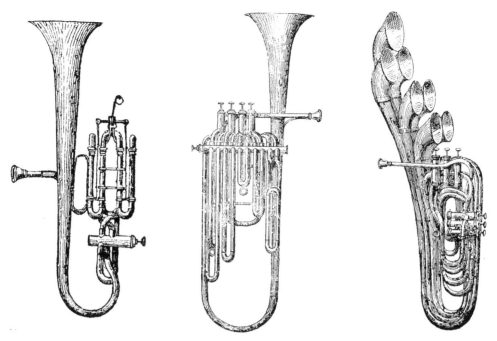

Fig. 1.4. Valve trombones from the 1893 Brussels Museum catalog: in C, in B♭, Sax multiple bell model.

The basic shape of the slide trombone has existed for centuries, but today's trombones are not quite like those of five hundred years ago. The bell profile and mouthpiece differ today from the earliest trombones (sackbuts). They have a greater proportion of conical tubing now than before, as the bore begins to widen before and not after the bell bow. The narrowest bore made today is wider than anything made in the Renaissance or indeed wider than many if not most trombones made through the first half of the twentieth century. Fixed tubular stays have replaced the earlier detachable flat stays. Figure 1.7 shows a few of the structural changes that have taken place, some of which have since fallen by the wayside.

Although the earliest trombones with flaring bells were made by Johann Karl Kodisch in the early eighteenth century, the design did not become commonplace until the nineteenth century. Some other innovations

might have caught on more quickly, but none of them instantly replaced earlier designs. Others failed entirely.

Of all the different sizes of trombones, the tenor in B♭ is the one to which all others are compared. Two sizes built in recent decades are mere toys: the piccolo trombone in B♭ (two octaves higher than the tenor) and the sopranino in E♭ (an octave and a half higher than the tenor). The soprano trombone in B♭ (one octave higher than the tenor), the smallest of any musical use, first appeared in the late seventeenth century. The relationship of all other sizes to the tenor varies by place and time.

In the early seventeenth century, Praetorius provided an illustration of an alto in D, a tenor in A, and basses in D and E.[2] It is different pitch standards since then, not different manufacturing or design, that account for the odd-looking basic pitches. By the late eighteenth century, some (but certainly not all) authors were beginning to write that the alto, tenor, and bass trombones were instruments in B♭. The only acknowledged difference was the size of the mouthpiece.

The practice of "alto" trombone in B♭ predates the earliest literary evidence of it. Familiar soloistic trombone parts from eighteenth-century Vienna and Salzburg, nominally for alto trombone, all lie better on a trombone in B♭ or A than on a smaller trombone in E♭ or D. It is convenient to think of music notated in alto clef as alto trombone music and music in tenor clef as tenor trombone music, but not necessarily correct. Even if that

Fig. 1.5. Selections from the Tom Izzo collection of trombones. Photograph by David M. Guion.

Fig. 1.6.   Slide trumpet. "Children of the Moon" *Das mittelalterlisches Hausbuch* (ca. 1480).

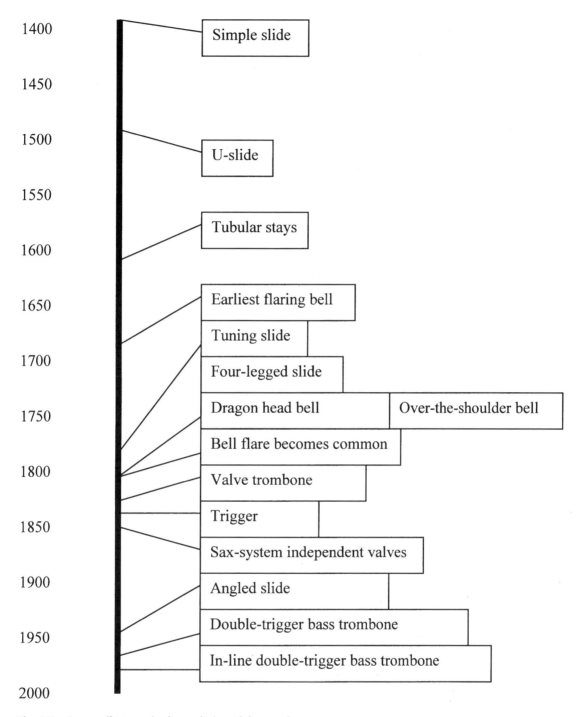

1400
1450
1500
1550
1600
1650
1700
1750
1800
1850
1900
1950
2000

Simple slide

U-slide

Tubular stays

Earliest flaring bell

Tuning slide

Four-legged slide

Dragon head bell

Over-the-shoulder bell

Bell flare becomes common

Valve trombone

Trigger

Sax-system independent valves

Angled slide

Double-trigger bass trombone

In-line double-trigger bass trombone

Fig. 1.7. **Some milestones in the evolution of the trombone.**

is what the composer had in mind, it is by no means a simple matter to determine if the "alto" trombone was in a higher key than the tenor or if the "bass" trombone was lower.[3]

From the end of the nineteenth century to the present, the alto trombone has been an instrument in E♭, although alto trombones in F exist. The bass trombone

has been more complicated. In England, Australia, and so forth, they were in G until after the Second World War. The old E♭ and F basses barely survived past the end of the nineteenth century in the rest of Europe, although Bartók wrote for an F bass in 1918 in *The Miraculous Mandarin* and apparently assumed it was still the standard bass trombone when he wrote *Concerto for*

Orchestra in 1945. Modern bass trombones are in B♭ with a very wide bore, a very large mouthpiece, and at least one trigger. It is still possible to buy new instruments made in F, but they are now called contrabass trombones, not bass trombones, and have a trigger. There are also contrabass trombones in B♭, an octave below the tenor, with a four-legged slide and, very likely, a trigger.

Repertoires and Traditions

More interesting, to me anyway, than the development of the trombone as an artifact is the history of its place in society, the music that it played, and the people who have played it. As it turns out, there is not a single history of the trombone; it has participated in several different traditions. It will clearly be impossible to follow the development of the trombone as an object and all of those traditions in a single chronological sequence. Figure 1.8 and the following general summary present the most important traditions from the beginning through the end of the twentieth century. The oldest of those traditions have ceased. If some newer uses had not been found for the trombone, it would have become obsolete.

The line labeled *Alta* Band Tradition in Fig. 1.8 is actually more ancient than the trombone itself. The term *alta* is never applied to any music later than the early Renaissance, but the tradition lasted much longer. Medieval towns needed watchmen to guard against invasion, fires, and other threats. Visible signals would have been sufficient during the day, but useless at night. Therefore the watchmen signaled with trumpets and shawms. Before long, they acquired musical duties—playing for civic ceremonies and dances—in addition to their watch duties. When the ruling classes established similar bands for their courts, these bands became an important and influential cultural institution. Over the course of the seventeenth century, however, the courts stopped supporting them, and they persisted only in certain German and Italian towns. The remaining Italian bands were abolished as a result of the Napoleonic conquest. Some of the German bands persisted until the middle of the nineteenth century.

In the late Middle Ages no instrument except the organ regularly participated in church services. Others, including the trombone, were heard in church on rare occasions, nearly always associated with the presence of the king or other ruler. Wider use of instruments gradually became acceptable, and churches began to sponsor their own *alta* bands early in the sixteenth century. Some continued to do so throughout the seventeenth century, but in general, churches that hired musicians at all grad-

ually adopted a newer ensemble, the orchestra. Church orchestras in Germany, Italy, and Austria regularly included trombones, so the demise of wind bands at church did not render trombones obsolete. In the nineteenth century, however, fewer royal courts retained their own chapels, but these chapels had made it possible for ambitious composers to make a career of church music.

Beginning in the nineteenth century, religious music composed for a professional chorus and orchestra was more often heard in the concert hall than in a church. Music suitable for church became at most a minor part of the output of any composer desirous of a wide reputation. But at about the same time, amateur volunteers began to play new kinds of music in church. In fact, the Moravian church started using amateur trombonists fairly early in the eighteenth century. The nineteenth and twentieth centuries ushered in new ways for amateur trombonists to participate in worship services. Many of these newer traditions continue to this day.

Sixteenth-century courts, especially in Italy, turned to theatrical entertainments to further their political aims. The trombone's role was considerably different from the old *alta* band. Trombones performed for the first time with solo voices, as well as in unprecedented instrumental combinations. The trend did not last long, however. Only a handful of similar entertainments occurred in the seventeenth century, but these extravaganzas were among the forerunners of opera. The earliest operas, including Monteverdi's *Orfeo*, were performed in the same settings as the older courtly entertainments.

Once commercial opera theaters began to operate in 1637, trombones were excluded until Gluck began to use them in 1762. Gluck's operas were so influential that by the end of the eighteenth century, the trombone had permanently joined the operatic orchestra. By that time, Viennese composers had long included trombones in the orchestra for oratorios, another kind of theatrical entertainment.

The symphony grew out of the operatic overture. It became necessary during Lent, when opera theaters were closed and instrumental concerts were among the few entertainments that continued to be offered. Only a tiny number of symphonies and similar pieces called for trombones until Beethoven chose to include them in his Fifth and Sixth symphonies. After that, they became permanent members of the symphonic orchestra.

Some time in the 1820s, public balls became very popular. Orchestra leaders like Johann Strauss Sr. became successful and famous by supplying the music for them. Before long, dance orchestras matched symphony orchestras in size. They made even greater use of trom-

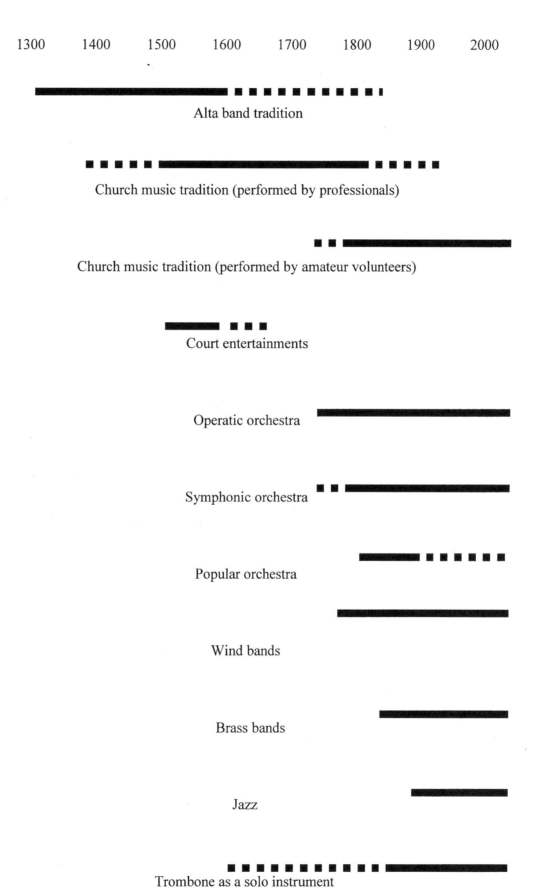

Fig. 1.8. Important traditions in the history of the trombone.

bones. In order to remain active during the off-season, these orchestras performed promenade concerts, which included symphonic music as well as lighter fare. The vogue for large dance orchestras did not long survive Johann Strauss Jr., but promenade concerts by various names are still common.

The next three lines on the graph show new traditions of wind band (which at first meant military band), brass band (which have nearly all been civilian bands), and jazz. The last line shows that while there were a few solo pieces for trombone from the seventeenth century onward, there was no widespread tradition of solo trombone playing until the nineteenth century. In fact, the bulk of the solo repertoire has been composed since 1940.

One thing clearly evident on the graph is that from the middle of the seventeenth century until the end of the eighteenth century, trombones did not participate in many kinds of music, and most of what they did play was at the margins of musical life. Not surprisingly, standards of performance suffered. If it was difficult to find places where the trombone was played at all, it was even harder to find places where anyone played it well. Also evident on the graph, most of the music in which trombones participate in the early twenty-first century represents various traditions that are no more than two hundred years old. The trombone very nearly disappeared before any of these traditions existed. That is perhaps one reason why so much historical writing about the trombone has been simply untrue.

A History of the History of the Trombone

Although the trombone is among the oldest instruments currently in use, it does not have quite the antiquity ascribed to it by eighteenth-century authors. Filippo Buonanni (*Gabinetto armonico*, 1722) passed on a careless translation error by Fortunato Scacchi a hundred years earlier that made it appear that the ancient Roman author Apuleus had described the trombone. Johann Philipp Eisel (*Musicus autodidactus*, 1738) claimed that Moses invented the trombone, citing ancient authors Philo and Josephus as his authority. William Tans'ur (*The Elements of Musik Display'd*, 1772) found it mentioned in the book of Daniel, where, indeed, the translators of the King James Version of the Bible misused the word *sackbut* to translate the Hebrew *sabbeka*, a stringed instrument. J. B. de la Borde (*Essai sur la musique ancienne et moderne*, 1780) and C. F. D. Schubart (*Ideen zu einer Aesthetik der Tonkunst*, 1784–85) likewise claimed that the ancient Hebrews knew the trombone. Perhaps the most scholarly treatment of the history of the trombone among eighteenth-century writers is found in Johann Zedler's *Grosses vollständiges*

Universal-Lexikon (1741), which contains four substantial articles on the trombone that cite Scripture and numerous ancient authors. For all of their erudition, hardly any of the statements in them are factual.[4]

Even in the late nineteenth century, Otto Langey's trombone tutor (1885) proclaimed "The peculiar characteristic of the Trombone consists of the means employed to produce a complete chromatic scale from the open notes of a simple tube; namely, by the use of what is termed a slide. There is much reason to believe that this contrivance is very ancient: it is said to have been invented by Tyrtaes about 685 B.C." Actually, this bit of "information" appeared in all seriousness at least once in the late twentieth century.[5]

The first task of modern scholarship has been to separate fact from fantasy. One early classic article by Francis Galpin takes evident delight in puncturing old legends, including an oft-repeated one that a Roman trombone was found in 1738 at an archeological dig in Pompeii and presented by the King of Naples to the British King George III.[6] Finding the facts requires a type of archeology of its own, sifting through layers of financial records, paintings, literature, and so forth. Much still remains to be uncovered. This painstaking archival and iconographic study is necessary because we have no surviving instruments built before 1551, no published descriptions before 1511, and no pictures of the modern trombone before about 1490, and yet its history can be traced back to the fourteenth century.

The efforts of Galpin and others of his generation mark the beginning of good historical writing about the trombone. Only slightly earlier than Galpin's article, Ernst Euting wrote the first doctoral dissertation on the history of wind instruments. Subsequent historical writing has depended on the science of organology. Victor Mahillon, curator of the musical instrument museum of the Brussels Conservatory, devised the first scientific taxonomy of musical instruments (since superseded by the Hornbostel-Sachs classification) and published a five-volume catalog of the museum's holdings, as well as a separate monograph on the trombone. Curt Sachs contributed greatly to the literature of organology, including, unfortunately, some new mistakes.

Especially over the past half century or so, there has been a flood of information published about the history of the trombone based on careful study of a wide variety of sources (as well as vast amounts of unsubstantiated misinformation). These sources include documents in some kind of written language, musical notation, and graphic arts, as well as trombones in museum collections. Recently, oral histories, recorded sound, and multimedia

Fig. 1.9. Pitch designations used in this book.

websites have become available as documents. Most of this research has been published in journal articles, doctoral dissertations, and books in which, likely as not, the trombone is incidental to the author's topic. More information and more kinds of documentation exist than can possibly fit into one volume. Every year, books, articles, and dissertations appear that add more to the mix. As I write this paragraph, someone is undoubtedly working on a project that I would have loved to use if it had been available. This is not the first book on the history of the trombone, and there is enough untapped information for several more.

In the following chapters, keys are printed in regular type and pitches in italics, with specific octaves designated as shown in Fig. 1.9. There is more than one way to designate the overtone series. I number the partials. The first partial is the fundamental to physicists and the pedal note to trombonists: in first position on an ordinary tenor trombone, *BBb*. The tuning note (*bb*) is the fourth partial and an octave higher (*bb'*) the eighth.

Notes

1. Patrick Tröster, "More about Renaissance Slide Trumpets: Fact or Fiction?" *Early Music* 23 (2004): 256–58.

2. This well-known illustration can be found (among other places) in Tom L. Naylor, *The Trumpet & Trombone in Graphic Arts, 1500–1800* (Nashville, Tenn.: Brass Press, 1979), plate 77.

3. For a very detailed explanation of this point, see Howard Weiner, "When Is an Alto Trombone an Alto Trombone? When Is a Bass Trombone a Bass Trombone?—The Makeup of the Trombone Section in Eighteenth- and Early Nineteenth-Century Orchestras," *Historic Brass Society Journal* 17 (2005): 37–79.

4. The relevant passages from each of these works are quoted and translated in David M. Guion, *The Trombone: Its History and Music, 1697–1811* (New York: Gordon and Breach, 1988), 28ff., 40ff., 47ff., 69ff., 83ff.

5. Someone sent me this quotation by e-mail. Langey's tutor is something of a bibliographic nightmare. The *National Union Catalog Pre-1956 Imprints* (315:185) has consecutive entries for *Newly revised tutor for the slide trombone, bass clef.* One is identified as the 7th ed., the other as the 15th. Both were published in New York by Carl Fischer with a copyright date of 1890. New editions of this text (along with dozens more by Langey for other instruments) appeared as late as 1948. I have no idea where a copy of the original edition might be located; Edward Kleinhammer, *The Art of Trombone Playing* (Evanston, Ill.: Summy-Birchard, 1963), 1.

6. Francis W. Galpin, "The Sackbut, Its Evolution and History," *Proceedings of the Musical Association* 33 (1906): 4–5. According to George Case, this legend first appeared in *Encyclopaedia Londeniensis* at the end of the eighteenth century. See *Grove's Dictionary of Music and Musicians*, 2nd ed., ed. J. A. Fuller Maitland (Philadelphia: Theodore Presser, 1916) s.v. "Trombone" by William H. Stone, with material added by David J. Blaikley. It was reported, minus the reference to the presentation to the king, in *Musical World* 29 Sept 1842, 311.

PART I

DEVELOPMENT OF THE INSTRUMENT

CHAPTER TWO

~

The Origins of the Trombone

Although many details still remain to be uncovered, the basic outlines of the origin of the trombone have been well known since Galpin's time. The trombone is a modified trumpet, an instrument used in ancient Rome and in other surrounding civilizations. The trumpet remained known in Europe in one form or another from Roman times into the Middle Ages, but the tradition of trumpet playing from which the trombone developed entered Europe from Arabic civilization during the Third Crusade (1189–92).

Some time during the fourteenth century, European instrument makers rediscovered how to bend brass tubing and make folded trumpets. The slide was invented somewhat later. At first the entire instrument moved along an elongated mouthpipe. The U-shaped double slide so familiar today was a still later development, which first appears in pictures at the end of the fifteenth century. While there is a general scholarly consensus, none of these statements lacks doubters.

Evolution of the Trombone

Straight Trumpet

The earliest trumpets were military and ceremonial instruments. They served as signaling instruments and as a rallying point in battle. In peacetime, they were used at banquets, jousts, processions, and other public occasions in order to add dignity and splendor, and especially to proclaim the glory and majesty of kings and other rulers. As long as trumpets were used for such occasions and not for private entertainment, and as long as they were not expected to play along with other instruments, natural trumpets were perfectly adequate. That they could play only the several notes at the bottom of the overtone series did not constitute a disadvantage for any of their purposes.

In about 1240, the emperor Frederick II presented four silver *tubae* and one *tubecta* to the town of Arezzo. That one of them is designated with the diminutive -*ecta* indicates that it was smaller than the other four. From this and other references, it is clear that there were two different sizes of trumpet in the Middle Ages. At the end of the twelfth century, a new word, *trumpa* (*trump*, *trompe*, *tromba*, etc.) entered the European vocabulary. It appears to denote an Arabic instrument twice as long as the *tuba*. King Richard I of England heard this instrument when he spent the winter of 1190–91 at Messina, Sicily, and began to use it for himself.[1]

The diminutive of *trompe* is *trompette*. Some time during the fourteenth century, the two terms merged, and both described the longer trumpet. The shorter became known as the clarion (*claro*, *clareta*, *clarino*, etc.), a distinction made in English records as early as 1348. At the end of the fourteenth century, the shorter trumpet was about four feet long. The longer, known not only as *trompe* or a cognate term, but also as *busawm* or some variant, was about six to eight feet long. The two instruments differed in more than length. The *clareta*, most often made of brass, had a greater proportion of conical tubing and a clearly defined bell. The *busawm*, on the other hand, a thin cylindrical tube whose bell had a rather small flare, was usually made of silver and otherwise of noticeably higher quality. Although the foregoing summary is fairly well accepted, Don Smithers has challenged parts of it.[2]

In March 1984, an archeological investigation at the location of the former Billingsgate Lorry Park in London, near the Thames, found a complete fourteenth-century

Fig. 2.1. Angel with trumpet. Detail from "Last Judgement," School of Montecassino (eleventh century). Fresco. S. Angelo in Formis, Capua, Italy. Photo Credit: Scala / Art Resource, NY.

trumpet. It was made in four sections, with total length of 1.61 meters, or 5 feet 3 3/8 inches. Measurement of the abrasions on each piece to determine how much the pieces overlapped yielded an estimate that it would be about 1.445 meters, or 4 feet 8 3/4 inches, when assembled. Because it shows signs of having undergone extensive repair at least twice, it was quite old whenever

it was last played. It was discarded or lost in the late fourteenth or early fifteenth century.[3]

If a short trumpet like the Billingsgate trumpet was made in sections, presumably for easier portability and care, the long instruments must certainly have been made in sections as well. Disassembling a six-foot-long instrument makes it more convenient to transport, but it is still six feet long while it is being played. A less cumbersome instrument must have been desirable for a long time.

Folded Trumpets

Folding a tube stretches the metal on one side and compresses it on the other. A hollow tube will merely break. If it is filled with lead or other hard substance with a lower melting point than the tube itself, however, it is possible to hammer out the wrinkles and preserve the shape of the bore. This technique was known both in ancient Rome and ancient Scandinavia, but not in Medieval Europe until it was rediscovered in the middle of the fourteenth century.[4]

A book of hours purchased in about 1405 by Charles III, King of Navarre, depicts two different trumpets with one fold, U-shaped trumpets that are sufficiently dissimilar in design that they cannot be two different views of the same instrument. There is also a picture of the later and more common S-shaped design, so whenever the U-shaped trumpet originated, it was already obsolete by the time Charles's book of hours was produced.[5]

It is necessary to bend only short lengths of tubing to make a folded trumpet. Two straight pieces, a pipe with either a built-in or detachable mouthpiece and a bell section, (collectively called yards) and a curved section (called a bow) would be sufficient to make a U-shaped trumpet. An additional yard and a second bow would allow the bell again to face forward. Such a trumpet could be assembled in at least two ways. The yards could be placed in three parallel lines in the same plane (the S-shaped trumpet, Fig. 2.3) or, by turning the second bow in the opposite direction, place the bell section close to the upper pipe (the loop-shaped trumpet, Fig. 2.4). The former shape began to appear in illustrations about 1375, and the latter about twenty years later.

The military uses of the trumpet are described in the *Yconomica* of Konrad of Megenberg, written between 1348 and 1352. Konrad also mentions that the trumpet and shawm "sound well together according to due proportions in 4ths, 5ths and octaves, just as the character of the melody requires." The shawm was likewise a military instrument. It is difficult to imagine how the greater number of notes it could play was any advantage in battle. It probably adapted itself to the limitations of the trumpet, which Konrad considers the greater of the two instruments. In peacetime, however, Konrad notes, "In modern times the shawms and loud trumpets generally banish the sober fiddles from the feasts, and the young girls dance eagerly to the loud noise, like hinds shaking their buttocks womanishly and rudely."[6] The natural

Fig. 2.2. U-shaped trumpet from Master of Brussels Initials and Associates (French). *Hours of Charles the Noble, King of Navarre (1361–1425): fol. 106r, Last Judgement,* c. 1405. Ink, tempera, and gold on vellum, 19.4 x 13.7 cm. © The Cleveland Museum of Art, Mr. and Mrs. William H. Marlatt Fund, 1964.40.106.

trumpet would soon prove inadequate for this new purpose as an instrument for entertainment.

Early Slides

Galpin suggested that the slide originated at the same time and place as the folded trumpet and that it may have been applied to the straight trumpet as well. Most scholars since his time have agreed with him and put forth various kinds of evidence. Sachs, whose doctorate was in art history, notes a slide trumpet made by Huns Veit in 1651 and used by *Stadtpfeifer* in Naumburg, Saxony. He refers to two artworks that, he says, prove that a similar instrument existed in the fifteenth century. In his first example, the painting "Adoration of the Magi" by

Fig. 2.3.   Angel playing a trumpet. Detail from the Linaiuoli altarpiece by Fra Angelico (1387–1455). Museo di
S. Marco, Florence, Italy. Photo Credit: Scala / Art Resource, NY.

Fig. 2.4. English clarions from the early fifteenth century. Francis W. Galpin, _Old English Instruments of Music._

Antonio Vivarini and Giovanni d'Allemagna (ca. 1444), he notes, "Two of the trumpeters in the retinue of Kings, waiting for their turn to play, shoulder their instrument bell-up with one hand and with the other hold the mouthpiece lest it should slip out. These mouthpieces, apparently the only ones ever shown unconcealed, have throats about as long as those of the Naumburg slide trumpet, and since so long a throat is useless for any other purpose, it must have served as a slide, too."[7]

Next, Sachs points out the St. Wolfgang altarpiece by Michael Pacher, completed in 1481, which has two nearly identical S-shaped trumpets. They are not held with the hands together, as one might expect, but with the one hand holding the mouthpiece and the other holding the first bow. Of greater interest to Sachs is that the two instruments are not of equal length; the one on the left is noticeably longer. The only difference is in the first yard, and consequently the distance between the mouthpiece and the bows. When Sachs compared the lengths of the two instruments, he found them in a ratio of 9:8 (a whole step in Pythagorean tuning) and concluded that they were two slide trumpets, the shorter one with the slide closed and the longer one with it extended. Sachs cites four other artworks that, he says, show instruments held in such a way that makes sense

only if the players are manipulating a slide. His illustrations are not very good. Better images of the Vivarini painting and the Pacher altar can be found in an article by Lorenz Welker.[8]

In a longer and more thorough exploration of the early history of the trombone, Heinrich Besseler examined several early fifteenth-century polyphonic pieces bearing the rubric _trompette_ or something similar. He concluded that these parts were played on some kind of trumpet. Noting that Burgundian court records made a distinction between _trompette de guerre_ and _trompette des menestrels_ from 1421 to 1468, when the term _trompette saqueboute_ replaced the latter, he concluded that the new term must refer to a new instrument, the modern trombone. Since the trumpet contratenors are not playable on a natural trumpet, Besseler argued that the _trompette des menestrels_ must have been a slide trumpet, an intermediate step between the natural trumpet and the trombone. Acknowledging Sachs's work, Besseler showed yet another picture, an illustration painted in the Bible prepared between 1455 and 1461 for Borso d'Este, ruler of Ferrara (see Fig. 2.5). Like Sachs, Besseler was persuaded by the way the instrument is held and the great distance between the player's mouth and the S-form that the instrument in the picture was a slide trumpet. Numerous scholars have used additional evidence to reach similar conclusions.[9]

Peter Downey has mounted a serious challenge to this hypothesis, claiming among other things that the slide trumpet did not exist until the middle of the seventeenth century.[10] Lorenz Welker has lately joined his skepticism. Therefore the article by Welker already cited no longer represents his viewpoint. Although he was a longtime advocate of the slide trumpet, having introduced it in modern _alta_ bands in the 1980s, he delivered a paper at a conference in 2006 in which he announced his agreement with Downey's position. That paper has not been published as yet.

I do not find Downey's claims persuasive, but he makes a good case that it is impossible to prove the existence of the slide trumpet by describing pictures. Now that the Billingsgate trumpet has been discovered and described, it is evident that the trumpets in the Vivarini painting are of this type. The mouthpieces that seemed so unnecessarily long to Sachs do not really appear to be long enough to serve as slides. The Veit trumpet, therefore, has nothing to do with the instruments in the painting. It is, as Downey demonstrated, not a late example of a Medieval instrument, but an example of a type of slide trumpet Veit invented in 1648. Downey dismisses the differences between the two trumpets in the Pacher altar as a carving error.

Fig. 2.5. Wind band with two shawms and trombone. Miniature attributed to Taddeo Crivelli in Borso's Bible (Modena, Biblioteca Estense, MS V.G.12 lat.429. f.280v), by permission of the Ministry of Cultural Heritage and Activities.

Indeed, Pacher was obviously more interested in symmetry than in real playing positions. Both angels face the center of the composition. The hand closest to the viewer holds the mouthpiece and the inside hand holds the bow. Sachs appears not to have noticed that the angel on the right would have to be left-handed; he holds his trumpet with the opposite hands from what was commonly reproduced in pictures. Downey also offers alternate explanations for every other artwork that anyone has claimed to show slide trumpets.

He is undoubtedly correct that reasoning based on descriptions of the appearance of pictures—measurements, playing positions, and so forth—cannot prove that any of the trumpets in them had moving parts. There are, however, two treatises (Agricola in 1529—see chapter 3—and Buonanni in 1722) that clearly and unambiguously describe a slide trumpet. Buonanni writes, "Also used is a straight trumpet with a single broken channel such that it inserts one part within the other, now shortening itself, now elongating itself, causing itself to sound more or less high or low, according to the rules of music; and it is particularly used by people who live in villages"[11] (see Fig. 2.6).

For earlier evidence of the slide trumpet it is necessary to compare the terminology in the archives of Ferrara, where the term *trombone* appears for the first time in 1439, with a picture of an *alta* band in Borso's Bible, a band much like many others from all over Europe: two shawms and an S-shaped trumpet. The trumpet is a straight pipe for most of its length, with the S-shaped bends occupying the thirty percent or so that is farthest from the player, who holds that portion at arm's length. Few other fifteenth-century pictures look so much like a slide trumpet, but no amount of description of the picture could ever prove conclusively that it is one.[12]

The proof comes from the fact that Borso himself had such a band in his household, and we know the identity of the players. Corrado de Allemagne played soprano shawm. Zoanne de Allemagne played tenor shawm. Pietro Agostino played *trombone*. That is the word used in court records throughout Borso's reign. It is tempting to speculate that the picture in question contains a portrait of those three men. In any case, the band in the picture is of the same type that would have been familiar to Borso and his court. Therefore, the S-shaped trumpet

Technical Resources of the Slide Trumpet

Sachs's explanation of the instrument's technical resources is as flawed as his analysis of his iconographic sources, but most later ones are based on it. He claims that a trumpet in F was "obviously the usual variety" and numbered the positions just as modern trombonists do. First position refers to the instrument's shortest length. Second position lowers the basic pitch by a semitone, third position by a whole tone, and so on. Because "stretching the arm to reach the fifth position (major third) would hardly be possible," he assumes a maximum of four positions, but offers no measurements or figures to justify his conclusion.[15]

Given this limitation, the instrument is fully chromatic above the fourth partial (compared to the natural trumpet, which is diatonic only above the eighth partial). There is one missing note ($c\sharp'/b'$) between the highest third partial and the lowest fourth partial. Sachs points out that a good player could easily lip this note if it was needed. He neglects to point out the three missing notes ($f\sharp/g\flat$, g, $g\sharp/a\flat$) between the highest second partial and the lowest third partial. (For an explanation of the pitch designations used in this book, see Fig. 1.9 in chapter 1.)

Smithers likewise assumes a limit of four positions, but unlike Sachs, he considers the possibility of trumpets in E♭, D, and C, as well as F. These other tunings would have the same gaps as far as the various harmonic series are concerned, but they would involve different pitches. He offers measurements of a slide trumpet in D, which he says would require the slide to be extended a little over five inches to lower the pitch by a semitone, or fifteen inches to reach "fourth" position. As Smithers describes the pictorial evidence, the arm is half extended in first position and fully extended in fourth.[16]

In order to lower the pitch of a sounding tube one semitone, its length must be increased by about six percent. The seventh (and last) position on a modern tenor trombone, which lowers its pitch by six semitones, requires an extension of about 23 inches or 58.5 cm. Because the slide has two different tubes, the movement out to seventh position actually adds 46 inches or 117 cm to the length of the tube.

On a slide trumpet in F, which is about 71 inches or 180 cm long,[17] an extension of just over 14 inches or 36 cm will lower the pitch by a minor third. A fifth position, ruled out by Sachs, would be out a little less than 18 inches or 45 cm. On the trumpet in C, the longest of those considered by Smithers, fourth and fifth positions would require extensions of 19 inches (48 cm) and 23 1/2 inches (60 cm) respectively.

VI *Altra Tromba Spezzata*

Fig. 2.6. Slide trumpet from Buonanni *Gabinetto armonico* (1722). Dover edition, 1964.

is the type of instrument played by Pietro Agostino, and its name in Ferrara was *trombone*. The name means "big trumpet." Although it was the same basic length as any other trumpet, it could be made bigger (longer) by means of the slide. It may have also been made with a somewhat larger bore to emphasize lower notes.[13]

Keith McGowan, working with a replica of a 1579 Schnitzer trombone, made as nearly as possible using sixteenth-century technology, has demonstrated that it is possible to disassemble it and put the parts back together as either a field trumpet or a slide trumpet.[14] While the fact that McGowan did so does not prove that sixteenth-century musicians ever got triple duty from the same instrument, it is certainly suggestive that perhaps we have had a few slide trumpets in our museums all along, without knowing it.

There is no reason, therefore, to rule out the possibility of five positions, although the fifth on a slide trumpet in C would certainly be awkward to reach. The extra available note in the third partial would be a chromatic note on trumpets in F, E♭, or C, but the one missing diatonic note could be lipped down from it by a skillful player. In other words, the slide trumpet could play a complete diatonic scale, with one problem note, beginning with the second partial. Exceptional players may have also managed to play the first partial (pedal) and/or bend the second partial down a fourth to a "false harmonic."

Reference to chromatically numbered slide positions on trumpets in some particular key is handy, but anachronistic. Music of the fifteenth century was diatonic music. The most practical slide trumpet would have been whatever length allowed the most convenient playing of a diatonic scale. No one would have cared about the name of the overtone series available when the instrument is at its shortest, which is what we mean by brass instruments in a particular key. The two main playing positions would have been with the right hand by the mouthpiece and a comfortable arm's length away, which would lower the basic pitch by a whole tone. Second position could be adjusted upward or downward as needed, and of course the diatonic note immediately above the highest second partial would require both an extreme lengthening of the slide and an uncomfortable embouchure adjustment.

The most likely length for a slide trumpet, therefore, would be the one in which the most notes of an ordinary diatonic scale would be available either in first or an unadjusted second position. Fig. 2.7 shows notes in the second through fifth partials for slide trumpets in four different keys. For convenience, the positions are numbered chromatically, and the basic positions are shown with open note-heads. Notes in parentheses are available only by lipping down the note in "fifth" position. The slide trumpet in D offers seven diatonic notes in these positions out of a total of twenty-one. These include five notes in the C-major scale. The C trumpet has six diatonic notes in basic positions, with four in the scale. The F trumpet has only five diatonic notes, two in the scale, and the E♭ trumpet only the highest two diatonic notes, neither of which are in the scale. It is also impossible to play *e* on a slide trumpet in E♭. It appears, therefore, that the slide trumpet in D would have been the most practical.

Chronology and Terminology of the Slide Trumpet

The earliest hints of the invention of the slide trumpet occur in the early 1360s; it began to become common by about 1400. There is, unfortunately, no consistent terminology to describe this new development. The bulk of available evidence comes in the form of civic and court records and chronicles, financial records, or descriptions of events in which music was but one constituent part.

Fig. 2.7. Technical resources of slide trumpets.

None of it was concerned with the technical aspects of music making. The clerks who kept the records had no more interest in organological distinction than did Konrad of Megenberg, who wrote that there was no difference between the trumpet and the shawm except for the largeness and smallness of their sounds.[18] The musical practices in question were everyday, mundane occurrences to the various writers. They had no need to write the distinctions and details that we would like to know. Most of the terms found in various archives can refer to instruments with or without a slide.

In 1363, Florentine chronicler Filippo Villani wrote that the English "have ladders, the main section of which is in three parts, with one fitting into the other in the manner of a trumpet."[19] We know from the Billingsgate trumpet that medieval trumpets were made in several sections that could be taken apart and fitted together at need. Villani probably meant that English ladders were constructed the same way, but if he meant some kind of extension ladder, he could be comparing it to a slide trumpet. This comment is one of the earliest that could by any stretch of the imagination be taken to refer to an instrument with a slide.

It is a similar stretch to interpret an item in the town records of Dortmund, also in 1363, as referring to a slide instrument. A group of three *Spielleute*, who were all issued the same livery and so presumably played together, included two *pfeiffers* and a *posauner*. The German term *posaune* is derived from *buisine*, an earlier Medieval straight trumpet. It was used to mean a straight trumpet as late as 1409, but once there is no question of the existence of a slide instrument, that is the word used to designate it in German-speaking countries. So did the *posauner* in 1363 have a slide instrument? Probably not, but there is no change in vocabulary between then and the later bands that definitely had an instrument with a slide. At the Council of Constance in 1416, it was reported that three *prusoner* "played together in three parts, as one ordinarily sings." *Prusoner* is recognizably related to *posauner*, and if "as one ordinarily sings" refers at all to a performance of a chanson or motet, it would require an instrument with a slide, but the comment is too ambiguous to bear much weight. Although German instrumentalists could be found in courts all over Europe, the term *posaune* seldom appears in non-German archives.[20]

Other payment records that imply an ensemble of shawms and a brass instrument, whatever it was called, can be found for 1368 (Augsburg), 1372 (Cologne), 1373 (Trier), 1377 (Dortmund), 1384 (Deventer), 1385 (Aachen), 1388–89 (Nuremberg), 1390 (Deventer),

1394 (Deventer), 1399–1400 (Maastricht), 1402 (Utrecht), 1403 (Utrecht, Braunschweig), 1405 (Braunschweig), 1408 (Audenaerde), 1409 (Ghent), 1410 (Aelst), 1412 (Leiden), 1419 (Hildesheim), 1421 (Nuremberg), 1427–28 (Hildesheim), and 1438 (Mechelen).[21] The later the reference, the more likely it is that the brass instrument had a slide.

The most common term in Flanders and Northern Germany for a slide trumpet was some form of the word trumpet, such as *trompette*, *tromp*, *trump*, *trummet*, and so forth.[22] If the instrument appeared with drums or in a military context, it was the older, slideless trumpet. If it played with shawms, it may have had a slide. Again, there is no clear demarcation between the earliest documents, where a slide is less likely, and later ones, where it is more likely.

Occasionally, a scribe felt the need for a more precise term. In 1386, records at the court of Philip the Bold, Duke of Burgundy, indicate payment to a musician visiting in the retinue of an unnamed German bishop who is identified as *menestrel de trompette*. Burgundian court records are very careful and consistent in terminology. Ordinarily, they show a clear distinction between Philip's minstrels and his trumpeters, who even wore different livery. The trumpeters' duties were military and ceremonial, while the minstrels were entertainers. One could either say that the bishop's trumpet player was a minstrel, or that the bishop's minstrel entertained with a trumpet. Either way, the careful distinction between trumpeter and minstrel maintained at Philip's court was obliterated in the person of this visitor.[23] Did his instrument have a slide? Maybe, but the term used here means a minstrel that played trumpet. The term for a special trumpet played by minstrels did not become common until much later.

Trumpets with a slide certainly existed by about 1410. Philip's son and successor, John the Fearless, hired Hennequin van Pictre in 1411. This musician, also known as Hennequin vander Pict and Hennequin Copetripe (a nickname he acquired after killing a colleague in a knife fight), served the duke as player of both *trompette de guerre* and *trompette des menestrels*. That is, he was capable of entertaining with the minstrels and also serving in battle with the other trumpeters. The term *trompette des menestrels* was the standard designation for slide trumpet/trombone in Burgundian court records from this time on for more than half a century, when it was replaced by *trompette saqueboute*.[24]

The distinction between *trompette de guerre* and *trompette des menestrels* is not limited to Burgundian court records. After the Battle of Agincourt in 1415,

Jehan Poulain, a minstrel and watchman of St. Omer, petitioned for indemnification for the loss of his two trumpets, "one for peace and one for war." Records for the royal court in Paris were not as well kept as those in Burgundy, owing to the chaos of the Hundred Years War and its aftermath and the madness of King Charles VI, but they do attest that the royal household included both *trompette de guerre* and *trompette des menestrels* in 1418. In Barcelona, the musical household established in 1413 by Prince Alfonso, heir to the throne of Aragon, included *trompeta dels ministrers*.[25]

The earliest term that seems to have been invented to describe an instrument with a slide appears to be *trombone*, which is first attested in Ferrara in 1439. By that time, Hennequin Copetripe had left the service of the Duke of Burgundy to join the court of Niccolò III of Ferrara, shortly after the duke made Niccolò a gift of a set of wind instruments that included a trombone. It was the slide trumpet, of course, and not the modern trombone to which the new term first applied. The document refers to a "tuba ductilis. . . trombonus vulgo dictus" (roughly, "*tuba ductilis*, or trombone in the vernacular").

The word *sackbut*, along with its French and Spanish cognates, is a later term than any of the foregoing. The earliest attested form is the French, derived from *saquier* (to pull) and *boter* (to push). Its first recorded use, in 1306, refers to a lance, a meaning it still had in the fifteenth century. It first appears as a name for the trombone in the *Memoirs* of Olivier de la Marche, a Burgundian court official. He used *trompette saqueboute* in his description of the 1468 wedding of Duke Charles to Margaret of York. Besseler and others give that date for the introduction of the term, but the passage was probably written at least twenty years later. Tinctoris, writing in Latin, mentioned the French word *saqueboute* in an undated treatise that may have been written in 1487. Therefore, the earliest datable use of a sackbut cognate comes from the Aragonese court in 1478, where Bartolomeo Gaço (or Gasso), "sacabuche domini regis," pledged to teach the technique of the instrument to a Castilian minstrel.[26]

Galpin and others attempted to find a Spanish origin for the term; Besseler doubted that such a politically and culturally marginal country as fifteenth-century Spain could have supplied a term used so widely in Western Europe.[27] Considering that Philip the Good of Burgundy married a Portuguese princess and also maintained close relations with the kingdom of Aragon, Spain was not as marginal as Besseler supposed.

The first use of the term in English occurs in records at the court of Henry VII in 1495. The actual form of the term, *shakbusshe*, suggests a Spanish rather than French origin, although it was eventually supplanted by *sackbut*, which more nearly resembles the French. In all three languages, the first use of the term merely meant the introduction of a new word, not necessarily a new instrument. Where the trombone had formerly been called some kind of trumpet (and indeed, La Marche's term is *trompette saqueboute*—*saqueboute* by itself is not attested before 1508), the appearance of the new word recognizes the same kind of distinction between the natural trumpet and the more flexible melody instrument already designated in Italy by *trombone* and in Germany by *posaune*.

In 1363, then, it is remotely possible that some trumpets may have been equipped with a slide. For most scholars, there is no question by about 1410. The distinction between ordinary trumpets and slide trumpets is unambiguous in French- and Spanish-language sources not long after 1410, while elsewhere, the pairing of some kind of trumpet with shawms and one reference to an actual performance invite the presumption that the instrument in question had a slide. Eventually, all languages had distinctly different terms for ordinary trumpet and slide trumpet. We might as well call the slide trumpet a trombone, as the Italians did.

The Modern U-Slide

On a slide trumpet, the old trombone, the first yard of the instrument is made with one tube contained in another with a slightly larger bore. The mouthpiece is inserted into (or hammered from) the near end of the narrower tube; the first bow and the remainder of the instrument are attached to the far end of the wider tube. On a modern trombone, the first and second yards both contain one tube inside another. The first bow connects the larger outer tubes, while the inner tubes are not connected to each other at all. In other words, the trombone slide as we know it today represents a new, improved design of existing technology. The older design continued to exist alongside the newer one and persisted well into the eighteenth century, although by that time it could be found mostly in villages.

Determining when and where the modern slide originated is just as difficult as determining when and where the slide trumpet originated, and for the same reasons. There are no written documents that herald the new invention and no surviving specimens earlier than the middle of the sixteenth century. What evidence we have comes mostly from paintings, engravings, woodcuts, and other pictorial evidence.

The chief difficulty in interpreting pictures of slide trumpets is that they cannot show movement. The problem in documenting the earliest U-slide is somewhat different. In order to evaluate that evidence, it is first necessary to determine the competence of the artists' draftsmanship, the artists' understanding of the subject matter, what kinds of details mattered to their conception of the picture, and whether there were artistic conventions that were more important than realistic accuracy. To make matters worse, many of the paintings have been restored since they were originally painted. Their value as evidence also depends on how well or poorly the restorations were performed.

It has long been supposed that the earliest picture of an instrument with a double slide is found on the so-called Adimari Wedding Chest (Fig. 2.8). For close to

Fig. 2.8. **The so-called Adimari Wedding Chest (detail). Accademia, Florence, Italy. Photo courtesy of Nicolo Orsi Battaglini / Art Resource, NY.**

two centuries, it was believed that the painting was a decoration on a chest made for the wedding of Florentine nobles Boccacio Adimari and Lisa Ricasoli in 1420. As it turns out, the painting has no verifiable connection with the Adimari family. It is far too large to have been painted for a wedding chest, and must have been painted some time between 1443 and 1465, not 1420. The setting is clearly Florentine, but does not depict any specific location.[28]

The subject of the painting is a dance of the type that frequently followed a banquet, with the town band providing the music. There are some oddities about the way the band is depicted. The three shawms are all soprano shawms, where one of them should have been a bombard. The banners hanging from the shawms would only get in the players' way. Such banners would have been more appropriate and common on trumpets. Although clearly shawms, they are more the color of brass than the dark wood used for shawms. (The color may have resulted from a later restoration, being chosen as a result of the erroneous but understandable belief that the instruments were trumpets.) Clearly, the painter, who deliberately painted a generalized suggestion of a Florentine cityscape rather than a specific location, was not concerned with a literal depiction of what the band would have looked like in real life. His artistic intent required banners, so he put them where it was convenient for him. It is in this context that the trombone (a term that first appears in Florentine civic records in 1443) must be considered.

The second bow of the instrument is drawn behind the player's ear, the first time such a construction occurs in an artwork. The bell extends beyond the first bow, which is not characteristic of the modern trombone. The picture therefore shows elements of both the modern trombone and the older slide trumpet. If the trombone (in either form) was a new and unfamiliar instrument, the artist may have had trouble drawing it. Just as likely, the shape may have been altered in the process of restoration. Since it is difficult to be sure whether the shape of the trombone is original or the result of a restoration, it is no longer possible confidently to regard this painting as the first picture of the modern trombone.[29]

In contrast with the many pictures of what may be slide trumpets from the fifteenth century, only a few pictures could possibly be modern trombones. The newer instrument would have a mostly stationary instrument with a moveable U-slide rather than most of the instrument moving along a single slide. Visual evidence would include the presence of at least two stays on the slide and one on the bell section, the bell bow extending behind the player's ear, and the bell itself not extending past the

end of the slide bow. A player would necessarily hold a modern trombone differently than he would a slide trumpet. There is something not quite right about every fifteenth-century picture up until 1490.[30]

It is generally considered that the first painting to show the trombone in its finished form is "The Assumption of the Virgin," a fresco by Filippino Lippi in the church of S. Maria sopra Minerva in Rome (Fig. 2.9). Here again, an angel is playing the trombone, with the slide extended to what would be modern fourth or fifth position, although the slide appears to be too short.[31] (The abnormally short slide seems to have been an artistic convention that lasted at least until the middle of the seventeenth century, when an engraving of a trombone with a foreshortened slide appears on the bell stay of a trombone by Sebastian Hainlein dated 1631 [Fig. 2.10]). The bell in the fresco has a pronounced flare (not encountered in real instruments until centuries later), and the second bow is hidden behind the angel's head and halo. The artistic license does not obscure the form of the modern U-slide. Therefore, it is certain that it existed by no later than 1490, when Lippi painted it. It probably existed some time earlier than that, but a date much before midcentury seems unlikely.

Eventually, the modern trombone displaced the slide trumpet. By the middle of the seventeenth century, the slide trumpet had been forgotten and reinvented in

Fig. 2.9. "Assumption of the Virgin" by Filippino Lippi (1490). S. Maria sopra Minerva, Rome, Italy. Photo Credit: Scala / Art Resource, NY.

Fig. 2.10. Bell stay and pin on a trombone by Sebastian Hainlein (1631). Photograph by Herbert W. Myers. Used by permission.

Germany. It could still be found among Italian villagers as late as the 1720s. During the late fifteenth century and well into the sixteenth century, however, the two instruments coexisted and were called by the same names. They may have even been two ways of assembling the same collection of parts. It would therefore be pedantic, probably even impossible, to distinguish between them except in iconographic sources.

The ensembles in which they participated and the music that they played during the fourteenth and fifteenth centuries are the subject of a later chapter. The term *trombone* will be used exclusively there except in issues limited to the very early fifteenth century, but it must be understood that even beyond the late fifteenth century, a trombone could have had either a single or a double slide.

Notes

1. Anthony Baines, *Brass Instruments: Their History and Development* (New York: Scribner, 1978), 87; Henry George Farmer, "Crusading Martial Music," *Music & Letters* 30 (1949): 244–45.

2. Keith Polk, *German Instrumental Music of the Late Middle Ages: Players, Patrons, and Performance Practice* (Cambridge: Cambridge University Press, 1992), 46; Don L. Smithers, "A New Look at the Historical, Linguistic and Taxonomic Bases for the Evolution of Lip-Blown Instruments from Classical Antiquity until the End of the Middle Ages," *Historic Brass Society Journal* 1 (1989): 3–64.

3. This find is described in Geoff Egan, "A Late Medieval Trumpet from Billingsgate," *London Archaeologist* 5, no. 6 (1986): 168; John Webb, "The Billingsgate Trumpet," *Galpin Society Journal* 41 (1988): 59–62; Grame Lawson and Geoff Egan, "Medieval Trumpet from the City of London," *Galpin Society Journal* 41 (1988): 63–66; and Grame Lawson, "Medieval Trumpet from the City of London, II," *Galpin Society Journal* 44 (1991): 150–56.

4. Geert Jan van der Heide, "Brass Instrument Metalworking Techniques: The Bronze Age to the Industrial Revolution," *Historic Brass Society Journal* 3 (1991): 140–41.

5. Ross Duffin, "Backward Bells and Barrel Bells: Some Notes on the Early History of Loud Instruments," *Historic Brass Society Journal* 9 (1997): 113–17.

6. Simul eciam bene concinunt secundum debitas proporciones in quartis, in quintis aut octavis, sicut qualitas exigit melodie.—Modernis etenim temporibus tibie ac tube altitone fidulas morigeras a conviviis communiter fugant, et altisono strepitu certatim iuvencule saliunt ut cerve clunes illepide ac effeminaliter agitando. Christopher Page, "German Musicians and Their Instruments: A 14th-Century Account by Konrad of Megenberg," *Early Music* 10 (1982): 193, 194–95.

7. Curt Sachs, "Chromatic Trumpets in the Renaissance," *Musical Quarterly* 36 (1950): 64.

8. Lorenz Welker, "'Alta Capella' zur Ensemblepraxis der Blasinstrumente im 15. Jahrhundert," *Basler Jahrbuch für historische Musikpraxis* 7 (1983): 133 and 129 respectively.

9. Heinrich Besseler, "Die Entstehung der Posaune," *Acta musicologica* 22 (1950): 11–18; Don L. Smithers, *The Music and History of the Baroque Trumpet before 1721*, 2nd ed. (Carbondale and Edwardsville: Southern Illinois University Press, 1988), 36–39; Welker, "Alta Capella," 131–39; Janez Höfler, "Der 'Trompette de Menestrels' und sein Instrument," *Tijdschrift van de Vereniging voor Nederlandse Muziekgeschiedenis* 29 (1979): 92–132; Edward Tarr, *The Trumpet*, trans. S. E. Plank and Edward Tarr (London: Batsford, 1988), 54–60; Patrick Tröster, "More about Renaissance Slide Trumpets: Fact or Fiction?" *Early Music* 23 (2004): 252–68.

10. Peter Downey, "The Renaissance Slide Trumpet: Fact or Fiction?" *Early Music* 12 (1984): 26–33. Downey restates and amplifies his objections in two later articles: "Adam Drese's 1648 Funeral Music and the Invention of the Slide Trumpet," in *Musicology in Ireland*, ed. Gerard Gillen and Harry White (Dublin: Irish Academic Press, 1990), 200–17; and "'In tubis ductilibus et voce tubae': Trumpets, Slides and Performance Practices in Late Medieval and Renaissance Europe," in *Music and the Church*, ed. Gerard Gillen and Harry White (Dublin: Irish Academic Press, 1993), 302–32.

11. Suole anche usarsi la Tromba dritta d'un solo Canale spezzato in modo che inserita una parte dentro l'altra, ora scortandosi, ora allungandosi si cagiona il suono più, ò meno acuto, ò grave, secondo che ricercano le regole della Musica, e si usa particolarmente da persone abitanti nelli Villaggi. Filippo Buonanni, *Gabinetto armonico* (Rome: Giorgio Placho, 1722), 51.

12. David M. Guion, "On the Trail of the Medieval Slide Trumpet," part 2. *Brass Bulletin* 110 (2000): 46–50.

13. Lewis Lockwood, *Music in Renaissance Ferrara, 1500–1595: The Creation of a Musical Center in the Fifteenth Century* (Cambridge, Mass.: Harvard University Press, 1984), 142; Keith Polk, "Ensemble Music in Flanders—1450–1550," *Journal of Band Research* 11, no. 2 (Spring 1975): 16–17.

14. Keith McGowan, "A Chance Encounter with a Unicorn? A Possible Sighting of the Renaissance Slide Trumpet," *Historic Brass Society Journal* 8 (1996): 92.

15. Sachs, "Chromatic Trumpets," 65.

16. Smithers, *Music and History*, 42–45.

17. Höfler, "Trompette des Menestrels," 112.

18. Page, "German Musicians," 193.

19. "Scale avevano artificiose, che il maggiore pezzo prendea l'altro a modo della trombe." Quoted in Keith Polk, "Instrumental Music in the Urban Centers of Renaissance Germany," *Early Music History* 7 (1987): 172.

20. Keith Polk, "The Trombone, the Slide Trumpet, and the Ensemble Tradition of the Early Renaissance," *Early Music*, 17 (1989): 393; Manfred Schuler, "Die Musik in Konstanz während des Konzils, 1414–1418," *Acta musicologica* 38 (1966), 165; Galpin, "Sackbut," 12.

21. Keith Polk, "The Trombone in Archival Documents, 1350–1500," *ITA Journal* 15 (Summer 1987): 28–29.

22. Polk, *German Instrumental Music*, 58; Polk, "Trombone, Slide Trumpet," 392–93; Polk, "Trombone in Archival Documents,"28.

23. Craig Wright, *Music at the Court of Burgundy, 1364–1419: A Documentary History*. (Henryville, Penn.: Institute of Medieval Music, 1979), 41.

24. Keith Polk, "The Invention of the Slide Principle and the Earliest Trombone; or, The Birth of a Notion," in *Perspectives in Brass Scholarship*, ed. Stewart Carter (Stuyvesant, N.Y.: Pendragon, 1997), 26–27; Wright, *Music at the Court of Burgundy*, 47–48.

25. Jeanne Marix, *Histoire de la musique et des musiciens de la cour de Bourgogne sous le règne de Philippe le Bon (1420–1467)* (Strasbourg: Heitz, 1939), 104; Downey, "In tubis ductilibus," 328, n. 99; Leeman L. Perkins, "Musical Patronage at the Royal Court of France under Charles VII and Louis XI (1422–83)," *Journal of the American Musicological Society* 37 (1984): 516; Higinio Anglés, *Hygini Anglés: Scripta musicologica*, ed. Joseph Lopéz-Calo, 3 vols., paged continuously (Rome: Edizione di Storia e Letteratura, 1975–76), 766, 970.

26. Anglès, *Scripta musicologica*, 890.

27. Galpin, "Sackbut," 2; Besseler, "Entstehung," 8.

28. Timothy J. McGee, "Misleading Iconography: The Case of the 'Adimari Wedding Cassone,'" *Imago musicae* 9–12 (1992–95): 144–46.

29. McGee, "Misleading Iconography," 152–54.

30. Herbert W. Myers, "Evidence of the Emerging Trombone in the Late Fifteenth Century: What Iconography May Be Trying to Tell Us," *Historic Brass Society Journal* 17 (2005): 17–23.

31. See Myers, "Evidence," 28.

CHAPTER THREE

~

The Trombone from the
U-Slide to the Invention of Valves

The use of valves aside, the trombone is very much the same instrument it was in the fifteenth century after the invention of the U-slide. Advancing technology has not brought substantial improvements to its basic design, although there have been critically important changes in detail that have altered both the sound and playing technique. The slide trombone as described in the early nineteenth century by Joseph Fröhlich and Andreas Nemetz differs only in minor details from what can be easily obtained from any manufacturer today. With the obvious exception of valve technology and the less obvious exception of bore size, the trombone as it appears by the end of this chapter is almost completely up to date.

Descriptions of the Trombone, 1511–1828

Sixteenth-Century Accounts

Sebastian Virdung's *Musica getutscht* in 1511 was the first book on musical instruments in a vernacular language. By most accounts, it is not very good, but if it did not succeed intellectually, it certainly succeeded commercially. A second edition appeared posthumously in 1521, followed shortly thereafter by translations into French and Dutch. Martin Agricola's *Musica instrumentalis deudsch*, which relies heavily on Virdung, appeared in 1529. Othmar Luscinius prepared an expanded translation of Virdung's book into Latin, which was published in 1536 under the title *Musurgia seu praxis musicae*. All of these derivative works were reprinted at least once, the latest of the reprints appearing in 1568.

Virdung apparently intended his little book as a teaser to build interest in a longer, more scholarly treatise that he did not live to see published. There were three brief references to the trombone. One is a quotation from Psalm 95:5–6 (Vulgate numbering) that translates the Latin "tubis ductilis" as "zehenden Busaune" (slide trombone). The other two promise detailed explanation in the larger treatise. The last one ends with such a complete non sequitur, however, that the typesetter may have omitted some key information. We will never know what Virdung knew about the trombone.[1]

Agricola, on the other hand, quite frankly admitted that he did not understand how the trombone, trumpet, or clareta really worked. According to his description (in the form of doggerel poetry), all three instruments had slides. When he published an expanded version of his treatise in 1545, he had evidently still not learned anything about the trombone. The little poem in the 1529 version remains unchanged.[2]

Strictly speaking, Luscinius did not prepare a translation. Instead, he produced a somewhat more scholarly treatise covering much of the same material and using the same illustrations. He added one interesting tidbit about the trombone:

> Furthermore, certain trombones are made, which, although they sound no more than a single tone at a time, nevertheless, they have mechanisms so that, if they were capable of producing many tones at once, each individual [fundamental] tone would suffice, rendering plainly up to four different tones. And indeed, in this aspect of Music, [these instruments] abound in such a variety of tones that you do not know whether you will wonder more at the beneficence of nature or of art.[3]

This comment alludes to the overtone series, which was known empirically but not yet understood theoretically. Perhaps Luscinius could pick out individual overtones in the sound. More likely, he meant that more than one

27

note can be played at any given length of the instrument without the use of tone holes. The comment, equally true of any brass instrument, enables us to deduce something of the range and playing technique of the instrument early in the sixteenth century. He wrote that it can render plainly up to four different notes.

Since Praetorius later singled out one player by name who could play the fundamental (pedal tone), it appears that it would not have been playable by most trombonists even half a century later than Luscinius. Taking the second partial as the lowest note, four notes in any given position would be the second through fifth partials, a range of a major tenth. The second partial itself may not have been playable in all positions by any but the best trombonists. It appears, therefore, that the typical trombonist was largely limited to a total range just over an octave. Virtuosos at a court could presumably play both lower and higher.

After Luscinius's book came out in 1536, it was more than fifty years before any other writer published a description of the trombone. Additional information can be gleaned from the business correspondence of the Nuremburg trombone maker Jorg Neuschel with the Prussian Duke Albrecht. The following trombone-related items are mentioned in two letters written in 1541: "Eyn Silberne Pussonen mit 4 Zugen" (a silver trombone with four slides, or four positions), "4 mundtstuck zu mittelbosaunen" (four mouthpieces for a middle trombone), and "II par bogen an die quart posaun" (two pair of crooks for the quart trombone).[4]

These terms are more than a little cryptic. Even Praetorius, who was trying to educate his readers about music, is sometimes ambiguous. Neuschel was merely trying to justify his pricing. Since the interpretation of what he meant is necessarily speculative and depends on comparing his terminology with later writers, it seems best to offer a range of possibilities rather than attempt a single answer.

The German word *Zug* has a wide variety of meanings, and here could conceivably mean either "slide" or "slide position." If the correspondence means a trombone with four slides, then it concerns a very unusual instrument, unlike any surviving trombone made in the sixteenth century. A four-legged slide seems unlikely in the 1540s, as does anything else that fits the description. Therefore, it seems more reasonable to suppose that "Pussonen mit 4 Zugen" means a trombone with four positions. That sounds very similar to the system of numbering positions first spelled out by Virgiliano in 1600 and elaborated by Speer in 1687. "Zug" is, in fact, the word Speer used for "position." Could the mention of four positions show a

distinction between the true trombone with a U-slide and the earlier slide trumpet, which had only two?

The reference to "mittelbosaunen" and "die quart posaun" indicates that Neuschel made at least three different sizes of trombone. In Praetorius's terminology, *quart posaune* means a bass trombone. A middle trombone would probably correspond to the tenor. If the tenor was a middle trombone to Neuschel, then there must have also been a smaller one in use at the time, which could mean either an alto trombone or a slide trumpet.

Praetorius is quite clear that there were two sizes of bass trombone and also a contrabass or two. He managed to imply, without ever explicitly stating, that there were two sizes of alto. With the tenor, that makes at least six sizes by 1619. Inventories taken in Stuttgart (1589) and Dresden (1593) list *Second-* and *Terz-Pusonen*. We could not expect any greater standardization in Neuschel's time. Therefore, his middle trombone may refer to one of the middle sizes as opposed to one of the larger or smaller sizes. "Middle" implies at least three sizes, leaving open the possibility of more. On the other hand, Fischer has noted that extant tenor trombones can be divided into large-bore and small-bore instruments. Possibly Neuschel's "mittelbosaunen" refers to bore size rather than, or in combination with, length.[5]

Describing a 1568 wedding banquet in Munich, Massimo Troiano mentioned that a madrigal was performed with "six large trombones, of which the bass was an octave lower than the other ordinary ones."[6] At the very least, this means five ordinary (tenor) trombones and a contrabass trombone, which Praetorius would later call an "octave trombone," but Troiano specified six large trombones after having mentioned trombones without an adjective for the previous course of the same banquet. "Tromboni grossi" indicates that perhaps the piece was played on six bass trombones, one of which was a contrabass. But what is meant, in this context, by the phrase "the other ordinary ones"? Ordinary trombones in general (tenors), or the other ordinary large (bass) trombones playing the madrigal? If he meant the latter, then the largest trombone, an octave below the ordinary bass trombone, would be an eye-popping monster, a sub-contrabass trombone!

No sixteenth-century writer after Luscinius attempted to describe and classify instruments for their own sake, but Italian writers who described them as adjuncts to other topics influenced later writers and thus can be seen as transitional figures between Virdung and Praetorius.

Gioseffo Zarlino sought to prove that singers used a particular tuning system, the diatonic syntonon described by Ptolemy, another name for which is just intonation. This tuning system gave a theoretical justification for considering thirds and sixths as consonant intervals, something that traditional Pythagorean theory did not allow. In fact, however, Zarlino devoted much of his energy as a theorist to championing a tuning system that does not and cannot work. His work on instruments must be understood in the context of his last defense of it, his views having been severely criticized both on mathematical grounds and for deficiencies in his understanding of his sources among the ancient Greeks.[7]

Zarlino's most important treatise, *Istitutioni harmoniche*, appeared in 1558 and established his reputation. He followed it with two lesser works, *Dimonstrationi harmoniche* (1571) and *Sopplimenti musicali* (1588). Incidental to his defense of his work on tuning, Zarlino proposed a new classification of instruments as a supplement to the ancient division into wind, string, and percussion groups. Because Zarlino cared about instruments only insofar as they affected the intonation of singers, he developed his classification gradually and piecemeal. In *Istitutioni*, he commented that once tuned, instruments cannot vary their pitch, and so singers must adjust to the instruments' tuning. Apparently recognizing that he had oversimplified, in *Dimonstrationi* he mentioned that some instruments are fixed in their tuning, but that others can play true, just intervals. He did not identify which instruments belonged to either category.[8]

It is only in *Sopplimenti* that Zarlino gave his thoughts about individual instruments in any detail. The trombone, bowed lira, and violins without frets can all play in the diatonic syntonon as perfectly as singers. Other instruments, including the important keyboard instruments, cannot, and so he grudgingly admitted the necessity of temperament. No one temperament could work for all instruments. Zarlino proposed a classification based on two different principles. He first divided wind instruments by physical form. The organ, which is put together of many pieces and played with a keyboard, is in a class by itself. Of the rest, some have holes, such as the flute and shawm, and others do not, such as the trumpet and trombone. The trumpet, being made of one piece, can be played only with the skill of the player's lips and breathing. The trombone, having a slide, can change its length.[9]

Zarlino's second principle of classification considers how much influence the player has over the tuning of particular pitches. On some instruments, notably keyboard instruments, the tuning is fixed and stable, and the player has no control over any pitch. On others, the bowed lira, violin, and trombone mentioned earlier, the player can freely vary the sizes of intervals as required

by the music and guided by his ears. Wind instruments with holes and stringed instruments with frets occupy a middle ground offering some limited possibilities for adjustment.

In addition to his work as a theorist, Zarlino was director of music at San Marco in Venice. In that capacity in 1584, he declined to hire a monk named Lodovico Zacconi to sing in the choir, partly on the grounds of Zacconi's insufficient knowledge of theory. Zacconi secured a court position in Graz and immediately began to write a treatise, *Prattica di musica*, which he published in 1592. He apparently wanted to prove to Zarlino that he knew enough theory to sing for San Marco. Zarlino, who died in 1590, never saw the book. He probably would not have been greatly impressed with it. Zacconi read Latin poorly, Greek not at all, and generally demonstrated that he had trouble understanding even the writings of Zarlino and other Italians.[10]

Where Zarlino excelled in speculative theory, Zacconi was interested in writing only about what a practicing singer would need to know. His interest in instruments was limited to their role in "imitating" the human voice, that is, either doubling vocal parts or substituting for them in liturgical polyphony. Like Zarlino, Zacconi attempted a classification based on whether the instrument had a fixed or stable sound, but drew the distinction very differently. Although his discussion of tuning principles is even less scientific than Zarlino's, it led him in a totally new direction. He appears to be the first writer to catalog the ranges of different instruments.

Zacconi mentioned the trombone in two different passages. He classed the trombone as both stable and alterable: stable because it does not go out of tune as stringed instruments do, and alterable because the slide allows limitless alterations. He gave the trombone's upper range as a' and commented that by using crooks it could go as low as anyone could want. As brief as they are, these comments constitute the fullest and most technically accurate description of the trombone ever published up to that time.[11] (Refer to Fig. 1.9 in chapter 1 for the pitch-naming conventions used in this book.)

Considering the references to a trombone with four positions in the Neuschel letters, it is not anachronistic to apply Speer's explanation of slide positions to Zacconi's range. Without using a crook, the lowest note on a tenor trombone in A, excluding pedal notes, would be E♭. Since later writers say that the crook lowers the instrument a fourth (but since the slide would then in fact allow only six positions by modern reckoning, not seven), the lowest note with the crook would have been BB. It would be interesting to know if Zacconi actually ever heard anyone play that low. Only a few years later, Praetorius was sufficiently impressed with someone who could play pedal *AA* that he mentioned him by name. If my interpretation of Luscinius is correct, there was an improvement in technique on the trombone of revolutionary proportions during the sixteenth century, with the upper range of the instrument growing by a sixth and the lower range by nearly a fourth, not counting the crook.

Ercole Bottrigari followed Zarlino's classification, not Zacconi's. He described instruments of stable pitch (keyboard instruments), alterable pitch (trombones and violins), and stable-alterable pitch (fretted string instruments and wind instruments with holes). Instruments of stable pitch were tuned according to mean-tone temperament, which uses two different sizes of semitone. Instruments of stable-alterable pitch were tuned according to two different principles. Bottrigari passed over wind instruments on the grounds that they cannot conform to any ancient tuning system, but said they come closer to mean-tone tuning than any other. Lutes and viols, on the other hand, had to be tuned with semitones all the same size: smaller than the major semitone of mean-tone temperament and larger than the minor semitone. A skilled player could adjust the notes a little bit in the direction of keyboard tuning, but could hardly play satisfactorily in tune with a keyboard instrument without great difficulty. Trombones, violins, and the human voice, on the other hand, were entirely alterable in tuning. They could use mean-tone tuning when they had to and could otherwise master any ancient or modern tuning system.

Bottrigari drew a very practical conclusion: the three categories of instruments cannot play in tune with each other and therefore should never be used in the same ensemble. In particular, wind instruments should never play together with string instruments. He did mention with approval the large mixed ensembles of the ducal court of Ferrara and the nuns of San Vito, also in Ferrara. These ensembles were made up of highly stable groups of musicians who performed as a large mixed group only rarely, rehearsed many times for each performance, and limited their repertoire to two pieces in the case of the duke's musicians and not much more than that in the case of the nuns. Therefore, he claimed, his glowing report of these concerts in no way contradicted his general disapproval of most mixed ensembles, which lacked both the stability and the discipline to overcome the severe problems caused by incompatible tuning systems.[12]

Giovanni Maria Artusi is most familiar nowadays for his controversy with Monteverdi, but the primary purpose of his best-known treatise was to refute Bottrigari. It begins, therefore, with a consideration of musical instruments based on a concert at San Vito. Artusi covered much the same ground as Bottrigari, but reached a different conclusion. If an instrumental ensemble does not please, the players are at fault, not the instruments—provided, of course, that they are well made. In reaching this conclusion, Artusi discussed the placement of tone holes in most wind instruments and various ways of tonguing. The trombone is entirely free to play in any tuning system. The cornett (a wooden instrument with tone holes and a cup mouthpiece that had replaced the shawm in wind bands), on the other hand, cannot truly play any of them. Artusi agreed with Bottrigari that wind-instrument makers have no mathematical basis for the placement and size of the holes, but denied that they approximate mean-tone tuning. The player can use his tongue and breath to raise or lower the pitch at any fingering.

Artusi rejected the concept of stable-alterable instruments as self-contradictory. An instrument can be stable or alterable, but not both. A much more useful classification, in his view, looked at tuning systems. His first category comprised instruments tuned with unequal semitones: keyboard instruments and double harps. His second included instruments that can bend notes in any direction: not only Bottrigari's voices, trombones, and violins, but also trumpets, cornetts, flutes, and dulcians. His third comprised instruments tuned with equal semitones: lutes, viols, and other fretted string instruments. Where Bottrigari concluded that wind instruments should never play along with fretted string instruments, Artusi contended that wind instruments could play harmoniously with either group. It is keyboard and fretted string instruments that could not play in tune with each other.[13]

In about 1600, Aurelio Virgiliano prepared a manuscript, *Il Dolcimelo* that gives examples of how to fill in intervals for divisions, unaccompanied ricercares for various soprano instruments, and fingering charts for many instruments, including the trombone.[14] It provides no text at all, but from the layout of his tablature (Fig. 3.1), it is clear that Virgiliano conceived the trombone as having four slide positions, producing series of pitches beginning with A, G, F, and E respectively. The notes in first position range from A to *a'*, or second to eighth partials. Not until André Braun, writing in the 1790s, did anyone offer a different enumeration and explanation of slide positions. Most likely, Virgiliano's explanation of slide positions reflects sixteenth-century thought as accurately as it does seventeenth- and eighteenth-century thought.

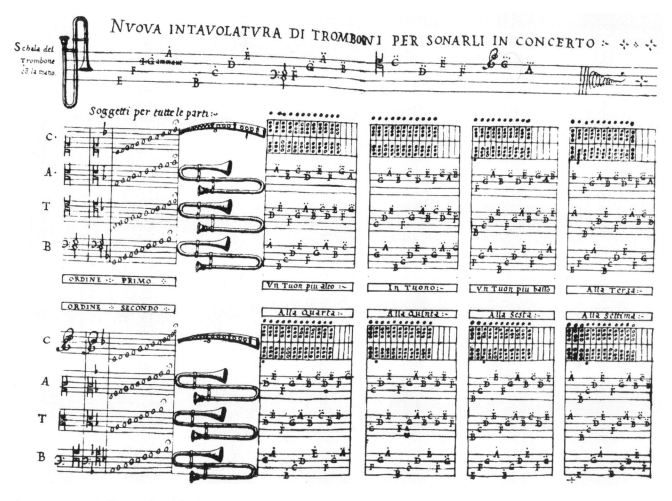

Fig. 3.1. From Virgiliano's *Il Dolcimelo* (ca. 1600). Tom L. Naylor, *The Trumpet & Trombone in Graphic Arts 1500–1800*, plate 74, © by Editions Bim /The Brass Press, www.editions-bim.com

Musical Encyclopedists of the Seventeenth Century

The seventeenth century saw encyclopedic treatises on music of truly monumental proportions. Pietro Cerone's *El Melopeo*, the earliest of these, was published in Naples in 1613. Possibly because it was written in Spanish (Naples being ruled by Aragon at the time), it is the least well known.[15] Unlike the treatises of Praetorius and Mersenne, Cerone's does not provide a detailed description of the various instruments.

Citing both Zarlino and Zacconi, Cerone based his ideas more on the latter. More explicitly than Zacconi, Cerone counted the trombone among the instruments of stable pitch. Where Zacconi said that it was impossible to tune such instruments without damaging them, Cerone merely observed that it is unnecessary, the maker having made them well and of proper proportion. Cerone also copied Bottrigari's contention that the incompatibility of tunings rendered performances of large

mixed ensembles unsatisfactory. His comments on the trombone, therefore, seem largely derivative.

Praetorius

Michael Praetorius' *Syntagma musicum* appeared in three volumes between 1615 and 1619. The first is a learned dissertation on ancient music, written in Latin and intended for scholars. Modern writers have not been greatly interested in it. The second and third volumes, however, written in German for practical musicians, are indispensable for understanding late sixteenth- and early seventeenth-century music. Praetorius was not only a great scholar, but also had considerable practical expertise as a performer and composer.

His descriptions of musical instruments comprise the second volume, subtitled *De organographia*. He divided wind instruments according to whether the wind is supplied by a bellows or the human breath. He further divided the latter into three groups. The trumpets play different notes with breath alone, and do not in any way move themselves. Trombones change pitches by the movement of the slide. All the others have finger holes.[16]

The chapter on classification concludes with three other methods of classification. First, regarding whether pitch stays constant, Praetorius seems to owe more to Zarlino than to Zacconi, although his conclusions differ from both. With all mouth-blown wind instruments, the pitch is not stable and goes out of tune readily. Second, in regard to how many parts of a composition various instruments can play, the trombone is among those that can play only one part. Third, it is explicitly for those whose range is greater, in the hands of a virtuoso, than when played by an ordinary musician.[17]

Praetorius pictured five sizes of trombone: alto, tenor, two sizes of bass, and on another page, contrabass.[18] He gave the alto trombone the alternate name of descant trombone, a term that would later refer to the soprano trombone. The fact that he used both names for the same instrument is sufficient proof that the soprano did not yet exist. Praetorius preferred the sound of the tenor trombone to that of the alto. He pointed out that the tenor could play equally high with practice. Although he never explicitly stated the relationship between alto and tenor trombones, the text implies that the alto is a fourth higher, and the table of ranges implies that it is a fifth higher. Perhaps there were two different sizes of alto trombone.

What we call the tenor trombone Praetorius called the ordinary trombone. He gave the range as *E* to *f'*. This upper limit, a major third lower than that given by Zacconi and Virgiliano, appears at first to be a misprint. Indeed, in his table of the ranges of the various trombones (Fig. 3.2), Praetorius gives *E* as the normal lowest note and *g'* and *a'* as the normal upper limit. Both the table and the text say that skilled players can play both higher and lower than the normal range. For an extended lower range, the table shows *D*, *C*, and *AA*. The *AA* would be the fundamental in first position. *C* and *D* would be available on a valveless tenor trombone only as falset tones. All of these notes would be relatively difficult to produce on the instruments of his day, and very difficult to gain sufficient control over to make them practical in performance situations. The extended upper range in Praetorius's table shows the notes *b'*, *c''*, and *g''*! Lest this last pitch seem like a typographical error, Praetorius claimed Fileno Cornazzani of Munich was but one of a number of trombonists who could comfortably play up to *e''*. Erhardus Borussus, whom Praetorius heard in

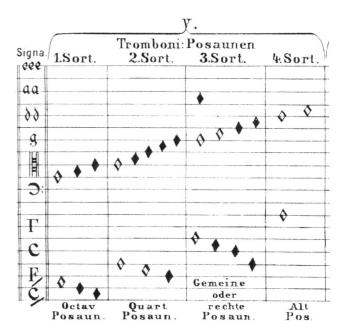

Fig. 3.2. Chart of trombone ranges from Praetorius's *De organographia* (1619).

Dresden, could even play *g''*, or nearly up to the top of the cornett's range. Borussus was also noteworthy for his ability to play pedal *AA* on a tenor trombone and fast coloratura divisions that were more typical of the cornett or viola bastarda.

These virtuosi, of course, were exceptional. Praetorius knew his share of mediocre trombonists. Therefore, he wrote in his third volume, "although some players manage to go up to *g'* on *Chorist*-bassoons, to *a'* on tenor trombones, and still higher yet, only a few are capable of doing this. Everyone else has to stop at *d'* on the bassoons and at *e'*, at the most *a'*, on trombones."[19] In other words, then as now, not everyone was able to get within an octave of certain of the best players.

How does one decide what is a reasonable range that any competent player ought to be able to command? The *f'* given in the second volume as the upper limit may not be a misprint so much as an example of an author changing his mind about something and not catching all instances of his earlier thought in the process of revising and proofreading. The *e'*, as low as it seems for an upper limit, is still one partial higher than the upper range implied by Luscinius. But it does seem, taking all relevant parts of Praetorius's writings into account, as well as his clear debt to Zacconi's work, that the *a'* represents the most accurate way of interpreting his final thoughts about the upper range of the tenor trombone.

Bass trombones were made either a fourth or a fifth lower than the tenor and an octave below the alto (again, implying two sizes of alto). Always using the tenor as the basic instrument, he called the basses quart- and quint-trombone (or fourth- and fifth-trombone). The bass trombone does not have the notes in the same positions as the tenor, but Praetorius considered it an easy transposition. One important feature of the bass trombone that he did not explicitly mention, but showed clearly in his illustrations, is the handle on the slide. The lowest notes on the tenor trombone are as far out on the slide as the human arm can reach. The handle makes up the difference in the length of the two instruments. Oddly enough, the chart shows a lower range for the quart-trombone that is a fifth and a sixth, not a fourth, below that of the tenor. The ordinary upper limit is likewise a fifth below the tenor, giving a normal range of GG to c′ and an extended range of *FF* to g′. The transposition mentioned in the text likewise works only for a bass trombone a fifth, not a fourth, below the tenor.

The contrabass, or octave trombone, "in earlier times was very rarely encountered." Praetorius's description of it is so vague that it was probably not very common in his own time, either. He wrote that there were two kinds, one an instrument proportionately the same as the tenor trombone but an octave lower. Praetorius was familiar with one made by Hans Schreiber and provided an illustration of this kind of contrabass trombone.[20] The Musikmuseet in Stockholm owns a remarkable example built in 1639 by Georg Nicolaus Oller (Fig. 3.3). The other type, Praetorius wrote, is not so long, but has a wider bore and a crook. It is possible that Praetorius had heard of such an instrument, but had not seen one, his claim to the contrary notwithstanding. In any case, he made no attempt to illustrate it.

But if Praetorius could not describe a contrabass trombone clearly, he was confident of how to use one effectively. He wrote that if enough musicians were available, a splendid tutti could be achieved with a tenor trombone, bass trombone, bassoon, or pommer at pitch on the bass line, doubled an octave lower by a contrabass trombone, double bassoon, double pommer, or double bass. He considered it sufficient justification of this practice that it was common in Italy.[21]

Praetorius's justly famous illustrations are not only the best that had been produced up to that time, they are also superior to anything that followed almost until the advent of photography. It is noteworthy that the bass and contrabass trombones have not only a handle, but also a loop of tubing (crook) where the bell section joins the slide. In his text, Praetorius mentioned the crook in passing, but said little about it.

Fig. 3.3. Contrabass trombone by Oller, with Nicholas Eastop, who is 5′10.5″ or 1.78m tall. Courtesy of Nicholas Eastop.

Mersenne

Marin Mersenne, a priest and philosopher, was no match for Praetorius as a practical musician, but he had broader knowledge of more subjects. His writings constitute major contributions not only to the understanding of music, but also physics, mathematics, and other subjects. Of his many writings on music *Harmonie universelle* (1636) is the most important. It consists of seventeen books, of which seven describe musical instruments. (An earlier work in Latin, *Harmonicorum libri*, covers very much the same ground.)

At the beginning of his description of the trombone,[22] Mersenne called it a kind of trumpet, one that is a little different from the military trumpet. His illustration shows the same kind of crook seen in Praetorius's illustrations. He pointed out that it lowers the basic pitch of the instrument by a fourth and was rarely used. Unlike Praetorius, Mersenne offered no scale, and it is not clear how far we can trust the proportions in his illustration.

Unlike almost any other seventeenth-century description of the trombone, Mersenne's does not allow us to discern what its basic pitch is. In the eighteenth century, Padre Martini interpreted Mersenne's "research" as found in *Harmonicorum libri* as supposing a trombone in C.[23] But in fact, when Mersenne described how to play a scale, he used solmisation syllables instead of note names. He did not number the positions. His instructions resemble how a modern trombonist plays a B♭ major scale without a trigger. Trombonists in the early part of the seventeenth century did not hold the instrument the same way modern trombonists do. The presence of a flat stay in Mersenne's illustration justifies presuming that the trombonists he knew had not adopted the new grip. Given the earlier way of holding the instrument, the slide was probably not long enough to play a scale following Mersenne's instructions using the crook.

The trombone was not nearly as common in Mersenne's France as it was at the same time in Germany, England, or Italy. He was quite capable of understanding it, but perhaps had little direct experience with it. That apparent lack of first-hand knowledge makes it difficult to interpret exactly what he was trying to describe. Modern readers and writers must therefore use extreme caution when studying Mersenne's writings in order to avoid being seriously misled.

Various Minor Authors

Pierre Trichet, in a manuscript treatise apparently written in the 1640s, described the construction of the trombone, and especially of the slide, with somewhat greater clarity than Mersenne. He had heard the instrument on more than one occasion and marveled at the cleverness of whoever invented it. He thought it must be a difficult instrument to play and that finding the right notes on it required great skill and long practice.[24]

Like Mersenne, Athanasius Kircher had wide scholarly interests. He wrote 37 voluminous works on many different subjects. Four contain information on music, the most important being *Musurgia universalis* (1650). It is an encyclopedic compendium of the historical, scientific, philosophical, and above all, theoretical knowledge of music of his time, comparable in scope, length, and ambition to the works of Cerone, Praetorius, and Mersenne, although much less informative and reliable.

Kircher made only passing reference to the trombone within his discussion of the trumpet, and it is evident that he had little interest in it.

> Slide trombones have the same nature as military trumpets, with this exception, that by pulling out and pushing in, or reversing the slide, all tones in order can be produced, which we said could not be done in the other. For the lengthening and shortening of the slide has the same effect as the closing or opening of holes in flutes. Since all these things are clear, it is quite unnecessary that we linger any longer over them.[25]

The reason for this lack of interest in the trombone is not difficult to discover. Wind instruments as a whole were less relevant to current trends in Italian music than perhaps at any other time in history. The trombone was in the process of disappearing from many Italian institutions. Kircher's lament on the demise of the cornett in Italian church music serves as well as anything to dramatize this disappearance. The bass instrument he recommended for a cornett ensemble is no longer the trombone, but the bassoon.

Throughout his discussion of instruments, Kircher harped on a point not stressed by any of the earlier writers in this survey: for instruments to sound their best, they must be provided with music that has been especially written for them. Music that is idiomatically written for one kind of ensemble cannot be effectively played by another.

Angelo Berardi wrote several important treatises on counterpoint. A minor work, *Miscellanea musicale* (1689), includes a brief description of musical instruments. "The trombone is a type of trumpet that plays the bass in concertos and symphonies [and] makes a very good effect."[26] In this brief sentence, Berardi mentioned two musical forms that hardly existed in Kircher's time, a mere generation earlier. They mark the first truly new use for the trombone in Italian music for more than a century.

James Talbot, Regis Professor of Hebrew at Trinity College, Cambridge, compiled a detailed description of all of the musical instruments used in England in the late seventeenth century.[27] He never published his findings, but the many additions and corrections to his manuscript show how seriously he was interested and how concerned he was about accuracy. Talbot was clearly familiar with some of the major treatises already cited. In addition to his reading, Talbot consulted with London's leading professional musicians for additional details. In his description of the trombone, he gave credit to Gottfried Finger and William Bull.

Unlike Mersenne, who merely gave the overall length of the instrument with the slide closed and fully extended, Talbot provided measurements for every segment of the trombone, beginning with the mouthpiece, in feet, inches, and eighths of an inch. He added the reference letters from Mersenne's illustration to his measurements. Although Talbot attempted to be accurate within an eighth of an inch, the numbers do not add up correctly. One measurement, which should start where the slide section joins the bell section, actually starts at the end of the slide. Therefore, the length of the second yard of the slide is counted twice.

It is interesting that Talbot chose to use the bass trombone for his measurements and noted that the tenor trombone is about 8/11 the length of the bass trombone. That would indicate that the trombone was by that time used only as a bass instrument. Talbot says that it was used in consort with the "English Hautbois," by which he appears to mean a shawm, in contrast to the "French Hautbois," which is essentially the modern oboe. He does not mention crooks.

A somewhat earlier English description of the trombone appeared in Randle Holme's *Academy of Armory* (1688). It can be found in Holme's manuscript, but was deleted from the published version.[28] It is interesting primarily as the earliest description of the trombone in English, but it is not especially informative. It simply lists the various parts of the instrument and makes a very clumsy stab at describing the slide.

Speer and His Followers

Among other prose works, Daniel Speer wrote the last of the Baroque musical behemoths.[29] But unlike the others, Speer's treatise is not at all concerned with ancient history or philosophical speculation. Even more than Praetorius's, Speer's treatise is the work of a practicing musician written for the sake of other practicing musicians, not scholars or amateurs. Speer's writing is entirely original, with no evident verbal dependence on any earlier author. His ideas, however, have much in common with those of Virgiliano and Praetorius. Like Praetorius, he considered the tenor trombone as the basic instrument, capable of playing both alto and bass parts. His understanding of slide positions is essentially the same as Virgiliano's, although explained in prose and musical notation. (It is analyzed at length below under Pitch.) He acknowledged the fundamental (*AA*) in first position, although not in any of the other positions. Speer also attempted to describe how to assemble a trombone, how to hold it, and how to play trills. He briefly considered the alto and bass trombones. Unlike Praetorius, who

described two sizes of bass trombone, Speer mentioned only the *Quint-posaunen*.

Throughout the eighteenth century, numerous dictionaries, encyclopedias, and treatises mentioned the trombone. Mersenne and Speer were the ultimate source for nearly all of them. In my first book, I quoted and described as many of them as I could find.[30] It is enough to say here that the majority of these authors quite evidently had no first-hand familiarity with the trombone, and the ones who did showed little interest in it.

It was during this time, however, that the soprano trombone made its first appearance in the literature. In 1713, Johann Mattheson may have had a soprano trombone in mind when he mentioned both a large and a small alto trombone, as well as a tenor and two basses. Johann Samuel Halle made a more explicit reference to the soprano trombone. Jean Benjamin de la Borde, the first French writer of the eighteenth century who had first-hand acquaintance with the trombone, mentioned both soprano and contrabass trombones.[31]

Alexandre Choron's revision of a treatise by Francoeur begins with the astonishing statement that the trombone was invented in Italy about forty years earlier (that is, in the 1770s) and introduced to France about thirty years earlier. An Italian trombonist, Antonio Mariotti, astounded French audiences with his skill on the trombone when he arrived in Paris in or shortly before 1789. Choron must have thought that Mariotti played a new instrument of his own invention. The rest of his explanation of the trombone appears to be largely copied from Othon Vandenbroek.[32]

New Ideas from Braun and Others

It is only at the very end of the eighteenth century that anyone offered a really new description of the trombone, when André Braun described a trombone in B♭ rather than A, with seven chromatic positions instead of four diatonic positions. He also explained how to assemble and hold the trombone more successfully than Speer did and provided the earliest published études. He described only one size of trombone, the bass, but his title promised a method for alto, tenor, and bass. There are only diagrams of the alto and tenor trombone, showing the notes in each position. These are sufficient indication that Braun conceived both the bass and tenor trombones in B♭ and the alto trombone in E♭. By the time Braun published his treatise, the trombone had come back from the brink of extinction. Trombone makers, and apparently especially French makers, began to introduce design changes for the first time since the introduction of the rounded stays in the early seventeenth century. Braun was the first author to describe the tuning slide.[33]

Joseph Fröhlich stated explicitly that the bass trombone was, like the tenor trombone, an instrument in B♭. The two instruments differed principally in the mouthpiece. The bass trombone had a large mouthpiece that emphasized the low register, and the tenor had a smaller mouthpiece that emphasized the higher notes. The alto trombone was a fourth higher, making the higher notes easier to play. Fröhlich was the first author to describe the mouthpiece in any detail and to advocate the use of alternate positions.[34]

Some years later Andreas Nemetz copied much of what Fröhlich wrote in his trombone method. Nemetz played a variety of instruments proficiently, like many musicians trained in the *Stadtpfeifer* tradition, but his principal instrument was trombone. He appears, therefore, to be the earliest writer on the trombone to specialize in playing it, although Speer and Braun, at least, certainly played trombone among other instruments. Nemetz's command of the instrument becomes apparent in the scales and études he provided, and also in details he added to what he copied from Fröhlich. He expanded the range of the instrument quite dramatically. Fröhlich showed only five notes in each position, second through sixth partials, implying a range of *E* to *f'*, although the scale he gave goes up to *g'*. Nemetz showed the fundamental through the twelfth partial for each position, and so added an octave to each end of Fröhlich's range. Nemetz explicitly stated that the alto, tenor, and bass trombones differ only in the size of the mouthpiece. In so saying, he went beyond Fröhlich, who only equated the bass and the tenor.[35]

Braun, Fröhlich, and Nemetz, each more explicitly than the last, either implied or stated that all trombone parts could be played on a B♭ instrument, and that the three traditional voices, alto, tenor, and bass, merely required different mouthpieces. It would be a mistake, however, to infer from these comments that alto and bass trombones in other pitches were no longer used. Fröhlich showed slide positions for an alto trombone in E♭. Nemetz showed them for a bass trombone in F.

Gottfried Weber first described the trombone in the context of an explanation of acoustics that was serialized in the *Allgemeine musikalische Zeitung* in 1816.[36] After describing the overtone series as it appears in a tube, Weber considered various means of filling in the gaps: the generally unsatisfactory expedient of bending a note up or down, muting, using a slide, and by means of tone holes. He also considered the alto, tenor, and bass trombones essentially the same instrument except for the

size of the mouthpiece. He hinted, but did not explicitly state, that the three varieties also could be built with different bores. He compared all three to a B♭ trumpet. Before the valve forever transformed the trumpet, trumpets and trombones had the same fundamental. When used as a melody instrument (that is, as a clarino), the trumpet had a very narrow bore and was the provenance of specialists in that range. The bass trombone had both a larger mouthpiece and wider bore and specialized in playing the lower partials. Weber claimed that the fundamental was not used and that the bass trombone never played higher than the sixth partial, a range comparable to that given by Fröhlich.

Because Weber described the trombone in the context of explaining various ways of filling in the gaps in the overtone series, he laid great emphasis on the number of positions needed for that purpose. That not enough positions are available to fill the octave between the highest fundamental (*BB♭*) and the lowest second partial (*E*) justified not using the fundamental. As the interval between adjacent partials becomes smaller, fewer different positions are required to fill in the gap and some notes can be played in more than one position. The tenor trombone specializes in the middle harmonics. Weber wrote that the second partial is not used on the tenor trombone, but that the seventh is added to the top. The alto trombone in B♭ specializes in the upper harmonics and uses nothing lower than the fourth partial.

Weber published a proposal for improving the trombone later the same year. He advocated a bass trombone with a four-legged slide. Although this proposal is well within the chronological limits of this chapter, conceptually it belongs in the next.

Augustin Sundelin wrote a manual on instrumentation for composers of orchestral music. Although it is more informative than Francoeur's or Vandenbroek's, it is not an outstanding work. What is forward-looking and unprecedented is that he also issued a similar manual for composers of music for military band.[37]

He gave the alto trombone's range as *c* to *b'*, the tenor's as *c* to *g'*. and the bass's from *C* to *e'*. He did not specify the fundamental pitch of each instrument, but evidently considered the alto and tenor trombones the same and the bass lower. Most likely, he thought of both the alto and tenor trombones as B♭ instruments and did not believe that the second partial was usable in either role. Since C is not available on a B♭ instrument, his bass trombone must have been in F, or less likely, E♭. As its upper note is only a third lower than the tenor's, the bass trombonist must have been the strongest player in the section. Neither alto nor tenor trombones are ever used without the other two sizes, although the bass trombone may occasionally play alone. Long sustained chords, short staccato chords, or sforzandos are suitable for the trombones, and rapid repeated notes work well, but not wide leaps or any kind of figuration.

It appears that Sundelin considered trombonists in general weaker musicians than the rest of the orchestra or band. He recommended against using trombones at the very beginning of a piece unless other instruments are playing, on the grounds that trombones have no other means of finding their notes and playing them in tune! No one ever suggested that violins or other stringed instruments could not play their first chord in tune without help from other instruments. Two hundred years earlier, Praetorius had recommended tuning to the tenor trombone, so Sundelin's suggestion that trombonists could not be trusted at the beginning of a piece implies a stunning deterioration of competence. That may in turn explain why so many trombone parts from the early part of the nineteenth century and before are so boring. The most interesting difference between Sundelin's recommendations for the orchestra and military band is that the latter often uses four trombones, with two being bass trombones that usually play in octaves.

Early Trombone Makers

There are 148 extant trombones made before 1800 in museums or private collections. Most were manufactured in Germany or Austria (especially Nuremberg). Several were made in Sweden, with one each from Italy, France, and possibly Switzerland.[38]

From the late fifteenth century well into the eighteenth century, Nuremberg was the most important center for the manufacture of trumpets and trombones. The city council, which maintained strict control over the brass industry, named Hans Neuschel the elder as a master craftsman in 1479. Before that, he had been a piece-worker, and his production had included slides (*Ziehstücke*). At such an early date, the slides could have been made either for trombones or slide trumpets. Neuschel, who also became a *Stadtpfeifer* in 1491, founded the oldest of Nuremberg's trumpet- and trombone-making dynasties. His son, Hans Neuschel the younger, is credited with improving the making of trombones in 1498. He was a trombonist and *Stadtpfeifer*, and important enough to be pictured and named in Maximilian's *Triumph*. (Refer to Fig. 5.3 in chapter 5.) Customers for his trombones included Pope Leo X. His reputation as a trombone maker remained strong long after his death. Nearly two hundred years later, an entry on Neuschel

appeared in J. G. Doppelmayr's overview of important thinkers and artists in Nuremberg's history. The last member of the dynasty, Jorg (or Georg) Neuschel was apparently an adopted son of Hans the younger. His customers included the kings of Denmark, Poland, and England. A trombone made by him in 1557 is the only surviving trombone made by this family, although not much is left of the original workmanship.[39]

Jorg Neuschel had no children, but he married the widow of a Munich *Stadtpfeifer* named Anton Schnitzer, whose son Anton took over his business. The Schnitzer family is difficult to describe. Anton Schnitzer may be a descendent of Albrecht Schnitzer of Munich, four of whose sons moved to Nuremberg.[40] Erasmus Schnitzer, whose connection with other Schnitzers remains undocumented, built what is now the oldest extant trombone in 1551, although not much of it is original. The Schnitzers specialized in elaborate ceremonial instruments of the most masterful construction, which may indicate the quality of instruments made by the Neuschels.

The Hainleins, another important family, descended from a long-established family of coppersmiths. Sebastian Hainlein the elder was the first to make brass instruments. Other members of the family are Sebastian the younger, his brother Hans, son Paul, and grandson Michael. Paul Hainlein, like his father, was a trombonist as well as instrument maker. Two generations of the Kodisch family made trombones. The most important member, Johann Karl Kodisch, made instruments with a higher degree of terminal flare than those of his contemporaries. Carter describes one made in 1701.[41] Compare the lower instrument in Fig. 3.4 with the more common profile above it. Flaring bells would not become common until the nineteenth century.

Johann Wilhelm Haas, the first of three generations of instrument makers, learned the trade from Hans Hainlein. The Ehe family lasted for five generations. Although the first three generations of Ehes prospered and produced excellent instruments, some members of the fourth and fifth generations died as paupers, reflecting the general decline in the fortunes of Nuremberg brass craftsmen in the late eighteenth century.

A number of factors drove the decline of Nuremberg's brass instrument industry. Social and political forces in the late eighteenth and early nineteenth centuries led to the elimination of many small courts, which had provided the main customer base for Nuremberg's craftsmen. In 1806, as a result of the dissolution of the Holy Roman Empire, Nuremberg lost its status as a free imperial city and became just another town. The kind of trumpet that the Nuremberg craftsmen made was obsolete by the end

Fig. 3.4. Above: Trombone by Michael Nagel (Nuremberg, 1656). Below: Trombone by Johann Karl Kodisch (Nuremberg, 1701). Note the flaring bell in comparison with Nagel's trombone. National Music Museum, University of South Dakota.

of the eighteenth century. The trombone had come perilously close to disappearing decades before that.

Had Nuremberg's craft guilds been more flexible and imaginative, however, they could have overcome these problems and continued to thrive in the new cultural conditions of the nineteenth century. Instead, while manufacturers elsewhere developed machinery and techniques for mass production, Nuremberg makers limited themselves to the old-fashioned hand techniques. Demand for the high-end products of a master craftsman had all but ceased. The lesser craftsmen producing the more ordinary instruments attempted to speed production using old instead of modern techniques, but at the cost of hasty, careless, and crude workmanship.[42]

The decline of Nuremberg as the main center of brass instrument making directly coincides with the rise of various workshops in Saxony. Elector Augustus II, the Strong (r. 1694–1733) was a major patron of the arts and encouraged trade. Where Nuremberg trumpet makers were limited by their guild in both technology and the size of their workshop, Saxon law allowed great flexibility in both. A workshop founded as a sideline in Pfaffendorf by George Schmied some time in the late seventeenth century seems to be the earliest of the important Saxon workshops.[43] Others went into business in Leipzig around 1710, Dresden after 1720, and Markneukirchen after 1760, to name only a few Saxon centers of brass instrument manufacture. By about 1800, there were fifteen brass workshops in Markneukirchen alone.

Schmied was a parish clerk and school teacher by trade. At his death in 1718, he was acknowledged as a skilled craftsman as well. Such a sideline was not uncommon when Nuremberg instruments were good but expensive, and demand for brass instruments was relatively small. His son, two grandsons, and a great-grandson continued the business.

Extant Schmied trombones include four sopranos, seven altos, four tenors, and seven basses. Except for an alto trombone probably made in 1692, all of them were made between 1773 and 1804. Most were made for local churches, but because of Pfaffendorf's proximity to Herrnhut, headquarters of the Moravian church, American Moravians became important clients as well. At least six of the Schmied trombones used in America are still extant. It appears that Schmied instruments were intended for average users, not the top virtuosos in important courts.

The earliest brass instrument maker authenticated in Berlin's archives is Hans Schrieber, appointed to the court in 1616. Very little is known of him, but he made a contrabass trombone in 1615, apparently to demonstrate his abilities at the time of his application. Praetorius mentioned this instrument as being twice as long as the ordinary trombone and pitched an octave lower.[44] The archives identify Schreiber as a "gross vnnd klein Posaunen, vnnd andere blasende Instrumentmacher" (maker of large and small trombones and other wind instruments). Not one of his trombones is extant.

No other brass instrument makers appear in the archives until 1691, when two Huguenot craftsmen, Abraham and Paul Blanvalet, settled in Berlin after having been forced out of France by the revocation of the

Edict of Nantes. The Blanvalet family held a monopoly on trumpet and trombone making in Prussia until 1780, when A. F. Krause opened a shop in Potsdam. Krause helped pave the way for Berlin to become a dominant center of brass instrument manufacture when, in 1792, he prevailed upon the government to raise the import tax on trumpets, trombones, and horns to a level that stifled competition.

The days of royal monopolies were over in Berlin, however. Almost immediately, other brass instrument makers set up shop, beginning with Elsner in 1794. Elsner's apprentice, Johann Caspar Gabler, is much better known. Christian Gottfried Eschenbach opened his business in 1804, and Johann Gottfried Moritz arrived in Berlin no later than 1808, in which year the firm of Griesling & Schlott began manufacturing brass instruments as well.[45]

Anthony Baines wrote that Cormery and Courtois "must have been among" the first French makers of trombones at the end of the eighteenth century.[46] Until someone undertakes a documentary study of early French makers, it will be impossible to do more than approve his speculation and present reasons for supposing that he may be correct.

If the trombone was not completely unknown throughout most of eighteenth-century France, it was essentially irrelevant until 1760, when Gossec included trombone parts in his *Messe des morts*. In the 1770s, Gluck produced five operas in Paris that require trombones, and French composers began to use them with increasing frequency. It was not until 1789, however, that trombones became permanent members of any French orchestra. The Revolution broke out in that year. Between operas and band music for revolutionary festivals, there was a surge of demand for trombones. There was also a strong desire on the part of the French government to minimize dependence on foreigners, which directly led to the foundation of the Conservatory and probably also to the beginnings of the manufacture of French trombones.[47]

Pierre noted 473 instrument makers active in Paris some time between 1775 and 1800, including 29 makers of wind instruments. Of these, seven can be identified as brass instrument makers, mostly of horns: Amboulevart, Brunet, Jean-François Cormery, the Courtois family, Lefèvre, the Raoux family, and François Riedloker, the first to make a tuning slide for the trombone. Some, if not all, of these firms probably made trombones some time before 1800.[48]

In 1804, Amboulevart sold his business to Jean Hilaire Asté, the first of three men to do business under the name of Halary. This firm was a distinguished maker

of brass instruments, including trombones, throughout most of the nineteenth century. Cormery sold his business to his pupil Riedloker in 1791. Riedloker in turn sold out to Halary in 1831.

In the early nineteenth century, members of the Courtois family established two different businesses. Courtois Frères (Courtois Brothers), established in 1803, became known as Antoine Courtois in 1844. This company exists to this day, although under different ownership. Courtois Neveu Aîné (Courtois, oldest nephew), probably also founded in or about 1803, eventually passed his business to his sons. This firm was briefly known as "Les trois fils de Courtois neveu" (the three sons of the Courtois nephew), but eventually became Auguste Courtois in 1847.

Although Nuremberg trombone makers sold their wares all over Europe, there is probably no place that did not produce at least some trombones locally. German trombone makers in districts not already mentioned include Petrus Goltbeck of Cottbus (fl. 1635) and Rudolf Veit of Naumburg (fl. 1650). Trombones made by Hanns Geyer of Vienna are extant from 1676 and 1702. The earliest extant bass trombone was made in 1593 by Pierre Colbert of Rheims, France.

In about 1584, Simon Brewer, a Dutchman living in England, complained that although his only source of income was making and repairing trumpets and trombones, George Landall had obtained a royal monopoly to conduct that business. Pointing out that, as one of the queen's trumpeters, Langdall had other sources of income, Brewer petitioned for relief from Langdall's monopoly and the right to continue to ply his trade. English makers of a later date who are still within the chronological limits of this chapter are more difficult to identify. Baines says that the Courtois design "stifled" native instruments by F. Pace and others.[49]

Jean Arnold Antoine Tuerlinckx began to manufacture instruments in Mechelin, Belgium, in 1771. He first established his reputation as a maker of clarinets and arrows. Eventually, he and his son employed 40 workers in two shops, one for woodwind and one for brass instruments. They could and frequently did supply the entire instrumentation of civil and military wind bands. Although they were not innovators, they kept their designs and processes up to date.

Early Manufacturing Techniques

Although occasional references can be found to other materials, such as silver, the vast majority of trombones have been made of brass, an alloy of copper and zinc.

Brass has been used for thousands of years, but the existence and nature of zinc was not known until well into the seventeenth century. Before that, brass was produced by melting copper and the mineral calamine, a zinc ore. After the slag was skimmed off the top and the metal poured out, it was hammered into sheets.[50]

Straight tubes, called yards, were made by bending sheet metal around a mandrel and soldering the seam. Bent tubes, called bows, required finished tubes to be filled with lead, bent on a jig, and hammered smooth. Bells were made from sheet metal wrapped around a special mandrel, soldered, and hammered into shape. Probably journeymen made all of the individual pieces, and the master craftsman assembled and finished them.[51]

Differences in how early and modern trombones are assembled have important implications for both sound and technique. Early bell sections were held together with only one flat stay instead of the modern three tubular stays. Early and modern slides both have two stays, but the early ones were flat and not soldered in place. That a few early instruments have fixed tubular stays is attributable to their having been repaired generations after they were first made.[52]

Mersenne noted that the stays could be removed easily, making trombones easy to make and to carry.[53] The mounted trombonists pictured in *The Triumph of Maximilian* have what appears to be some kind of case hanging from their horses. (See Fig. 3.5.) It would not seem possible to put a trombone in such a case without disassembling it more completely than is necessary today. Trombones must have required more frequent and drastic repairs in those days. The ability to dismantle a trombone easily must have certainly made fixing it faster and easier. When he sent me the picture of a slide stay (refer to Fig. 2.10 in chapter 2), Herbert W. Myers pointed out the pin and chain, the typical method of attachment.

In the early sixteenth century, there may have been an additional reason for trombonists to disassemble their instruments, although so far it is entirely speculative; the same parts that can be put together to make a trombone with a U-slide suitable for performing along with voices can be assembled differently to make a field trumpet for military use or a single-slide trombone (slide trumpet) suitable for traditional *alta* band functions![54] The loose construction also allows the bell to resonate more, although it is not clear whether that is an additional reason for removable stays or an accidental by-product.

The different construction of the Renaissance trombone requires a fundamentally different approach to playing it. While not impossible to hold and play it in the modern way, it is awkward and uncomfortable. First,

the one bell stay is too far from the player's left hand to grip it with the thumb. Second, the flat stays cut into the player's hand, generating tremendous pressure on a small area. Third, with no counterweight at the bell bow, and with the bell extending further than the modern bell, the instrument is front-heavy. Fourth, the loose construction allows movement in all directions and offers little resistance to rotational torque.

It is quite evident from sixteenth- and seventeenth-century artworks that contemporary trombonists did not hold the trombone the way we do. McGowan has studied pictures and other evidence and proposed a more comfortable grip.[55] This alternative has a number of consequences besides the player's comfort. It allows the ornate stays to remain visible. It facilitates removing the outer slide to empty out condensation—an important advantage before the invention of the water key—and it makes it impossible to close the slide all the way while the instrument is being played. The latter fact is not a disadvantage, but has important implications for tuning and pitch.

The earliest depiction of the modern way of holding a trombone appears to be on the ceiling of the Rosenberg Castle in Copenhagen, which shows the trombonists of King Christian IV. It was probably painted between 1610 and 1620. The earliest extant trombone clearly made with round stays as original equipment is a tenor made by Sebastian Hainlein in 1631. It seems likely that the round stay came about because players were changing the way they held their instruments. That in turn may be because changing pitch standards made it desirable to close the slide all the way in order to play B♭ in first position.[56]

Pitch

Most of the earliest extant tenor trombones produce an overtone series on B♭ according to modern pitch standards in what is now considered first position. For this reason, many authors who have not taken the trouble to investigate further have claimed that Renaissance and Baroque tenor trombones were in B♭, just like modern trombones. Nicholas Bessaraboff even dismissed the claims of better scholars than he, who had actually studied documentary evidence, as fiction. Although the arrogance was his own, his information and reasoning appear mostly to be copied from Sachs. There was no one standard pitch in the late Renaissance and Baroque periods. Instead, there were choir pitch, used for church music, and chamber pitch, used for secular music. Choir pitch was usually either two or three semitones higher

Fig. 3.5. *Triumph of Maximilian I*, plate 78, showing mounted trombonists. Dover edition.

than chamber pitch, but in some times and places, chamber pitch was higher than choir pitch. The actual frequency of these pitches varied widely. Each town had its own local pitch, which changed over the course of time. Because of this complexity, playing period instruments to find out which notes are in first position cannot possibly tell us their key in Baroque terms.[57]

Sachs assumed that the lowest notes given by Praetorius were to be understood as the second partial in seventh position. Since the alto trombone had *B* as its lowest note, the first position note in that partial would be *f*. Therefore, he concluded that the alto trombone was in F. Similarly, Praetorius gave the lowest note of the tenor trombone as *E*. If *E* is the second partial in seventh position, then *B♭* is the second partial in first position, meaning that the tenor trombone was in B♭.

In this reasoning, he failed to notice two important differences between the seventeenth-century and twentieth-century mind and at least one important difference between the form and construction of early and modern trombones. First, trombonists in Praetorius's day would not have understood the concept of seventh position. As far as they were concerned, the trombone had only four. Virgiliano's tablature showed the four positions as having a lowest note of A, G, F, and E respectively. The difference between A and E is a perfect fourth. The difference between a modern first and seventh position is an augmented fourth.

It would almost seem like the slide of the early trombone was a half step shorter than the modern trombone except for the second concept that Sachs neglected. Seventeenth-century musicians thought in diatonic terms. Acknowledgement of chromatic notes would have seemed a needless complication. Sachs missed one key comment by Praetorius:

> I humbly believe that there is no better instrument for finding correct pitch than a trombone, especially those formerly and presently made in Nuremberg; for if one extends the slide the width of two fingers, it gives, in true choir pitch, exactly the right and proper tenor *a'*.[58]

Praetorius's illustrations clearly show detachable flat stays, which made it necessary to hold the trombone in such a way that the slide could not be fully closed. If that grip resulted in a first position with the slide extended the amount that Praetorius recommended, then the inability to close the slide fully was no disadvantage, but something taken for granted in determining correct tuning. Carse supposed, although without any apparent knowledge of this particular passage in Praetorius, that the slide in a seventeenth-century first position was extended far enough to correspond to a modern second position.[59]

At the end of the seventeenth century, Speer provided the most detailed explanation of the four-position system ever written. (See Fig. 3.6.) The notes and positions are exactly the same ones given by Virgiliano at the beginning of the century, but Speer describes them in prose. The first position notes show three octaves of the familiar overtone series, although there was not enough room on the page for the music typesetter to show the high *a'*. It is important to note two deviations from the strict overtone series.

First, it includes *c'* rather than *c♯'*. Although the overtone series as a set of ratios and as the series of notes produced by a trumpet or by dividing a monochord had been known since the time of Pythagoras, the physics of overtones was not discovered until an experiment by John Wallis in 1677,[60] and the concept of an overtone series as we now understand it did not enter the realm of music theory until the publication of Rameau's *Traité de l'harmonie* in 1722. In terms of seventeenth-century theory, therefore, the *c'* was entirely proper, but it cannot be played with the slide in the same place as the other notes. Speer points out that it must be played with the slide extended about three inches. He also comments that *f♯'* is played in the same place. This rather offhand remark is one of only two references to a chromatic note in Speer's entire discussion of the trombone.

The second deviation from the overtone series in Speer's notated first position is simply a misprint. The note *g'* in the example is erroneously shown as *g♯'* in the caption, a note that is not playable in first position. The notated *g'* agrees with Virgiliano's tablature. Perhaps the typesetter was thinking of the *f♯'* that Speer mentions in his commentary. In the extended first position, GG♯ would be the fundamental and *f♯'* the seventh partial. Of the two notes, *f♯'* is a more basic and common note in late seventeenth-century music than *g♯'*. Oddly enough, the misprint was copied without comment for more than a century.[61]

The outer positions show progressively less of the overtone series. Only one position is given for each note. Seventeenth-century trombonists were probably aware that some notes are available in more than one position, but if any of them actually used alternate positions, no documentary evidence survives. By Speer's fourth position, only the second and third partials are necessary. But here, he found it necessary to introduce a second chromatic note, B♭. He pointed out that it is necessary to extend the slide somewhat beyond where it is for the other two notes (about four inches, actually). With the introduction of this note, we can correctly compare Speer's numbering system with the modern system:

Erster Zug	First position (A overtone series)
Extended *Erster Zug*	Second position (A♭ overtone series)
Anderer Zug	Third position (G overtone series)
Extended *Anderer Zug*	Fourth position (F♯ overtone series)
Dritter Zug	Fifth position (F overtone series)
Vierdte Zug	Sixth position (E overtone series)
Extended *Vierdte Zug*	Seventh position (E♭ overtone series)

Why trombone in A? Is that not odd for a basic pitch? We need to lay aside our modern assumptions and think diatonically. As Virgiliano's and Speer's treatises make clear, trombones were considered to have four basic positions. On a trombone in A, all but one of the notes in a C major scale is available in one of the first three basic positions. The *c* is in third position, *d* in second, *e* in first, *f* in third, *g* in second, *a* in first, and *b* in second. The *c'* in the extended first position is the only diatonic note that cannot be played in a basic position.

The modern way of holding the instrument, which made a BB♭ overtone series available for the first time, first appears in the early seventeenth century in Denmark. It seems to have taken almost two centuries before theorists began to explain the trombone as having seven chromatic positions, with the first in B♭, rather than four diatonic positions with the first in A. Writing in 1811, Fröhlich made it clear that many of his contemporaries still thought of the trombone in the old-fashioned, diatonic way.[62]

Something more than tradition and habit kept the older view alive for so long. Given the multiplicity of pitches all over Europe, the old way of numbering positions may have been a more sensible explanation in some places. For example, soloistic trombone parts are usually in sharp keys in eighteenth-century Salzburg, but in flat

Erſtlich iſt zu wiſſen/ daß eine Poſaun in zwey Theilen beſtehet/ nemlich im Hauptſtuck und in Stangen/ welche in einer Scheide ſtecken/ es wird aber das Hauptſtuck auf die Stangen eingezäpfft/ und mit der lincken Hand die gantze Poſaun gehalten/ welche bräuchliche Haltung der Informator ſeinem Lehrling ſchon zeigen wird/ mit der rechten Hand aber ergreifft man die Scheide zwiſchen die Finger; dieſe hat nun drey vornemliche Züge/ der erſte Zug iſt beym Mundſtuck/ und beſtehet in folgenden Buchſtaben/ ſo das beygeſetzte Exempel weiſet:

Erſter Zug.

A c á c e g♯ und a.
A

Dieſer Buchſtaben Thon werden alle im erſten Zug gefunden/ auſſer/ daß das c. um zwey quehr Finger etwas vorwarts muß gezogen werden/ bey welchem Zuge auf das f. ♯. ſich befindet.

Der ander Zug iſt beym Hauptſtuck/ und befinden ſich folgende Buchſtaben darinnen/ wie zu erſehen:

Anderer Zug.

G d g ♮ d

NB. Bey dieſem Zug iſt zu mercken/ daß das b. mol, um zwey quehr Finger hinaußwarts muß gezogen werden.

Der dritte Zug iſt vier quehr Finger außwarts deß Hauptſtucks/ und hat folgende Buchſtaben/ wie zu erſehen:

Dritter Zug.

F c f

Der vierdte Zug auf einer Tenor-Poſaun/ ſo man einen Baß darauf tractiret/ iſt ſo weit drauſſen/ als mans mit dem Arm faſt erſtrecken kan/ und ſeyn folgender Thon-Buchſtaben/ wie zu erſehen:

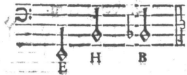

E H B

NB. B. mol muß noch um etwas weiters als die fördern zwey Buchſtaben E. und H. gezogen werden.

Wie werden die Semitonia gezogen?

Die harten als mit ♯. bezeichneten hohen Semitonia werden von ihrem natürlichen Thon hineinwarts/ die mit b. aber bezeichneten nidrigen Semitonia, werden um zwey quehr Finger hinaußwarts gezogen. NB. Die Triller werden mit dem Kien/ wie fornen bey der Trompeten gedacht worden/ gemacht; theils ſchleiffen auch den Poſaunen-Schall mit dem Athem/ kommt aber beſſer herauß und lebhaffter/ wann er mit der Zungen fein friſch geſtoſſen wird; die moderation im forte und piano wird durch den ſtarcken und ſchwachen außlaſſenden Athem gemacht/ wie auf allen blaſenden Inſtrumenten/ und braucht dieſes Inſtrument keine ſonderliche Leibs-Kräfften/ ſondern es kan ein Knab von acht/ neun oder zehen Jahren/ ſchon kecklich/ Leibs-Kräffte halber/ lernen/ ſonderheitlich einen Baß auf einer Tenor-Poſaun/ welcher gar ſchlechten Wind gebrauchet.

Fig. 3.6.   Explanation of slide positions in Speer's *Grundrichtiger. . .unterricht. . .* (1697). Courtesy of the Rita Benton Music Library of the University of Iowa.

keys in Vienna. In fact, Vienna's pitch changed near the end of the first decade of the eighteenth century.[63] Therefore, it may have been more natural to think of slide positions in the old way in Salzburg but the new way in Vienna.

In Paris, Gossec wrote E♭ in his *Messe des morts* in 1760, but by the end of the century, the score was marked with an 8[va] sign.[64] It appears that pitch in Paris more nearly resembled that of Vienna than that of Salzburg. Given that Paris was a magnet that drew composers from all over the world to have their works performed and published there, and given the worldwide influence of the Viennese composers Gluck, Haydn, Mozart, and Beethoven, it is not surprising that something like this pitch level, at which it is more natural to think of trombones in B♭ than in A, eventually became the worldwide standard. Trombone in B♭ and trombone in A are different ways of thinking about the trombone, not different ways of designing or making one. As a physical object, they are the same.

Notes

1. Sebastian Virdung, *Musica getutscht* (Basle, 1511); facs. ed. by Robert Eitner (Berlin: Trautwein, 1882), fol. Aiii, Biv, E; English translation by Beth Bullard, *Musica getutscht: A Treatise on Musical Instruments (1511) by Sebastian Virdung* (Cambridge: Cambridge University Press, 1993), 98, 107, 121–22. The illustration can also be found in Tom L. Naylor, *The Trumpet & Trombone in Graphic Arts, 1500–1800* (Nashville, Tenn.: Brass Press, 1979), plate 75.

2. Martin Agricola, *Musica instrumentalis deudsch* (Wittenberg: Georg Rhau, 1529, 1545); facs. ed. by Robert Eitner (Leipzig: Breitkopf & Härtel, 1896); English translation by William E. Hettrick, *The 'Musica instrumentalis deudsch' of Martin Agricola: A Treatise on Musical Instruments, 1529 and 1545* (Cambridge: Cambridge University Press, 1994). The illustration can also be found in Naylor, *Trumpet & Trombone*, plate 76.

3.

Fiunt praeterea quaedam tubae ductiles ne qua in parte Musicae desit modulanei facultas. Quae Quanuis monophona sint tantum, tament habent systema: ut si polyphona essent, sufficerent plane ad quadrifaria uoces reddendas singulae: adiadeoq[ue] in hac parte Musicae uoces multiphariam exuberant, ut nescias artis beneficia, an naturae mireris magis.

Ottmar Luscinius, *Musurgia seu praxis Musicae* (Strasbourg: Joan Schott, 1536), 22–23. Bullard, *Musica getutscht*, 219, n. 24.

4. "Briefe von Jorg Neuschel in Nürnberg, nebst einigen anderen (Im Besitze des kgl. geh. Archivs in Königsberg i/Pr.)," *Monatshefte für Musikgeschichte* 9 (1877): 150, 151, 152.

5. Anthony Baines, "Two Cassel Inventories," *Galpin Society Journal* 4 (1951): 34; Henry George Fischer, *The Renaissance Sackbut and Its Use Today* (New York: Metropolitan Museum of Art, 1984), 43–44.

6.

sei tromboni grossi, ch'il Basso uà otto uoici piu basso de gli altri comuni

Massimo Troiano, *Dialoghi di Massimo Troiano* (Venice, 1569), facs. ed. by Horst Leuchtmann, *Die Münchner Fürstenhochzeit von 1568: Massimo Troiano; Dialoge* (Munich: Katzbichler, 1980), 63.

7. See Claude V. Palisca, "Scientific Empiricism in Musical Thought," in *Seventeenth Century Science and the Arts*, ed. Hedley Howell Rhys (Princeton, N.J.: Princeton University Press, 1961), 91–137.

8. Gioseffo Zarlino, *Istitutioni harmoniche* (Venice: Senese, 1558), 157–58; Gioseffo Zarlino, *Dimonstrationi harmoniche* (Venice: Senese, 1571), 256.

9. Gioseffo Zarlino, *Sopplimenti musicali* (Venice: Senese, 1588), 216.

10. Gerhard Singer, "Lodovico Zacconi's Treatment of the 'Suitability and Classification of All Musical Instruments' in the *Prattica de musica* of 1592" (Ph.D. diss., University of Southern California, 1968), 1–6.

11. Lodovico Zacconi, *Prattica di musica* (Venice: Bartolomeo Carampello, 1596), fol. 215v, 218r; Singer, "Lodovico Zacconi's Treatment," 85, 113–14.

12. Ercole Bottrigari, *Il desiderio, overo De' concerti di varii strumenti musicali* (Venice, 1594, 2nd ed., 1599); facs. ed. of 1599 ed., ed. Kathi Meyer-Baer (Berlin: Martin Breslauer, 1924), 39–43, 48–49; English translation by Carol MacClintock (s.l.: American Institute of Musicology, 1962), 49–54, 59–60.

13. Giovanni Maria Artusi, *L'Artusi, ouero Delle imperfettioni della moderna musica* (Venice: Giacomo Vincenti, 1600), fol. lr–11v; English translation by Malcolm Litchfield, "Giovanni Maria Artusi's L'Artusi, overo Delle imperfettioni della moderna musica" (M.A. thesis, Brigham Young University, 1987), 69–119.

14. Aurelio Virgiliano, *Il dolcimelo* (Ms), facs. ed. (Florence: Studio per Edizioni Scelte, 1979), 102–04.

15. Pietro Cerone, *El melopeo y maestro* (Naples: I. B. Gargano and L. Nucci, 1613), 1037–43, 1061–64, 1068–69; See Ruth Hannas, "Cerone, Philospher and Teacher," *Musical Quarterly* 21 (1935): 408–22.

16. Michael Praetorius, *Syntagma musicum: Tomus secundus; De organographia* (Wolffenbüttel, 1619); facs. ed., Berlin: Trautwein, 1884), 1–2; English translation by David Z. Crookes (Oxford: Oxford University Press, 1986), 21–22.

17. Praetorius, *De organographia*, 6–8; Crookes, 25–26.

18. Praetorius, *De organographia*, 31–32; Crookes, 43–44; illustrations also in Naylor, *Trumpet & Trombone*, plates 73, 77.

19.

Denn obwol etliche Instrumentisten uff Chorist Fagotten, biß ins g', uff Tenor-Posaunen biß ins a', und noch höher hinauf kommen können: So ist es doch in gemein allen nicht gegeben, sondern müssen in den Fagotten im d', in den Posaunen im e', und zum höchsten im a', commoriren und verbleiben.

Michael Praetorius, *Syntagma musicum: Tomus tertuis; Termini musici* (Wolffenbuttel: Holwein, 1619; facs. ed., Berlin: Trautwein, 1884), 164; English translation by Hans Lampl, *The Syntagma Musicum of Michael Praetorius, Volume Three: An Annotated Translation*, ed. Margaret Boudreaux (United States: American Choral Directors Association, 2001), 177.

20. See Naylor, *Trumpet & Trombone*, plate 73.

21. Praetorius, *Termini*, 96; Lampl, *The Syntagma Musicum of Michael Praetorius*, 110.

22. Marin Mersenne, *Harmonie universelle, contenant la theorie et la practique de la musique* (Paris: Sebastian Cramoisy, 1636; facs. ed., Paris: Centre National de la Recherche Scientifique, 1963), 3:270–72; English translation by Roger E. Chapman, *Harmonie universelle: The Books on Instruments* (The Hague: Martinus Nijhoff, 1957), 341–43; illustration also in Naylor, *Trumpet & Trombone*, plate 81.

23. David M. Guion, *The Trombone: Its History and Music, 1697–1811* (New York: Gordon and Breach, 1988), 63.

24. Pierre Trichet, "De la saquebout ou trompette harmonique (vers 1640)," *Brass Bulletin* 45 (1984): 10–12.

25.

Tube ductiles eadem cum tubis militaribus habent, hoc excepto, quod eductione, & intrusione, siue retroactione hyposalpingis omnes ordine toni exprimi possint, quod in priori fieri non posse diximus, ideq; praestat prolongatio, & decurtatio hyposalpingis, quod in fistulis orificiorum clausura, vel apertura. Quae cum omnia   clara sint, ijx nequaquam diutius immorabimur.

Athanasius Kircher, *Musisurgia universalis* (Rome: Francisci Corbelletti, 1650), 503; English translation by Frederick Baron Crane, "Athanasius Kircher, Musurgia universails (Rome, 1650): The Section on Musical Instruments," (M.A. thesis, University of Iowa, 1956), 96.

26.

Il Trombone è vna specie di Tromba, che suona il basso, ne concerti, e Sonfonie fà bonissimo effetto.

Angelo Berardi, *Miscellanea musicale* (Bologna: Giacomo Monti, 1689), 16.

27. Anthony Baines, "James Talbot's Manuscript (Christ Church Library Music MS 1187). I. Wind Instruments," *Galpin Society Journal* 1 (1948): 21–22.

28. Trevor Herbert, "The Trombone in Britain before 1800" (Ph.D. diss., Open University, 1984), 279.

29. Daniel Speer, *Grundrichtiger kurtz- leicht- und nöthiger Unterricht der musikalischen Kunst* (Ulm: Kühnen, 1687); revised and enlarged as *Grundrichtiger kurtz- leicht- und nöthiger jetzt wol-vermehrter Unterricht der musikalischen Kunst oder Vierfaches musikalischen Kleeblatt* (Ulm: Kühnen, 1697); English translation by Henry Howey, "A Comprehensive Performance Project in Trombone Literature with an Essay Consisting of a Translation of Daniel Speer's *Vierfaches musikalisches Kleeblatt*" (D.M.A. essay, University of Iowa, 1971).

30. Guion, *Trombone*, 11–117.

31. Johann Mattheson, *Das neueröffnete Orchestre* (Hamburg: Author, 1713), 266–67; Johann Samuel Halle, *Werkstätte der heutigen Kunst* (Brandenburg: J. W. Halle, 1761–65), 3:371; Jean Benjamin de la Borde, *Essai sur la musique ancienne et moderne*, 4 vols. (Paris: Ph.-D. Pierres, 1780), 1:275–76; Guion, *Trombone*, 25, 64, 73–74; Howard Weiner, "The Soprano Trombone Hoax," *Historic Brass Society Journal* 13 (2001), 153, cites two works that I was unable to locate: Christoph Weigl, *Abbildung der Gemein-Nützlichen Haupt-Stände* (Regensburg, 1698) and Johann Daniel Berlin, *Musikalische Elementer* (Trondheim, 1744).

32. Louis Joseph Francoeur, *Traité général des instruments d'orchestre*, new ed. by Alexandre Choron (Paris: Aux adresses ordinaires de musique, 1813), 72–73; cf. Othon Vandenbroek, *Traité général de tous les instrumens à vent à l'usage des compositeurs* (Paris: Louis Marchand, 1794?), 54–55. Facsimile, transcription, and English translation in Guion, *Trombone*, 76–78.

33. André Braun, *Gamme et méthode pour les trombonnes alto, tenor et basse* (Paris: Sieber, 179–; Offenbach: André, 1811); transcription, translation, and commentary in Howard Weiner, "André Braun's *Gamme et méthod pour les trombones*: The Earliest Modern Trombone Method Rediscovered," *Historic Brass Society Journal* 5 (1993): 288–308.

34. Joseph Fröhlich, *Vollständige theoretisch- pracktisch Musikschule* (Bonn: Simrock, 1811), 3:27–35; Guion, *Trombone*, 94–117.

35. Andreas Nemetz, *Neuste Posaun-Schule* (Vienna: Diabelli, 1827); transcription, translation, and commentary in Howard Weiner, "Andreas Nemetz's *Neuste Posaun-Schule*: An Early Viennese Trombone Method," *Historic Brass Society Journal* 7 (1995): 12–35.

36. Gottfried Weber, "Versuch einer praktischen Akustik," [pt. 2] *Allgemeine musikalische Zeitung* 24 (January, 1816): col. 50–56.

37. Augustin Sundelin, *Die Instrumentirung für das Orchester* (Berlin: Wagenführ, 1828); *Die Instrumentirung für sämmtliche Militär-Musik-Chöre* (Berlin: Wagenführ, 1828).

38. Trevor Herbert, *The Trombone* (New Haven, Conn.: Yale University Press, 2006), 311–18. Much of the information in this section comes from William Waterhouse, *The New Langwill Index: A Dictionary of Musical Wind-Instrument Makers and Inventors* (London: Tony Bingham, 1993) and *Grove Music Online*.

39. Martin Kirnbauer, "Die Nürnberger Trompeten- und Posaunenmacher vor 1500 im Spiegel Nürnberger Quellen," in *Musik und Tanz zur Zeit Kaiser Maximilian I*, ed. Walter Salmen (Innsbruck: Helbling, 1992), 135; Johann Gabriel

Doppelmayr, *Historische Nachricht von der Nürnbergischen Mathematicis und Künstlern* (Nuremberg: P. C. Monath, 1730), 284; "Briefe von Jorg Neuschel," 158–59; Henry G. Fischer, "The Tenor Sackbut of Anton Schnitzer the Elder at Nice," *Historic Brass Society Journal* 1 (1989): 73, n. 4.

40. Markus Raquet and Klaus Martius, "The Schnitzer Family of Nuremberg and a Newly Rediscovered Trombone," *Historic Brass Society Journal* 19 (2007): 11–12.

41. Stewart Carter, "Early Trombones in America's Shrine to Music Museum," *Historic Brass Society Journal* 10 (1998): 95, 105.

42. Robert Barclay, *The Art of the Trumpet-Maker: The Materials, Tools, and Techniques of the Seventeenth and Eighteenth Centuries in Nuremberg* (Oxford: Clarendon Press, 1992), 26–32.

43. Herbert Heyde, "The Brass Instrument Makers Schmied of Pfaffendorf," in *Perspectives in Brass Scholarship: Proceedings of the International Historic Brass Symposium, Amherst, 1995*, ed. Stewart Carter (Stuyvesant, N.Y.: Pendragon, 1997), 91–113.

44. Praetorius, *De organographia*, 32; Crookes, *Syntagma musicum*, 43.

45. Herbert Heyde, "Brass Instrument Making in Berlin from the 17th to the 20th Century: A Survey," trans. Steven Plank, *Historic Brass Society Journal* 3 (1991): 43–45.

46. Anthony Baines, *Brass Instruments: Their History and Development* (New York: Scribner, 1978), 42.

47. Guion, *Trombone*, 168–91.

48. Constant Pierre, *Les facteurs d'instruments de musique: Les luthiers et la facture instrumentale; Précis historique* (Paris: Sagot, 1893; repr. Geneva: Minkoff, 1971), 150–53.

49. Fischer, *Renaissance Sackbut*, 43–45; Herbert, *Trombone*, 66; Baines, *Brass Instruments*, 243.

50. See Karl Hachenberg, "Brass in Central European Instrument-Making from the 16th through the 18th Centuries," *Historic Brass Society Journal* 4 (1992): 229–52.

51. Barclay, *Art of the Trumpet Maker*, passim.

52. Fischer, *Renaissance Sackbut*, 45.

53. Mersenne, *Harmonie universelle*, 3:270; Chapman, *Harmonie universelle*, 341.

54. Keith McGowan, "A Chance Encounter with a Unicorn? A Possible Sighting of the Renaissance Slide Trumpet," *Historic Brass Society Journal* 8 (1996): 90–101.

55. Keith McGowan, "The World of the Early Sackbut Player: Flat or Round?" *Early Music* 22 (August, 1994): 447–51.

56. McGowan, "World," 460–61.

57. Nicholas Bessaraboff, *Ancient European Musical Instruments* (Cambridge, Mass.: Harvard University Press, 1941), 412, n. 410; Curt Sachs, *Handbuch der Musikinstrumentenkunde*, 2nd ed. (Leipzig: Breitkopf & Härtel, 1930), 298; *History of Musical Instruments* (New York: Norton, 1940), 326; Arthur Mendel, "On the Pitches in Use in Bach's Time," *Studies in the History of Musical Pitch* (Amsterdam: Frits Knuf, 1968), 190–93, reprinted from *Musical Quarterly* 41 (1955).

58.

Auch halte ich vor meine Wenigkeit kein besser Instrument den rechten Thon auerfahren als eine Posaune, sonderlich die von der ziet und noch, zu Nürnberg gefertiget seyn: Daß man nemblich den Zug umb 2. Finger breit vom ende außziehe, so gibe es gar recht und just, in rechter Chormasse, das alamire im Tenor.

Praetorius, *De organographia*, 232.

59. Adam Carse, *Musical Wind Instruments* (1939; repr. ed., New York: Da Capo, 1965), 255.

60. John Wallis, "Of the Trembling of Consonant Strings," *Philosophical Transactions* 134 (April 23, 1677): 839–44.

61. Guion, *Trombone*, 27, 35, 38, 80.

62. Guion, *Trombone*, 104–05.

63. Stewart Carter, "Trombone Pitch in the Eighteenth Century: An Overview," in *Posaunen und Trompeten: Geschichte, Akustik, Spieltechnik*, ed. Monika Lustig and Howard Weiner (Blankenburg: Stiftung Kloster Michaelstein, 2000), 62–65.

64. Baines, *Brass Instruments*, 242.

CHAPTER FOUR

~

The Valve Era

The nineteenth and twentieth centuries witnessed an explosion of written documentation. When I wrote my doctoral dissertation, I included the text and translation of every published primary source that I could find that appeared between 1697 and 1811. I found a few more while preparing it for publication. There would have been plenty of room for other documents from that time. Attempting to deal with either nineteenth or twentieth century materials as exhaustively would be madness. The nineteenth century saw the dawn of new kinds of musical literature, including periodicals, method books devoted to the teaching of single brass instruments, and orchestration treatises. Museums, manufacturers, and retailers all issued catalogs. Encyclopedias grew in both number and length and focused on increasingly narrow specialties.

The Industrial Revolution began an explosion of technological innovation that has not subsided to this day. New processes and materials changed the manufacture of musical instruments. The application of valves to brass instruments revolutionized the design of brass instruments. In the twentieth century, changes in the design and manufacture of trombones were more evolutionary than revolutionary, but still demonstrated advancing technology.

Descriptions and Prescriptions: Documents from 1816 to 2000

When Gottfried Weber wrote his "Versuch einer praktischen Akustik," he described the trombone as he found it, but later the same year, he expressed great dissatisfaction.[1] He was either unaware of the recent invention of the valve or did not recognize its possibilities, but

in proposing a four-legged slide, he was the first person in at least four hundred years to consider a radical new design of the trombone. The chronological approach used in the previous chapter will not work here. What follows is a summary of various kinds of literature about the trombone.

Periodicals, General Reference, and General Works on Instruments

The *Allgemeine musikalische Zeitung*, founded in 1798, was among the earliest financially successful musical periodicals. Within half a century of its founding, comparable journals existed in nearly every European language, along with general-interest newspapers and magazines. They included advertisements, reviews of concerts and new printed music, descriptions of new inventions, and musical news from around the world. Berlioz's orchestration treatise grew from a series of journal articles.[2]

Periodicals have become increasingly specialized. *Wright & Round's Brass Band News* (1881–1958) is but one of the journals published for the British brass band movement. *Die Posaune* (1912–1939, 1953–) is but one of the journals published for the German Posaunenchor movement. Recent journals aimed at brass players generally include *Brass Quarterly* (1957–64), *Brass Bulletin* (1971–2003), and *Historic Brass Society Journal* (1989–). At least four journals specifically have trombonists as their target audience: *ITA Journal* (1973–), *The Trombonist* (1985–), *Das Schallstück* (1990–), and the *Online Trombone Journal* (1996–2008). Other information about the trombone, trombonists, and music that uses trombone appears in periodicals covering such specialties as music education, jazz, early music, American music, the wind band, and so forth.

Most general encyclopedias have articles on the trombone. *Encyclopaedia Britannica*, 11th edition (1910–11) probably has the best in English. Encyclopedias devoted entirely to music began to appear in the nineteenth century. *Musikalisches Conversations-Lexikon* by Hermann Mendel was first issued in 11 volumes beginning in 1870 and went through three editions. Hugo Riemann's *Musik-Lexikon*, first published in 1882, is now in its 12th edition.

George Grove's *A Dictionary of Music and Musicians* was published in four volumes between 1879 and 1889. It contains articles on both sackbut and trombone by William H. Stone, an enthusiastic amateur musician. Both articles pass on the story about finding an ancient trombone at Herculaneum. The eminent acoustician David Blaikley revised the article on trombone for the second edition, which appeared in 1916. The revision is especially fascinating for quoting a lengthy memorandum from George Case, professor of trombone at the Royal College of Music, who debunked the Herculaneum story. Stone's article on sackbut was replaced with a new one by Francis Galpin, which was reprinted in the third through fifth editions.

In the third and fourth editions, the article on trombone merely reorganized material from Stone and Blaikley and incorporated information on the valve trombone, formerly relegated to brief comments in the article "Valve." Anthony Baines contributed the article to the fifth edition and rewrote it for the New Grove. As befitting the first professional musicologist to write about the trombone for Grove, his articles are excellent, both in terms of historical and organological detail.

Two other highly regarded encyclopedias disappoint. The article by Flandrin in the so-called Lavignac encyclopedia is opinionated and riddled with historical errors. The articles in two editions of *Die Musik in Geschichte und Gegenwart* were not written by specialists in the history of brass instruments. They are both full of errors and internal contradictions.

When Victor Mahillon, curator of the musical instrument museum of the Brussels Conservatory, issued a five-volume catalog of the museum's holdings, a new era in the discipline of organology began. It described dozens of both slide and valve trombones, made by such ancient makers as Ehe and Hainlein of Nuremburg and such contemporary makers as Tuerlinckx and Sax. Descriptions are in prose, with no measurements and few illustrations. Mahillon divided instruments into four classes: I. solid wood or metal bodies usually set in motion by percussion (which he called autophonic), II. membranes stretched on frames, III. wind instruments, and IV. stringed instruments. He divided and subdivided each of these classes. Trombones are class III (wind instruments), branch D (mouthpiece instruments), section c (chromatic, of variable length), subsection aa (with a slide) or subsection bb (with valves). This pioneering classification was greeted with enthusiasm, but not total acceptance. Mahillon's colleague François-Auguste Gevaert (citing an edition that appeared beginning in 1878) rearranged it for his orchestration treatise. Hornbostel and Sachs, while praising the basic division into four classes, found the subdivisions illogical, especially for non-Western instruments. Today, their classification is far better known than Mahillon's.[3]

Sachs is a towering figure in musicology, especially in the disciplines of organology, musical iconography, and ethnomusicology, but he studied art history for his doctorate. This background gave him a different perspective from other musicologists. His arguments are often based on interpretation of works of art, and not without controversy. Some persistent historical errors in twentieth-century writings about the trombone can, in fact, be traced to Sachs.

His *Real-Lexikon* remains the standard against which dictionaries of musical instruments are measured. It is the earliest book I have yet seen that has a picture of a trombone with a trigger (thumb valve), yet the article on trombone, just less than a page long, does not acknowledge the application of valves to the trombone in any way. To my knowledge, Sachs's reference to a trumpet made by Hainlein, erroneously dated 1460, marks the first citation of an extant instrument in a museum in any writing about the trombone.[4]

The *Handbuch der Musikinstrumentenkunde*, which has Sach's most comprehensive examination of the trombone, first appeared in 1920 and was revised in 1930.[5] No previous work examines musical instruments according to so many different disciplines, including art history and acoustics. Sachs declined to speculate on where the trombone was invented, but proposed that it happened early in the fifteenth century. As many footnotes as Sachs used in this work, he simply asserted the date without evidence. He made another undocumented claim, with more serious consequence, that in the sixteenth century, there was a whole family of trombones: descant (soprano) in B♭, alto in F, *gemeine rechte* (i.e. tenor) in B♭, *quartposaune* in F, *quintposaune* in E♭, and *oktavposaune* in B♭. All of these pitches are incorrect, and there was no soprano trombone in the sixteenth century. For nearly half a century afterward, other writers repeated these errors, as likely as not attributing them to Praetorius, whom Sachs did not mention in this context.

In his description of the modern trombone, he commented that all sizes except alto, tenor, and bass were eventually abandoned, and that these still formed the standard trio in the late nineteenth century. By that time, the alto was being replaced with a second tenor because of its inferior tone, and the awkward bass, which required a handle to manipulate the slide, was being replaced by the trigger, invented by Sattler in 1839. Except for the announcement of its invention in *Allgemeine musikalische Zeitung* (see Document 5, in the appendix) and rather offhand references by Berlioz and Marx, this comment is the earliest mention of the trigger I have found. Sachs noted that the contrabass trombone occupied the attention of instrument makers and that Weber invented the four-legged slide. He briefly mentioned the valve trombone (with strong disapproval on account of its inferior intonation and tone) and the short vogue for over-the-shoulder bells.

After moving to the United States before the Second World War, Sachs wrote books in English on various subjects, including *The History of Musical Instruments*. There are no footnotes, so it was apparently intended as a popular rather than scholarly book. The description of the trombone is very similar to that in the *Handbuch*. Besides repeating the error about the pitch of early trombones, it contains numerous other factual mistakes, most of which are attributable to careless editing. More seriously, he asserted that the early trombones had thicker walls than modern trombones, misleading a generation of English-language scholars.[6]

Many museum catalogs have appeared since Mahillon's. The more useful ones are profusely illustrated and contain detailed descriptions of the instruments. Unfortunately, no two catalogs measure quite the same aspects, which makes it impossible to compare instruments at two different museums. The closing years of the twentieth century saw a resurgence of interest in the taxonomy of instruments and a new interest in investigating the acoustic behavior of instruments. Both of these areas of research require careful, accurate measurements.

Heyde's catalog of the music instrument museum of Karl Marx University in Leipzig and Myers' catalog of the collection at Edinburgh University have some of the most detailed measurements. Heyde even includes the angle of the bell flare.[7]

After the invention of the Internet and good web browsers, whole new sources of information (or misinformation, as the case may be) came into existence. Entering "trombone" in any search engine results in literally millions of pages, including personal web pages for everyone from leading professionals to high school students. Recent doctoral dissertations can be found via the Web. Increasingly, they are not even issued on paper any more. Some websites are portals, with more or less well organized links to other pages. Trombonists can exchange information and opinions on e-mail lists and online forums. Finding information about the trombone, or any other subject, has become easier than ever before in history. Finding accurate and authoritative information or any particular detail remains as difficult as ever.

Orchestration Texts
In many ways, Georges Kastner's 1837 *Traité général d'instrumentation*[8] simply carries on the tradition of authors from Virdung onward in writing about a large variety of instruments. It also marks a significant departure, being written as a textbook for use in orchestration classes at the Paris Conservatory. This section examines his and other orchestration texts, along with a more general textbook for composers (by Marx), a book intended as much for conductors as composers (by Fétis), and some others about scoring for bands.

Kastner's treatise was immediately adopted by the Conservatory as a textbook in its composition classes. A companion volume, *Cours d'instrumentation* appeared in 1839. Supplements to both books appeared in 1844. It appears that most of the *Traité* was actually written in Strasbourg, before Kastner moved to Paris. Its supplement indicates that he had changed his mind about some important details.[9] It is unfortunate that he chose to issue a supplement rather than a new edition. It merely refers to page and line numbers where new prose should be added, resulting in a very disorganized text.

Kastner copied some ideas from the writings of Sundelin and Weber. His ranges are considerably different from Sundelin's, however: *e* to *c″* or *d″* for alto, *E* to *B♭′* for tenor or buccin, and *C* to *f′* or *g′* for bass. He did not consider the three trombones essentially the same instrument, as did Braun and his followers. The lowest note he gives for the alto is the third partial in seventh position on an E♭ instrument, which implicitly conforms to the advice of later writers to ignore its unsatisfactory low register. The low notes given for the bass means that it must be in a key lower than B♭. He mentioned the "quart" bass (in F) and the "quint" bass (in E♭), saying both were rare in France and the tenor must frequently play the lowest part. All of his ranges go a few notes higher than Sundelin's. He was not favorably impressed with pedal notes, but acknowledged that Berlioz used them.

Kastner regretted that French orchestras rarely had alto or bass trombones. While an occasional piece may call for only one trombone, the usual section was three.

He noted that it is necessary to write complete chords for the trombones, because it does not sound right for a trumpet or horn to supply missing harmonies. Echoing Sundelin, Kastner cautioned composers not to make trombones begin a piece without other instruments as they had no way to find the right notes.

Trombones can play long notes or short notes. Repeated notes work well. Because the trombone plays all of the notes in the scale, it should not be given the unnatural leaps necessary on the trumpet or horn. (That is one reason why Kastner disapproved of using pedal notes, which cannot be approached except by leap.) Trombones cannot play rapid passages, and composers

must know the slide positions in order to avoid long slide shifts.

Kastner was one of the first writers to describe the valve trombone. In the main volume the description is very brief, consisting mostly of a drawing depicting an over-the-shoulder bell, a chart showing the fingerings for a chromatic scale for a tenor trombone, and the comment that this nearly unknown instrument could be played more rapidly and accurately than the slide trombone. A valve alto trombone was also available and had the same advantages.

The supplement greatly expanded the discussion. Kastner observed that execution on the valve trombone

Fig. 4.1. Valve trombone and fingerings from Kastner's orchestration treatise (1837).

is faster and more accurate. In principle, it is possible to play with better intonation on a slide trombone, but in practice he considered the intonation of the valve trombone superior. He knew of hardly anyone who played slide trombone in tune. The valve trombone had the additional advantage that with the length of the player's arm no longer being a limitation, manufacturers could extend the lower range by adding more valves. German trombones with five valves were able to play chromatically down to BB♭. He also reported that Sax had recently introduced a new design of valve, such an improvement over the older design that he made a distinction between the older "pistons" and Sax's "cylinders."

Finally, Kastner devoted several paragraphs to a summary of Weber's new slide. Where Weber proposed an improvement to the bass trombone, Kastner gave positions for tenor-bass (which he defined as an instrument with the dimensions of a tenor trombone, but a bass trombone mouthpiece), tenor, and alto trombones with the new slide. Each chart shows nine positions.

Later orchestration texts differ in important details from Kastner, but generally speaking, they make similar recommendations. It would be redundant to describe any of them at length. As an indication of how many there are, Lapie lists 27 treatises published in France after Berlioz and before 1914.[10] The summary that follows is based on the chronological list of works below:

1837 François-Joseph Fétis, *Manuel des compositeurs, directeurs de musique, chef d'orchestre & de musique militaire, or* [sic] *Traité méthodique de l'harmonie, des instrumens, des voix et de tout ce qui est relatif à la composition, à la direction et à l'execution de la musique* (Paris: Schlesinger, 1837), 78–80, 107–12.

1843 Hector Berlioz, *Grand traité d'instrumentation et d'orchestration modernes* (1843, 1855), ed. Peter Bloom (Kassel: Bärenreiter, 2003), 300–42; English translation Hugh McDonald, *Berlioz's Orchestration Treatise: A Translation and Commentary.* (Cambridge: Cambridge University Press, 2002), 208–29.

1847 Adolf Bernhard Marx, *Die Lehre von der musikalischen Komposition: Praktisch theoretisch*, Vierter Theil (Leipzig: Breitkopf & Härtel, 1847), 62–77, 99–100, 504–8; this text came out in five editions, the last, edited by Hugo Riemann, appearing in 1888. It is not exactly the same as the first edition, but the differences are not substantial.

1853 Allen Dodworth, *Dodworth's Brass Band School* (New York: H. B. Dodworth, 1853), 11–22, 33.

1877 Ebenezer Prout, *Instrumentation* (London: Novello, Ewer, 1877; repr. New York: Haskell House, 1969), 87–91.

1883 Oscar Coon, *Harmony and Instrumentation* (New York: Carl Fischer, 1883), 36, 72–76. 175.

1885 François-Auguste Gevaert, *Nouveau traité d'instrumentation* (Paris: Lemoine & Fils, 1885), 235–57, 282–83; English translation *A New Treatise on Instrumentation*, trans. E. F. E. Suddard (Paris: Henry Lemoine, 1906), same pagination.

189- Nikolay Rimsky-Korsakov, *Principles of Orchestration* [189-], ed. Maximilian Steinberg; English translation Edward Agate (Berlin: Éditions russe de musique, 1922; repr. New York: Dover, 1964), 24–25.

1897 Ebenezer Prout, *The Orchestra. vol. 1, Technique of the Instruments.* (London: Augener, 1897), 220–34.

1898 Gabriel Parès, *Traité d'instrumentation et d'orchestration à l'usage des musiques militaires d'harmonie et de fanfare* (Paris: Lemoine, 1898), 82–89.

1904 Hector Berlioz, *Instrumentenslehre*, revised and enlarged by Richard Strauss (Leipzig: C. F. Peters, 1904), 302, 329–30; English translation as *Treatise on Instruments* by Theodore Front (New York: Kalmus, 1948), 327, 353–54.

1904 Charles-Marie Widor, *Technique de l'orchestre moderne*, 5th ed. (Paris: Henry Lemoine, 1925), 95–112; English translation of the 1st (1904) ed. *The Technique of the Modern Orchestra*, trans. Edward Suddard (London: Joseph Williams, 1906), 78–90.

1914 Cecil Forsyth, *Orchestration*, 2nd ed. (London: Macmillan, 1935), 133–51. [1st ed. 1914]

1918 Gaston Borch, *Practical Manual of Instrumentation* (Boston: Boston Music Co., 1918), 25.

1935 Stanislao Gallo, *The Modern Band* (Boston: Birchard, 1935), 1: 64–65, 74.

1935 Denis Wright, *Scoring for Brass Band* 5th ed. (London: Studio Music, 1986), 28–30. [1st ed. 1935]

1951 Bernard Rogers, *The Art of Orchestration: Principles of Tone Color in Modern Scoring* (New York: Appleton Century-Crofts, 1951), 61–66.

1952 Kent Kennan, *The Technique of Orchestration* (New York: Prentice-Hall 1952), 136–42. Later editions: 2/1970, 3/1983, 4/1990, 5/1997,

6/2002. Editions 3–6 co-written with Donald Grantham.

1955   Walter Piston, *Orchestration* (New York: Norton, 1955), 268–81.

1982   Samuel Adler, *The Study of Orchestration* (New York: Norton, 1982), 239–52, 285–92. Later editions 2/1989, 3/2002.

1985   Andrew Stiller, *Handbook of Instrumentation* (Berkeley: University of California Press, 1985), 67–89.

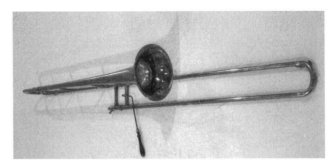

Fig. 4.2.   Bass trombone in G from Tom Izzo's collection. Photograph by David M. Guion.

Beginning with Braun, several earlier authors considered alto, tenor, and bass trombones as B♭ instruments that differed only in such details as the size of the mouthpiece or bore, although each of them acknowledged the existence of other sizes. According to Kastner, the three kinds of trombone all had different fundamentals. Fétis, publishing in the same year, acknowledged only bass and alto. His bass is in B♭, and the alto is a fifth higher. He mentioned that the Germans have a bass trombone that can play down to C and that the invention of valves made a contrabass trombone possible.

Later authors follow Kastner's example rather than Braun's, but over time, new options became available. Marx and Prout considered soprano trombones obsolete, but Widor noted that some manufacturers were beginning to make them. Berlioz wrote that the alto was rare. Widor called it obsolete. Not every author mentioned it, but nearly all who did found it tonally inferior to the tenor. Adler noted that it was making a comeback.

No other size of trombone has existed in more forms than the bass. As noted by Gevaert and all English authors, the English bass trombone was in G. Easier to play than larger sizes, it lacked some low notes that continental composers called for. Forsyth observed that when this bass trombone was equipped with a trigger in D, the advantage of the larger sizes disappeared. To most continental authors of the nineteenth century, the true bass trombone was in F, although E♭ basses existed. To Berlioz, it was the other way around. Most authors mentioned that it is physically taxing to play. Gevaert also complained about the handle necessary to reach the outer positions, noted that "a less primitive contrivance" (probably meaning Weber's four-legged slide) makes it unnecessary by reducing the distance between positions.

Braun's idea of the bass trombone as a B♭ instrument was, however, the wave of the future. Marx bewailed the tenor-bass trombone, a B♭ instrument with the bore of a bass trombone in F, complaining that it showed the grievous influence of French and Italian music. Using a large-bore tenor trombone as if it were a bass is easier to play, but loses the lowest notes. Gevaert observed that the term *bass trombone* sometimes applied to a B♭ instrument, which was called a tenor-bass trombone in Germany.

The only way a trombone in B♭ can make a satisfactory bass trombone is for it to have at least one trigger. Sattler made the first such instrument in 1839. Marx knew about it by hearsay. In the second edition of his treatise, Berlioz commented on Sax's piston trigger. Rimsky-Korsakov implicitly described a trigger; in his scale for a tenor-bass trombone, he said that C, D, and E♭ were rare notes and BB did not exist. Piston still called such an instrument a tenor-bass trombone and said that when it is intended to serve as a bass trombone, it had a larger bore, a larger bell, and a tuning slide on the valve that could be pulled out to E. Stiller regarded the B♭/F trombone as the standard tenor trombone, although the "old, simplex tenor trombone" still had its uses. For him, a bass trombone had two triggers, with the second in E, or preferably D. Kennan's description of the bass trombone is different in each of the first three editions. From his third edition onward, he described in-line double-trigger trombones with F and G (or G♭) triggers.

From the time Wagner introduced the contrabass trombone in his *Ring* cycle, it became necessary for orchestration texts to mention it. Implicitly or explicitly, it is an instrument in BB♭ with a quadruple slide. Forsyth wrote that it sometimes has a trigger. He also noted that it reaches or exceeds the ability of human lungs to produce low notes on a cylindrical instrument. Adler admonished students not to write for it, as it is too taxing.

Although not every author repeated Kastner's ranges, the differences are not worth describing in detail. Several authors acknowledged that the alto trombone could play lower than Kastner's bottom note, but because these notes are tonally inferior, recommended avoiding them. By the twentieth century, most authors gave a higher upper limit for the tenor. Widor and Piston gave *d"*, Adler and Stiller *f"*. Indeed, Adler noted that many professionals can play even higher. For Rogers, it was especially jazz players who "display no fear of extremely high notes," but said they use a different mouthpiece from orchestral players. Marx specified a narrower range than most, on grounds that the highest and lowest playable notes lack the trombone's true character. Widor commented that trombonists, like hornists, must specialize in either the upper or lower register, as the lips cannot play both with equal ease. At the low end of the tenor range, nearly all but the most recent authors agreed with Kastner in disapproving of pedal notes if they mentioned them at all. Berlioz, of course, considered them an important new resource.

No later writer repeated Kastner's caution that trombones could not find their notes without hearing other instruments. Berlioz strongly regretted that French trombone sections consisted of three tenor trombones, as it either deprived composers of certain notes and tone colors or caused French orchestras to distort the composers' original intentions. He castigated French composers for labeling their three tenor parts alto, tenor, and bass instead of first, second, and third. Expressing strong disapproval of the older French practice of one trombone playing the bass line, he considered a single trombone out of place and criticized the solo in Mozart's *Requiem*; trombones needed either harmony or unison. The normal trio in England and Germany was alto, tenor, and bass, although by 1897, Prout suggested two tenors and bass as a common alternative. Coon noted that alto and bass trombones were rare in the United States, where three tenor trombones comprised the normal section, with the same disadvantages as in France.

Marx considered and rejected the idea of a section of four trombones, alto, two tenors, and bass, pointing out that none of the great masters had done so. Gevaert agreed with Berlioz that there was no point in using only one trombone, but suggested that composers should write more often for only two.

If there is one universal recommendation in orchestration texts, it is not to write fast passages for trombones. Marx is somewhat disconcerting to read because he numbered the positions 0–6 rather than 1–7. Other than that, he gave probably the clearest explanation of slide technique. Gevaert pointed to passages from *William Tell* and *Les Hugenots* as examples of how not to write for trombone if hearing the parts played accurately is important, although composers need not avoid short, rapid scale passages. (See Document 7, in the appendix.) Coon also warned against rapid slide shifts, but his example of good trombone writing, from Meyerbeer's "Fackeltanz no. 1," includes a descending G♭ major scale

for three trombones in unison that requires a shift from 7th position to 1st in a triplet figure; they are doubled by the tuba. Rogers recommended "deliberate movement," but also noted that he had heard *Flight of the Bumblebee* as a trombone solo on the radio.

There is much less agreement on the subject of legato. Fétis flatly stated that a slide trombone cannot slur. Gevaert agreed, calling slurs in a Wagner excerpt "delusive." Trombones cannot play legato, he insisted; they can only play sostenuto. Widor, on the other hand, wrote that at a soft dynamic, trombones can play legato as well as any other instrument. Stiller commented that "the smoothest possible legato" on a trombone rivals what any other brass instrument can play. Piston claimed that "a perfect legato is obtained only between two adjacent harmonies in the same position." (While that is more nearly correct than Fétis or Gevaert, it is possible to play a natural slur with a change of position, provided that different harmonics are involved.) He went on to describe the special legato tonguing necessary between two notes of the same harmonic in different positions, saying that the notes are as well connected that way as when strings change the direction of the bow. Rogers likewise observed that "when the slide has to be employed the performer's art comes subtly into play."

Berlioz noted that valves give the trombone agility at the expense of good intonation. Apparently French trombonists used only the valve alto trombone at that time, although he said that the Germans also had a valve tenor. Marx heard a valve trombone once, and wrote that they were not common. He thought that the added facility came at the cost of lack of power and severity. Prout warned that it would be an "evil day" if the tonally inferior valve trombone ever supplanted the "legitimate instrument." Forsyth questioned whether any instrument needed valves less than the trombone, although he did approve of the Sax system of independent valves. Gevaert, then, is in a distinct minority. He thought that valves were preferable to slides in every respect, and Sax's system was even better than the older additive system. He pointed to a solo from Thomas's *Hamlet* as an example of an expressive melody playable only on a valve trombone.

In the United States, Coon noted that valve trombones were used in amateur bands, but not by professionals. Borch said that valve trombones were rarely used in the United States. Piston considered them suitable for bands, but not the orchestra. Works by Dodworth, Parès, Gallo, and Wright specifically concern bands, not orchestras. Gallo's book is primarily interesting as the earliest text I have located on either orchestration or band arranging that explicitly defines a bass trombone as a large-bore B♭ instrument with a trigger.

Dodworth's book does not greatly resemble any of the orchestration texts. Written in response to a rapidly growing number of amateur bands, it more nearly resembles the tradition of American singing school books started by William Billings and his contemporaries. It opens with a chapter on the rudiments of music, followed by a very brief classification and description of brass instruments. Since the bands often had at least some ties to the local militia and therefore important ceremonial roles, Dodworth described formations, reviews, matters of etiquette and ceremony, and the meanings of various drum beats and bugle calls. His arrangements of eleven pieces for full brass band occupy more than half of the book.

Dodworth divided all of the instruments into six classes according to vocal range, from soprano to contrabass. He listed the alto, tenor, and bass trombone among the tenor, bass, and contrabass instruments respectively. He also divided instruments into families: first, saxhorns, cornets, and ebor cornos (tenor or bass horns of his own design); second, bugles and ophicleides; and third, trumpets, post horns, and trombones. Dodworth considered the first two families the most important instruments and the third, along with French horns, as supernumeraries not needed for the principal parts. In his introduction to the arrangements, he mentioned that the trombone and trumpet parts were a concession to popular taste. He complained that these instruments were abused by most of the people who played them in both bands and orchestras. They were overblown until they cracked or snarled, not making music, but an annoying noise calculated to alarm the audience.

Parès's work more nearly resembles an orchestration treatise. He said there were three kinds of orchestras: the symphony orchestra, the *harmonie* or infantry wind band, and the *fanfare* or cavalry brass band. The symphony orchestra is the most rich and varied. While the *harmonie* is less perfect, it gains in power of sonority. The *fanfare* has the fewest resources of the three. Because military bands primarily play outdoors, they must have three main qualities: sonority, variety of timbres, and power.

Since the idea that original concert music could be written for band was a generation in the future (aside from the already forgotten repertoire of the Revolutionary period), Parès described in detail how to distribute original orchestral parts among the instruments of the two military bands. In *harmonie*, besides the original trombone parts, trombones sometimes reinforced bassoon parts or horn parts. There was no tuba in *harmonie*,

so its part was taken by a bass trombone or a fourth tenor. Parès divided the instruments into five distinct groups (one combining trombones with trumpets, cornets, and horns), each of which could be used separately as a little band. In *fanfare*, trombones still did not replace any of the string parts, but occasionally served as soloist.

Parès acknowledged every size trombone from soprano to contrabass, but described only the tenor, which he declared was the best of them. In both kinds of band, there were usually four trombones, the equivalent of a male choir. He said their parts must be written like choir parts, complete in harmony and with no unprepared dissonances or other part-writing errors. While it is necessary to write for trombones with restraint in a symphony orchestra in order to avoid overpowering the strings, in a band, which has saxhorns on the principal parts, the power of the trombones is a suitable counterbalance. Still, they should not be overused. In a general crescendo, the trombones should be among the last instruments to enter the texture.

The slide trombone has a noble timbre and is therefore suitable for every kind of melody. Although it is somewhat agile in the middle and upper registers, he considered it best to write melodies, especially solos, with sobriety. Parès strongly disapproved of writing variations for trombone; no matter how good the player, the effect is always painful for the audience. Trombones are perfectly capable of playing an excerpt like *William Tell*, but the effect is detestable unless the bass and baritone saxhorns play along.

He commented that valve trombones, easier to play than slide trombones, are debased and lacking in nobility, tolerable only in the case of absolute necessity. If a band has only valve trombones, then an alto should be given any solos. Even though valves offer greater flexibility, arrangers should never write anything for them that would not be suitable for slide trombones.

Unlike French military bands, British brass bands have only three trombones: two tenors and a bass. Even in the 1986 edition of his book, Wright implicitly thought of the bass trombone as an instrument in G. Unlike most authors, who stressed the importance of complete harmonies within each section, Wright described how to get four-part harmonies from three trombones by augmenting them either with a cornet in the top voice or an E♭ bass on the bottom. He did not consider it necessary to limit the bass trombone to the true bass of the texture. Three trombones in closed harmony in the middle or upper register have a brilliant effect.

The first trombone is as important a solo voice as the cornet or euphonium. The bass trombone is also a useful solo instrument on occasion. Wright expected the second part to be taken by a weaker player, giving separate ranges for the two tenor trombones. While smooth melodies are possible, declamatory ones are more characteristic. Like all the other authors, Wright warned against using the trombones only to make a loud noise. Trills and pedal notes, though possible, are best left to professional players and not a useful resource for amateur bands.

Berlioz's book has been much more successful than Kastner's, and not merely because it is better organized. Although he carefully described the technical possibilities and limitations of various instruments, he spent more effort describing their character and the emotional possibilities of different voicings, dynamics, articulations, and combinations of instruments. Indeed, the presence of such material distinguishes a true orchestration text from a compendium on instruments.

Textbooks often lag behind practice. After Marx and Berlioz noted the existence of a trombone with a trigger, none of the other texts explicitly mentioned it until Gallo, writing in 1935. Even after Mahler and Schoenberg expanded the size of the trombone section, textbooks have not considered how to use more than three trombones. Piston mentioned the trombone solo in Mahler's Third Symphony, but said that solos are much less common in symphonic music than unison melodies. He did not acknowledge that they had become more common than in earlier music. Rogers's book is probably the most up-to-date for its time. Writing in 1951, he had good things to say about jazz, which seems to have been a rare attitude for an academic.

Nevertheless, many textbooks acknowledged new techniques and equipment. Strauss mentioned mutes in 1904 as a recent introduction. He described their effect at both loud and soft dynamics. Thereafter, most texts mentioned only the straight mute, but Adler and Stiller each described at least seven kinds of mutes plus the effects of playing into one's hand or music stand. Widor was the first to describe the glissando, although not as an orchestral device. Besides the regular slide glissando, Piston noted a glissando of the overtone series in a single position, giving an example from Bartók's violin concerto. Rogers, Piston, and Stiller described flutter tonguing, although only Stiller described the more common technique of double tonguing.

Hamilton Clarke wrote a manual on orchestration, not for composition students but for amateur listeners. Perhaps its most interesting aspect is his attempt to compare orchestration with the use of color in a painting. Trumpets and trombones, he says, are "approaching to

scarlet, purple, deep blue, and rich brown." These colors should be used sparingly in the orchestra as in a landscape painting. A painting with only these four colors would be just like a movement played only on trumpets and trombones. "It is this which renders it impossible to listen with much pleasure for any length of time to a band composed entirely of brass instruments."[11]

Musicology as an academic discipline is a product of the nineteenth century. Ernst Euting wrote the first doctoral dissertation on the subject of brass instruments. Faculty at American universities are generally required to have a doctorate in order to gain promotion to full professor. That put performers at a disadvantage until a special degree, Doctor of Musical Arts, was created for them. It demands a research project in addition to recital performances. Joseph Nicholson was awarded the first D.M.A. in trombone. Dissertations and theses constitute a significant body of research relevant to the history, literature, and pedagogy of the trombone. Many biographical dictionaries were published in the last two centuries. Even some not specifically musical occasionally include articles on brass players. Two have brass players as their entire subject matter.[12]

Method Books and Trombone Textbooks

There must have been a great hunger to learn trombone in France during the 1830s. There was no trombone class at the Paris Conservatory until 1833, yet Victor Cornette published a method for trombone in 1831. A provisional class was formed under Félix Vobaron in 1833, and his method appeared in 1834. When the Conservatory established a permanent class in 1836, Dieppo became its professor. He had already co-written a method book with Frédéric Berr in 1835, but after his appointment, he repudiated it and published a new one. Lesser-known methods by Schiltz, Foraboschi, and Muller also appeared before the end of the decade.[13]

According to Herbert's "indicative list" of slide trombone methods, nearly all of the methods issued before about 1870 were first published in Paris. As the heading indicates, it is not an exhaustive compilation. In particular, it does not include later editions. The more important French works, beginning with Braun, were soon published in translation. Editions of Cornette and Vobaron, at least, are still available to this day, but without the original text. I have been able to obtain useful early editions of Cornette, Vobaron, and Dieppo, but not copies or even adequate bibliographic descriptions of any other nineteenth-century works.[14]

This section will be limited to a description of the three methods already mentioned, one by André Lafosse, and a number of textbooks by British and American authors. Cornette's comments are very brief. Vobaron wrote more, but his remarks seem to be in random order. Of the three, Dieppo provides the most extensive and best-organized verbal description of the trombone and how to play it. In terms of the prose content, each work is more useful than the last. The modern usefulness of the études seems to be just the reverse. Cornette's method, in an edition by Jerome Proctor, is widely used in this country. Vobaron's method is available, but not highly regarded. I am unaware of any modern edition of Dieppo's method.

Cornette wrote that the bass and tenor trombones were essentially the same instrument, both in B♭. His alto trombone was in E♭. Vobaron noted trombones in B♭, D♭, and E♭. Presumably, the bass and tenor trombones were both in B♭ and the alto in E♭. The D♭ trombone was an ordinary tenor with a shorter tuning slide, which Vobaron said he had used himself. As he said nothing more about it, he must have considered it a mere curiosity. Dieppo wrote that older composers like Gluck wrote for alto, tenor, and bass trombones of different sizes, but that modern composers preferred the unity of timbre that comes from using only one size. They still wrote three parts in three different clefs, but expected all parts to be played on a tenor trombone.

As for how to hold the instrument, Cornette merely says that the left hand holds it and the right hand moves the slide. Vobaron's description is the longest. He advocated keeping the end of the slide level with the chin. Dieppo advocated holding it at a somewhat downward angle to avoid putting too much pressure on the upper lip. Only Cornette and Vobaron described the mouthpiece. Cornette said that bass trombones use a larger mouthpiece than tenor trombones. He advocated using an ivory mouthpiece in the orchestra. Vobaron preferred a metal mouthpiece, noting that mouthpieces of ivory or horn mute the sound of the instrument.

All three authors instructed students to put the mouthpiece on the center of the mouth and to be careful not to puff out the cheeks. Dieppo further advocated placing half of the mouthpiece on each lip. He also commented on the aperture of the mouthpiece and mouthpiece pressure, and instructed the student to keep the mouthpiece on the lower lip while taking a breath. Cornette advocated tonguing with the syllable "da" for soft passages and "ta" for loud. Implicitly commenting on legato, he said that articulation is more difficult on trombone than other instruments. Slurs are easy enough if the slide is on one position, but the trombone cannot play them if the notes are moving in the same direction as the slide. Vobaron assigned different syllables to every

pitch between F and f'; from low to high notes, "dou." "dau" "da," "ta" for soft playing, but only "da" and "ta" for loud playing. He complained that some trombonists tongue very little, so the notes in the passage vanish.

That comment comes in the context of his discussion of portamentos, which turn out to be slow glissandos. He advocated playing them as wide as a major third or fourth, just as singers do. Lest that recommendation seem entirely unmusical, comparison of today's singers with the earliest generation of recording artists shows that scooping was once much more prevalent than we would tolerate today. Audiences of the 1830s might very well consider our performance practice inexpressive and unmusical. In the same context, Vobaron gives examples of good and bad articulation. Anything more than two notes under a slur is invariably marked bad. Most of the "good" slurs are "against-the-grain," but several of them would result in a glissando without legato tonguing, which no one would think of for nearly a century.

According to Dieppo, there is no particular syllable to use. One tongues as if spitting something off the tip of the tongue. The stroke must be proportionate to the desired sound. The tongue and slide must be perfectly coordinated. Any delay in either one produces a bad effect and reveals a player with little ability. His comments on the portamento come in the context of solo playing, but he, too, advocated introducing a slight glissando whenever the slide would permit it. If the two notes were in the same position, the player should anticipate the second in lieu of a portamento.

Dieppo's range is the most conservative, E to $b♭'$. Cornette took the tenor and bass trombone up to d''. For the alto, he did not acknowledge seventh position or the lower partials, yielding a range of f to $e♭''$. Vobaron's position chart shows the pedal $BB♭$ up to f'' in first position, although he insisted that students should not try to play higher than f' until after they have achieved a thorough knowledge of all seven positions and a good sound.

Cornette and Vobaron did not comment on breathing, and Cornette did not describe slide technique. Dieppo described both a full breath, to be done slowly at a rest, and a half breath, when there was no rest. A half breath takes time from the preceding note. In either case, he cautioned that the note after the breath must start with an appropriate attack and must be exactly in time. His method of taking a full breath would not be acceptable today. He said to raise the chest while flattening the belly. Regarding slide technique, he said that the forearm must be flexible and the wrist must have no stiffness. The upper arm and shoulder do not move, but must not be rigid. The slide must be moved in a straight line, with no fumbling, slowness, or hesitation. Vobaron's comments, in the context of holding the trombone, are similar.

Only Cornette and Vobaron dealt with cleaning out the instrument. Cornette noted that it is necessary to clean the inside of the slide by attaching a cloth to a piece of strong wire, dipping it in boiling water, and running it through the slide. Vobaron said to wipe the inner slide with a cloth every day. The inside of the slide needs frequent cleaning by filling it three quarters with hot water and moving a wire with a rag at the end back and forth. He noted that the bow must also be cleaned out, as a lot of filth can accumulate there. Only Cornette wrote instructions on lubricating the slide. He said to use watchmaker's oil. Implicitly, Vobaron also advocated oiling the slide; oil was one of the specific things that needed to be cleaned away periodically.

Dieppo's method is divided into two parts, the first intended for training orchestral trombonists and as preparation for the second part, the training of trombone soloists. Most of the comments so far described are from the first part. It appears that he considered a good basic technique and musicianship sufficient for what he called accompaniment. There is not a syllable about how to play in an ensemble. Students with any ambition would want to become soloists, although they would need to master the first part of the method before going on. The second part covers different kinds of articulation (including legato playing, but not legato tonguing), ornamentation (including trills and grupettos), nuances, and phrasing.

In all three of these methods, the earliest exercises require the second through sixth partials. Absolute beginners would not be able to play them. Cornette's "Six grandes études" are more advanced than anything in the other two methods and far more difficult than any surviving solo literature of the time. Most of Vobaron's advanced études are in the form of duets. Dieppo provided a number of operatic arias.

Lafosse first issued his method in 1921 and revised it in 1946.[15] Much had changed since Dieppo's method appeared, but some of Lafosse's recommendations are very similar. He acknowledged the full trombone family of alto, tenor, bass, and contrabass, but except for an appendix on the bass trombone, the method covers only the tenor; the alto was obsolete, the contrabass more often played by tubists than trombonists, and the bass was nothing but a large-bore tenor with a trigger. Triggers were available in F and E. Lafosse recommended the E trigger for the sake of obtaining BB.

Lafosse's comments on the mouthpiece go far beyond earlier writers in their detail. The choice of mouthpiece depends on a player's natural peculiarities. Players with thick lips will need a wide cup diameter. A narrow throat makes high notes easier, but at the expense of richness of sound. Whoever can play high notes easily will benefit from a larger mouthpiece. The cup should be rather deep and cone shaped for a tenor trombone, but basin shaped for a bass trombone. The mouthpiece should be placed in the center of the mouth, roughly half on each lip, although placement often varies from player to player. Like earlier writers, Lafosse warned against puffing the cheeks. He advocated stretching the lips tight.

Lafosse said less about breathing than Dieppo, but it was necessary for him to describe articulation at greater length. To start a note, he advocated placing the tongue between the teeth and withdrawing it sharply while pronouncing the syllable "'tu." He struggled to describe a special kind of legato tonguing to avoid the glissandos that would otherwise result. He considered glissandos always tasteless, even though some composers called for them. Somewhat unwillingly, therefore, he described them at length, as well as multiple tonguing and flutter tonguing. He also described vibrato and mutes, both of which he attributed to jazz players. He made no particular value judgment about the straight mute, but considered other mutes and vibrato vulgar for classical music.

Within twenty years of the publication of the 1946 revision of Lafosse's method, English-language texts began to appear that differ more from Lafosse than Lafosse from Dieppo. Edward Kleinhammer, long-time bass trombonist of the Chicago Symphony Orchestra, published his first book in 1963. In 1997, in collaboration with a former student, Douglas Yeo of the Boston Symphony Orchestra, he issued another. It is not a new edition of the earlier text, which remains in print. In the discussion that follows, "Kleinhammer" refers to the earlier text, and "Kleinhammer and Yeo" to the later. Texts by Denis Wick and Reginald Fink are also widely read and cited, as are works by Philip Farkas and Donald Reinhardt that are aimed at brass players in general, not just trombonists.[16]

Reinhardt dealt only with the embouchure, and Farkas only with the embouchure and breathing. Otherwise, these authors considered a wider range of topics than the earlier books and went into much more detail. Except for Reinhardt's, the books include photographs, which enable the authors to illustrate things never before possible. (See Fig. 4.3.)

All of these authors displayed a much more sophisticated knowledge of human physiology than the earlier writers. They have been much more cognizant of the role of particular muscle groups and variations in human dentition in the development of the embouchure.

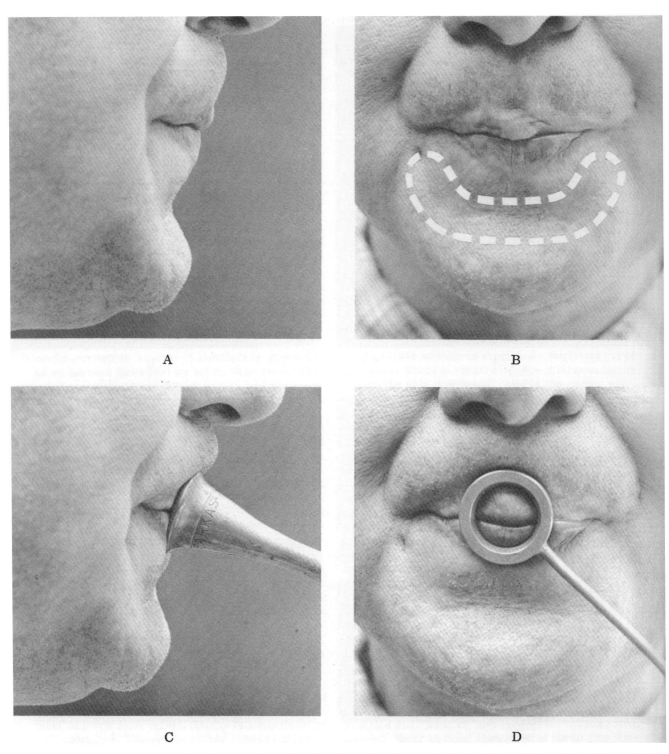

Fig. 4.3.   Photographs of Philip Farkas demonstrating embouchure formation, from Farkas's *Art of Brass Playing.* Used with permission of the Farkas family.

(See Fig. 4.4.) Physiological differences between two players likewise mean that the best embouchure for one will not achieve good results for another. Reinhardt introduced the concept of down-stream and up-stream players and developed the pivot system in order to find the most suitable embouchure for any facial structure. These ideas were very controversial in his lifetime, but had won considerable acceptance by the end of the

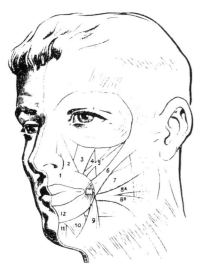

Scheme of musculature of embouchure, lateral view.

FIG. 9.--M, modiolus. 1, orbicularis oris (upper lip portion). 2, levator labii sup. alæque nasi. 3, levator labii superioris. 4, levator anguli oris. 5, zygomaticus minor. 6, zygomaticus major. 7, buccinator. 8a, risorius (masseteric strand). 8b, risorius (platysma strand). 9, depressor anguli oris. 10, depressor labii inferioris. 11, mentalis. 12, orbicularis oris (lower lip portion).

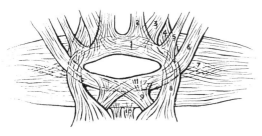

Scheme of musculature of embouchure, front view.

FIG. 9A.—1, orbicularis oris (upper lip portion). 2, levator labii sup. alæque nasi. 3, levator labii superioris. 4, levator anguli oris. 5, zygomaticus minor. 6, zygomaticus major. 7, buccinator. 8, depressor anguli oris. 9, depressor labii inferioris. 10, mentalis. 11, orbicularis oris (lower lip portion).

Fig 4.4. Medical drawing showing muscles of the face, with original caption, from Farkas's *Art of Brass Playing*. Reused with permission of *British Dental Journal*.

century. Awareness of physiology also informs discussions of breathing.

The emphasis on physiology led to recognition that musicians must train like athletes. Although Lafosse included four pages of daily exercises, it was American teachers who developed the concept of a systematic warm-up and first stressed the importance of avoiding excess tension. Each of these texts emphasizes relaxation in all aspects of playing. They also mention a new technique, practice with the mouthpiece alone.

Tonguing as if spitting something off the end of the tongue is not acceptable to any of these authors. More

successfully than Lafosse, they described tonguing in legato, which, according to Gordon Pulis, originated with Gardell Simon.[17] More than the tongue is required for a successful legato on the trombone. Where earlier discussions of slide technique hardly described more than the seven positions, these texts describe the very different kinds of slide movements required for legato passages and rapid staccato passages.

Regarding lubrication of the slide and cleaning of the instrument, the primitive equipment described by Cornette and Vobaron was no longer necessary. By 1963, Kleinhammer could explain the use of a flexible brush and a straight cleaning rod made specifically for cleaning a trombone. In addition to oil, he mentioned Pond's™ cold cream and Cuticura™ ointment. By the time Wick's book first came out, products made especially for lubricating trombone slides had appeared. He recommended Superslick™.

Many other new tools and practice aids became available (and in some cases quickly obsolete) in the last half of the twentieth century. For working on intonation, Kleinhammer and Fink both recommended the Stroboconn™ or its smaller version, the Strobotuner™. These large machines were probably only found in school bandrooms or teaching studios. They were too expensive and cumbersome for individuals to own, but they provided a way to see if a note was in tune, which helped the student learn to hear it. By the time Kleinhammer and Yeo appeared, it was obsolete. Inexpensive and reliable portable digital tuners had become available.

For embouchure development, Kleinhammer, Farkas, and Fink recommended a mouthpiece visualizer, a mouthpiece rim with a handle on it. The student could buzz into it while looking into a mirror and see the embouchure at work. Kleinhammer and Yeo add some newer tools: a cutaway mouthpiece, a Buzz Extension Resistance Piece or B.E.R.P.™, and a Forced Air Resistance Tube or F.A.R.T. The latter is simply eight inches or so of plastic tubing fitted at the end of the mouthpiece. The B.E.R.P.™ fits into the receiver of the trombone and the mouthpiece fits into an attached receiver, making it possible to combine mouthpiece practice with holding the instrument. Each of these tools enhances mouthpiece buzzing. For developing breathing, Fink advocated using a spirometer and described an exercise using a glass of water and a drinking straw. Each of these texts encourages using a tape recorder to record practice sessions.

Texts by David Baker and Stuart Dempster[18] cover various kinds of new and extended techniques demanded by the music of the late twentieth century. As Baker wrote primarily for jazz performers, he put great emphasis on different scale and chord patterns. Rhythmic issues include non-metric music, mixed meters, polymeters, multimetric music, and metric modulation. He shattered the ancient suggestion that the trombone can play neither rapid patterns nor legato with attention to what he called "tud-ul" tonguing, across-the-grain exercises for both scales and chords, and what he called "fretted playing."

Both described extremes of range, microtones, various kinds of vibrato, various trills, effects with mutes, and multiphonics (singing or making other vocal sounds while playing). Dempster wrote chapters on other body sounds, effects from disassembling the instrument, various percussive devices and accessories, extending the trombone's sound with piano resonance or electronics, and various theatrical considerations. Baker listed numerous recordings that illustrate the different techniques he describes. He included études for many of the techniques. Most of them are much more difficult and sophisticated than those in the other works described in this section, although his exercises for angular lines are actually less extreme than some of Cornette's études. In addition to a discography, Dempster included a recording.

Technological Tinkering: Evolution and Revolution in Designing Trombones

Valves

In the last chapter, Nemetz's 1827 text was the culmination of literature about the trombone written before the advent of valves. Some time after 1830, he issued a second edition, which includes one of the earliest descriptions and illustrations of a valve trombone. I have not seen this edition. Prussian wind players Stölzel and Blühmel invented the valve in 1814. It overcame the trumpet's and horn's limitation to notes in the overtone series. Trombones, being already chromatic instruments, did not need them. Nevertheless, the Berlin firms of Gabler and Griesling & Schlott began to make all three instruments with valves in 1818.[19] There were many different valve designs over the course of the nineteenth century, but only two need to be mentioned here: piston valves and rotary valves. There are primarily three ways that valves have been applied to the trombone: additive valves, the trigger, and independent valves.

After some experimentation, trumpets, horns, and valve trombones were equipped with three valves. The first lowers the basic pitch of the instrument by a tone, the second by a semitone, and the third by a tone and a half. The system fills in the gaps in the overtone series, making trumpets and horns completely chromatic. Com-

pared to the slide, it increases flexibility and enables fast passages to be played with greater ease.

On the other hand, valve instruments have generally been considered tonally weaker than their natural counterparts, and combining valves introduces problems of intonation. Lowering the pitch of a tube by a semitone requires an increase in length of about 6%. The second valve is the right length to lower the basic pitch of the instrument, but not enough to lower it an entire semitone if either or both of the other valves are engaged at the same time. One simple expedient for the lower brasses is to use four or more valves. In the supplement to his orchestration treatise (1844), Kastner noted that Germans had made tenor trombones with five valves. To this day, however, the three-valve design predominates. Valve trombones have been marketed mostly to amateur players, for whom extra valves are merely extra complication and expense. A three-valve trombone makes an easy double for a trumpet or cornet player.

Most valve trombones maintain the familiar shape of the slide trombone, a long form in which the valve section is added to what otherwise looks like the slide, but many have been made in various short forms that do not look anything like a slide trombone. (Refer to Fig. 1.4 in chapter 1.) The visual shape does not affect the acoustic quality of the instrument; all shapes of valve trombones sound alike.

The valve trombone was used exclusively for a while in some countries, so no distinction needed to be made there between slide trombones and valve trombones. But even in countries where slides and valves coexisted, nineteenth-century writers did not always differentiate clearly between them. An offhand reference to the quietness of the "keys" is the only indication that the following announcement of a new contrabass instrument concerns a valve trombone:

> A new brass instrument under this name, [contrabass *Posaune*] was lately tried at St. Phillip's church, Liverpool, the invention of Mr. Roe of that place. It is a powerful instrument, containing three octaves, the bottom note (E natural) being four notes below any wind instrument ever made. The performance, accompanied on the organ, was very creditable to Mr. Jeffreys. Eminent professors have inspected this instrument, and have expressed their unqualified admiration and astonishment at the very powerful and melodious tone which is produced upon it. It is so very ingeniously contrived, that not the slightest noise is heard with the keys.[20]

Valve trombones have been built in every size from alto to contrabass, but the tenor predominates. The alto valve trombone was a popular solo instrument for a while, at least in France and England, but the vogue did not last long. An English journal announced a contrabass valve trombone, but the most useful one today originated in Italy. Verdi intensely disliked the sound of the tuba with trombones. In 1881, he asked the Pelitti firm to design a contrabass trombone. They provided an instrument with four valves initially called the *trombone contrabasso Verdi*, but later called the *cimbasso*. That term, unfortunately, has caused a great deal of confusion, as it had been used earlier in the century for various other brass or even wooden instruments. I have been unable to locate an image of one built by Pelitti, but pictures of "cimbassos" of more recent manufacture show an instrument with the standard trombone shape, except that the mouthpiece receiver and the connection between the bell and the part that resembles the slide are bent so that the "slide" rests on the floor, but the bell still points forward.[21]

In 1839, Sattler introduced an innovative design in which a single valve operating with the player's left thumb, commonly called a trigger, was added to the bell section of a slide trombone. At the time, German tenor trombones were slide instruments in B♭ and bass trombones were ostensibly in F. A B♭ instrument with a larger bore was called a tenor-bass trombone (or very likely a bass trombone), and it was to this instrument that Sattler added his valve. With the valve engaged, the instrument had a fundamental of *FF*, just like the bass trombone in F. It provided six overtone series, thus filling in most of the gap between the first position pedal and the lowest second partial. It also made the sixth and seventh position series available in first and second, increasing the number of useful alternate positions.

The same acoustic principle that makes valve combinations too sharp makes it impossible to play *BB* and extremely difficult to play *C* in tune with a trigger in F. Lafosse recommended a trigger in E, which makes those two notes available at the expense of losing the advantage of having *F* and *c* available in first position. Not long afterward, some manufacturers made F-valves with a long tuning slide that could be pulled out enough to provide a temporary E-valve.

The modern bass trombone dates from the 1960s, when Allen Ostrander, Kauko Kahila, and Edward Kleinhammer (bass trombonists of the New York Philharmonic, Boston Symphony, and Chicago Symphony Orchestras respectively) persuaded manufacturers to make trombones with two triggers. A single thumb lever operated either the F valve or both valves together. At first the second valve was in E, but second valves in E♭ and D soon followed. By the 1970s, independent valves

became available. The first was still in F, but the second was in either G or G♭. Using this valve alone gives the player additional alternate positions, while using both together puts the instrument in D or D♭. (Combinations with the first valve in G are also available.) It is very awkward to operate two valves with the thumb. Therefore, they are commonly built so that the thumb plays the first valve and the middle finger plays the second. In about 1850 Adolphe Sax designed a trombone with a piston trigger, added to a small-bore French trombone. In the United States, Frederick Neil Innes designed a piston trigger that lowered the pitch of the instrument a semitone, making otherwise impossible trills practical. The trigger is most often a rotary valve. In the closing years of the twentieth century, several designers attempted to improve on it. Gary Greenhoe and Christian Lindberg have introduced new rotary valves. O. E. Thayer invented

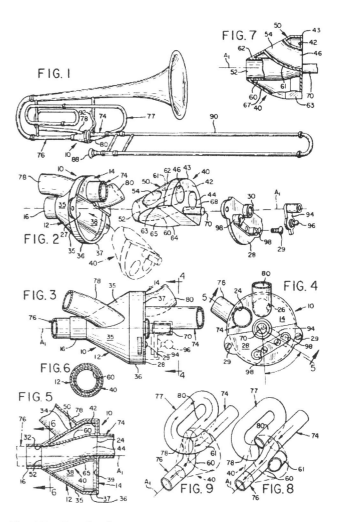

U.S. Patent   Sep. 4, 1984   Sheet 1 of 3   4,469,002

Fig. 4.5.   Drawing from U.S. Patent no. 4,469,002, one of five patents for the Thayer axial flow valve (1984).

something completely new, the axial-flow valve. (See Fig. 4.5.) More recently, René Hagmann and Robert Miller introduced new valve designs.[22]

It is difficult to find any documentation of the use of the trigger in the nineteenth century, although it stands to reason it had to be fairly successful then in order to survive into the twentieth century. In recent decades, it has become so well accepted that it is applied not only to tenor, bass, and contrabass trombones, where it is needed, but also to alto trombones. Thein even manufactured an alto trombone with two triggers that each lower the pitch a semitone in order to make trills easier to play. One of the valves is removable and the other can be fitted with a longer valve slide in order to lower the pitch a perfect fourth.[23]

In 1852, Sax introduced perhaps the most radical redesign of the trombone in history, a trombone with six valves, each independent of the others. Since the valves are used only one at a time, it avoids the intonation problems created by the additive system. In theory, it can always play perfectly in tune. According to Mahillon, in the first and most successful design each valve had a double channel and eight holes. With no valve engaged, the air column crossed all of the valves from one to six, passed through a length of tubing, and then re-crossed all of the valves from six to one. This length was the equivalent of a slide trombone in seventh position. Each valve shortened the sounding length of the tube by a certain amount. The sixth valve subtracted a semitone, the fifth valve a whole tone, and so forth, so that each valve represented the same-numbered slide position. (See Fig. 4.6.)

Not only is this instrument very heavy, but it is difficult to make such long double-channel valves airtight, an absolute prerequisite for good functioning. So in 1867, Sax introduced a new model. Each valve was pierced with only four holes and ended with its own bell. (Refer to the far right instrument in Fig. 1.4 in chapter 1.) It became, therefore, a bundle of seven natural instruments

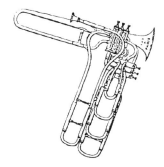

Fig. 4.6.   Trombone by Sax with six independent valves, from an advertisement in *Revue et gazette musicale de Paris* **(31 March 1872).**

of different lengths. For accuracy and craftsmanship, Mahillon considered this design a great improvement, but it was even heavier than the earlier one. It still did not allow the subtle variations in pitch necessary to make its intonation as good in practice as it was in theory.[24] Despite Sax's confidence that his design would render all earlier designs obsolete, it was never used much except in France, Belgium, and England, and then not for very long. It provided no advantages for the top professional slide trombonists and had no chance at penetrating the amateur market. It turned out to be a design that many were eager to try, but quick to abandon.

Some slide trombones have been built with fully functioning additive valves operated by the player's left hand. Early in the twentieth century, Conn marketed them as "Valide" (valve + slide) trombones. In the 1970s, Maynard Ferguson popularized this design as "Superbone." It is somewhat useful as a transposing device, although the intonation difficulties inherent in the additive valve system become even worse when combined with the slide. Only the most expert players can take whatever advantage there is of the design.

The double-belled euphonium is a duplex instrument, a combination of a tenor tuba and tenor valve trombone with an additional valve enabling the performer to decide which of two distinctly different sounds to evoke. Benny Sluchin described a similar duplex slide trombone, a large bore tenor with an additional small bell that points back over the player's shoulder. With a mute in one bell or different mutes in both bells, possibilities of coloristic echo effects are endless. Such a trombone would seem most useful for an improviser, although some pieces have been composed for it.[25]

Other Innovations

Although valves represent the most important new technology of the industrial era, inventors have continued to lavish attention on the slide trombone. Many of their ideas quickly fell by the wayside, but some have become commonplace features.

The modern era of trombone design began not with the valve trombone, but in 1816 with Weber's new slide. (See Document 2, in the appendix.) He was dissatisfied with the centuries-old slide mechanism because it is necessary to move the slide as much as two feet to get from one note to the next. It was even worse for the bass trombonist, who needed a handle to reach the outer positions. Weber considered it fatiguing to play.

Because the standard trombone slide has two legs, when the trombonist moves the slide out one inch, he has actually increased the total length of the tube by two inches. So Weber proposed a slide with four legs. A one-inch outward movement of the slide increases the sounding length of the trombone by four inches. The trombonist would need to move the slide only half as far between notes. If the entire slide were more than half the length of a regular slide, making more than seven positions available, it would make lower notes available to fill the gap between the highest pedal notes and the lowest second partial that he found so objectionable in his earlier article. It would also increase the number of alternate positions for many of the regular notes and make the movement of the slide even more efficient.

The four-legged slide is used to this day for BB♭ contrabass trombones, but there is no sign that it ever met with widespread favor. The invention of the trigger not many years later accomplished many of the same purposes without forcing the player to learn a whole new set of positions. It probably had less impact on the overall balance of the instrument as well. Some confusion has been caused by the existence of a four-legged slide on a bass trombone made in 1612 by Jobst Schnitzer. It is not authentic. The bell is by Schnitzer, but the slide conversion was done in the nineteenth century.[26]

Other innovations, though introduced with less fanfare, have proven more useful. The water key, invented by Halary in 1845, enabled the player to rid the trombone of condensation efficiently. Around the middle of the century, slides acquired stockings (an expansion of the lower end of each inner slide, which significantly reduces the friction with the outer slide).

Boosey & Company made trombones in 1885 with a tuning slide at the end of the playing slide. There are some acoustic advantages to tuning in the slide. Because the bore of a modern trombone begins to expand before the bell bow, the bell bow is conical in shape, but only imperfectly if the tuning slide is there. More recent design of tuning in the slide relies on a screw mechanism attached to an extra brace. Such slides are heavier and more difficult to maintain, so they remain less common.

In 1897, the London branch of the Besson Company patented spring slide buffers.[27] They provide two advantages. They provide a cushion if the player brings the slide into first position too abruptly. If the instrument is tuned with the end of the slide barely touching the spring, there is room left to sharpen first position by pressing against the spring, making even the very flat seventh partial available.

In the early twentieth century, manufacturers started to supply screw mechanisms in place of friction joints to join the bell section with the slide section. The 1927 King catalog lists it as an extra option and attributes its

necessity to the use of effects that require players to put their left hand by the bell; without the screw lock, the slide could become separated from the bell.[28] The slide lock, another screw mechanism near the mouthpiece, prevents the slide from moving at all, an important safety feature.

Possibly the most important new design feature of the twentieth century, the lead pipe, is a small pipe that is often soldered to the inside of the inner slide as a receiver for the mouthpiece. Narrower at the mouthpiece end, it opens up over a length of seven to nine inches. The amount of taper directly affects the quality of sound, the resistance, and response of the instrument. Several models are now available with detachable and interchangeable lead pipes.

Unsuccessful innovations continued into the twentieth century. Olds marketed a fluted slide in order to reduce friction still more than stockings. It proved easy to damage and difficult to repair. In 1952, Davis Shuman introduced a slide that moved to the player's right at an angle. (Refer to Fig. 8.14 in chapter 8.) He claimed that it resulted in a more natural movement of the arm, thus saving wear and tear on the player's elbow. Young students could more easily reach the outer positions. In crowded orchestra pits, he claimed that the trombonist was less likely to hit someone in front. He recommended a 45-degree angle for children and a 15-degree angle for professionals.[29] In practice however, these instruments were worse in pits than ordinary trombones. No one else shared his enthusiasm for the design.

Some of the earliest extant tenor trombones have bores of 10 mm (.394 inches) or less, although others are as large as 12.1 mm (.476).[30] Dieppo wrote that French composers used only one size of trombone, implicitly the tenor, which had a bore of 10 mm.[31] It appears that instruments that narrow were still made in England, but that German trombones were already somewhat larger. Manufacturers continued to make instruments with small bores as late as the middle of the twentieth century.

Sattler introduced the tenor-bass trombone, a B♭ tenor trombone with the bore of a bass trombone in F, and subsequently added the trigger to it in 1839. The term tenor-bass trombone therefore can and often does refer to an ordinary slide trombone. Once the tenor-bass trombone, with or without the added valve, became common in Germany, German orchestras routinely used trombones with a larger bore than any other country except Austria, where Červený popularized large-bore valve trombones. That only began to change when American orchestral players started to adopt the large bore early in the twentieth century. After the Second World War, large-bore trombones, mostly of American design, became the instruments of choice in orchestras worldwide.

By the end of the nineteenth century, at least one author complained that modern trombones had too large a bore, and blamed military bands. Baines provided dramatically different measurements in his two articles for Grove. In 1954, he defined narrow bore as .45 inches, medium as .49, and wide as up to .52. The metric equivalents are 11.4 mm, 12.4 mm, and 13.2 mm. In 1980, he wrote that the bore was usually between 12.3 and 13.8 mm, with bass trombones being larger than 14 mm. The English-system equivalents are .472, .543, and more than .551. The narrowest measurement he gave in 1980 was barely smaller than the medium bore of 1954, and the widest was much wider than the earlier wide bore. Today's orchestral tenor trombones have a .547 bore (13.9 mm) and bass trombones are .562 (14.3 mm).[32] Table 4.1 lists the measurements of various trombones.[33] For each instrument listed, the top row of measurements is expressed in millimeters, the bottom row in inches. I doubt if the Courtois alto trombone made in the 1930s with the 10.0 mm bore really has a 320 mm (12.60 in.) bell, but that is what is printed in the catalog. Even 230 mm (9.06 in.) seems too large.

Table 4.1. The Measurements of Various Trombones

Date	Museum	Number	Maker and Where Made	Size	Bore	Bell	Angle
1594	Edinburgh	2695	Schnitzer Germany	Tenor	8.9 0.350	102/05 4–4.13	
1631	Leipzig	1914	Hainlein Germany	Bass	12.5 0.492	122 4.80	40°
1635	Leipzig	1909	Goltbeck Germany	Bass	13.6 0.535	122 4.80	31°
1650	Leipzig	1910	Birckholtz Germany	Bass	12.5 0.492	129.5 5.10	31°
1668	Leipzig	1896	Ehe Germany	Tenor	11.8 0.464	105 4.13	40°
1690	Leipzig	1884	Starck Germany	Alto	12.3 0.484	98.5 3.88	
1720/24	Leipzig	1897	Ehe Germany	Tenor	12.1 0.476	110 4.33	40°
1720/24	Leipzig	1886	Ehe Germany	Alto	11.9 0.469	99.5 3.92	41°
1789	Leipzig	1887	Schmied Germany	Alto	11.8 0.464	110 4.33	53°
1794	Edinburgh	3205	Huschauer Austria	Tenor	10.8 0.425	117 4.51	
1796	Leipzig	1879	Anon. Germany	Sopr.	11.8 0.464	110.5 4.35	74°
1796	Leipzig	1880	Eschenbach Germany	Sopr.	11.3 0.445	104 4.09	58°
1796	Leipzig	1899	Eschenbach Germany	Tenor	11.9 0.469	130 5.12	54°
1810	Edinburgh	3534	Riedlocker France	Tenor	10.7 0.421	119 4.69	
1820	Edinburgh	3227	Anon. England	Tenor	10.5 0.413	148 5.83	
182-?	Edinburgh	3738	Anon.	Tenor	11.5 0.453	139 5.47	
1820/30	St. Petersburg		Devaster Brussels	Tenor	12.8 0.504	169 6.65	
1820/30	St. Petersburg		Kretchmann Strassbourg	Tenor (OTS)	13.0 0.512	130.3 5.13	
ca. 1825	Nuremberg		Hilaire-Asté Paris	Tenor	11.8 0.465	(buccin)	
1830/40	Leipzig	1913	Anon. Germany	Bass	13.8 0.543	175 6.89	64°
1835	Edinburgh	3026	Green England	Bass	12.8 0.504	167 6.57	

Table 4.1. (*Continued*)

Date	Museum	Number	Maker and Where Made	Size	Bore	Bell	Angle
1838/39	Leipzig	1915	Anon. Germany	Bass 4-leg	14.7 0.579	152 5.98	76°
1840	Rome		Apparuti Modena	Tenor	12.0 0.472	172 6.77	
1841	Leipzig	4137	Sattler Germany	Alto	11.5 0.453	125 4.92	72°
1841	Leipzig	4138	Sattler Germany	Tenor	13.1 0.516	195 7.68	66°
1841	Leipzig	4139	Sattler Germany	Tenor-Bass	14.6 0.575	230 9.06	68°
1850	Edinburgh	901	Anon. Britain?	Bass	12.5 0.492	158 6.22	
1855	Leipzig	3303	Penzel Germany	Tenor	13.8 0.543	230 9.06	
1855	Leipzig	3164	Schöngarth Germany	Bass	15.3 0.602	215 8.46	66°
1865	Edinburgh	3747	Courtois France	Tenor	11.3 0.445	151 5.94	
1869	Edinburgh	581	Courtois France	Bass trigger	12.1 0.476	191 7.52	
1872/78	Edinburgh	3849	Courtois France	Tenor	10.9 0.429	169 6.65	
1880	Edinburgh	2500	Riviere/Hawkes England	Tenor	10.3 0.406	138 5.43	
1885/86	Edinburgh	1556	Boosey England	Alto	10.8 0.425	141 5.55	
1890	Edinburgh	519	Besson England	Bass	11.8 0.465	204 8.03	
1895	Edinburgh	1770	Pace England	Tenor	9.6 0.378	147 5.79	
1895	Edinburgh	2840	Woods England	Tenor	10.5 0.413	150 5.91	
1900	Edinburgh	521	Hawkes England	Alto	10.8 0.425	130 5.12	
1900	Edinburgh	2991	Besson England	Tenor	11.0 0.433	156 6.14	
19--	Edinburgh	578	Anon. England	Tenor	10.6 0.417	182.0 7.17	
1900/10	Edinburgh	3665	Courtois France	Tenor	10.5 0.413	152.0 5.98	
1904/10	Edinburgh	1865	Courtois France	Bass	11.0 0.433	187/89 7.40	
1910	Edinburgh	3207	Schopper Germany	Tenor	12.4 0.488	232 9.1	
1920	Leipzig	3474	Anon. Germany	Tenor	13.0 0.512	227 8.94	66°
1921	Edinburth	211	Boosey England	Tenor	12.1 0.476	190 7.64	
1924	Edinburgh	3093	Boosey England	Tenor	11.2 0.441	150 5.91	
1925	Leipzig	3610	Anon. France	Tenor	12.3 0.484	172 6.77	66°
1925	Edinburgh	2802	Conn U.S.	Tenor	10.7 0.421	177 6.97	
1925	Edinburgh	3706	Couturier U.S.	Tenor Conical	10.9 0.429	202 7.95	
1925	Edinburgh	3671	Higham England	Bass	10.8 0.425	186 7.32	
1930s	Edinburgh	3692	Courtois France	Alto	10.0 0.394	320 [!] 12.6 [!]	

(*Continued*)

Table 4.1. (*Continued*)

Date	Museum	Number	Maker and Where Made	Size	Bore	Bell	Angle
1933	Edinburgh	2496	Boosey/Hawkes England	Tenor	11.2 0.441	154 6.06	
1934	Edinburgh	1122	Boosey/Hawkes England	Tenor trigger	11.2 0.441	185 7.28	
1935	Edinburgh	2151	Horst Germany	Tenor	11.8 0.465	235 9.25	
1940	Edinburgh	2782	Besson England	Alto	10.4 0.409	150 5.91	
1940	Edinburgh	839	Conn U.S.	Tenor	10.4 0.409	176 9.63	
1946	Edinburgh	2853	Boosey/Hawkes England	Bass	11.4 0.449	187 7.36	
1948	Edinburgh	3751	Besson England	Tenor	10.2 0.402	158 6.22	
1957	Edinburgh	3752	Besson England	Tenor	10.6 0.417	196 7.71	
1962	Edinburgh	1866	Besson England	Bass trigger	12.0 0.472	203 7.99	

Late in the seventeenth century, Johann Karl Kodisch began to make trombones with a wider terminal flare than the standard cone shape. (Compare the two instruments in Fig. 3.4, in chapter 3.) That design did not begin to become common until the end of the eighteenth century. Shortly thereafter, it became universal. The last column in the table above shows the angle of flare in trombones at the Leipzig museum; only Heyde supplies such a measurement. In a more subtle design change, late eighteenth- and early nineteenth-century trombone makers started expanding the bore profile before rather than after the bell bow, resulting in a larger proportion of conical tubing. The tuning slide also appeared in the late eighteenth century, first made in Paris by Riedlocker and described by Braun.

Most other changes to the bell have had no more than a temporary vogue. Anticipating possible objections to his new slide, Weber conceded that the extra winding would cause the sound to lose some strength. He suggested that the bow that directed the bell forward was unnecessary. Strength lost from the extra bends in the slide could be regained by allowing the bell to point back over the player's shoulder. This suggestion was more successful than his slide. Vobaron's method includes a drawing of such a bell. (See Fig. 4.7.) Dodworth claimed to have introduced it to the United States. Partly because nineteenth-century trombonists had a reputation for a blaring sound that covered more important parts, the over-the-shoulder bell seemed like a way to restore balance. Saxhorns and other low brass instruments were likewise built that way, and the use of over-the-shoulder bells lasted past midcentury on both sides of the Atlantic.

At about the same time as the over-the-shoulder bells were introduced, some French and Belgian makers, including Guichard, Courtois, and Tuerlinckx, began to make trombones for their military customers that ended in a gaudily painted dragon's or serpent's head. (See Fig. 4.8.) This form of trombone, known as the buccin, had a deader sound than the regular bell, but it must have looked very impressive on parade. The same makers also put monster's heads on serpents, serpent bassoon, and other precursors of the ophicleide. Kappey's history of military music includes this recollection:

> I distinctly remember having seen in childhood a large Austrian band, which made a lasting impression upon me; it had about 5 or 6 brass serpents in the front rank, the bell of each being shaped like an open mouth of a huge serpent, painted bloodred inside with huge white teeth, and wagging tongue which moved up and down at every step! For "picturesque" effect—I never forgot *that*; as to what or how the band played, I remember nothing except those terrible open jaws!![34]

In the twentieth century, some straight tenor trombones are equipped with a counterweight that helps balance the instrument. Holton and Thein, at least, have made trombones with a screw bell. Being able to remove the rim of the bell enables the instrument to fit into a more compact case, which is a great advantage for air travel.

Fig. 4.7.   Trombone with over-the-shoulder bell from Vobaron's method (1834).

The extra weight also helps hold the sound together at loud dynamic levels.

Mouthpieces have nearly always been made of metal. Most today are of silver-plated brass. In the 1830s, some were made of ivory. Cornette recommended them for orchestral work, probably because, as Vobaron pointed out, ivory (or horn) mutes the sound.[35] In the twentieth century, plastic mouthpieces have proved useful for playing outdoors in cold weather. Teflon rims and gold plating are both useful for trombonists who develop an allergy to silver plating.

There has been great variation in mouthpiece design over the years, at least in part because of the personal preferences of different players. Rims can be flat or rounded, wide or narrow. There is as much variation in the shape and depth of the cup and the size of the throat. Vincent Bach was the first maker to develop tools to duplicate mouthpieces. Numerous manufacturers now use similar processes to mass-produce large catalogs of mouthpieces. Each variation in rim, cup, throat, backbore has advantages for some aspect of playing and corresponding disadvantages. Many players prefer to choose one mouthpiece and stick with it while others select different mouthpieces on different occasions. Doublers who prefer to use the same rim for everything have special problems. One solution is to have various custom-made

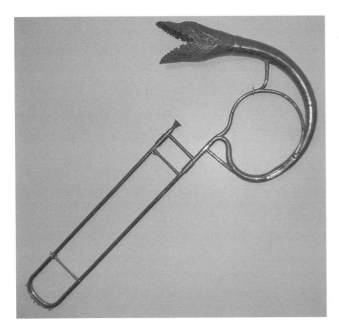

Fig. 4.8. Buccin. Bell (1820s?) by François Sautermeister; new slide by Jim Becker. Photograph by Douglas Yeo. Used by permission.

mouthpieces, each with the identical rim. Elliot and Giardinelli both sell an ingenious alternative: mouthpieces that come in three parts, with separate rims, cups, and shanks. The player can mix and match at will, using the same rim for everything or not.

Cornette advocated oiling the slide with watchmaker's oil. Later in the century, Holton marketed oil especially formulated for trombone slides. By the middle of the twentieth century, many players preferred to rub a small amount of cold cream on the stockings and keep it moist by spraying water from an atomizer. By the end of the century, a wide variety of products became available, including creams, oils, and liquid silicon.

Those in the nineteenth century who complained about the weight of the long bass trombone would be utterly appalled at the weight of modern trombones. It has reached a point where trombonists can suffer pain in their wrists, elbows, or shoulders. Gary Greenhoe has designed a rest bar that can be custom fitted to a player's hand. Some trombonists use straps made of fabric to bear the weight of the instrument and relieve muscle strain. More recently, the Ergobone™, a rod that attaches to the trombone at one end and rests either on the floor or in a plastic pouch on a harness worn by the player, enables one to play the trombone without holding it with the left hand at all. Besides bearing the weight of the instrument, it probably facilitates mute changes.

There is some evidence of the use of mutes as early as the fifteenth century, but they were rare until late in the nineteenth century. Only in the twentieth century did a collection of mutes become a necessity for every trombonist. Orchestral music frequently requires a straight mute, which can be made of various kinds of fiber, metal, or plastic. Other mutes are less common in the orchestra, but cup mutes and Harmon mutes are occasionally required. Jazz players need all of those plus at least a bucket and a plunger. Practice mutes block nearly all of the sound. They are handy for practicing in hotels, dorm rooms, or otherwise to avoid disturbing other people. Yamaha makes Silent Brass™, an electronic practice mute with headphones that also allows players to practice with play-along records or to record their practice sessions.

During rests, between pieces, or even between practice sessions, trombonists can keep their instruments on a stand. In most cases, it essentially consists of a rod resting on three legs, with a curved pad on which the bell rests. Some stands hold the instrument by the slide braces instead, so that it is not necessary to remove mutes. Players today have a choice between hard cases of various materials and padded gig bags.

Manufacturers

Already before the end of the eighteenth century, the labor-intensive techniques of the Nuremburg craftsmen became economically unsustainable. Modern trombones are made very differently. The differences can be summarized under four headings: the choice of materials, use of machinery, mass-production techniques, and division of labor.

The process of making brass using pure zinc rather than calamine was patented in 1781. Greater control over the zinc content of brass made different specific ratios of copper to zinc easier to achieve and gave manufacturers of brass instruments a greater choice of kinds of brass to use. But zinc was not the only newly available pure metal. Aluminum became economically feasible in the 1850s, and in 1857 Besson patented aluminum valves. It did not turn out to be an acceptable substitute for brass. Neither have other new materials introduced since then. Steel is not a suitable material for trombones, but it is superior for mandrels and other tools and machines used in making them. Nickel or chromium, on the other hand, became very useful on valves and slides once the process of electroplating was invented.[36]

Modern machinery requires power far beyond what can be supplied by human or animal muscle, a millstream, or other pre-industrial sources. Steam power provided the first breakthrough. Electricity has since supplanted it. Machinery for rolling out sheet metal replaced the older hammer mills after about 1800. Machines also enable seamless, drawn tubes, and new processes of joining parts together. The twentieth century saw the development of hydraulic forming techniques to bend tubes into the most intricate shapes quickly.[37] Bells are usually now spun on a lathe. Machines enable much greater control of the thickness of the metal and the bore of the tubes, which in turn enables standardization and interchangeable parts.

It is expensive to tool up the various new processes, but once all of the machinery is in place, it enables assembly lines and mass production. By the end of the nineteenth century, craftsmen were allowed up to one hundred hours to produce a top of the line instrument. That is probably less time than the Nuremberg craftsmen needed, but by the end of the twentieth century a professional instrument required half that time. Cheaper mass-produced instruments come off the assembly line after only about six man-hours of work.[38] Older methods have not been abandoned entirely. Smaller companies cannot afford the machinery for some of the newer processes, and in other cases, the older methods achieve better quality.

The Tuerlinckx factory, large for its time, was soon dwarfed by other larger, more efficient firms. On the modern assembly line, each person works on only a small part of the production of an instrument. That is not new in itself. Hans Neuschel the elder was a piece-worker before becoming a master craftsman. Modern factories divide the tasks differently and among more people. In 1897 the Mahillon factory hired fourteen different categories of brass instrument makers. Bell makers, valve makers, and fitters were the highest paid. Filers, scrapers, and polishers, among others, earned much less.[39]

Prussia became a major center for the manufacture of brass instruments late in the eighteenth century when tariffs rose high enough to make imported instruments prohibitively expensive. At about the same time, the practice of royal monopolies ended. Important Prussian brass instrument makers included Elsner, Eschenbach, Gabler, Griesling & Schlott, Krause, and Moritz.[40] Although the first valve trombones were made in Berlin, they never supplanted slide trombones in Germany. The Moritz firm, which lasted until 1955, built a slide contrabass trombone to Wagner's specifications.

Elsewhere in Germany, Sattler of Leipzig is best known as inventor of the trigger, but before that he was apparently among the first to make a wide-bore tenor-bass trombone. Other important non-Prussian trombone makers include several members of the Stowasser family,

Altrichter, Penzel (Sattler's son-in-law and successor), and especially Kruspe, whose trombones are often considered the epitome of German design of the Romantic era. None of these firms is still active. The most prominent German makers today are the brothers Max and Heinrich Thein, admired both for their ability to recreate the Kruspe design and for their own innovations.

Austrian orchestras quickly abandoned the slide trombone in favor of the valve trombone, so nineteenth-century Austrian manufacturers made only valve trombones. When slide trombones were reintroduced to the Vienna Philharmonic in 1883, it was necessary to import German-made instruments. Uhlmann, whose firm dates from 1834, patented a new valve design in 1830, known as the Vienna valve. Bohland & Fuchs, founded in 1870, was the first Austrian instrument manufacturer to use steam power and mass-production techniques. It quickly became the largest in the empire. It employed 500 workers in 1940, but ceased operations in 1945. Among its unique offerings was a double alto/tenor trombone designed by Serafin Alschausky in 1920.

Václav Červený founded a very important company in Prague in 1842, which is credited with introducing large-bore designs to the entire German-speaking world. (Sattler made large-bore trombones earlier, but it is not clear how influential they were.) It made trombones with rotary valves, Červený's own refinement of Uhlmann's design. Some of the earliest pictures of Červený trombones show a standard long-form valve trombone, but in 1867 he introduced an *Arméeposaune* for military use, which does not at all resemble the traditional appearance of the trombone. The firm continued to thrive when the empire was broken up after the First World War and Prague became the capital of the new republic of Czechoslovakia, but it was nationalized when the Communists took control after the Second World War. It still continues to make brass instruments, although the name was abandoned.[41]

Italy abandoned the slide trombone as soon as valve trombones became available. Gioacchino Bimboni began to manufacture valve trombones in Florence in 1831. That he was also Italy's leading trombone soloist probably helped gain acceptance for the new instrument there. Other important factors include Austrian political dominance and the difficulty of Rossini's trombone parts. In 1850 he introduced the "bimbonifono," a vertical trombone with seven rotary valves.

The leading Italian firm, however, was Pelitti. Five generations of this family made brass instruments until 1905. The firm ceased operation shortly before the Second World War. Pelitti was famous for duplex and even triplex instruments (two or three instruments in one). It also designed and built a valve contrabass trombone for Verdi.[42]

Of the various French manufacturers mentioned in the previous chapter, only Courtois, established in 1789, is still in business. The founder, whose first name is not known, apparently died in 1803. At that time, a number of successors appeared, with names such as Courtois, the Oldest Nephew; Three Sons of Courtois' Nephew; Auguste Courtois; and Antoine Courtois. The latter was the most successful. Antoine Courtois's son died without heir in 1880, but the firm continued with the same name under the leadership first of Auguste Mille and eventually under various members of the Gaudet family. The slide trombone was one of Antoine Courtois's main specialties. He gave trombones to winners of the Paris Conservatory contests beginning in 1838. His successors have continued to work closely with leading performers and to give special attention to keeping their trombone designs up to date.[43]

Three other French firms manufactured trombones into the twentieth century. Couesnon, successor to a firm founded in 1827 by Guichard, was the largest musical instrument manufacturer in the world in the first quarter of the twentieth century, employing 1000 workers and producing 60,000 instruments (brass, string, and woodwind) annually. After a long decline, it ceased to exist by 1995.

Gustave Auguste Besson founded his firm in 1837 or 1838 and established a London branch in 1851. He was among the makers involved in litigation against Sax. When it failed in 1858, he moved his operations to London to avoid paying damages to Sax, but left his wife in charge of the Paris office. That office remained in business until the death of Besson's granddaughter. By 1957, it had been absorbed by Couesnon. Among its innovations was a duplex trombone with both a slide and valves (ca. 1864).

Henri Selmer established his firm as a woodwind manufacturer in 1885. It took over what was left of Sax's workshop in 1928 and began manufacturing brass instruments, including trombones. In 1931 it acquired two more brass instrument firms, Raoux and Millereau. Branches in both the United States and Britain operated separately.

Sax established his firm in Brussels in 1835, but moved operations to Paris in 1842. His innovations in trombone design include a slide trombone with a piston trigger, and most notably, the concept of independent valves. The most important Belgian firm was founded in 1836 by Charles Boromée Mahillon, father of the better-known Victor-Charles Mahillon, who also worked for the firm. Mahillon continued to make brass instruments until it closed in 1999.

Frederick Pace and other British firms made a few trombones early in the nineteenth century, but ceased after French instruments became popular. Courtois sold trombones in the English market, and Besson established a branch of his company in London. Boosey & Co. purchased patent rights to Besson's contrabass trombone in 1862 and acquired the firm of Distin & Co. in 1868, thus becoming a major manufacturer of brass instruments. (Distin had started as a distributor for Sax's instruments and subsequently began manufacturing saxhorns on a large scale.) In collaboration with George Case, Boosey made slide trombones from E♭ alto to F bass that had their tuning slide at the end of the playing slide. Its output included both slide and valve trombones, and in 1929 it made a B♭/F model with a trigger. The firm merged with Hawkes & Son in 1930 to become Boosey & Hawkes and later absorbed the London branch of the Besson Company, as well as the firm of Rudall Carte.[44]

In the late nineteenth century, most British instruments for band use were built at "Old Philharmonic" or "Kneller Hall" pitch (a' = 452.5 Hz), while orchestral wind instruments were built at "International Pitch" (a' = 439 Hz). In the twentieth century, these became known as high pitch and low pitch. In 1964 the two remaining British manufacturers of band instruments (Boosey & Hawkes and the Salvation Army) decided to stop making high pitch instruments, forcing bands to change to low pitch if they wanted new instruments.[45]

Boosey & Hawkes was the only remaining large-scale British manufacturer of trombones at the end of the twentieth century, but Michael Rath started a small shop in 1996 that specializes in modular design (allowing customers to choose individual components) and hand craftsmanship. Boosey & Hawkes is both a manufacturer of a wide variety of instruments and a leading music publisher, but Rath makes only trombones and trombone mouthpieces.

Although evidence of trombonists in the United States is slim before the middle of the 1820s, American shops began to produce trombones not long afterward. In October 1835, the *American Musical Journal* noted, "The Trombones and other brass instruments exhibited at the Fair in Castle Garden, and manufactured by Mr. John Rosenbeck of Utica, have been pronounced by Mr. Norton and Signor Cioffi, superior in point of tone and neatness of workmanship to any hitherto made in this country. Signor Cioffi immediately purchased the alto and tenor trombones for his own particular use."[46]

SLIDE TROMBONES,

—— Manufactured by ——

C. G. CONN,

Elkhart, Indiana, and Worcester, Mass.

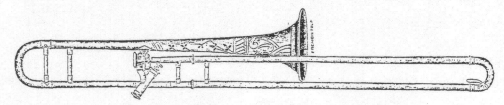

Innes Model Tenor Slide Trombone.

From Frederick N. Innes. The famous Trombone Soloist and Bandmaster.

C. G. CONN:—It is the most marvelous, perfect trombone it has ever been my good fortune to play upon. There is a rich brilliancy of tone, together with a totally unprecedented freedom and ease of blowing, that your would-be competitors will strive in vain to approach.

Guaranteed to be superior to any other Slide Trombone Manufactured

IN THE WORLD.

The Artists' Model Tenor Slide Trombone.

From E. BROOKS, Trombone Soloist and Musical Director, Nantasket Beach, Boston, Mass., Composer of Rip Van Winkle Overture, Christmas Chimes, etc.

C. G. CONN:—The Trombone I ordered of you came to hand, and I have given it a six weeks' trial. Allow me to compliment you, and will say I have used nearly all makes, and this is the finest trombone I ever had, and gives me perfect satisfaction. It certainly is a beautiful instrument, and I am happy now that I have an instrument that suits me. Please accept my sincere thanks for promptness in filling my order. You can rely on my order for future times. This is the third trombone purchased of you.

Fig. 4.9.   Page from an early Conn catalog, showing Innes's trill valve.

Other important early makers include Graves & Co. (1837–1869) and Isaac Fiske (1842–1887).

The earliest American manufacturer still in existence, Conn, began modestly in 1874 as a maker of rubber-rimmed mouthpieces, but expanded aggressively when it began to produce instruments the following year. Conn purchased Fiske's factory and recruited several craftsmen who had worked for Distin. With his very large facilities and excellent designers and technicians, Conn dominated the American band instrument market. Ultimately, he combined the best features of French and German designs.

He worked closely with such leading trombonists as Innes and Pryor, realizing that endorsements from well-known professionals would boost sales in the more lucrative amateur market. The company continued to flourish and expand for decades after Conn's retirement in 1915 because of its strengths in both research and marketing. Conn was the leading manufacturer of instruments for professionals, amateur bands, and schools. As American orchestral trombonists began to use larger equipment, most of them preferred Conns.

During the Second World War, Conn, like many other manufacturers, retooled for war production and sold no instruments to civilians for several years. After the war, it did not reconvert quickly and lost some of its market dominance to other manufacturers. On the other hand, Conn's aggressive marketing in England when Boosey & Hawkes stopped making high pitch instruments led to the adoption of large-bore instruments in British brass bands. The Conn 8H and 88H models became the instrument of choice as both British and French orchestral trombonists began to abandon narrow-bore instruments.

Although Conn was the largest American company, many others flourished. Henderson White founded the King company in 1893. Because he was unwilling to begin production on any instrument that did not represent an improvement over what was already on the market, his instruments were immediately successful. Frank Holton, the first solo trombonist with the Sousa band, stopped touring in 1898. The manufacture of trombone slide oil was not profitable enough, so he began to make trombones. The popularity of these instruments enabled him to begin making other brass instruments as well. Vincent Bach began to manufacture mouthpieces in 1918, trumpets and cornets in 1924, and trombones in 1928. The Bach Stradivarius model provided Conn with some of its stiffest competition. Other noteworthy American makers of trombones include Benge, Blessing, Getzen, Kanstul, Martin, Olds, and Reynolds.[47]

As of this writing, most American brands are now sold by a single conglomerate, Conn-Selmer, a subsidiary of the Steinway Corporation. A number of smaller companies custom design trombones for individuals, including Edwards (founded in 1989) and Shires (founded in 1995). For example, tenor trombone bells can be made in several sizes from several different kinds of brass of several different weights. Mass-production techniques allow these companies to stock many different kinds of bells, which can be combined with as many different kinds of slides, lead pipes, trigger configurations, and so forth. Customers visit the factory for a consultation in order to determine which options will be combined for their trombone.

Torakasu Yamaha began to manufacture reed organs in Japan in 1887. The company began to make pianos in 1900 and brass instruments in 1959. It retained Renold Schilke, an important manufacturer of trumpets, cornets, and mouthpieces, as a consultant in 1966, and by 1969, Yamaha instruments were available worldwide. Yamaha makes both professional and student trombones, and like European and American makers, consults with leading professional players in the process of designing new instruments.

Jupiter trombones, made in Taiwan, are acceptable student instruments. Their professional instruments have been less successful, but they, too, are consulting with professional musicians to improve their designs. Trombones manufactured in China have generally been regarded as trombone-shaped objects, not musical instruments, but it seems only a matter of time before some Chinese manufacturer designs and markets trombones that will be competitive with other brands.

Notes

1. Gottfried Weber, "Ueber Instrumentalbässe bey vollstimmigen Tonstücken," *Allgemeine musikalische Zeitung* 18 (1816), no. 41: col. 694–702; no. 42: col. 709–14; no. 43: col. 725–29; no. 44: col. 749–53; no. 45: col. 765–69. See Document 2, in the appendix.

2. The tenth article of the series describes the trombone: *Revue et gazette musicale de Paris* 9 (March 6, 1842): 92–94.

3. Victor Mahillon, *Catalogue descriptif et analytique du Musée instrumental du Conservatoire royal de musique de Bruxelle: Avec un essai de classification méthodique de tous les instruments anciens et modernes*, 2nd ed., 5 vols. (Ghent: Ad. Hoste, 1893–1912; v. 5, Brussels, Th. Lombaerts, 1922; repr., Brussels: Les Amis de la Musique, 1978); François-Auguste Gevaert, *Nouveau traité d'instrumentation* (Paris: Lemoine & fils, 1885), 3–13; Erich M. Hornbostel and Curt Sachs, "Classification of Musical Instruments: Translated from the original German by

Anthony Baines and Klaus P. Wachsmann," *Galpin Society Journal* 14 (1961): 3–29. (Originally published in 1914.)

4. Curt Sachs, *Real-Lexikon der Musikinsntrumente zugleich ein Polyglossar für das gesamte Instrumentengebiet* (1913; rev. and enl. repr., New York: Dover, 1964), 304.

5. Curt Sachs, *Handbuch der Musikinstrumentenkunde*, 2nd ed. (Leipzig: Breitkopf & Härtel, 1930), 297–300.

6. Curt Sachs, *The History of Musical Instruments* (New York: Norton, 1940), 325–27; Henry George Fischer, *The Renaissance Sackbut and Its Use Today* (New York: Metropolitan Museum of Art, 1984), 1.

7. Herbert Heyde, *Trompeten, Posaunen, Tuben* (Leipzig: Deutscher Verlag für Musik, 1980); Arnold Myers, ed., *Historic Musical Instruments in the Edinburgh University Collection*, 2nd ed., vol. 2, part H, fasc. iii: *Trumpets and Trombones* (Edinburgh: Edinburgh University Collection of Historic Musical Instruments, 1998).

8. Georges Kastner, *Traité général d'instrumentation* (Paris: Prilipp, 1837; 2nd. ed. with suppl., Paris: Prilipp, 1844).

9. Stewart Carter, "Georges Kastner on Brass Instruments: The Influence of Technology on the Theory of Orchestration," in *Perspectives on Brass Scholarship*, ed. Stewart Carter (Stuyvesant, N.Y.: Pendragon, 1997), 84, 186.

10. Raymond Lapie, "Le trombone d'après les traités d'orchestration (France, 1700–1914)," *Brass Bulletin* 105 (1999): 130.

11. Hamilton Clarke, *A Manual of Orchestration* (London: J. Curwen, 1888), 76–77.

12. Ernst Euting, *Zur Geschichte der Blasinstrumente der 16. und 17. Jahrhundert* (Ph.D. thesis, Friedrich-Wilhelms-Universität Berlin, 1899; published Berlin: A. Schulze, 1899); Joseph Nicholson, "A Historical Background of the Trombone and Its Music" (D.M.A. thesis: University of Missouri at Kansas City, 1967); Glenn Bridges, *Pioneers in Brass*, (CD-ROM, Trescott Research, 2001); Michael Meckna, *Twentieth-Century Brass Soloists* (Westport, Conn.: Greenwood Press, 1994).

13. Benny Sluchin and Raymond Lapie, "Slide Trombone Teaching and Method Books in France (1794–1960)," *Historic Brass Society Journal* 9 (1997): 9–12; *Revue et gazette musicale de Paris* 3 (Nov. 20, 1836): 467; *Times* (Feb. 22, 1839), 2; (Mar. 4, 1839), 1.

14. Trevor Herbert, *The Trombone* (New Haven, Conn.: Yale University Press, 2006), 327–28; Victor Cornette, *Méthode de trombone* (Paris: Richaut, 1831). I have seen only the German/French edition published by Schott some time between 1832 and 1835. I am grateful to Howard Weiner for sending it to me; Félix Vobaron, *Grand méthode de trombonne* (Paris: Gambaro, 1834), 2–12; Antoine Dieppo, *Méthode complète pour le trombonne: Adoptée pour l'enseignement de cet instrument dans les classes du Conservatoire de Musique* (Paris: Troupenas, 1837), 2–7, 53–60.

15. André Lafosse, *Méthode complète de trombone à coulisse*, Nouvelle édition, 3 vols. (Paris: Alphonse Leduc, 1946).

16. Edward Kleinhammer, *The Art of Trombone Playing* (Evanston, Ill.: Summy-Birchard, 1963); Edward Kleinhammer and Douglas Yeo, *Mastering the Trombone* (Hannover,

Germany: Edition Piccolo, 1997); Denis Wick, *Trombone Technique*, 2nd ed. (Oxford: Oxford University Press, 1984); Reginald H. Fink, *The Trombonist's Handbook* (Athens, Ohio: Accura Music, 1977); Philip Farkas, *The Art of Brass Playing* (Bloomington, Ind.: Brass Publications, 1962); Donald S. Reinhardt, *The Encyclopedia of the Pivot System for All Cupped Mouthpiece Brass Instruments*, augmented version (New York: Charles Colin, 1973).

17. Gordon M. Pulis, "On Trombone Technique," *Symphony* (New York) 2 (1948): 5.

18. David N. Baker, *Contemporary Techniques for the Trombone* (New York: Charles Colin, 1974); Stuart Dempster, *The Modern Trombone: A Definition of Its Idiom* (Berkeley: University of California Press, 1979).

19. Herbert Heyde, "Brass Instrument Making in Berlin from the 17th to the 20th Century: A Survey," *Historic Brass Society Journal* 3 (1991): 45.

20. "Miscellaneous: The Contra-Bass Posaune," *Musical World* (July 5, 1838), 169.

21. Renato Meucci, "The Cimbasso and Related Instruments in 19th-Century Italy," trans. William Waterhouse, *Galpin Society Journal* 49 (1996): 143–62. Images can be found through Google Images.

22. Orla Edward Thayer, "The Axial Flow Valve Update," *ITA Journal* 10 (April 1982): 34–35; Robert Miller, "The Miller Valve," *ITA Journal* 28 (Summer 2000): 43.

23. Max Thein and Heinrich Thein, "Neues über Alt-Posaune," *Brass Bulletin* 40 (1982): 33.

24. Victor Mahillon, *Le trombone: Son histoire, sa théorie, sa construction* (Brussels: Mahillon, 1906), 42–44.

25. Benny Sluchin, "Les instruments 'duplex'—hier et aujourd'hui," *Brass Bulletin* 115 (2001): 114–15.

26. William Waterhouse, *The New Langwill Index: A Dictionary of Musical Wind-Instrument Makers and Inventors* (London: Tony Bingham, 1993), 360.

27. Arnold Myers and Niles Eldridge, "The Brasswind Production of Marthe Besson's London Factory," *Galpin Society Journal* 59 (2006): 50, 57.

28. *King Trombones and Accessories: Sectional Catalog 735* (Cleveland: H. N. White Co., 1927).

29. *New York Times* (August 18, 1952), 19.

30. Fischer, *Renaissance Sackbut*, 43–44.

31. Dieppo, *Méthode*, 3.

32. *A Dictionary of Music and Musicians*, ed. George Grove (London: Macmillan, 1889 [v. 4]), s.v. "Trombone," by William H. Stone, 4:177; *Grove's Dictionary of Music and Musicians*, 5th ed., ed. Eric Blom (London: Macmillan, 1954), s.v. "Trombone," by Anthony Baines, 8:552; *The New Grove Dictionary of Music and Musicians*, ed. Stanley Sadie (New York: Macmillan, Grove's Dictionaries of Music, 1980), s.v. "Trombone," by Anthony Baines, 19:164.

33. Most of these instruments are selected from one of two catalogs: Myers, ed. *Historic Musical Instruments*, or Heyde, *Trompeten, Posaunen, Tuben*. The rest of the measurements were supplied by Stewart Carter.

34. J. A. Kappey, *Military Music* (London: Boosey, ca. 1894), 45.

35. Cornette, *Méthode*, 5; Vobaron, *Grand méthode*, 3.

36. Arnold Myers, "Design, Technology and Manufacture since 1800," in *The Cambridge Companion to Brass Instruments*, ed. Trevor Herbert and John Wallace (Cambridge: Cambridge University Press, 1997), 115–16; Ignace De Keyser, "The Paradigm of Industrial Thinking in Brass Instrument Making during the Nineteenth Century," *Historic Brass Society Journal* 15 (2003): 234.

37. "Hydraulic Forming Techniques Applied to the Manufacture of Musical Instruments: Interesting Methods Developed by Boosey & Hawkes, Ltd. Edgeware, Middx.," *Machinery* (London) 82 (1953): 1089–99, 1194–96. This article provides an excellent description of the process, but other manufacturers used hydraulic techniques decades earlier than Boosey & Hawkes did.

38. Myers, "Design," 120.

39. De Keyser, "Paradigm of Industrial Thinking," 38–39.

40. For the rest of this chapter, information on particular manufacturers who were active before about 1950 comes from Waterhouse, *New Langwill Index* and *Grove Online* unless otherwise noted.

41. Gunther Joppig, "Vàclav František ervený: Leading European Inventor and Manufacturer," trans. Veronica von der Lancken, *Historic Brass Society Journal* 4 (1992): 224.

42. Renato Meucci, "The Pelitti Firm: Makers of Brass Instruments in Nineteenth-Century Milan," trans. Enrico Pelitti, *Historic Brass Society Journal* 6 (1994): 321–23.

43. Jean-Pierre Mathez, "Antoine Courtois, Paris," *Brass Bulletin* 97 (1997): 76–85.

44. Baines, *Brass Instruments*, 245; Arnold Myers, "Brasswind Innovation and Output of Boosey & Co. in the Blaikley Era," *Historic Brass Society Journal* 14 (2002): 404, 410.

45. Arnold Myers, "Brasswind Manufacturing at Boosey & Hawkes, 1930–1959," *Historic Brass Society Journal* 15 (2003): 57–58.

46. "Fair of the Mechanics Institute, Castle Garden," *American Musical Journal* 1 (October, 1835): 264.

47. Richard J. Dundas, *Twentieth Century Brass Musical Instruments in the United States*, rev. ed. (Norwood, Mass.: Bryant Altman, 1998), passim.

PART II

PERFORMANCE HISTORY

CHAPTER FIVE

~

Minstrelsy and the Wind Bands of the Late Middle Ages

The modern U-slide was first depicted in art around 1490 and must have existed earlier. The slide trumpet is attested in pictures as late as the early seventeenth century, or as a folk instrument, as late as 1722. The slide trumpet and the trombone coexisted for more than a hundred years before professional musicians abandoned the older instrument. Today we consider the two as distinctly different instruments, but musicians of the Renaissance did not. In fact, the word "trombone" was first applied to what we would call a slide trumpet. The slide trumpets depicted in the title page of Hermann Finck's *Practica musica* (1556) and in a drawing by Valentin de Boullogne (before 1632—see Fig. 5.1) were probably identified by their contemporaries as trombones (or *Posaunen*) rather than as some kind of trumpet.[1]

From the middle of the fifteenth century until after 1550, there is an increasing probability that an instrument called the trombone (or *posaune* or sackbut in its various forms) had a modern U-slide, but no certainty that it did not have the old single slide. It is impossible to distinguish between trombone and slide trumpet in contemporary literature. Therefore, only the term *trombone* will be used for most of this chapter.

Beginnings: Minstrelsy and the *Alta* Band

The earliest instrumental musicians did not devote their careers to a single instrument. The term *trombonist* in this chapter and the next two refers to anyone who is known to have played trombone on some occasion. Most of them could just as accurately be referred to as shawmists or cornettists. Modern scholars refer to the ensemble in which these instruments played as an *alta* (Latin for *loud*) band.

Professional musicians of the Middle Ages routinely performed a variety of non-musical tasks. They could be poets, chamber valets, diplomats, or spies at the higher end of the social scale; jugglers, acrobats, or bear wardens at the lower; and watchmen or clock tenders somewhere in the middle. "Minstrel" has become the most frequent term used by modern writers to designate professional musicians with basically secular training and education. The minstrels who played in *alta* bands were also distinguished by surnames derived either from their chief instruments (piper, *pfeifer*, *piffaro*), or from important non-musical tasks (wait, *wachter*).

Medieval minstrels were descended both from the lowly and despised Roman *mimus* (an itinerant entertainer who mocked respectability) and the highly respected Teutonic *scop* (a class of poet-singers of the ruling class who eulogized great men and deeds). The tension that resulted from the mingling of low-status and high-status traditions continued throughout the Middle Ages and beyond. Variables that contributed to relatively high or low status for musicians included whether they had a permanent home, their ancestry, their level of skill and education, the status of their employer if any, what kinds of music they were able to provide, and what instruments they played.[2]

Additional tension resulted from the ambivalence of the medieval church. Scripture, especially the Psalms, gives high importance to instrumental music. The image of angelic minstrels playing various musical instruments was commonplace in medieval churches and the illuminations of medieval books. Minstrelsy, in other words, served as a powerful symbol of the divine order. On the other hand, the behavior of human minstrels fell far short of angelic standards. Many musicians served at

Fig. 5.1. Valentin de Boullogne (d. 1632), tinted pen drawing of musicians with woodwind instruments and trumpet. Graphische Sammlung Albertina, Vienna.

a town or court, but most minstrels of the early Middle Ages were itinerant, and itinerancy, which endured long after the chronological limits of this chapter, was not socially respectable.

As early as the thirteenth century, medieval writers typically divided musical instruments into two groups, loud and soft (or, respectively, *haut* and *bas*). Soft instruments including flutes, keyboard instruments, and various plucked and bowed string instruments, played indoors in intimate settings. They frequently accompanied singing and took part in a wide variety of instrumental ensembles. Some, especially the lute, emerged as solo instruments. Loud instruments, on the other hand, included drums, shawms, bombards, trumpets, and eventually trombones. They played either outdoors or in large banquet halls, and invariably in ensembles. One standard ensemble, used for military purposes, consisted of field trumpets and drums. Another, often used for

dancing or other entertainment, consisted of shawms and a trumpet or trombone.

Socially, the distinction between *haut* and *bas* meant more than volume of sound. Once sovereign rulers adopted the loud band, they used it to enhance their own dignity and magnificence. The musicians, however, did not gain higher social status from the association. As late as 1537, someone could write, "The entertainer and the juggler are not people like other men, but have only a semblance of humanity, and are almost comparable to the dead."[3]

Three was the preferred minimum number for a loud band, but some smaller towns and courts never had a budget for more than two. A duo was most often a shawm and a bombard (a lower-pitched shawm), less frequently a shawm and a trombone, playing descant and tenor respectively. The standard trio, as described by Tinctoris,[4] consists of a shawm playing descant, a bombard playing tenor, and a trombone playing contratenor. Archival and iconographic evidence shows that an alternative grouping of a shawm and two bombards was sometimes used.

Although a three-part texture predominated in early fifteenth-century polyphony, four-part music with a high and a low contratenor became increasingly common as the century progressed. A four-member *alta* band of shawm on descant, bombards on the tenor and high contratenor, and a trombone on the low contratenor would be consistent with Tinctoris's description. Alternatively, a four-member group could have consisted of two shawms, one bombard, and trombone. Given that an *alta* band was not infrequently required to play all night and that the descant player was expected to provide elaborate ornamentation, having an extra shawmist for an essentially three-part texture had obvious practical benefits. In fact, the Burgundian court band consisted of five players according to archival records, but iconographic evidence from the same court rarely shows more than three. The fifth member was usually another trombonist. Occasionally, records indicate a six-part band, with the last added part being another bombard, but such a large band was rare until the sixteenth century.[5]

The *Alta* Band in Towns and Courts

Before 1400
Towns began to sponsor bands earlier than courts did, but not, at first, as musical ensembles. Watchmen from a multitude of gates and towers protected towns from fires or military threats. Flags and other visual signals that were adequate communication during the day were useless after dark. Night watchmen, therefore, began to use trumpets as signaling instruments. Bologna hired its first trumpeters in 1250. By the early fourteenth century, towns were beginning to hire both trumpeters and shawmists.

By that time, the watchmen were also expected to function as musicians. In 1310, the first year their existence is recorded, the watchmen of Bruges performed for civic festivities. About midcentury, the technical standards of shawm playing improved dramatically.[6] Perhaps for that reason, many more towns began to sponsor bands. Because trumpets could play so few different pitches, they could not keep up with the new shawm techniques. By the early fifteenth century, scribes began to seek vocabulary to differentiate between a signaling trumpet and a musical trumpet, which we now know as the slide trumpet. *Trompette des menestrels* is the term most often cited in the musicological literature.

Various ruling households likewise began to change the way they patronized music. In addition to giving gifts to itinerant minstrels, they started to support resident ensembles, and none more extravagantly than King John II of France. Even before he became king, he supported minstrels. In 1364, when he made his youngest son, Philip the Bold, duke of Burgundy, Philip already had four minstrels and a trumpeter on his payroll. His payment to a visiting *menestrel de trompette* in 1386 is one of the earliest records of a trumpet used for entertainment.

1400–1450
Watch duty continued to be an important function of loud bands in fourteenth-century towns. The mounting of the guard became a public spectacle, one of the occasions on which the watchmen were expected to provide entertainment. In Malines, guards were expected to have both good eyesight and musical ability. Enough applicants with those attributes greeted every vacancy that the town had to institute a system of juried examinations to select new personnel. Keeping a good band was likewise a matter of urgent concern. Bruges required members of its band to swear an oath not to accept employment from a court or another town for a specified length of time. Both auditions and oaths became common and remained so for centuries.

Perhaps because the town bands descended from watchmen who signaled from towers, much of their music-making took place from raised areas such as church belfries, the city gates, or balconies on the town hall, a practice that persisted as long as this kind of band did—into the nineteenth century in Germany. Equally important, however, were street-level activities. Processions made up an important part of middle-class life in towns from at least as early as the middle of the thirteenth century, throughout the fifteenth century and beyond. They could have political significance, such as a welcome to a visiting dignitary, or religious significance, such as the patronal feast of a large church.

Professional entertainers also presented street dramas, including elaborate mystery and morality plays as well as shorter, often comical pieces. Special occasions frequently included lavish *tableaux vivants*. Like processions, these dramas and *tableaux* were organized for a wide variety of civic and religious observances. Many different musical instruments took part in these productions. Loud instruments such as the trombone often made unearthly noises fit to accompany Satan. They also participated in scenes of the Last Judgment, conveying fear and terror at the end of the world, and in coronations and regal entries, much as they would in real life. In the shorter comic plays, instruments also accompanied dancing. Rubrics such as "pause" or "silete" in the plays often indicated instrumental interludes. All of the instrumental music would have been supplied by a small group of minstrels playing a variety of instruments.[7]

The court of Charles VI of France (r. 1380–1422) was among the most important musical centers in Europe, rivaled only by the Burgundian court and the Papal court at Avignon. It included both *trompette de guerre* and *trompette des menestrels* as early as 1418. Unfortunately, French records are very deficient, at least in part because of the chaos of the Hundred Years War and the king's madness. His son Charles VII began his reign with less power, prestige, and money than perhaps any monarch in European history. Because ostentatious display of wealth was necessary to persuade both a king's subjects and foreigners that he personally commanded the respect due his office, it would seem that Charles could not afford not to have a musical household. He must have had an *alta* band at one point; in 1428, he gave Alfonso V of Aragon three minstrels in order to pay off a debt. Otherwise, whether he had one any time before his throne was secure is unclear; a trumpet ensemble would have been more important and possibly sufficient to meet his ceremonial obligations.[8]

John V, Duke of Brittany, was also a music lover. In 1426–27, court records name seven minstrels, including a *trompette des menestrels*. French towns hired both civic wind ensembles and trumpet corps, although apparently not to the same extent as towns elsewhere in Europe. Towns in southern France (Montpellier, Toulouse, Avignon, and Marseilles) did not provide full-time employment. During the period of time when it is possible that these bands included trombones, from 1400 onward, minstrels are identified in the archives by such terms as *menestrier, trompeta, trompayer, tubissinator, ault menestrier, charmayre, tubicinator,* and *trombador.* Unlike northern areas, they make no distinction between minstrel trumpet and war trumpet in their terminology, but the band at Montpellier, at least, apparently used a slide trumpet as early as 1403.[9]

Four members of the Valois dynasty ruled as dukes of Burgundy from 1364 to 1477. Philip the Bold, the first duke (r. 1364–1404), was the youngest son of the French king John II, brother of Charles V, and uncle of Charles VI. He was de facto ruler of France during his nephew's minority and episodes of madness. Philip inherited Flanders upon the death of his father-in-law, the last Count of Flanders, in 1384. Thereafter, the dukes of Burgundy spent more time and energy in Flanders than in Burgundy. Nominally vassals of the French king, they were

often stronger and had a much more impressive court. Many other European courts organized their musical establishments on the Burgundian model.

The shawm/trombone ensemble seems to have been one of the more notable musical features at the Burgundian court. This combination was called "the Burgundian pipers" in the *Triumph* of Maximilian I nearly forty years after the end of the duchy. In Prudenzani's novella (1429), the highest compliment available to describe the hero's musical skills was that he sounded like a Flemish piper.

Philip's resident minstrels received a daily wage, food and clothing, two horses, and even their own personal valet, as well as lavish gifts at irregular intervals. In addition to housing at court, they owned their own homes. Such largesse was hardly typical of medieval noblemen. It made the Burgundian court a highly desirable place to work and enabled Philip to demand a high degree of musical competence. In 1412, Duke John the Fearless hired Hennequin van Pictre, who played both field trumpet and *trompette des menestrels.* He killed another trumpeter in a knife fight, thus acquiring the nickname by which he is best known, Hennequin Copetripe (which roughly means "cut gut").[10]

Whenever a ruler paid a state visit to a town, the town paid for a welcoming ceremony. The dukes of Burgundy visited Bruges regularly; both city and court musicians took part in the ceremony, which always included a procession. Other honored visitors included various bishops and secular rulers from as far away as Italy. Bruges took pride in how well it staged such welcomes and regularly sent spies to rival towns. The major occasion for public music making in Bruges was the May Fair, which began on May 3 with the procession of the Holy Blood and continued for two and a half weeks, with a procession nearly every day. On three specified days during the fair, no taxes were charged for buying or selling. Loud minstrels entertained the crowd from the belfry of the town hall.[11]

In Antwerp, the town band participated in processions for all of the usual religious and civic occasions. Several were annual events that included the town's entire ecclesiastical community, its confraternities and guilds, its government, as well as the band. One such was held at least from 1324 on Trinity Sunday. Antwerp's Corpus Christi procession was established by 1398. Its most splendid annual procession, that of Our Lady on the Sunday in the octave of Assumption, began in 1399. All of these persisted well into the sixteenth century.[12]

Given the close alliance between England and Burgundy, the common claim that Henry VII was the first English king to hire trombonists is probably incorrect.

Andrew Ashbee's monumental transcription of royal court documents contains nothing earlier than that reign. But at least the names of the royal minstrels are known from the time of Edward I onward, and not only in the kings' households, but also in the households of queens, princes, and dukes. Among the minstrels of Henry IV's queen in 1406 are Richard Trumper and John Trumpington. As minstrels were often called by the name of their instrument, these men may have played *trompette des menestrels*. Rastall tentatively identifies William Baldwin as trumpeter with the king's minstrels; there was a separate group of trumpeters. Baldwin may have served the Prince of Wales both as trumpeter and minstrel. One strong indication of the presence of trombones at the English court comes in a description of music at the Council of Constance in 1416, when an English choir sang Vespers with the participation of organ and trombones.[13]

Several English towns established their own waits during this time, including Norwich (1408), Salisbury (1409), Coventry (1423), Kingston-on-Hull (1429), Southampton (1433), Shrewsbury (1437), and Maidenhead (ca. 1450). Coventry's band was unusually large, with four members. In 1435, an ordinance in Coventry designated the trumpet player as the chief of the waits. Terminology is murky this early, but it seems likely that the ordinance refers to the *trompette des menestrels*, that is, a slide trumpet or trombone.[14]

Herbert expressed doubt that the waits of London used trombones before 1526. In that year, the band purchased one, and the secretary wrote "hakbush" and "hakbussh" before settling on "sakbutte" to describe the purchase.[15] The document certainly demonstrates that the word was unfamiliar, more than 30 years after it was introduced at court. At such a late date, it may refer to an instrument with a U-slide replacing the older slide trumpets. If "trumpet" indeed meant *trompette des menestrels* in 1435, there is no reason to suppose that the trombone in some form, by whatever name, was not used in England throughout the fifteenth century.

Alfonso V of Aragon (r. 1417–1458) had *trompeta dels ministrers* from the time he first established his household in 1413. This term, cognate with the French *trompette des menestrels*, undoubtedly refers to the same instrument, a trombone. Significantly, Alfonso, not yet king, hired his first trombonist at about the same time Hennequin Copetripe's presence is documented at the court of Burgundy. As it seems unlikely that a young prince would include any completely unprecedented instrument in his first establishment, the trombone must have been known in Barcelona some time before 1413.[16]

In 1426, Duke Philip the Good of Burgundy commissioned the manufacture of twelve wind instruments ("quatre grans instruments de menestrelz, quatre douchains et quatre fleutes") as a gift to "M. le Marquis de Ferrare" (Niccolò III d'Este). The first four instruments mentioned were evidently *trompettes des menestrels*, and it appears that no one in Ferrara knew how to play them. This date seems to be the earliest record of the presence of a trombone any place in Italy. In 1428, Niccolò succeeded in recruiting Hennequin Copetripe, who became one of the few minstrels ever to leave the service of the dukes of Burgundy to work for another court. He remained in Niccolò's service until 1433. The term *trombone* appears to have originated in Ferrara. At least, its earliest attested use occurs in a Ferrarese document of 1439. By 1452 it was used regularly in Ferrarese records.[17]

Most Italian towns of any size and pretension boasted active wind bands. Bologna, which had hired a trumpet ensemble since 1250, established a separate group of *piffari* in 1399, although they do not appear regularly in the records until 1428. Florence had a separate group of *piffari* in 1383. Both of these bands (and probably similar ones in other Italian cities) played daily concerts at the palace where the city council was in residence and provided special music for various important civic occasions.[18]

Germany was a recognized ethnic and linguistic entity in the fifteenth century, although not a political one. Nominally, the Holy Roman Emperor was the German ruler, but the office was elective, and in practice the emperor's power was no greater than that of any of the other German princes. Some towns managed to attain considerable autonomy. Emperor Ruprecht von Wittelsbach (r. 1400–1410) had a retinue of sixteen instrumentalists. Records are not explicit on the internal structure of this group, but most likely it consisted of a six-part field trumpet ensemble, four players of soft instruments, and a loud band of four shawms and two trumpets or trombones.[19]

In 1452, Friedrich III (r. 1440–1493) of the house of Habsburg became emperor. Every subsequent emperor was a Habsburg until the War of Austrian Succession after the death of Charles VI in 1740. Friedrich favored loud instruments. His band was standardized at five players: three shawms and two trombones. In the first half of the fifteenth century, shawm bands were conspicuous at the courts of the dukes of Guelders and Bavaria Straubing. Their trumpeters appear to have divided their time between playing with the shawmists and playing as a trumpet duo. If so, they probably played both slide trumpet and field trumpet.

German towns likewise had their own musical establishments. By 1430, nearly all of them had bands, mostly three-part ensembles (shawm, bombard, trombone). Smaller towns struggled to support a shawm duo. A few larger towns boasted a four-member band. It appears that German town musicians at this time played shawm and trombone almost exclusively.

From the foregoing survey, it is apparent that the early decades of the fifteenth century saw the development of an essentially international style. Wars, dynastic marriages, and other political and diplomatic activities all allowed rulers to hear and imitate each other's musical establishments. Urban confraternities, not courts, sponsored minstrel schools, another internationalizing influence, that were held annually during Lent in such cities as Paris, Malines, Bruges, and Cambrai. The earliest known meeting took place in 1313, the last in 1447. The journey to these schools was both expensive and dangerous, so besides local minstrels, only those attached to an important and prosperous court attended. There seem to be two major reasons for a monarch to send musicians to such a gathering: to buy new instruments and learn the latest music and performing styles.[20]

1450–1520

By midcentury, the *alta* band was entrenched in towns and courts all over Europe. The last half of the century saw a tremendous growth in its maturity and sophistication. Although the three-piece band remained standard, four-piece bands became more numerous, and even larger bands could be found not only in the major courts, but also in a few towns such as Nuremburg, Bern, and Cologne.

Bands continued to be important symbols quite apart from their musical significance. Visually, as well as sonically, they showed off the splendor and prestige of the court or town. The musicians wore ornate livery, exquisitely tailored and made from the most expensive of fabrics. In the 1490s, in order to protect this visual distinction, many jurisdictions passed sumptuary laws

Fig. 5.2. "Dance of Salome for the Birthday Celebration of Herod" by Israhel van Meckenem (ca. 1500), showing an *alta* band playing from a raised platform. Jerome Robbins Dance Division, The New York Public Library for the Performing Arts, Astor, Lenox and Tilden Foundations.

forbidding ordinary citizens from wearing or purchasing the kinds of fabric worn by the nobility—or used for the bandsmen's livery.[21]

Little biographical detail is available for earlier instrumental musicians, but by the beginning of the sixteenth century, a number of them became well enough respected as artists in their own right that it is possible to trace their movements in some detail. The best trombonists served at the same courts, towns, and churches as the leading players of soft instruments, singers, and composers of the day. Several, in fact, were also skilled in these other areas of music, including composition.

A number of important changes in musical style and performance practice are noticeable by or shortly after 1450. These include the growing prevalence of a four-voice texture and the tremendous expansion of the importance and sophistication of imitative counterpoint. The leading court trombonists interacted with their colleagues as equals and clearly played a role in the development of the new style, although the more average wind players eventually found themselves outside the mainstream of musical development and increasingly marginalized.[22]

Burgundy and the Empire

The last two dukes of Burgundy, Philip the Good (r. 1419–1467) and Charles the Bold (r. 1467–1477), worked diligently to acquire the land between their Burgundian and Flemish holdings, which were 150 miles apart at their closest points. Philip maintained between twelve and fifteen minstrels. However much he personally enjoyed them, they had no social standing. There is a remarkable painting of an outdoor reception by Jan van Eyck that on the one hand shows the suspension of some of the usual indicators of the social hierarchy, but on the other hand clearly shows that the only person actually paying any attention to the loud band is the court fool.[23]

In 1430, Philip married Isabella of Portugal and obtained the services of some Portuguese minstrels. Two of them, Adrian and Jacob de Rechter, played trombone, although it is not clear whether they played it in Portugal or learned it after their arrival at the Burgundian court. Other trombonists in Philip's service included Hennequin Jansone, Rogier de Bey, Jean Pentin, and Hennequin Copetripe, until he left the court for Ferrara in 1428. Throughout most of Philip's reign, these men appear in the records as players of *trompette des menestrels*. This term was eventually supplanted by *trompette saquebute*, which first appears in the *Memoirs* of Olivier de la Marche when he described Charles's wedding to Margaret of York in 1468.

As yet, there has been no major musicological study of the reign of Charles the Bold, but he was renowned as a music lover and even had sufficient musical training and talent that he composed a motet in 1460.[24] The Burgundian court under these two dukes enjoyed a sacred music establishment that was second to none, a loud band with few if any rivals, and a good group of soft minstrels, in which they seem to have taken less interest. It was also a major center for the development of the basse danse, the leading court dance of the fifteenth century, spreading from there to other courts. Accompanying dances was one of the most important duties of the loud band.

After the death of Charles the Bold in battle in 1477, his Burgundian lands and title escheated to the French throne. His only child, Mary, found herself ruler of his Flemish territories. Within a year, she married Maximilian, son of Holy Roman Emperor Frederick III. The couple had two children, Philip the Fair and Margaret of Austria, but Mary died in a hunting accident after only five years of marriage. Maximilian eventually became emperor, and Philip, who married the daughter of Ferdinand and Isabella of Spain, eventually became King of Castile, but died a month later. Until Philip came of age, Maximilian ruled Flanders as regent, maintaining the traditional structure and opulence of the Burgundian court.

Unfortunately, the quality of record-keeping under Maximilian's administration is no match for the excellent documentation of the Valois court. It does, however, reflect his lavish spending. Doorslaer mentions his largesse toward "his drummer, his lute player, master Augustin, his trumpets, and minstrels."[25] "Augustin" here refers to Augustein Schubinger. It is not by accident or whim that he is mentioned separately. Although he may have played with the minstrels, he is best known for playing cornett along with the singers of the chapel.

As emperor, Maximilian inherited an excellent wind band from his father, but the nucleus of his musical household was built around the establishment at Innsbruck he inherited from his uncle Sigismund, Archduke of Tyrol. Minstrels had been on the payroll of the noblemen of this area since the thirteenth century.[26]

To present himself to posterity in the best possible light, Maximilian commissioned several biographical works.[27] The best known of these is *The Triumph of Maximilian*, a series of woodcuts by Hans Burgkmair and others. Two different pictures show five trombonists mounted on horseback (refer to Fig. 3.5 in chapter 3). Another shows a five-piece wind ensemble with two shawms, two crumhorns, and trombonist Hans Neuschel the Younger (see Fig. 5.3). One picture of the singers of

Fig. 5.3. *Triumph of Maximilian I*, plate 20, showing trombonist Hans Neuschel. Dover edition.

the chapel also includes Augustein Schubinger, cornett, and Hans Stewdlin, trombone (refer to Fig. 5.5, later in this chapter).[28]

Neuschel appears never to have actually been a part of Maximilian's household. He became a member of the town band of Nuremberg in 1491. Maximilian had a legal right to require the temporary services of any town musician. He called frequently for Neuschel, who appears to have taken a dim view of the honor. (He preferred not to be taken away from the shop where he made trumpets and trombones.) Other German courts with loud bands include Brandenburg, Bavaria, Austria, Württemburg, numerous families of the minor nobility, and several bishops.[29]

Philip the Fair, not Maximilian, inherited and controlled the Flemish lands and institutions once he attained majority. He was as passionate a music lover as any of the Valois dukes of Burgundy. Court records indicate the gifts he lavished on individual musicians,

nearly all of them to instrumentalists, not singers. These include the musicians of his own household, musicians wherever he visited, and the musicians attached to visiting rulers. The most important events of Philip's reign were his two trips to Spain in 1501 and 1506. His retinue included trombonists Hans Nagel and Hans Broen, formerly in the service of King Henry VII of England, as well as Augustein Schubinger.[30]

Towns continued to be major patrons of wind bands. The town band of Augsburg had a decisive influence on the course of instrumental music in the last half of the fifteenth century and beyond. In 1457, Ulrich Schubinger was admitted to the band. He became one of a small number of musicians of his generation who could play loud instruments, lute and viol, and also read music. Eventually, town records designated him as "master," and judging from the taxes he paid, he was one of its wealthiest citizens. Beginning in 1471, he served three years in the court of Duke Sigismund in Innsbruck. He may have spent three years in Italy before returning to Augsburg in 1477. He remained a town musician there until his death in 1492.[31]

A master musician's duties included passing the secrets of his craft to the next generation. Ulrich Schubinger's four sons, Michel, Augustein, Ulrich, and Anthon, all traveled widely. The first three named became renowned court musicians. Augustein and Ulrich, at least, were notable trombonists, in addition to their other attainments. Their activities, as told in this chapter, show the importance of town bands in general and that of Augsburg in particular as a training ground for court musicians.

Italy

Italy was perhaps more politically diverse than any other part of Europe, including as it did the Kingdom of Naples, the Republic of Venice, other North Italian city-states with or without the court of a ruling family, and, dividing north from south, territory directly ruled by the pope. In many respects, the courts of the popes and other church dignitaries were indistinguishable from secular courts.

By the accession in 1492 of the first of the so-called Renaissance popes, Alexander VI, the papacy was especially rich and powerful. Alexander and his successors (especially Julius II, Leo X, Clement VII, and Paul III) must be counted among the major arts patrons of their time. Their chapels served both private and public functions. They used both local musicians and outsiders. Like other rulers, they employed a variety of secular musicians in addition to the singers of the chapel. The Castel Sant' Angelo was among the preferred residences of these popes. It had a loud band of cornetts, trombones, and drums that functioned like any other court band, playing for various solemn processions as well as for the private entertainment of the pope. Several Roman cardinals likewise had their own court establishments. Churchmen loved secular culture and worldly pomp and splendor as much as any king or duke.[32]

Leo X (born Giovanni de' Medici) is the most notable music lover among the Renaissance popes. His love of instrumental music is amply documented. He was a skilled amateur lute player and commissioned Hans Neuschel the Younger to make silver trombones for him. On at least two occasions while he was pope, instrumentalists participated along with the papal choir in services at the Sistine Chapel, a group otherwise known for not even admitting the organ.[33]

For a celebration of the Feast of St. Peter in Chains in 1520, Leo spent an enormous sum on a luncheon and dinner for the cardinals and other dignitaries. The after-dinner concert included at least four groups of performers, one group of boys and the other three consisting of probably ten musicians, each half singers and half instrumentalists. One of them alternately sang a German song and played it on trombones and cornetts. At the end, all four groups performed together in ten parts. At another luncheon the pope hosted in the Castel Sant' Angelo, a trombone served as the bass to seven flutes.[34]

Just as the papal court was indistinguishable from contemporary secular courts, the city of Rome was, in many ways, just like any other city, and its government maintained its own band of *piffari*. It was probably these musicians that performed when Leo had his brother Giuliano invested with Roman citizenship in 1513.

From 1434 until 1737, with a brief interruption, the Medici family controlled Florence. Until the sixteenth century the city was nominally a republic, and therefore the Medici rulers, most notably Lorenzo the Magnificent, held no title. Although Lorenzo lavishly patronized literature and the visual arts, the town continued to be the major patron of music. German players continued to dominate the *piffari* and appear to have specialized in improvised polyphony. The Republic maintained a band of four players. The skill of the trombonists was especially noteworthy.[35]

Once the Medici were firmly reestablished as hereditary dukes, their patronage of music became an important political tool. Opera eventually grew from the entertainments that they sponsored. Most of these entertainments properly belong in the next chapter, but an important one occurred in 1518. As early as the 1460s, old Latin comedies were revived and performed in Rome, Ferrara, and Florence. Simple musical interludes, both vocal and instrumental, filled up the time between the acts. By 1487, modern comedies by Coreggio and Polizano were presented in Ferrara, likewise with musical interludes. As these interludes became more elaborate, they grew into theatrical events in their own right, known as *intermedii*. An *intermedio* can be defined as a spectacle comprising music, dance, dialogue, pantomime, elaborate scenery, and splendid costume, performed between the acts of a comedy.[36]

Such spectacles grew out of popular carnival entertainments, but were presented at Italian courts with a new richness and splendor, invested with political significance. Especially in Florence, *intermedii* became a conspicuous part of state occasions such as weddings, entries, and baptisms. Minor and Mitchell have identified thirty occasions between 1471 and 1539, not all in Florence, at which music is known to have been used. This list cannot be considered exhaustive as it lacks the 1518 celebration in Florence: *intermedii* for Lorenzo Strozzi's *Commedia in versi* were performed in the Palazzo Medici as part of wedding festivities for Lorenzo II de' Medici and Madeleine de la Tour d'Auvergne. The music is no longer extant, but contemporary descriptions show that trumpets, bagpipes, and *piffari* played before the first act, and a group of four trombones played during the fifth act.[37]

Ferrara boasted an excellent *alta* band. Ferrarese archives (which become truly adequate only during Borso's reign, 1450–71) describe separate groups of instrumentalists: trumpeters, *piffari*, and players of soft instruments. The *piffari* were a remarkably stable group. Corrado de Alemagna, the leader of the group, who played soprano shawm, joined the court in 1441, the first year of the reign of Leonello (r. 1441–50). He kept his position as leader of the *piffari* until 1481, well into the reign of Ercole I (r. 1471–1505). Zoanne de Alemagna (tenor shawm) and Pietro Agostino (trombone) first appear in the personnel lists of 1456 (the first extant records from Borso's reign, 1450–71). Pietro Agostino continued to play at least until 1503, although he does not appear on every list. (These three musicians may even be the subject of a well-known picture in a Bible prepared for Borso. Refer to Fig. 2.5 in chapter 2.) At least four other trombonists appear in Ferrarese records.[38]

Borso's taste in music favored instrumental over vocal music and improvisation over written polyphony. In this, he differed from other Italian rulers, including his successor. Ercole I increased the number of *piffari* from three to four or five. He preferred written polyphony and had a chansonnier known as Casanatense 2856 copied for his band to play from. That the same musicians were able to satisfy two rulers with such different tastes and expectations indicates that they were highly skilled and versatile. A contemporary chronicler wrote that they were the best *piffari* in Italy.[39]

The Gonzaga court at Mantua likewise had an excellent wind band. Records indicated the presence of *piffari* in Mantua by 1434. Other groups of instrumentalists were the trumpet ensemble and, for dancing, pipe and tabor players. When Isabella d'Este married Francesco II Gonzaga in 1490, she became a leading patron of the arts, and Mantua became one of the most important centers of Italian Renaissance music. The *piffari*, at least, must have been highly regarded even before Isabella's time. In 1468 they traveled to Milan to take part in festivities for the wedding of Galeazzo Maria Sforza and Bona di Savoia.[40]

Court records name more than half a dozen trombonists. Some studied with Pietro Agostino in Ferrara.

At any given time, there were no more than two trombonists on the payroll, and they were all expected to be proficient on other instruments as well. Especially noteworthy are Bernardino Trombone (usually styled Bernardino Piffaro), Enrico Tedesco Trombone (that is, Ulrich Schubinger the Younger), and the best known of all in modern times, Bartolomeo Tromboncino. He was respected as a trombonist, but records mention him as such only up to about 1497. At about that time, he seems to have given up instrumental playing for the more prestigious roles of singer and composer of *frottole*.[41]

A major reorganization of civic music in Bologna included the hiring of trombonist Bartolomeo Juliani on 6 December 1469. From that time until well into the seventeenth century, the wind band (known as the Concerto Palatino) was among the most highly regarded wind bands in Italy. In the late fifteenth century, it was expected to provide music for both religious and secular communities, including the university. It played for worship services, banquets, the comings and goings of the *Signoria*, and regularly performed from the balcony of the palace of the ruling Bentivoglio family.[42]

Most of the payment records and other documentation from 1439 to 1503 are missing, making it impossible to document changes in the size of the group during that period. In 1503 it consisted of 4 trumpets, 5 *musici* (3 shawms, 2 trombones), a harper, and a drummer. By 1537, it had grown to 19: 8 trumpets, 8 *musici* (4 cornetts in place of the earlier shawms and 4 trombones), and one each of harper, lutenist, and drummer. From then until 1779, there was little variation in these numbers.[43]

The Venetian Republic, led by a doge, strived for a dignity equal to that of courts led by hereditary rulers. Philip the Fair gave a gift to a trombonist in the service of a Venetian ambassador in 1505, one small sign of the diplomatic success of its musical establishment.[44]

The doge's band (three shawms and two trombones) was officially established in 1458. One charter member of that group, and perhaps its leader, was Zorzi Trombetta di Modon. As a young man, he had served as trumpeter on a Venetian merchant ship and between 1444 and 1449 kept a diary that is well known to historians. It includes instructions on seafaring, notes on the payments he received in his dual career as musician and wine merchant, and some written polyphonic music, undoubtedly similar to what he played on ship and in various ports of call. Along with Ulrich Schubinger the elder, he was one of the first musically literate wind musicians. Careful examination of the notation shows that he did not play natural trumpet, but slide trumpet. If not at the founding of the doge's band in 1458, then certainly several years later he exchanged his slide trumpet for a modern trombone. By the end of his illustrious career in 1494, he played not only in the doge's band, but also for three of the city's *scuole grande*.[45]

In 1495, Giovanni Aloixe, another Venetian trombonist, sent an arrangement of a motet by Obrecht to the Duke of Mantua. The motet was originally for four voices, arranged for six parts, by adding two lower parts for trombones. A six-part band was large for the time. That one of its members could arrange four part vocal music for a six-part instrumental ensemble that was worthy of submission to one of the leading musical patrons in northern Italy speaks highly of the overall musicianship of the band. By 1505, Aloixe was trying to interest the duke in an eight-part arrangement. By the end of the century, the doge officially had a six-part wind band, but a well-known painting, "Procession on the Piazza San Marco" by Gentile Bellini, painted in 1496, depicts a 10-piece band (see Fig. 5.4).[46]

A group of Venetian wind players successfully auditioned for a job at the English court of Henry VIII in 1528, presumably having failed to find steady employment in Venice.[47] This fact would seem to be another indication that the doge had very good musicians in his household if he had other musicians in preference to such an excellent band. On the other hand, it would seem to indicate that, at the time, Venice had few other opportunities for a wind band to find full-time employment.

Venice had a number of confraternities, large and small, connected with particular churches. The smaller confraternities met in chapels inside their church. The *scuole grandi* had their own halls and more independence from the churches. The confraternities existed primarily for religious and charitable purposes. They typically hired choruses and organists on a regular basis and other instrumentalists as needed.

In 1503, Scuola San Marco hired six players of shawm and trombone for the vigil and feast of San Marco

Fig. 5.4. "Procession on the Piazza San Marco," detail of musicians, by Gentile Bellini (1496). Accademia, Venice, Italy. Photo Credit: Cameraphoto / Art Resource, NY.

and the feast of Sant' Agnese. In 1515, "trumpets and shawms" were commanded to accompany the singers during processions held the first Sunday of every month, and apparently at the Mass as well. The document mentions *trombetti* rather than *tromboni*, but iconographic evidence points to the use of the trombone. The local economy forced cutbacks in expenditures in 1527, and the Scuola San Marco decided that the wind players were superfluous as regular employees. They would no longer be used for the Mass on the first Sunday of every month, but only hired for processions on a per-service basis. All hiring restrictions were rescinded in 1534 when the need for austerity had passed.[48]

The Scuola San Marco was affiliated with the doge's chapel, the basilica of San Marco. The musicians mentioned in the 1515 document included one member of the doge's wind band and the son of another. The church itself did not hire its own band until 1568. Most likely, it depended on the confraternity's band, the doge's band, or that of visiting dignitaries, when wind instruments were wanted. Scuola San Marco made the most conspicuous use of wind instruments, but it was not alone. San Teodoro, a *Scuola Piccola* until 1552, hired winds for a procession in 1490. Although San Marco was the only Venetian confraternity to hire a wind band on a permanent basis, the fact that even one of the smaller ones hired one for a particular occasion indicates the possibility that the others did so as well.[49]

Unlike most major musical centers, Bergamo was not politically independent. It was under Venetian rule. Bergamo established its band in 1491, having had town trumpeters for nearly two centuries. It was an all-shawm band until 1500, when Martinus de Besutio was hired to play trombone. Dire military conditions forced the temporary disbanding of this group in 1515, but not the better-paid trumpet corps.[50]

Other northern Italian towns where regular wind band concerts took place include Sienna, Lucca, Genoa, and Perugia. Naples, in the south, likewise had an important royal court with a wind band. As Tinctoris worked for that court, his description of the *alta* band may well be based on its band.

Spain

Throughout most of the fifteenth century, several independent kingdoms shared the Iberian Peninsula. In 1469 Ferdinand II, son and heir of Juan II of Aragon, secretly married Isabella I, half-sister and heiress of Enrique IV of Castille. Aragon and Castille had very different cultural and legal traditions and remained administratively separate throughout the reigns of these monarchs.

Ferdinand and Isabella came to their respective thrones in the midst of political instability, and neither of them had a firm grip on power. They genuinely liked music, but their need to appear more powerful than they really were was an important factor in their patronage of the arts. Like many other rulers of the time, they modeled their courts after that of Burgundy, although Isabella's pious nature caused the two Spanish courts to be less exuberant and more austere than their model.

Ferdinand's first musical household, established in 1462, included a three-piece wind band. In the early 1490s, his band had six or seven pieces. After 1496, the minimum size of the band was usually eight. When Isabella died in 1504, Ferdinand added three of her *ministriles altos* to his own band, temporarily giving him as many as 11 players, although the number dropped back to eight or nine after 1506. Isabella's *alta* band had eight players in 1492, although from 1498 until her death she usually had only six. At Ferdinand's death in 1516, all of the members of his loud band continued in royal service under Charles I (son of Philip the Fair and the later Holy Roman Emperor Charles V). The records rarely identify minstrels according to what instrument they played until after the beginning of the sixteenth century. These bands must have included trombones; trombones are attested in earlier reigns and in numerous contemporary bands, including one belonging to Prince Juan.[51]

In 1505, four of Ferdinand's players can definitely be identified as trombonists: Bartolomeo Gaço (or Gasso), Jos de Bruxelas, Anton Lucas de Borbon, and Juan Galiano. It appears that most of the musicians in both Ferdinand's and Isabella's courts were native Spaniards, although there were foreign players at both courts; Jos de Bruxelas was obviously Flemish. Gaço had served at the court of Juan II of Aragon as early as 1478. He is also known to have taught trombone, and not only at the Aragonese court; his pupils included a Castillian minstrel and a townsman in Barcelona.[52]

Of all the cities in late medieval and Renaissance Spain, only Barcelona has been the subject of any systematic musicological research. It had no town band; the government payroll included only a single trumpeter. Although there were ample political and economic reasons why Barcelona did not patronize music to any greater extent, it will be impossible to know if it was following a typical Spanish practice or a local idiosyncrasy until more research has been done on other towns. It appears from notarial documents, however, that musicians existed in abundance and were officially recognized as legitimate professionals.[53]

Most references to civic ceremonies refer simply to trumpets. Recalling that Konrad of Megenberg had written that the trumpet and shawm were pretty much the same, it is apparent that those who kept civic records in Barcelona either did not know one instrument from another or preferred the simple expedient of using "trumpet" as a generic term for all wind instruments. Even so, there are a few documents as early as 1391 that refer to shawms or minstrels or juglars (which is nearly synonymous with minstrel). In 1436, when an armada was sent out against Genoa, the procession included "tres xeremies e una trompeta" (three shawms and a trumpet), that is, a standard four-piece *alta* band. The same document later refers to "les dites trompetas e ministres" (the said trumpets and minstrels). The trumpet that played with shawms must be understood as *trompeta dels ministrers*.

When Duke Alfonso of Calabria entered Barcelona in 1477, the procession was led by "ab coble de ministrés e trompetes" (a band of minstrels and trumpets). When Grenada fell to Ferdinand's army in 1492, Barcelona celebrated with "moltes desfresses, momos, e grans balls ab trompes e juglars per casa e carreres" (many masquerades, mimes, grand balls with trumpets and minstrels in houses and streets). Just as documents that mention only trumpets may actually refer to a shawm band, documents that refer to minstrels may refer to soft minstrels as well as (or instead of) loud minstrels. Even with all the ambiguity, however, it appears that trumpet ensembles and shawm bands both participated in processions. Occasionally a band would be assembled instead of a trumpet ensemble to make announcements throughout the city. Both loud and soft bands would have been appropriate for dancing, a role apparently not shared by trumpet ensembles. The term *sacabuche* occurs only once in Barcelona's civic records, when Gaço included a citizen of the town among his trombone students.[54]

France

After about 1450, Charles VII was firmly in control of his kingdom. France prospered enough by the end of the fifteenth century to begin military interference in Italian politics. As yet surviving records do not allow us to identify minstrels by name or even document minstrels in the royal households of Charles VII or Louis IX (r. 1461–83). That hardly means that they did not have minstrels. It may not even mean that they did not simultaneously have both the means and the desire to patronize music on the same scale as the dukes of Burgundy.

The division of the royal musical establishment into the Chapel (sacred music), the Chamber (soft instruments), and the Stable or *Ecurie* (loud instruments), usu-

ally associated with the reign of Francis I, actually began no later than the reign of Charles VIII (r. 1483–98). The trombone first appears in these records in 1491, when Charles helped pay off a debt incurred by Françoys de Malle, "sacqueboute de Monsieur de Bourbon." The Duke of Bourbon was the king's brother-in-law, and there is no indication that the trombonist was ever on the royal payroll. The earliest hint of the establishment of a royal *alta* band is in 1495, after the invasion of Italy. Pierre de Modène (or Modaine), evidently a native of Modena, became court trombonist in June or July 1496 at a salary equal to that of the highest paid trumpeter. There is no record of shawmists at the French court until Louis XII hired six players of shawm and trombone from Milan. These first appear in the payroll of October 1502, although they may have been hired as early as 1499.[55]

Records from the reign of Francis I (1515–1547) are nearly complete. From 1516–38, the Chamber was divided into three groups: domestic officers (*valets de chambre*), cornett players, and fife and drum players. By 1540, singers began to be included with the Chamber, and no longer exclusively with the Chapel. Thereafter, the Chamber was divided into five groups, with singers and players of other instruments being added to the original three. The Stable consisted of trumpets, shawms, trombones, and violins, although occasionally players of these instruments appeared on the rolls of the Chamber instead. All of the trombonists and all but one of the cornettists were Italian.[56]

If the Chamber was supposed to consist of soft instruments and the Stable loud instruments, it seems odd to have the fife and drum consistently listed with the Chamber and the violins with the Stable. As difficult as it is to ascertain the personnel of these two groups, their separate roles seem clear enough. The Chamber was a collection of virtuosos who entertained a select audience: the king, his family, and honored guests. The Stable, on the other hand, performed at festivals, balls, tournaments, and parades and similarly public settings.

Francis traveled constantly and widely throughout France and Italy. The musicians of the Stable accompanied him and played wherever he went, including worship in the cathedral of Notre Dame. His trombones and flutes were noted as having played most excellently in the church of San Marco in Venice. Pope Leo X heard a group of Francis's musicians, consisting of flutes and a trombone, in June 1519 and paid them a reward. The Stable undoubtedly upheld the very highest standards of excellence in the performance of its repertoire, but neither under Francis I nor under any of his successors did it regularly participate in the more artistic side of

French court life, as comparable groups did in Italy and Germany. [57]

In 1520, Francis met with English King Henry VIII at the Field of Cloth of Gold, where both monarchs sought to outdo each other in splendor and extravagance. Cardinal Wolsey, the chief English minister, celebrated a Mass on June 23 that featured both royal choirs. As part of the intent of the meeting was to proclaim peace between the two countries after generations of hostility, the two choirs sang in alternation, each with the other country's organist. "The Patrem omnipotentem [was sung] by those of France, to which singers were added the sackbuts and shawms of the king, which produced an agreeable sound."[58]

The almost complete absence of French towns from any published discussion of civic wind music in the fifteenth and sixteenth centuries is striking. It appears that the trombone and *alta* band, so important elsewhere, were no longer cultivated there.

England

Whatever musical documentation of the English court exists from before Henry VII (r. 1485–1509) has not been transcribed and published. There may not be very much available for much of the fifteenth century because of instability and wars. John de Peler, who is listed as a trumpeter at the end of Edward IV's reign (1470–82) and the beginning of Richard III's (1483–85), served in the households of Henry VII and Henry VIII under the heading of "sackbuts and shawms." It is only the name "sackbut" that first appears during Henry VII's reign. Some kind of trombone, whether the old slide trumpet or the newer one with a U-slide, must have been at court for most of the century, and John de Peler very likely played it from the beginning of his service at court. Galpin and others have written that the sackbut was introduced to the English court in 1495, probably based on accounts of the treasurer of the king's chamber. The account for May 3, 1495, says, in part, "Item to 4 Shakbusshes for their wages £7."[59] This, in fact, is the earliest record of payment of monthly wages of the minstrels. That "shakbusshe" makes its first appearance here cannot be taken to mean that it is a new instrument.

This entry also marks a reorganization of the king's household. In medieval times, the king's chamber had been one large room in which he conducted all public and private business. Henry VII decided to make a distinction between the Chamber, for public business, and the Privy Chamber, where only the king's closest confidants were admitted.[60] It appears that Tudor monarchs had little informal contact with their official musicians, who were not among those welcome in the Privy Chamber.

A document that requisitions mourning livery for the funeral of Henry's queen is the earliest in Ashbee's collection that lists individual musicians and their duties at court. John de Peler, William Burgh, Hans Naille, Edward Peler, and Adryan Wilmorth are identified therein as "Sakbusshes and Shalmeys." Another warrant for livery, dated 17 June 1503, lists Maister Johannes de Peler, Maister Guyllame vander Bourgh, Hans Nagel, Edward de Peler, and Adrian Willeme as "lowde mynstrelles." These are recognizably the same people, designated by an older term. Nagel began his career as a town musician in Leipzig before joining the English court some time before 1503. By 1506, he had left England to serve Philip the Fair on a trip to Spain. When Philip died, Nagel served his sister Margaret as a musician and continued to accept diplomatic missions for Henry VIII.[61]

English (and Scottish) towns continued to establish their own bands, including Darlington (1457), Doncaster (1457), Colchester (1469), London (1481), Chester (1484), Canterbury (1492), Dover (1492), Maidstone (1492), Sandwich (1492), Northampton (1493), Dartford (1494), Aberdeen (1500), and Cambridge (1511).[62] The year 1481 may seem surprisingly late for the capital to establish its own town band, but the royal musicians lived there. When they were not in personal attendance to the king, they took every opportunity for freelance work they could find.

The Trombone in Church

Throughout most of the Middle Ages, musical instruments other than the organ were not used in church services. From the earliest times, Christian worship services were modeled on Jewish synagogue services, where instruments were essentially irrelevant, and not on temple services, where, judging from frequent references in the Psalms, they were used extensively. Patristic authors one and all, up through St. Augustine, found musical instruments inherently immoral, something for Christians to avoid under all circumstances.[63]

Inevitably, the early objections were forgotten. The fact that instruments were rarely used in church can be attributed more to practical circumstances than to theological objections. Instrumental musicians as a group had a poor reputation as late as the thirteenth century, but occupied important posts both in towns and courts by the end of the fourteenth century. The organ gained acceptance in the liturgy by the thirteenth century, and nearly all churches had organs by the middle of the fifteenth century. By that time, the trombone, among other instruments, was beginning to appear in the worship service on special occasions.

If we take the term *Mass* as meaning the service of worship from its beginning until the words of dismissal, and *liturgy* as meaning the prayers of the Ordinary and Proper, then some music in a Mass would not have been part of the liturgy. Some kind of extra-liturgical music took place during processions or during parts of the service when there was no specific prayer or text, such as the Elevation of the Host. Instruments would have been useful, although not strictly necessary, for such music.

The singers in churches were usually musically literate clerics, while instrumentalists were laymen who, until late in the fifteenth century, could not read music. Chant, which constituted the entire liturgy under normal circumstances, had been sung quite successfully without accompaniment during the time minstrelsy's reputation was at its lowest. Once minstrels were welcome in church, they had nothing to contribute to the performance of chant. Polyphonic music, always exceptional in the medieval worship service, occurred only in certain mass movements and only on high feast days. Written polyphony may have been beyond the sophistication of musically illiterate instrumentalists whose performance practice depended on improvisational ability or rote memorization.

Beginning in the twelfth century in France, however, the Elevation of the Host became the focal point of the Mass, and there is no chant during that part. As early as 1389, Philippe de Mezières recommended the use of the trumpet during the Elevation. His comment comes in a warning to the French king Charles VI (who at the time had only recently begun to rule in his own right and was not yet beset with the madness that ruined his reign) not to spend too much money on frivolities. It is a concession, not a recommendation to do anything new:

> What can be said of the money wasted on gifts to heralds and minstrels and entertainers? I don't say you can't have music for the honour of God and Your Majesty, such as trumpets and clarions to be sounded at the Elevation of the Host or to assemble your soldiery, and you can have minstrels playing for your recreation and to help your digestion, but not to excess. Sometimes, indeed, you may be led by sweet sounds to think of minstrels in Paradise and to be, as it were, transported by God's grace.[64]

In this regard, it is important to keep in mind that the early trombone was always designated as some kind of trumpet in French sources. The use of any kind of trumpet at the Elevation was probably limited to special occasions at only the most important churches, but on these occasions, the use of *trompette des menestrels* seems likely, if not in 1389, then certainly not long after 1400. If, as Bowles pointed out, the organ and the trumpet were the first instruments to gain a role in the liturgy, the "trumpet" soon must have been a trombone.[65]

A Mass was celebrated in 1412 at St. Innocent at which one observer noted that participants included "the best singers which could then be found in Paris and an organ and a large quantity of soft instruments, so that the people said it was the finest mass they had ever seen said or sung." Whether loud instruments participated in this way is a matter of controversy. Certain Burgundian and French composers wrote music with the contratenor parts indicated for "trompette," which will be described at the end of this chapter. One of these pieces is a mass by Estienne Grossin. If in fact these parts were actually played on a slide trumpet, Wright suggests that the mass was most likely intended for the church of St. Merry in Paris.[66]

The disaster of the Hundred Years War put an end to expensive experiments in France. Over the next hundred years, instruments other than the well-established organ were probably not used in French churches. The chapter at Notre Dame appears to have been hostile to instruments and instrumentalists well into the fifteenth century.

Trombones participated in the liturgy at the Field of Cloth of Gold in 1520, but it is a matter of speculation whether they, or any other instrument besides the organ, ever participated within the walls of any French church until well after the chronological limits of this chapter. What is not conjectural is that Francis's instrumentalists accompanied him wherever he went, even within the walls of Notre Dame itself, and played fanfares to signal his entries and exits. Francis had a larger personal entourage and greater personal splendor than any French king since Charles VI. He ruled as an absolute monarch. No opposition from the canons of the cathedral or any church council could dissuade him from having his own way. He even caused an interior wall of the cathedral to be demolished to make room for a large number of visiting dignitaries. The cathedral had to tolerate Francis's instrumentalists and those of his successors in the sixteenth century. It was not until the seventeenth century that it began to hire its own instrumentalists for use when the king was not in attendance.[67]

Spain appears to have led the way in admitting instruments into the Mass. In 1420 Alfonso V of Aragon commissioned Jacme Gil to supply an organ for the royal chapel in Barcelona. One of the requirements for this organ was that it could be tuned with the instruments of the minstrels, and so the minstrels were expected to play sacred music with the organ in worship services at least occasionally. Anglès noted that the Aragonese court was following a practice begun by the Avignon papacy in the fourteenth century.[68]

According to the *Hechos del Condestable don Miguel Lucas de Iranzo*, a loud band played at the Elevation of the Host at a Mass in Jaén for Christmas 1463 and Epiphany 1464. At the Easter Monday service it played while the procession was moving, for the Elevation of the Host, and as the priest departed after saying Mass. It does not appear that the use of instruments on such occasions was a novelty or innovation. It is, in fact, an account of how Lucas observed a typical liturgical year.[69]

On May 15, 1502, Augustein Schubinger, in the service of the visiting Philip the Fair, accompanied the singers on cornett during a Mass celebrated in Toledo. This performance was apparently unprecedented, but not the only time that Schubinger's cornett was heard

Fig. 5.5. *Triumph of Maximilian I*, plate 26, showing trombonist Hans Stewdlin and cornettist Augustein Schubinger. Dover edition.

in Spanish churches before Philip returned home. I have found no earlier instance where the sources clearly state that an instrument accompanied the choir, that is, participated in the liturgy. Knighton found no record of such a practice among Spanish musicians, but noted that in a war between Navarre and France in 1512, the Duke of Nájera heard both Mass and Vespers with participation of loud minstrels to encourage his men. Although this is not "church" practice, it did its part in gaining acceptance for the use of instruments in the liturgy.[70]

On the way back to Flanders, Philip the Fair and his entourage visited his father, the emperor Maximilian I. Records indicate the participation of Philip's and Maximilian's instrumentalists in a Mass on September 17, 1503, and another the following week, playing the Gradual, the Deo gratias, and the Ite missa est. From that occasion, instrumental participation in the liturgy spread throughout Germany, but not without opposition. Erasmus complained about it regularly, beginning as early as 1516. He disliked not only the sound of instruments competing with the sound of voices, but also the expense to the church. From the vehemence of his complaints, as well as the number of his writings in which they occur, it appears that by his time, instrumental participation in the Mass was no longer limited to non-liturgical parts on special occasions at exceptionally important churches, but had become a regular feature of many services.[71]

Trombones appeared in Italian churches as well. *Piffari* and *tubicini* frequently performed in the cathedral of Ferrara as early as the 1430s when the marquis or city dignitaries were in attendance. When the French king Francis I visited Venice in 1519, his trombonists played in the doge's chapel of San Marco. By that time, the confraternity associated with the basilica had apparently been using trombones in its own services for at least four years.[72]

Repertoire

The question of what trombonists would have played in the course of their various duties has an easy answer and a more complicated one. The easy answer is that the trombone was an ensemble instrument that, as Tinctoris described it, played the contratenor line in the *alta* band. Music for the *alta* band can be divided into three major categories: dance music, music originally for voices, and a small amount of instrumental music not intended for dancing. The latter category included fanfares and flourishes suitable to announce the arrival of important persons or for interludes in street dramas. Any attempt to elaborate on this easy answer becomes complicated by

the fact that hardly any music exists that can clearly be associated with the *alta* band. Professional musicians did not play from written music; the ability to read music was essentially irrelevant. What mattered much more was their ability to memorize and improvise.

It appears that the general level of musical sophistication rose during about the first half of the fifteenth century. One of the earliest sources to contain any written music that can be linked to loud instruments is the Mondsee manuscript of ca. 1400, also known as the Spörl Liederbuch, which contains pieces by Hermann, Monk of Salzburg. Three of the polyphonic pieces are named for brass instruments: "Das Nachthorn," "Das Taghorn," and "Das haizt dy Trumpet." All bear the rubric "gut zu blasen," or good for wind instruments. They consist of a tune and an accompanying line that is little more than a drone, which bears the legend "Das ist der pumhart dazu" (this is its bombard). A natural trumpet could easily play such a part in place of a bombard. If some kind of trumpet played the melody, it would have to be a slide trumpet.[73]

It would be easy to read too much into these pieces. On the one hand, they show a very simple tune with the most rudimentary of counterpoint. The rubric "gut zu blasen" may indicate that wind bands at the end of the fourteenth century and very early fifteenth century played similarly primitive music. On the other hand, French and Flemish musicians had long been the leaders in the development of polyphony. Salzburg, although it had a magnificent musical establishment, was off the beaten path. Hermann's pieces represent about the earliest polyphonic music in Austria. They cannot be used to establish the practice in more advanced centers. Zorzi Trombetta was writing out contratenors that showed familiarity with the conventional rules of counterpoint in the 1440s.

Tinctoris noted that improvised and written counterpoints were based on the same principles and rules. Other contemporary writers indicated that little theoretical distinction was made between singing music and playing it on instruments, although instrumentalists were more closely associated with certain techniques of embellishment.

At least as early as the 1350s, as attested by Konrad of Megenberg, ensembles of shawms and trumpets played dance music. By the end of the century, the trombone began to supplant the trumpet as the standard brass instrument in the shawm band. An anonymous poem from the 1370s, "Echecs amoureux," lists both loud and soft instruments. Its author considered loud instruments especially suitable for dancing, but preferred soft instruments when less noise was wanted.[74]

Of the wide variety of dances that existed in the late Middle Ages and early Renaissance, the *basse danse* has attracted the greatest amount of scholarly attention, largely because it is the earliest for which sufficient instructions have been preserved to reconstruct the steps. It was named as early as 1340 by the troubadour Raimond de Cornet and became the principal courtly dance of the fifteenth century. By the middle of the sixteenth century it had disappeared from the courts, but the steps and much of the musical practice survived as the German *Hoftanz*.

The *basse danse* is best understood as a family of dances, not a single dance. Its name described the dignified, striding motion of the steps, as opposed to the vigorous leaps of the *alta danse*, or *saltarello*. The long shoes affected by the nobility, as shown in Fig. 5.6, would have certainly been unsuitable for anything else. The musical basis of the *basse danse* is a cantus firmus of long notes of equal length, often derived from the fashionable chansons of the day. Each note of the tune corresponds to one complete dance move, which requires three or four seconds to execute. Many tunes survive, but only as the tenors on which the band improvised faster-moving counterpoint.[75]

An important manuscript of German lute tablature, dated 1512, includes a piece called "Der annder statpfeifer danntz." Tracing the history of this tune provides a clue to the *Hoftanz* and the ensemble practice of the German *Stadtpfeifer*. Evidence comes in a painting by Narziss Renner ("The Augsburg Couples Dance," 1522). It was destroyed in the Second World War, but a photograph is still extant.[76] (See Fig. 5.7.)

Fig. 5.6. Marriage of Renaud and Clarissa (Wedding procession), from "Renaud de Montauban" by Loyset Liedet (ca. 1460–1478). Flemish. Ms.5073, fol.117v. Bibliotheque de l'Arsenal, Paris, France. Photo Credit: Giraudon / Art Resource, NY.

Fig. 5.7. Detail from "The Augsburg Couples Dance" by Narziss Renner (1522).

It is one of at least three from early sixteenth-century Augsburg that show couples dancing in historical costume. All of them show some of the same costumes and similar dance movements: gliding steps in a procession similar to representations of the French *basse danse* and the Italian *bassadanza*. Renner's painting shows the history of the imperial city of Augsburg from about 1200 and identifies many historical personages by means of name tags. A number of musicians are depicted playing on a raised platform. Three of them, dressed in the town livery, can be identified as the *Stadtpfeifer* of Augsburg: Georg Eyseln and Bernhard Hurlacher (shawms) and Jacob Hurlacher (trombone). They are flanked by a flute player, a bagpiper, and two military figures playing a drum. Also pictured, but not playing, are a harper and a lutenist. The trombonist gazes intently at the two shawmists, suggesting that members of the band helped each other with visual cues. Just as Renner informs viewers of the identity of several of the figures, he also shows exactly what tune the band is playing: the same cantus firmus that "Der annder statpfeifer danntz" was based on. It is one of three tunes that Heartz traced from their origin as *basse danse* tunes into various German lute and organ manuscripts.

The bombard would play the tenor, with the shawm and trombone playing lines above and below it. Not only in this painting, but in all others that depict instrumental ensembles of the time, the players are not using music. By the 1520s, it is fairly clear that professional musicians could read music, but they did not use it in performance. Like their illiterate predecessors, they memorized hun-

dreds of tunes and then either improvised counterpoint or worked something out in rehearsal, memorized it, and probably embellished it profusely.

Besides dance music, the *alta* band was expected to know a wide range of vocal music: chansons, motets, and even portions of the Mass. This vast repertoire was likewise played from memory and probably embellished. Possibly the bandsmen learned the basic tune and improvised, or they may have learned to play pieces as written, learning them either from notation or by rote.

It is hardly possible to make any widely acceptable generalizations about how chansons were performed in the fourteenth and fifteenth centuries. Composers left to performers such basic elements as which syllable of the text matched which note of the music, accidentals, and how or whether instruments and voices should be used together. The presence of a complete text beneath a part does not necessarily mean that it had to be sung. Conversely, the absence of a text does not necessarily mean that it was not sung. The style and texture of chansons from Machaut to the generation of Ockeghem indicate that they were conceived for solo voice with instrumental accompaniment, but other combinations were not only possible but common.

The most likely instruments to combine with voices were soft instruments, especially the lute and harp. The number of existing intabulations of chansons indicates that they made up much of the repertoire of the organ and other keyboard instruments, and possibly also the lute. With chansons being such popular and common fare for such a wide variety of music making, *alta* bands playing for concerts, weddings, banquets, and street dramas would have included many in their repertoire.

Now that the date and geographic provenance of all of the important manuscripts of the late fifteenth century are known with reasonable certainty, it is possible to deduce from the amount of text given which pieces were intended for vocal or instrumental performance. Something may have been composed as a vocal piece, but copied in a particular manuscript for use by an instrumental ensemble.

French manuscripts of the 1480s have *forme fixe* chansons with text only in the superius. *Forme fixe* chansons in manuscripts from thirty years later are supplied with text in all parts. Apparently, they were sung by a solo singer accompanied either by instruments or singers who vocalized without text in the 1480s, but sung with text in all parts in the 1510s. In Italian sources, however, a growing number of manuscripts abandon a fully texted superius and supply only an incipit when the music is of French origin. At the same time, Italian music is carefully supplied with texts. Here, the absence of a text points to instrumental performance rather than vocalization. The earliest Italian manuscript that has no text besides incipits, Casanatense 2856, is described in the record of payment to the copyist as having been prepared "a la pifaresca." It was intended specifically for the *alta* band in Ferrara. Even in texted manuscripts, French texts are so corrupt that performance was more likely instrumental than vocal—not for want of French singers, who were available in abundance, but because of the Italians' apparent antipathy for hearing music in the French language.[77]

The Casanatense chansonnier consists of one hundred three-voice pieces and ten four-voice pieces, all of which are supplied with attributions, voice rubrics, and text incipits. Although its pages are not large, it is written so that it is legible from several feet away. Twenty-seven composers are represented, some active at Ferrara or other nearby courts and some from as far away as Antwerp. Comparison of the arrangements in the chansonnier with the same pieces in other sources shows that the ranges and tessituras of the music were adjusted to fit the ranges of the shawm and trombone. The largest number of pieces is by Ferrarese composer Johannes Martini. Other composers include Josquin, Agricola, Busnois, and Ockeghem.[78]

Another Italian manuscript of instrumental music, Bologna Q18, most likely copied in 1502–05, contains more than 70 textless pieces: one in five parts, some in three, and most in four. None of the music is attributed, but by comparing the manuscript with other sources, it is possible to identify works by Isaac, Josquin, Compère, Tromboncino, and others. It was compiled for use in Bologna; titles of at least eight pieces allude either to Bologna or the ruling Bentivoglio family. The Concerto Palatino probably used it, but there was also a group of aristocratic amateurs capable of playing the music.[79]

The Segovia Codex, possibly copied at the court of Isabella of Castille from the repertoire of the visiting Philip the Fair, also includes music suitable for a wind ensemble. Three of the pieces also appear in the Casanatense manuscript. In Germany, the Schedel, Glogauer, and Augsburg song books, while not primarily instrumental books, contain much material of more use to players than singers. Motets are carefully provided with Latin texts. Many German songs have texts, but French chansons have only incipits, implying that outside of French-speaking areas French secular music was normally played on instruments rather than sung.[80]

There even appear to be chanson-like pieces, including some by composers of the stature of Josquin and Isaac, that were conceived from the start as instrumental pieces. Some of them set borrowed material against new lines that feature quick rhythmic motion and motivic manipulation. Others are not based on any pre-existing material that has yet been identified, and given titles like "La martinella" or "La morra" rather than text incipits.

Although today the term *motet* is closely associated with church music, it has not always been a sacred form. It originated as a liturgical trope, but during the late Middle Ages it was the supreme form of secular art music. Secular music does not exclude a sacred text. Christian thought and symbols—and even scripture—were not confined within the walls of the church. Motets, performed both vocally and instrumentally, formed an important part of the various civic processions, mystery plays, tableaux vivants, and other street entertainments. Exceptionally, but with increasing frequency over the course of the fifteenth century, wind instruments also participated in the liturgy. Most performances of late fifteenth-century polyphonic mass settings were by unaccompanied choir, but occasionally instruments took part, either in alternation with the choir or doubling it.[81]

A small body of works, mostly but not exclusively mass fragments, contains the word *trumpet* or something similar either in the title or in a rubric for the contratenor line. Besseler believed that the composers of these works intended for the contratenor to be performed on a trombone. (Actually, these pieces are all early enough that the trombone existed only in the form of the slide trumpet. To avoid ambiguity, I will use the latter term for the rest of the chapter.)

Besseler's list of pieces comprises "Dy trumpet" by Hermann, Monk of Salzburg, the so-called *Missa trompetta* of Estienne Grossin, a setting of "Et in terra" by Richard de Loqueville, another setting of the same text by Arnold de Lantins, a motet "Ave virgo" by Johannes Franchois, Dufay's "Gloria ad modem tubae," an antiphon "Virgo dulcis" (alternately titled "Tuba heinrici") by Heinricus de Libero Castro, a chanson "J'ayme bien celui qu s'en va" by Pierre Fontaine, and an anonymous textless piece called "Tuba gallicalis." Wheat added two more pieces by Hermann and *Missa Tube* by Jean Cousin. Hermann's pieces, the earliest, originated around 1400, Cousin's, the latest, about 1450.[82]

Upon closer examination of these pieces (except for Cousin's mass), Ramalingam determined that they represent not one repertoire, but two contrasting tendencies. Those whose contratenors are labeled "trumpet" or some such term, she decided, are actual slide trumpet parts, but the rest are imitations of the trumpet idiom. On this view, the Dufay piece is of the latter type. It uses reiterated figures that Tinctoris called *redictae*, which, he said, should be avoided except to imitate trumpets or bells. Music "in the manner of a trumpet" was intended to evoke the idea of a trumpet, but need not be played on one. *Trumpetum* was a recognized idiom in the fifteenth century. Ramalingam identified two aspects of it: the frequent use of the intervals of fifth and octave, and a freer treatment of dissonance than allowed by normal rules of counterpoint.[83]

Two of the pieces, the "Tuba heinrici" and the "Tuba gallicalis," exhibit a dissonant style. The term *tuba* in these pieces, and also Cousin's mass, appears in a title that applies to all parts, not in a rubric that applies only to one part. Therefore, according to Ramalingam, it indicates a genre, not a performance instruction. The utter simplicity of the works of the Monk of Salzburg, with the limitation of the trumpet parts to fifths and octaves, likewise set them apart from the trumpet contratenors.[84]

The remaining pieces examined by Ramalingam are those by François and Fontaine, composers at the Burgundian court; Loqueville, a teacher of Dufay who spent most of his career at the cathedral of Cambrai, the Burgundian capital; Grossin, who worked in Paris at a time when the Duke of Burgundy was a leading political figure there; and Lantins, who appears to have been originally from Liège and who sang with Dufay in the papal choir in the 1430s. In other words, all of the composers had ties to the most innovative court of their time.

Are Besseler and Ramalingam correct that the rubrics associating the contratenor part with the trumpet mean that these are actual trumpet parts? It almost seems too much to expect, in a time when even text underlay and accidentals were left to the performers' choices, that composers would specify a particular instrument for a specific line.

Several authors have raised objections to this idea. Some have alleged that slide trumpets were technically incapable of playing the parts.[85] They contend that a player's arm would not be sufficiently long to extend the slide enough to lower the fundamental pitch of the instrument by more than a minor third, leaving key pitches unplayable. As shown in an earlier chapter, however, the slide trumpet was capable of playing an unbroken diatonic scale from the top to the bottom of its range (excluding the half-octave above the fundamental), although there was one note that was very awkward to produce. On the most likely slide trumpet ("in D"), *e* must be lipped down from chromatic note in "fifth position" according to a chromatic numbering of theoretical positions.

By this reasoning, the pieces by Grossin, Loqueville, and Lantins are playable on a slide trumpet. Francois's piece requires A, however, and Fontaine's requires D, F, G, and A. Ramalingam points out that A could be played either in the same position as *e* or as a falset tone in first position. G and F would have to be falset tones in longer positions; D is available only as a pedal tone.[86]

Considering that a century after these pieces were written Luscinius implied that the trombone played only the second through fifth partials, falset tones and pedals would have required exceptional virtuosity on a slide trumpet. If such a virtuoso lived at the time, he would not have been able to read the parts, but he could have either learned them by rote or they could be transcriptions of his improvisation.

It is further objected that instruments did not participate in the liturgy and that loud instruments did not play with singers. Surely this is too sweeping a generalization. Instruments did not *ordinarily* participate in the liturgy. Singers did not *ordinarily* perform with loud instruments. Composers did not *ordinarily* supply anything beyond notes and rhythms. But if the rubric did not prescribe the manner of performing the line, what did it mean? These are not ordinary pieces; they are exceptional. They are few in number and appeared over a short span of time and limited geographical provenance.

All of these pieces would have been potentially part of the repertoire of the duke's *alta* band. Once the technical resources of the slide trumpet are correctly understood, the only controversy concerns whether the composers intended that a trumpet play along with the singers. The occasional participation of trombones and other instruments in the liturgy, be it ever so rare, cannot be ruled out. Also, liturgical pieces were played out of church for private devotions or entertainment in noble households, where standards of liturgical propriety would have been relaxed. One of the pieces is a chanson. It does not appear possible either to prove or disprove that these five pieces have slide trumpet parts, but if the composers did intend for mixed vocal and instrumental performance, it hardly counts as an important step in the evolution of musical performance. In that case, these pieces would represent an innovation that did not catch on.

Notes

1. For Finck's *Practica musica*, see Tom L. Naylor, *The Trumpet & Trombone in Graphic Arts, 1500–1800* (Nashville, Tenn.: Brass Press, 1979), plate 71.

2. See Walter Salmen, "The Social Status of Professional Musicians in the Middle Ages," in *The Social Status of the Professional Musician from the Middle Ages to the 19th Century*, ed. Walter Salmen (New York: Pendragon, 1983), 3–29.

3. Spieleut und gaukler sind nicht leut wie andere Menschen, denn sie nur ein Schein der menschheit haben, und fast den Todten zu vergleichen sind. *Sächsiches Weichbidrecht*, quoted in Keith McGowan, "The Prince and the Piper: *Haut, Bas* and the Whole Body in Early Modern Europe," *Early Music* 27 (1999): 230.

4. See Anthony Baines, "Fifteenth-Century Instruments in Tinctoris's *De Inventione et Usu Musicae*," *Galpin Society Journal* 3 (1950): 20–21.

5. Keith Polk, *German Instrumental Music of the Late Middle Ages: Players, Patrons, and Performance Practice* (Cambridge: Cambridge University Press, 1992), 81; Keith Polk, "Ensemble Music in Flanders: 1450–1550," *Journal of Band Research* 11 (Spring 1975): 18.

6. Keith Polk, "Instrumental Music in the Urban Centers of Renaissance Germany," *Early Music History* 7 (1987): 164.

7. Edmund A. Bowles, "The Role of Musical Instruments in the Medieval Sacred Drama," *Musical Quarterly* 45 (1959): esp. 77, 79, 81—at least some of the times when Bowles uses the term *buisine*, the instrument probably had a slide; Howard Mayer Brown, *Music in the French Secular Theater, 1400–1550* (Cambridge, Mass.: Harvard University Press, 1963), 74–75, 140.

8. Leeman Perkins, "Musical Patronage at the Royal Court of France under Charles VII and Louis XI (1422–83)," *Journal of the American Musicological Society* 37 (1984): 516; Kenneth Kreitner, "Music and Civic Ceremony in Late Fifteenth-Century Barcelona" (Ph.D. diss.: Duke University, 1990), 172.

9. L. de la Laurencie, "La musique a la cour des ducs de Bretagne aux XIVe et XVe siècles," *Revue de musicologie* 14 (1935): 3; Gretchen Peters, "Urban Minstrels in Late Medieval Southern France: Opportunities, Status, and Professional Relationships," *Early Music History* 19 (2000): 202–03, 229–35.

10. Craig Wright, *Music at the Court of Burgundy, 1364–1419: A Documentary History* (Henryville, Penn.: Institute of Medieval Music, 1979), 25, 35, 49.

11. Reinhard Strohm, *Music in Late Medieval Bruges* (Oxford: Oxford University Press, 1985), 79–80, 85, 100.

12. Kristine K. Forney, "Music, Ritual and Patronage at the Church of Our Lady, Antwerp," *Early Music History* 7 (1987): 26–27.

13. Richard Rastall, "The Minstrels of the English Royal Households, 25 Edward I–1 Henry VIII: An Inventory," *R. M. A. Research Chronicle* 4 (1964): 26–27; Manfred Schuler, "Die Musik in Konstanz während des Konzils 1414–1418," *Acta musicologica* 38 (1966): 159.

14. Lyndesay G. Langwill, "The Waites: A Short Historical Study," *Hinrichsen's Musical Yearbook* 7 (1953): 181.

15. Trevor Herbert, "The Trombone in Britain before 1800," (Ph.D. diss.: Open University, 1984), 395.

16. Higinio Anglés, *Hygini Anglés: Scripta musicologica*, ed. Joseph Lopéz-Calo (3 vols., continuously paged, Rome: Edizione de Storia e Letteratura, 1975–76), 766, 774, 899, 940, 970, 972, 974, 982, 987–88, 1011.

17. Jeanne Marix, *Histoire de la musique et des musiciens de la cour de Bourgogne sous le règne de Philippe le Bon (1420–1467)* (Strasbourg: Heitz, 1939), 105; Keith Polk, "The Trombone in Archival Documents, 1350–1500" *ITA Journal* 15 (Summer 1987): 27.

18. Osvaldo Gambassi, *Il Concerto Palatino della signoria di Bologna: Cinque secoli di vita musical a corte (1250–1797)* (Florence: Olschki, 1989), 589–610; Keith Polk, "Civic Patronage and Instrumental Ensembles in Renaissance Florence," *Augsburger Jahrbuch für Musikwissenschaft* 3 (1986): 54, 59.

19. Polk, *German Instrumental Music*, 88.

20. Maricarmen Gomez, "Minstrel Schools in the Late Middle Ages," *Early Music* 18 (1990): 213–15.

21. See for example Tess Knighton, "Music and Musicians at the Court of Fernando of Aragon, 1474–1516" (Ph.D. diss.: University of Cambridge, 1983), 1:46, 49.

22. Keith Polk, "Patronage and Innovation in Instrumental Music in the 15th Century," *Historic Brass Society Journal* 3 (1991): 157–59.

23. Described in McGowan, "Prince and the Piper," 219–25.

24. Georges van Doorslaer, "La chapelle musicale de Philippe le Beau," *Revue belge d'archéologie et d'histoire de l'art* 4 (1934): 24.

25. Doorslaer, "La chapelle musicale," 34.

26. Walter Senn, *Musik und Theater am Hof Innsbruck: Geschichte der Hofkapelle vom 15. Jahaarhundert bis zu deren Auflösung im Jahre 1748* (Innsbruck: Österreichische Verlagsanstalt, 1954), 1–7.

27. See Louise Cuyler, "Music in Biographies of Emperor Maximilian," in *Aspects of Medieval and Renaissance Music*, ed. Jan LaRue (New York: Norton, 1966), 119–21.

28. *The Triumph of Maximilian I: 137 Woodcuts by Hans Burgkmair and Others*, with a translation of descriptive text,

introduction, and notes by Stanley Appelbaum (New York: Dover, 1964), 4–5, descriptions of plates 20, 26.

29. Martin Kirnbauer, "Die Nürnberger Trompeten- und Posaunenmacher vor 1500 im Spiegel Nürnberger Quellen," in *Musik und Tanz zur Zeit Kaiser Maximilian I.*, ed. Walter Salmen (Innsbruck: Helbling, 1992), 131; Polk, *German Instrumental Music*, 97–107.

30. See Doorslaer, "La chapelle musicale," 50; Keith Polk, "The Schubingers of Augsburg: Innovation in Renaissance Instrumental Music," in *Quaestiones in musica: Festschrift für Franz Krautworst zum 65; Geburtstag*, ed. Friedhelm Brusniak and Horst Leuchtmann (Tutzing: Schneider, 1989), 501.

31. Keith Polk, "Augustein Schubinger and the Zinck: Innovation in Performance Practice," *Historic Brass Society Journal* 1 (1989): 84; Senn, *Musik und Theater*, 7.

32. William F. Prizer, "Bernardino Piffaro e i piffari e tromboni di Montova: Strumenti a fiato in una corte italiana," *Rivista italiana de musicologia* 16 (1981): 169; Giancarlo Rostirolla, "Strumentisti e costruttori di strumenti nella Roma dei papi: Materiali per una storia della musica strumentale a Roma durante i secoli XV–XVII," in *Restauro conservatione e recupero di antich strumenti musicali* (Florence: Olschki, 1986), 174–75.

33. Anthony M. Cummings, *The Politicized Muse: Music for the Medici Festivals, 1512–1537* (Princeton, N.J.: Princeton University Press, 1992), 11–14; André Pirro, "Leo X and Music," *Musical Quarterly* 21 (1935): 15.

34. Bonnie J. Blackburn, "Music and Festivities at the Court of Leo X: A Venetian View," *Early Music History* 11 (1992): 5–6, 18.

35. Polk, "Civic Patronage," 60.

36. Federico Ghisi, "La tradition musicale des fêtes et les origines de l'opera," in *Les fêtes du mariage de Ferdinand de Médicis et de Christine de Lorraine, Florence 1589*, ed. D. P. Walker (Paris: Centre National de la Recherche Scientifique, 1963), xi.

37. Andrew C. Minor and Bonner Mitchell, *A Renaissance Entertainment: Festivities for the Marriage of Cosimo I, Duke of Florence, in 1539* (Columbia: University of Missouri Press, 1968), 46; Howard Mayer Brown, *Sixteenth Century Instrumentation: The Music for the Florentine Intermedii* (s.l.: American Institute of Musicology, 1973), 87.

38. Lewis Lockwood, *Music in Renaissance Ferrara, 1500–1595: The Creation of a Musical Center in the Fifteenth Century* (Cambridge, Mass.: Harvard University Press, 1984), 183, 314–28.

39. Lockwood, *Music in Renaissance Ferrara*, 142.

40. William F. Prizer, *Courtly Pastimes: The Frottole of Marchetto Cara* (Ann Arbor, Mich.: UMI Research Press, 1980), 1–3; Guglielmo Barblan, "Vita musicale alla corte sforzesca," in *Storia di Milano*, ed. Giovanni Treccani degli Alfieri (Milan: Fondazione Treccani degli Alfieri, 1961), 9:793–94.

41. Prizer, "Bernardino Piffaro," 159–60; Prizer, *Courtly Pastimes*, 55–61.

42. Susan Forscher Weiss, "Musical Patronage of the Bentivoglio Signoria, c1465–1512," in *Report of the 14th Congress of the International Musicological Society (Bologna, 1987)*.

(Turin: Editioni de Torino, 1990), 3:704; Gambassi, *Concerto Palatino*, 122, doc. 163.

43. Gambassi, *Concerto Palatino*, 8–9.

44. Doorslaer, "La chapelle musicale," 41.

45. Rodolfo Baroncini, "Zorzi Trombetta and the Band of *Piffari* and Trombones of the *Serenissima*: New Documentary Evidence," trans. Hugh Ward-Perkins, *Historic Brass Society Journal* 14 (2002): 59–82; Rodolfo Baroncini, "Zorzi Trombetta da Modon and the Founding of the Band of *Piffari* and *Tromboni* of the *Serenissima*," *Historic Brass Society Journal* 16 (2004): 1–17.

46. Carl Gustsav Anthon, "Music and Musicians in Northern Italy during the Sixteenth Century," (Ph.D. diss.: Harvard University, 1943), 239–40; Eleanor Selfridge-Field, *Venetian Instrumental Music from Gabrieli to Vivaldi*, 3rd rev. ed. (New York: Dover, 1994), 14.

47. David Lasocki, *The Bassanos: Venetian Musicians and Instrument Makers in England, 1531–1665* (Hants, England: Scolar Press, 1995), 5–6.

48. Jonathan Glixon, "Music at the Venetian 'Scuole Grandi,' 1440–1540" (Ph.D. diss.: Princeton University, 1979), 1:92–99, 189–90, 210.

49. Lasocki, *The Bassanos*, 3–5; Glixon, "Music at the Venetian 'Scuole Grandi,'" 1:179.

50. Gary Towne, "Tubatori e piffari: Civic Wind Players in Medieval and Renaisssance Bergamo," *Historic Brass Society Journal* 9 (1997): 177, 181–82.

51. Knighton, "Music and Musicians at the Court of Fernando of Aragon," 1:200–201, 204; a table of the *alta* musicians at both courts and their years of service is in 2:79–100.

52. Knighton, "Music and Musicians at the Court of Fernando of Aragon," 1:201–3; Anglès, *Hygini Anglés: Scripta musicologica*, 890; Kreitner, "Music and Civic Ceremony," 51.

53. Kreitner, "Music and Civic Ceremony," 130–31, 157, 170.

54. Kreitner, "Music and Civic Ceremony," 51, 53, 160–69.

55. Stephen Bonime, "The Musicians of the Royal Stable under Charles VIII and Louis XII (1484–1514)," *Current Musicology* 25 (1978), 7, 9, 10, 14–15.

56. Henri Prunières, "La musique de la chambre et de l'écurie," *L'année musicale* 1 (1912): 219–21, 232–33.

57. Craig Wright, *Music and Ceremony at Notre Dame de Paris, 500–1550* (Cambridge: Cambridge University Press, 1989), 231; Glixon, "Music at the Venetian 'Scuole Grandi,'" 1:220; Pirro, "Leo X," 15.

58. Theodore Godefroy, ed., *Le ceremonial françois* (1649), quoted in Wright, *Music and Ceremony*, 227.

59. Andrew Ashbee, *Records of English Court Music* (Hants, England: Scolar Press, 1986–95), 7:153.

60. Andrew Ashbee, "Groomed for Service: Musicians in the Privy Chamber at the English Court, c. 1495–1558," *Early Music* 25 (1997): 186.

61. Andrew Ashbee and David Lasocki, *A Biographical Dictionary of English Court Musicians 1485–1714* (Aldershot, England: Ashgate, 1998), 817–21; Bruno Bouckaert and

Eugeen Schreurs, "Hans Nagel, Performer and Spy in England and Flanders (ca. 1490–1531)," in *Tielman Susato and the Music of His Time: Print Culture, Compositional Technique, and Instrumental Music in the Renaissance*, ed. Keith Polk (Hillsdale, N.Y.: Pendragon, 2005), 101–15.

62. Langwill, "Waites," 181.

63. See James McKinnon, "The Meaning of the Patristic Polemic against Musical Instruments," *Current Musicology* 1 (1965): 69–82.

64. Philippe de Mezières, *Le songe du vieil pelerin*, ed. G. W. Coopland (Cambridge: Cambridge University Press, 1969), 2:26–7. The original French, of which the quoted passage is a paraphrase, is on p. 243.

65. Edmund A. Bowles, "Were Musical Instruments Used in the Liturgical Services during the Middle Ages?" *Galpin Society Journal* 10 (1957): 48–52.

66. des meilleurs chantres ui pour lors fussent à Paris, et avoit orgues et grant quantite de bas instrumens, tant que le [peuple] disoit que c'estoit la plus belle messe que oncques ilz eust [veu] dire ne chanter. Quoted in Wright, *Music at the Court of Burgundy*, 52; Wright, *Music and Ceremony*, 302–03.

67. Wright, *Music and Ceremony*, 218–19, 230–31.

68. Anglés, *Hygini Anglés: Scripta musicologica*, 767.

69. Kenneth Kreitner, "Minstrels in Spanish Churches, 1400–1600," *Early Music* 20 (1992): 534; Kreitner, "Music and Civic Ceremony," 159.

70. Doorslaer, "La chapelle musicale," 50–52; Knighton, "Music and Musicians at the Court of Fernando of Aragon," 1:102, 199.

71. Leslie Korrick, "Instrumental Music in the Early 16th-Century Mass: New Evidence," *Early Music* 18 (1990): 360, 364.

72. Enrico Peverada, "Vita musicale nella cattedrale di Ferrara nel quattrocento: Note e documenti," *Rivista italiana di musicologia* 15 (1980): 4–6.

73. Christopher Page, "German Musicians and Their Instruments: A 14th-Century Account by Konrad of Megenberg," *Early Music* 10 (1982): 198 and n. 42; Vivian Safowitz [Ramalingam], "Trumpet Music and Trumpet Style in the Early Renaissance," (M.M. thesis: University of Illinois, 1965), 53–67.

74. Page, "German Musicians," 194–95; Wright, *Music at the Court of Burgundy*, 51–52.

75. See Daniel Heartz, "The Basse Dance: Its Evolution circa 1450 to 1550," *Annals musicologiques* 6 (1958–63): 287–340.

76. Daniel Heartz, "Hoftanz and Basse Dance," *Journal of the American Musicological Society* 19 (1966): 25–27. This article also includes the entire photograph and some other details.

77. Louise Litterick, "Performing Franco-Netherlandish Secular Music of the Late Fifteenth Century," *Early Music* 8 (1980): 480.

78. Lockwood, *Music in Renaissance Ferrara*, 269–77.

79. See Susan Forscher Weiss, "Bologna Q18: Some Reflections on Content and Context," *Journal of the American Musicological Society* 41 (1988): 63–101, for an extensive description of this manuscript. Other collections of similar size, repertoire, and format, besides Casanatense 2856, include Odhecaton, CantiB, Florence Panciatichi 27, and Paris Rés. Vm7676.

80. Jon Banks, "Performing Instrumental Music in the Segovia Codex," *Early Music* 27 (1999): 305–8; Polk, *German Instrumental Music*, 138, 144–45.

81. Howard Mayer Brown, *Music in the French Secular Theater* (Cambridge, Mass.: Harvard University Press, 1963), 149–50; Willem Elders, "The Performance of Cantus Firmi in Josquin's Masses Based on Secular Monophonic Song," *Early Music* 17 (1989): 330–41; David Fallows, "The Performing Ensembles in Josquin's Sacred Music," *Tijdschrift van den Vereniging voor Nederlandse Muziek Geschiedenis* 35 (1985): 32–35.

82. Heinrich Besseler, "Die Entstehung der Posaune," *Acta musicologica* 22 (1950): 13; James Raymond Wheat, "The Tuba/Trompetta Repertoire of the Fifteenth Century," (D.M.A. essay: University of Wisconsin-Madison, 1994), 8–11.

83. Vivian S[afowitz] Ramalingam, "The *Trumpetum* in Strasbourg M222 C2," in *Le musique et le rite sacré et profane: Transactions of the 13th Congress of the International Musicological Society, 1982*, ed. Marc Honneger Christian Meyer and Paul Prévost (Strasbourg: Association des Publications près les Unversités de Strasbourg, 1986), 2:143, 148, 156–57.

84. Ramalingam, "Trumpet Music," 94; Ramalingam, "Trumpetum," 146–47, 149–50; Wheat, "Tuba/Trompette Repertoire," 44.

85. Don L. Smithers, *The Music and History of the Baroque Trumpet before 1721*, 2nd ed. (Carbondale and Edwardsville: Southern Illinois University Press, 1988), 43–49; Janez Höfler, "Der 'Trompette de Menestrels' und sein Instrument," *Tijdschrift van de Vereniging voor Nederlandse Muziekgeschiedenis* 29 (1979): 114–18; Wheat, "Tuba/Trompette Repertoire," 65–73.

86. Ramalingam, "Trumpet Music," 126.

CHAPTER SIX

~

The Renaissance Trombone

The last chapter is a story of growing professionalism among wind players. By about 1520, no longer was the ability to read music superfluous for minstrels. No longer did members of *alta* bands toil in anonymity, with no personal reputations of their own. There were two basic paths to follow through the sixteenth century.

First, the band continued to play its traditional role, with expansion into church music. Some outstanding bandsmen became known as composers and leaders in major musical establishments. Playing wind instruments was among the skills that they had, but not the core of their professional identity. They did not compose music especially for their own performance, or for that matter, very much music especially for instruments. Early in the seventeenth century, similarly prominent violinists and keyboard players wrote a considerable body of very influential music based on the idioms and characteristics of their instrument. Eventually, as tastes changed, the traditional wind band became increasingly marginal and irrelevant to the latest developments in music, to which wind musicians had contributed nothing.

Second, certain courts developed elaborate theatrical entertainments for political purposes. The producers experimented with new combinations of instruments. Traditional distinctions between loud and soft instruments were cast aside as trombones participated in ensembles with soft instruments and singers. Opera developed from these practices, but it soon abandoned colorful instrumentation in favor of a string orchestra. Other simpler mixed ensembles also enjoyed only a short vogue. Both of these paths therefore turned out to be dead ends.

Aristotle and other ancient Greeks had disapproved of wind instruments, and numerous Renaissance thinkers adopted much the same reasoning. Alessandro Piccolo-

mini is but one of a number of authors of books about the proper conduct of the nobility. He considered wind instruments unsuitable for honorable people to play because it distorted their faces.

> The same thing applies to music you make with instruments, which is that some is plebian and blameworthy and some other is honorable. Different kinds of music move different affects. Plebian and unworthy of the civil man are all those instruments that make parts of the body of those who play them twisted and ugly. It is truly impossible to use them for any noble purpose, because we have no report of ancient instruments like panpipes, auloses, petads, heptagons, symponias, sambucas and the like that we might have accommodated to our ways in these times. I say that the vile and vulgar instruments, whose use vilely twists some parts of the body and which are maladapted to any virtuous purpose are those like trumpets, shawms, bagpipes, cornetts, flutes, trombones, drums, and the like, most of which require blowing and forcing of the breath or some similar servile act. The effort aggravates and forces the breath and the spirit, makes the face extremely ugly and disgusting, and by weakening the chest, exhausts the person; and because of the disturbance and agitation of the spirit, does not dispose one to moderation in one's habits.[1]

Vincenzo Galilei more explicitly cited the authority of the ancients. Cornetts and trombones, he observed, were loved by the common people, but never heard in the private chambers of gentlemen with good taste. Indeed, the puffing of cheeks, shown in numerous pictures, and the energetic and jerky movements of the slide served to show the difference between the serene nonchalance of the truly noble person and the laborious efforts of the working classes.[2]

From the 1620s to the 1640s, economic conditions, war, and plague devastated musical life. When recovery from those disasters began, the string orchestra was firmly entrenched, and wind instruments were not welcome in it. This chapter begins as trombonists were emerging from obscurity and ends with the onset of the instrument's decline.

The Traditional Wind Band

France

The basic division of the royal musical household into Chapel, Chamber, and Stable remained in effect until the French Revolution, but the exact composition and function of each unit changed over time.

In 1530, two sons of Francis I (r. 1515–47) who had been held hostage by Emperor Charles V since 1526 were released, an event marked by three days of celebration in Lyons. One of at least three processions included "trumpets and shawms playing very melodiously polyphonic musical chansons that were very good to hear." At the head of another were "trumpets and clarions, while between the mendicants and seculars were shawms and other instruments playing sweetly." The final procession was led again by trumpets and clarions, followed by "shawms, trombones, and other instruments sounding sweetly and melodiously."[3]

It appears that whoever wrote the description of the first procession did not know or care about the difference between a trumpet and a trombone. By this time, trumpets did not play in shawm bands and were incapable of playing polyphonic chansons. The combination of shawm and trombone was a tradition of such long standing by this time that the trombone must have been included among the "other instruments" in the second procession.

The entry of Henry II (r. 1547–59) into Lyons on September 21, 1548, tried to duplicate the ancient Roman triumphs, which had been in vogue in Italy for some time. Where *tableaux vivants* had a prominent place in earlier triumphs, obelisks and triumphal arches were built for this and later ones. Bowles reproduces pictures of two arches, with instrumentalists playing from the top. In one of them, at least, a trombonist is discernable.[4] Although triumphal arches were new to French culture, elevating a band so high above street level was by this time commonplace—not only in France, but all over Europe.

Henry entered Rouen in a similar triumph on October 1–2, 1550. The procession stopped at several points along the route for music. For the last of these, the contemporary description merely observes, "Led by the music of a galliard, the goddess Flora, accompanied by two of her nymphs. . . [passed by]. There followed six instrumentalists, dressed in silk satin." The illustration, however, specifically shows a band, including a slide trumpet.[5]

It is difficult to escape the conclusion that the trombone's role in these French productions was limited to traditional *alta* band ceremonial music. It was, in other words, part of the aural wallpaper with no artistic significance. This impression gathers strength from descriptions of politically important processions in Paris in the early 1580s. Sets of commemorative drawings, some of which depict musicians, exist for two of them. And yet apparently none of the source material acknowledges the presence of a wind band.[6] Would the king have neglected to throw all of his resources into such occasions? More likely, with so much novelty in these processions, no one thought the ordinary parts were worth documenting.

The trombone also took part in the funeral ceremonies for Duke Charles III of Lorraine (r. 1545–1608) in 1608. The duke's chapel comprised "20 singers and 10 players of cornetts, dulzians and sackbuts, by which the music for high masses, vespers and vigils was performed."[7]

French towns never cultivated the wind band to the extent German, Italian, and English towns did, but the trombone was not completely unknown. Few instrumental musicians could derive their entire income from playing their instruments. When the wife of Thomas Boullant died in 1534, an inventory taken of his household effects included two trombones, two shawms, two tambourines, and four flutes, but he was identified as a master pin maker. Trombones or parts of trombones were noted among the effects of two instrument makers at their deaths in 1551 and 1557 respectively. In Paris in 1561, a court case involved failure to pay for trombone lessons. Pierre Colbert of Rheims made the oldest extant bass trombone in 1593.[8]

Spain and Germany

On the death of Maximilian I, the empire passed to his grandson Charles V (r. 1516–56, emperor from 1519), already king of Spain. Charles abdicated in 1556. Because ruling all of the various Habsburg holdings had proved too much for him, he made his son Philip II (r. 1556–96) king of Spain and his brother Ferdinand (r. 1558–64) Holy Roman Emperor. Again, "Germany" means here a cultural and linguistic entity, recognized as such at the time, and not a political entity.

Fig. 6.1.   Musicians on a triumphal arch in Heidelberg during welcoming ceremonies for Elector Friedrich V of the Rhine Palatinate and Princess Elizabeth of England. Spencer Collection, The New York Public Library, Astor, Lenox and Tinden Foundations. See Bowles, *Musical Ensembles in Festival Books*, pp. 187–89 for a description of the event.

Fig. 6.2. Flora and her nymphs, with an *alta* band. Triumphal visit to Rouen of King Henry II and Queen Catherine of France, October 1–2, 1550. Lessing J. Rosenwald Collection, Library of Congress, Washington, D.C.

Spain

Charles inherited Spanish minstrels from his grandfather Ferdinand of Aragon and Flemish singers from his father Philip the Fair, and these two groups continued to serve throughout his reign. He traveled widely, especially in Italy, an important battleground in his rivalry with the French king Francis I. His minstrels constantly attended him. Charles must have especially loved instrumental music; in 1539, when the queen died, Charles divided her musical establishment among his children, but kept the instrumentalists for himself.[9]

Spanish churches were among the first to include trombones and other instruments during the celebration of the Mass. Charles's minstrels took an active part in sacred music at the court throughout his reign, and indeed until 1572, when Philip II dismissed them. It appears, however, that Philip merely stopped using them for sacred music. He probably did not dispense with their

services entirely. As late as 1655, the court minstrels consisted of four soprano shawms, two alto shawms, two tenor shawms, and four trombones.

According to a 1558 inventory, Charles's sister Mary owned 5 violins, 20 violas da gamba, 10 trombones (one of silver), 39 fifes, 59 cornetts, 19 recorders, 12 shawms (plus 2 contrabass shawms and 2 small shawms), 7 transverse flutes, 7 *bordone*, 4 clavichords, 4 lutes, a dulzaina, 2 otherwise unidentified *ynstruments de música*, one case of recorders and one case of cornetts (the number of instruments in each case not being identified), and a piece of an onyx horn. An inventory of instruments at the court in 1602 included 55 fifes, 30 cornetts, 9 trombones, 8 shawms, 12 flutes, three bass flutes, 16 bagpipes, and a dulzaina.[10]

Philip III (r. 1598–1621), generally considered a pleasure-loving nonentity, left the government in the hands of Francisco Gómez de Sandoval, Duke of Lerma. While the king was progressive in his musical taste, establishing a salaried violin band for his own entertainment, the trombone continued to play some role at the court, most likely for religious music and ceremonial music. Bartolomé de Selma, the royal wind instrument maker from 1612 to 1616, repaired trombones and may even have made some.[11]

Lerma, a generation older, preferred traditional Spanish and Flemish polyphony. As soon as he had the reins of government in his hands, he began to establish his own ducal court. In 1607, he hired four minstrels: a shawmist, two trombonists, and a *bajonista*. A cornett player joined the group a year later.[12] By the time Lerma was driven from power in 1618, he had provided his chapel with an ample repertoire of manuscript and printed music, including two large manuscripts for the instrumentalists.

The Empire

The emperors Ferdinand I (r. 1558–64), Maximilian II (r. 1564–76), Rudolf II (r. 1576–1612), Matthias (r. 1612–19), and Ferdinand II (r. 1619–37) were all, to varying degrees, important patrons of music. Ferdinand I, before becoming emperor in 1558, held the titles of Archduke of Austria and King of Hungary and Bohemia. In 1528, five trombonists in the service of Archduchess Anna agreed to serve Ferdinand as well. The king and queen maintained separate households and separate treasuries. The trombonists received payments from each.

One of them, Stephan Mahu, served as Ferdinand's assistant chapel master from 1530 to 1539. In that capacity, he wrote a considerable quantity of mostly sacred music in the style of the contemporary Flemish compos-

Fig. 6.3. Funeral ceremonies for Duke Charles III of Lorraine. Detail showing the loud consort in the near balcony and the soft consort in the far one. The Metropolitan Museum of Art, The Elisha Whittelsey Collection. The Elisha Whittelsey Fund, 1959 [59.570.163(25–26)] Image © The Metropolitan Museum of Art.

ers. Although his compositions are little known today, they had sufficient merit for entries in the biographical dictionaries of Eitner, Fétis, and Schmidl, none of whom mention that he was a trombonist. It appears, however, that he continued to play trombone throughout his career. In fact, he apparently resigned his position as assistant chapel master in 1539, but is mentioned in court records as a trombonist until 1541.[13]

In his study of the imperial chapel, Ludwig Köchel erroneously concluded that Ferdinand II had dissolved much of it. He had not found records of payments to musicians during this reign in the same accounts where they were found for other reigns. Ferdinand maintained a huge chapel, but chose to pay for it as Archduke of Austria rather than from imperial accounts.[14] Most literature on music in the empire is limited to sacred music. By analogy with other courts, a certain minimum of secular music, specifically including a wind band, must have been indispensable to the reigning emperor even if he did not personally care for it.

Other German Courts

Lesser members of the house of Habsburg reigned as archdukes in Innsbruck. As it is unlikely that they would have richer, more splendid courts than the emperors, the court at Innsbruck indicates what the imperial establish-

ment may have been like. Archduke Ferdinand II, son of Emperor Ferdinand I and younger brother of Emperor Maximilian II, reigned from 1564 to 1595. His singers and instrumentalists were divided into two groups, the *Hofkapelle* and *Hofmusik*. Although administratively separate, they performed as one body for important occasions, both religious and political. An inventory made after Ferdinand's death included 37 viols, 27 trumpets, 20 trombones, 23 cornetts, and lesser quantities of other instruments.[15]

It is possible to name some trombonists from later reigns. Christoph Gerner and Andreas Gerlaschitz played trumpet and trombone under Archduke Maximilian II (r. 1602–18). Paul Zieglgruber served the separate household of Ferdinand's widow Anna Catherine Gonzaga. Georg Karl, Gregor Richter, and Johann Bischof played trombone under Archduke Leopold V (r. 1619–32). Leopold, younger brother of Emperor Ferdinand II, was bishop of Strasbourg before he became archduke and continued in that office until 1625. At that time, he renounced his bishopric to marry Claudia de' Medici, widow of the duke of Urbino. Their wedding was celebrated with the usual ostentation, and trombones participated in the music.

The Protestant Reformation ended whatever chance there had been for the development of a unified imperial government. Most other German rulers besides the emperors became Protestant. Even those who remained Catholic pursued policies independent of the empire. A wind band would have been part of the minimum requirement for any court's musical personnel. Several courts became major cultural centers that equaled or even eclipsed the splendor of the imperial court. Bands are mentioned in connection with festivities that provide a glimpse of how the trombone might have been heard in these courts on more ordinary occasions.

Bavaria's importance as a musical center roughly coincides with the tenure of Orlande de Lassus as chapel master from 1563 until his death in 1594. He served during the reigns of Dukes Albrecht V (r. 1550–79) and Wilhelm V (r. 1579–97) and recruited musicians for the duke's household. Wind players were paid more than string players.[16]

The marriage of the future Duke Wilhelm V and Princess Renée of Lorraine in 1568 served as the occasion for one of the most splendid festivals in Renaissance Germany. According to Troiano's description, the first Sunday of the festival began with a six-voice mass by Lassus for voices and winds. The party started with a "Battaglia à 8" for trombones and cornetts by Annibale Padovana. During the first course of a banquet, a motet for seven voices by Lassus was performed with five cornetts and two trombones. Guests enjoyed the second course to a madrigal by Alessandro Striggio Sr., with six large trombones, probably including a contrabass trombone. Music by Padovana accompanied the fourth course, performed with six violas da braccio, five trombones, a cornett, and a regal. The sixth course included unidentified music with one each of harpsichord, trombone, flute, lute, cornamuse, mute cornett, viola da gamba, and fife.

Later, a large ensemble provided table music in 24 parts. The piece was played once by instruments only and again with eight singers joining the ensemble. The instruments were arrayed in three choirs: eight violas da braccio, eight violas da gamba, and a mixed ensemble of bassoon, cornamuse, mute cornett, alto cornett, large twisted cornett, fife, dulcian, and bass trombone. Six *fifferi* provided background music for a card game. If this term means the same as the more common *piffari*, it was a group of shawms or cornetts and trombones.[17]

The Bavarian court included ten musicians capable of playing the various wind parts. Annibale Morari, Cerbonio Besutio, Mathais Besutio, Lucio Terzo, and Christoforo da Cremona specialized in wind instruments. Domenico Aldigeri, Francesco Guami, Fileno Cornaz-

zani, Sebastiano da Treviso, and Simone Gatto each played all sorts of instruments.[18]

Guami's career is traced elsewhere in this chapter. Cornazzani was born some time between 1543 and 1545. As a boy, he was recruited to study to become an instrumental virtuoso. He arrived in Munich in 1559 or 1560 and became a salaried member of the court chapel in 1568. He must have been exceptionally good, because he received almost the same salary as the veteran members of the chapel. He was always among the highest paid musicians at the court.

Available documentation usually refers to him either simply as an instrumentalist or as a cornett player. Praetorius, however, singled him out as an exceptionally good trombonist, capable of playing from a bottom D (a falset tone on a tenor trombone) to c″, d″, or e″ in the soprano register. In a letter written in 1606 or 1607, Cornazzani reminded the duke that he taught many students on trombone, bassoon, flute, and violin.[19]

Dresden, the seat of the Elector of Saxony, did not become an important musical center until after the Reformation, but by that time, there had been some minimal level of court music, including a wind band, for generations. Elector Moritz (r. 1541–53, elector from 1547) founded the *Hofkantorei* in 1548. Among its earliest members were trombonists Antonio Scandello and the Besutio brothers Cerbonio and Matthias, who had lately left Bergamo after a salary dispute. The Besutios returned briefly to Bergamo in 1557 and eventually joined the Bavarian court in Munich. Scandello remained in Dresden and eventually became chapel master in 1568. By his death in 1580, he was a well-respected composer. It is not clear how long he continued to perform instrumental music, but if he composed any, it does not survive.

In 1574, Elector Augustus (r. 1553–86) hosted a festival in conjunction with that year's carnival. The procession included two separate bands among many different ensembles. The first was an eight-part ensemble of cornetts, shawms, and trombones, and the other a four-part ensemble of cornetts and shawms. Later in the procession, an eight-part mixed ensemble included a trombone and a cornett. A procession as part of the marriage celebration for the future Elector Christian I (r. 1586–91) in 1582 included a four-part *alta* band consisting of cornett, tenor shawm or bombard, and two trombones. Two years later, Christian hosted wedding festivities for two members of his court. A trombone participated in a mixed ensemble of eight instruments.[20]

All of the occasions described so far show the wind band playing what wind bands had always played everywhere else. During the early years of the seventeenth century, Saxon wind players had the opportunity to play the latest style of music from Venice. Much of it was composed by the first generation of truly great German composers, including Michael Praetorius, Johann Hermann Schein, and Heinrich Schütz.

Two inventories that survive from the smaller Hessian court in Kassel and one from Stuttgart have some interesting implications. The 1573 Kassel inventory lists 7 trombones, 3 slide trumpets, 4 Welch trumpets, 10 flutes, 2 bass flutes, 17 *Pfeifen*, 14 cornetts of various descriptions, 7 crumhorns, 4 pommers, 2 shawms, 1 *vagant*, 6 violins, 4 viols, 18 *Geigen*, 2 virginals, and a regal. The trombones consist specifically of one *Quart* trombone with crooks and mouthpiece, 3 *Second* trombones, one of which was missing a crook, and 3 small trombones, likewise one of which was missing a crook. The three small trombones are most likely the ordinary tenor trombones. In that case, the *Second* trombones would have been a step lower.

The Stuttgart inventory (1589) lists *Terz-Pusonen*, which would have been built a third lower than the ordinary tenor, comparable to the later British bass trombone in G. It was most common to lower the basic pitch of a trombone using crooks or tuning bits. In these two courts, apparently someone preferred to have them made longer in the first place. The Stuttgart inventory does not mention crooks.

In the second Kassel inventory of 1613 for the landgrave Moritz (r. 1592–1627), wind instruments comprised the majority of the collection. Trombones included one "great" trombone, one "bad" trombone (with slide and crooks), four tenor and alto trombones (with seven crooks and shanks), two small alto or discant trombones, with three crooks and shanks, and a bass (*Quart*) trombone with crooks and slide. Moritz sent Schütz to study with Giovanni Gabrieli and had several of his works, including some unique manuscripts, in his music library.[21]

The baptism of Prince Friedrich on March 10, 1616, was followed by a week of celebration that included banquets, tournaments, processions, and a ballet. For the baptism itself, trombones participated in at least two sacred numbers. A *Laudate Dominum* by Gregor Aichinger was performed by eight voices, two cornetts, four trombones, and two bassoons. Performance of Tobias Salomon's *Te Deum* required three separate ensembles, one of which included two trombones and another three.[22]

German and Flemish Towns

Town bands continued to flourish throughout the sixteenth century and beyond. The repertoire remained the same as described in the last chapter, mostly adaptations of music originally written for a vocal ensemble. One set of part books greatly clarifies standards of instrumentation. Titled "1579 Orlandi Lassi sexta vocum," it begins with a set of motets by Lassus and also contains 20 Italian madrigals and some other motets: 120 pieces in all. About half of them contain some indication of what instruments were supposed to play them: cornett, bombard, and trombone. Comparing the specific numbers of instruments given, the clefs for each part, and the information in Praetorius's *Syntagma musicum*, it is possible to reconstruct not only what instrument played which part, but also gain a clear idea of what sizes of each instrument were probably used.[23]

In Antwerp, the annual Corpus Christi procession, established some time before 1398, remained a lavish occasion until 1544, when a town ordinance decreed that it should be converted to a purely devotional procession. The even more elaborate procession of Our Lady continued to be conducted with its original splendor at least as late as 1567.[24]

Antwerp's town musicians included trombonist Tielman Susato, best remembered now as a music printer. He was born in about 1510 near Cologne and moved to Antwerp in 1529. At first he worked as a calligrapher, joining the town band in 1531. In addition to the trombone, he played trumpet, crumhorn, flute, and recorder. His religious leanings were strongly Calvinist. After years of good relations with Charles V (hereditary overlord of Flanders, as well as king of Spain and Holy Roman Emperor), he was dismissed, along with the entire band, a few days after Charles's triumphal entry in 1549. The other musicians were soon reinstated, but Susato was permanently replaced. That year marks his last known performances with the Confraternity of Our Lady, but not the end of his playing career. Records in the town archives refer to him as a working instrumentalist as late as 1555. He moved to North Holland in 1561 because of the repressive policies of King Philip II.[25]

Susato is best known as a printer and music publisher. He established his business in 1543. Over the next 18 years, he published 25 books of chansons, 3 of masses, 19 of motets, 2 of Flemish songs, 8 of psalter songs, and one volume of his own arrangements of dances based on popular songs. His compositions include a mass, several motets, chansons, and Flemish songs. Most of this music would have been suitable for performance by a wind band.

Numerous other Flemish towns maintained bands. Noteworthy trombonists include the well-traveled Hans Nagel. Even small cities, such as Oudenaarde, supported bands well enough that at least three trombonists served there for more than 20 years each.[26]

Nuremberg is well known as the city where most of the best brass instruments were manufactured, but its band was not very good. Its weaknesses became apparent in 1570 as the town prepared for a visit from Emperor Maximilian II. The following year, the city council increased the band from four to five members. In 1572, it increased salaries and ordered the band to conduct weekly rehearsals. Throughout much of the century, all bandsmen were locally born and trained, but in 1574, the council hired a cornettist from Ghent. He played so much better than the native Nurembergers that the city council took steps to improve the education of local wind musicians, including sending several young players to Venice for study.[27]

Perhaps one reason why low standards of performance persisted so long is that Nuremberg was a free city governed by businessmen. There was neither court nor citizens who patronized their own private musical establishments. In fact, the council maintained strict sumptuary laws specifically to prohibit such practices. Their tradition as a free city was more important than excellence in music until mediocrity became an embarrassment. It is also worth recalling that Hans Neuschel the Younger, who must have been an excellent player, resented his frequent summonses to play trombone for the emperor. They took him away from his workshop too much. Perhaps other city musicians, and not only in Nuremberg, regarded their civic duties as sidelines, pouring most of their energy into other pursuits.

Italy

The duties of Italian town and court bands remained as described in the previous chapter: accompanying public officials, performing in processions (often on horseback) and playing daily concerts for the populace. Unofficially, they remained available for weddings and private parties on a freelance basis. They were expected to take students. Occasional archival documents imply that towns, especially, regarded these students as free musical labor. In 1546, a group of six musicians offered their services to the Duke of Parma, claiming that they could all play trumpet, trombone, shawm, cornett, bagpipe, recorder, flute, and violin, and therefore provide a six-part consort of any of those instruments. Such versatility was by no means uncommon.[28]

By 1537, the Concerto Palatino of Bologna had grown to 19 musicians, including a band of 4 cornetts and 4 trombones (collectively known as the *musici*). Because of quarrelling among the trumpets and the *musici*, the town

council created the office of dean for both ensembles. The deans' duties included settling disputes, maintaining professional behavior, and, for the *musici*, leading rehearsals and choosing a pleasing variety of music.

The *musici*'s duties included two daily concerts from the balcony of the palace, one shortly before noon and the other about an hour before sunset. On Sundays and special occasions, however, the morning concert was canceled so that the musicians could join the lute and harp in playing table music for the *Signori* and their guests. Whenever the civic leaders left the palace on official business, the trumpets and the *musici* were required to go with them and play music suitable to the occasion. There were 78 annual occasions when the band was required to go out, including the annual lecture of the city's leading judge at the university. They also had to be prepared to go out on an unscheduled basis whenever they were required.[29]

For particularly lavish celebrations, especially the feast of San Petronio, it was necessary to hire additional musicians. The account books are full of payments to musicians from other cities and courts. These payments, first documented in 1450, went to musicians both from large cultural centers such as Venice, Milan, Mantua, Rome, Perugia, Lucca, Modena, and Florence, and smaller towns such as Piombino, Mirandola, and Pistoia. Bologna returned the favor, sending its musicians to other towns for special occasions. In 1538, Pope Paul III took musicians from the Concertino Palatino, among others, to a peace conference in Nice.[30]

The town band of Lucca, an independent republic, was founded in 1372 and reorganized in 1543 under Nicolao Dorati, who continued to lead it until his death in 1593. Dorati was both a highly regarded trombonist and composer of six collections of madrigals. The document that decreed his appointment contains interesting details about the musicians' tendency to quarrel and their need for regular rehearsals. As of 1543, the band had five players: Dorati and Nicolao di Ferrara were the trombonists.[31]

When Dorati died in 1593, no one was designated leader of the band until 1598, when Francesco Guami returned to Lucca to close out an illustrious career. His reputation has always been overshadowed by that of his brother Gioseffo. They were born in or near Lucca, Gioseffo in about 1540 and Francesco in about 1544, and were sent to Venice for musical study under the patronage of two politically connected merchants. Both of them served the court of Duke Albrecht V in Munich.

Gioseffo, a virtuoso organist and composer, eventually became Lassus's assistant director. Francesco, highly regarded as an instrumentalist and composer, did not achieve an administrative position. He left Munich in 1580, probably to be chapel master at the court of Margrave Philip II at Baden-Baden. His salary was as much as he and his brother together had made in Munich, but when Philip died in 1588, the chapel was dissolved. Guami's next known job was chapel master at San Marciliano in Venice. Between 1587 and 1597, he also appears to have been part of the band at San Marco in Venice.[32]

In Lucca, he was *maestro di cappella*, a title usually associated with leadership of either a cathedral or a court chapel. There are two possible explanations. First, it may be a courtesy title in recognition of his previous cathedral service. Second, the band had been known as the Cappella Palatina at least since its reorganization 50 years earlier. After Guami's death in 1601, the town did not designate a leader for the band again until 1609. Perhaps

the council believed that the title should only be given to someone of similar stature to Dorati or Guami.[33]

Politically, Venice was a republic, headed by an elected doge. The doges, especially Marin Grimani (r. 1595–1605), maintained a musical establishment that was the equal of most princely courts. Ceremonial music appears to have been even more important in Venice than elsewhere. For example, Lassus wrote more than a thousand works, but barely two dozen ceremonial motets. The extant works of Giovanni Gabrieli are only about a hundred, but nearly all of them were in one way or another composed for ceremonial use.

Bergamo submitted to a succession of different overlords beginning in 1331. By 1491, when it established its first band of *piffari*, it was under Venetian rule. The new band probably consisted entirely of shawms of various sizes until 1500, when trombonist Martinus de Besutio joined it.[34] He was also a member of the trumpet corps,

Fig. 6.4. Excerpt from "La Processione del Doge, nella Domenica della Palme" (The Procession of the Doge on Palm Sunday) by Mattio Pagan (1556–1569). Print Collection, Miriam and Ira D. Wallach Division of Art, Prints and Photographs, The New York Public Library, Astor, Lenox and Tilden Foundations.

and so became the first person to serve in both ensembles. His instrument as a member of the *piffari* is listed in the archives as *tuba major*, certainly a Latin equivalent of the Italian word "trombone." As in much of the rest of Europe, the fortunes of the band were intimately connected with economic and military conditions. Thus, as a result of war and plague, the *piffari* had to be disbanded in 1515.

In 1538, the band was reconstituted, with members drawn from local families of wind players. This time, it appears that the instrumentation was two shawms and three trombonists: Hieronymus de Morarijs, Cerbonio Besutio (son of Martinus), and Antonio Scandello. The last two named later became internationally famous, but only after they left Bergamo. The city ceased to support the band after 1548. Statutes forbidding or limiting various musical activities prove that wind music continued to be heard even without an official town band.

In contrast to the instability of the town band, Bergamo had supported a corps of trumpet players beginning no later than the early fourteenth century and continued to do so throughout the sixteenth century without interruption. It was paid twice as much as the town band. Playing simple trumpet calls was but a necessary prelude to their real job of making official proclamations. All that was required of them by statute was the ability to play with a sustained and resonant sound in order to attract attention for the proclamation.

In this difference of status between the trumpets and the band, Bergamo's practice was typical of its time. While to twenty-first-century eyes the trumpet corps is a musically inferior ensemble, to sixteenth-century eyes it had the more prestige and social importance. The trumpets were associated mostly with the dignity of the town council, whereas the band was associated with entertainment and decoration for special occasions.

During the reign of Marquis Francesco II Gonzaga (r. 1484–1519), especially under the influence of his wife, Isabella d'Este, Mantua became an important center of musical patronage and innovation. There are few surviving references to music in the court of his son and successor Federico (r. 1519–40, duke from 1530). It is evident, however, that the *piffari* were maintained throughout his reign, indicating that it was more a necessary image of the dignity of the court than an expression of his taste. After 1558, the dukes were again important patrons of music. The death of Vincenzo II (r. 1626–27) touched off a succession war that forever ended Mantua's importance as a cultural center.[35]

The Gonzagas held their musicians to the highest standards and paid them as little as they could get away with. As a result, turnover was high. Notable among the recruits was the Pelizzari family: Antonio, his daughters Lucia and Isabetta, and his sons Annibale and Bartolomeo. They joined the court in 1588, and some of them served as late as 1615, partly, no doubt, as a result of Vincenzo I's willingness to pay female singers lavishly. In addition to being fine singers, however, Lucia and Isabetta performed on cornett and trombone.[36] Although it was not unusual for primarily instrumental performers to sing from time to time, it was very unusual for people who were primarily singers—especially women—to play wind instruments.

In 1609, Claudio Monteverdi, the Gonzagas' musical director, was asked to recruit wind players. Writing to Alessandro Striggio (court counselor as well as the librettist for *Orfeo*), Monteverdi noted that he had begun negotiations with a father and two sons, who wanted considerably more money than the duke was likely to pay. Striggio instructed him to string them along, neither hiring them nor dashing their hopes entirely. There is no indication of the outcome, but two years later, he requested that Monteverdi find a wind player who could play recorder, cornett, trombone, flute, and bassoon to bring the wind band up to five members. Monteverdi reported that he had found a young man who could play all of those instruments plus gamba and viola, and who was agreeable to the duke's requirements: "to hear a variety of wind instruments play in private, in church, in procession, and atop city walls; now madrigals, now French songs, now airs, and now dance songs."[37]

Ceremonial occasions for which the wind band played included coronations of a new duke, the election of a new emperor, weddings of dukes or members of their family, and visits by high-ranking dignitaries. Besides a wide variety of vocal works, possible repertoire for the band on various occasions included sinfonias and canzonas by Giovanni Gastoldi and Ottavio Bargnani and the opening toccatas of Monteverdi's *Orfeo* and *Vespers*.[38] Trombones also took part in the new medium of opera. Monteverdi called for them at least in *Orfeo* (1607) and possibly *Ariana* (1608) and other lost works as late as *Andromeda* (1618).

The Este family continued to rule Ferrara until Duke Alfonso II died without heir in 1597, at which time it was annexed to the Papal States. There is no general survey of music in Ferrara to follow up on Lockwood's study of the court of Ercole I, but it continued to be one of the more glamorous of Italian courts up to the very end. The trombonists of the court surely played exactly the same kinds of music for the same kinds of occasions as any other court. There is, however, one particular large ensemble at which Ferrara excelled.

In 1549, Cristoforo da Messisbugo, a steward in the Este household, published a cookbook, intended in part to provide a pattern for how to plan a successful entertainment. He described ten banquets, three lunches, and a party that he had organized. Music played a prominent role in three of these. For each course, a different combination of voices and instruments performed. All three of these banquets used a six-piece band of trombones and shawms or cornetts. During the first two, a single trombone played at least one piece along with a mixed ensemble of soft instruments and, sometimes, voices.

Each banquet ended with the kind of grand concerto for which Ferrara became famous by the end of the century. In the first case, a piece by the concertmaster Alfonso della Viola, was performed by six voices, six viols, a lute, a lira, a "citara," a trombone, tenor and bass recorders, a flute, a "sordina," and a large and small harpsichord. The second ended with an ensemble of five voices, five viols, a harpsichord, and one each of bass recorder, lira, trombone, and flute. Messisbugo did not specify the instruments used on the last occasion, but says that it was most divine music by various instruments.[39]

Although Bottrigari wrote an entire treatise to explain and justify his disapproval of large mixed ensembles, he acknowledged that the Ferrarese grand concerto always made a good effect. There were three chief reasons: the duke commanded such a concert only rarely; the musicians rehearsed much more for them than for other performances; and the repertoire was limited to two pieces that had been especially composed for such an occasion. One of them was the piece by Alfonso della Viola mentioned above. The other was by his successor, Luzzasco Luzzaschi. Therefore, with no new music to learn, the entire rehearsal time could be spent on ironing out the inevitable problems of intonation and balance.

Ferrara was not the only court where such a grand concerto was performed. Bottrigari mentioned Venice and Verona with approval. Other observers may not have agreed with Bottrigari that the Ferrarese group was the most impressive. A Florentine visitor sniffed that the Ferrarese might not be so proud of an ensemble of fifty players if they knew that Florence assembled a hundred musicians for similar occasions.[40]

After the death of Lorenzo de' Medici in 1492, members of the Medici family contended against anti-Medici republican factions for control of Florence for forty years. Although the Medici were not the only Renaissance rulers to use theatrical extravaganzas for political ends, they did so more thoroughly and more spectacularly than anyone else.

Pope Clement VII (Giulio de' Medici) and Emperor Charles V reached an important agreement in 1529 that included recognizing the Medici family as hereditary rulers of Florence. Alessandro de' Medici, designated the first Duke of Florence, was murdered in 1537 before he held power securely. Duke Cosimo I (r. 1537–74) came from a minor branch of the family that had not previously been involved in politics. Upon Alessandro's murder, he had himself elected as head of the Florentine republic and only began to call himself the Duke after he was certain of imperial backing. His marriage in 1539 was therefore critical to his ability to hold on to power. The elaborate wedding festivities included a comedy with *intermedii*. This play and all of the music associated with it are still extant and have been issued in a modern edition. Some numbers required one to four trombones.[41]

Cosimo's long reign was very prosperous and successful. He was succeeded by his sons Francis (r. 1574–87) and Ferdinand I (r. 1587–1609), who had to renounce a cardinalship in order to get married in 1589. This wedding likewise featured a comedy with *intermedii* which has survived and been issued in a modern edition. It likewise requires trombones.[42] Cosimo II (r. 1609–20) died leaving a ten-year-old son as heir, Ferdinand II (r. 1620–70). During his minority, his mother and grandmother ruled as regents. As Ferdinand proved to be a weak ruler, the death of Cosimo II marks the beginning of a long decline of Tuscan power and influence.

Of four musicians Cosimo I retained from Alessandro's household, two were trombonists. Four of the eleven musicians Cosimo hired were trombonists. At least two of these early trombonists were outstanding musicians. A group of students known as the Franciosini initially came from the Spedale degli Innocenti (the orphanage of Santi Annunziata). In 1586, two of them played cornett, transverse flute, viola, and trombone at the wedding of Cesare d'Este and Virginia de' Medici in Florence. Eight Franciosini were among the musicians for the 1589 *intermedii*. Four trombonists among the Franciosini eventually became salaried members of the court.[43]

The major composer of Florentine instrumental ensemble music in the early years of the seventeenth century, Lorenzo Allegri was among the first to write orchestral suites. The instrumentation of these pieces, written for court ballets between 1608 and 1616, is unspecified, but the preface indicates that they can be performed with a mixed ensemble of strings and winds. Using the titles in the table of contents, it is possible to identify music used in eight different court ballets. Antonio Lassagnini is known to have played trombone in the first of them, for the wedding of Crown Prince Cosimo.[44]

After Cosimo II became duke, there is a noticeable decline in the number of wind players. Of 24 musicians hired during his reign, Kirkendale identifies only three as wind players. It appears that few musicians of any description were hired during the regency that followed his death. Many musicians joined the Florentine court during the long reign of Ferdinand II. Only Lorenzo Buti, hired in 1640, is identifiable as a trombonist, and his primary instrument appears to have been the violin.[45]

An inventory of instruments at the Accademia Filarmonica of Verona, taken in 1585, lists 6 keyboard instruments of four different kinds, 37 stringed instruments of four different kinds, and 80 wind instruments: 30 recorders, 15 transverse flutes, 4 bagpipes, 4 crumhorns, 1 bassoon, 23 cornetts, and 3 trombones. An inventory of the musical instruments owned by Count Mario Bevilacqua, taken at his death in 1593, listed one each of 4 different keyboard instruments, 22 stringed instruments of five different kinds, and 52 wind instruments: 16 recorders, 6 transverse flutes, 6 *bassanelli*, 6 rackets, 4 crumhorns, 1 bassoon, 11 cornetts, and 2 trombones, one large and the other small (probably tenor and bass).[46] These instruments were used for concerts for Bevilacqua's private pleasure and that of a highly exclusive audience.

In both inventories, wind instruments outnumbered stringed instruments. Recorders, viols, and cornetts were the most common instruments. It seems odd that there would be so many treble instruments and so few bass instruments. Inventories of music books indicate that most of the music was vocal music, such as madrigals and motets, performed by a mixed group of voices and instruments. The instruments had to be able to blend with the voices and not cover them.

England

Although the royal court was not the only notable musical center in England, it flourished at the expense of other institutions. The court appropriated the best musicians for the pleasure of the reigning monarch and left the rest of the country to do the best it could with lesser talent. Noble households seem not to have employed musicians as permanent retainers, although they hired them on a freelance basis and owned large collections of various instruments.

Most musicians in England, as elsewhere, did not have steady employment. They played in taverns and depended on a succession of weddings, dances, and other similar occasions. The majority had been itinerant minstrels most of the way through the Middle Ages, but found increasing pressure to settle in one place. In England, much of that pressure came in the form of strict

laws against vagrancy. As the sixteenth century opened, however, itinerant musicians still commonly competed against a town's permanent residents.

Henry VIII (r. 1509–47) replaced the earlier minstrel structure with the King's Musick, household musicians in daily attendance on the king. Henry loved music passionately and spent money on it freely. The trombone played a very important role in Tudor secular music. From his accession until the English Civil War, there were always trombonists on the payroll, usually at least six and sometimes as many as twelve. Trombonists were usually paid more than other instrumentalists. The importance of the trombone did not die with Henry. Five years after his death, trombonists' wages accounted for about 9% of the court's spending on secular music.[47]

The King's Musick was divided into a number of discrete groups, which were organized at different times in his reign. In addition to the trombone/shawm band he inherited from his father, he hired a new trombone consort from Venice, which included members of the Bassano family. The distinction between the two is carefully maintained in the records, so they must have had different functions. Henry also had a viol consort, a recorder consort, and a flute consort. Before the end of his reign, most of the members of the flute consort could also play cornett. A trombone may have been used as a bass instrument in this consort. The combination of cornetts and trombones grew in importance until the organization of the King's Musick into discrete consorts could no longer be sustained.[48]

Neither Edward VI (r. 1547–53) nor Mary I (r. 1553–58) were important musical patrons, although they kept the same basic structure. At Mary's death, she passed 41 musicians (not counting the Chapel Royal and the trumpet corps) to Elizabeth I (r. 1558–1603). The day before her coronation in 1558, Elizabeth made a triumphal entry into London, with allegorical pageants presented at twelve triumphal arches. A contemporary description mentions "a noyse of loude instruments upon the top" of one of them. Elizabeth loved music, but being less willing to spend money on it, patronized it on a smaller scale than her father had. She had 41 musicians in 1558, 33 in 1570, 24 in 1580, 29 in 1590, and 38 at her death in 1603. The larger numbers at her accession and death may represent a temporary enlargement of the household for the royal funerals and coronations of those years.[49]

James I (r. 1603–25) kept an average of 40 musicians. His wife and son each had 15 musicians in their personal households. When Charles I (r. 1625–49) became king, he augmented the King's Musick, temporarily bringing its total to 78 musicians. On average, he appears to have kept 65 musicians until the Civil War. Although the number of musicians at court increased significantly during these two reigns, there were fewer trombonists.

In 1630, Charles reorganized the King's Musick, combining all of the previously autonomous consorts into one group. It is possible to discern two very different bodies of music that used trombones. The traditional wind band consisted of shawms (or by 1630, cornetts) and trombones. It played for ceremonial occasions, for dances, and in the theaters. One printed collection illustrates the kind of music it played. In 1621, John Adson published a collection called *Courtly Masking Ayres for violins, consorts and cornets.* The title page proclaims that it was "framed only for instruments; of which kind, these are the first that have ever been printed." The collection consists of 21 five-part pieces and 10 six-part pieces. Three of the five-part pieces specify cornetts and trombones.

Plenty of similar music that does not specify instrumentation was at least useful to and possibly intended for the wind band. One especially noteworthy example is a set of part-books now known as Fitzwilliam Mus. MSS 24. E.13-17, prepared for and by the band of James I. It consists of Italian and English pieces. Some of the English pieces were composed by wind players in the king's household, who each played a variety of instruments. The music could have been played by any of the groups of instruments in which the composers took part, one of which was the shawm and trombone band. With the addition of newer pieces, the collection was used after the Restoration by Charles II (r. 1660–85).[50]

The other body of music, the mixed consort, was associated with a smaller group of trombonists who specialized on the instrument. Mixed consort does not refer here to a mixture of wind instruments, but rather to wind instruments participating in an ensemble with stringed instruments. Because this repertoire is distinct from the traditional wind band, it will be described elsewhere.

In response to challenges from itinerants, London's resident musicians complained to the city council in 1500 and obtained an ordinance that served as a charter for the Company of Musicians. Desiring more protection and authority than was available from the city, they obtained a royal patent of incorporation from James I in 1604.

Members of the Company of Musicians had two opportunities to secure steady employment. They could strive to qualify either for the King's Musick or for a position among the city waits. London boasted the largest and most prestigious group of waits in the country. From 1475 until the middle of the seventeenth century, London officially had positions for six. From 1502 to 1548,

each one was allowed to keep one apprentice, making as many as twelve musicians available for official functions. After 1548, each wait was allowed two apprentices, making eighteen musicians available. Apprentices were a lucrative benefit for the waits. A good one could be sent as a substitute for some performances. And whether the apprentice played with or in place of the wait, the wait pocketed the money thus earned.

From 1605 to 1635, there were still officially six waits, but the city began to make special appointments that in effect increased the number of both waits and apprentices. Unofficially, there may have been as many as 10 or 11 waits and 20 apprentices. They never performed as a single large ensemble. Various groups of them performed for whatever function required their presence. They also competed for casual work with other London musicians. (Members of the King's Musick may have also done so, at least in the neighborhoods where they lived.)[51]

From the earliest times, the waits played primarily shawms and trombones, although they were certainly expected to be able to play other instruments as needed. Vestiges of the ancient watch duty persisted into the sixteenth century, but their duties consisted chiefly of processions and public concerts. By the opening of the seventeenth century, however, they had largely ceased to play in processions. Instead, they took up fixed positions along the route, implying that they were no longer primarily a wind ensemble, but expected to play viols or lutes, instruments unsuitable for marching.

In the last quarter of the sixteenth century, there is ample evidence that trombones were used in theatrical performances, although it is not clear who played them. The Admiral's Men, England's most important theater company, owned at least one trombone. The trombonist spoke the prologue to Ben Jonson's *Every Man Out of His Humor* (1599). There was a wide variety of music that would have been appropriate in English drama, played both on stage and off. Instrumental music was also played before the play began and possibly between the acts.

In the beginning, the waits improvised their music. Once they started playing from notation, their music was in manuscript, which has since been lost. Between 1590 and 1638, at least 23 collections of music consisting of, or at least including, instrumental ensemble music were published in England. There is no reason to suppose that it was essentially different in style or function from the unpublished music. It therefore gives us a window on the kinds of music played by London's waits.

Among these collections, John Adson's *Courtly Masking Ayres* has already been mentioned. The reference to the court in the title should not obscure the fact that, as published music, these pieces were available to any band whose musicians were good enough to play them. The title page of Anthony Holborne's *Pavans, Galliards, Almaines, and Other Short Aeires* mentions "viols, violins, or other musicall winde instruments." This odd phrase is a reminder that the string and wind idioms had not yet diverged and that, regardless of the instruments specifically named in these collections, they were playable by any instruments then current. Presumably, gentlemen amateurs would play them on viols and professionals would play them on violins and/or wind instruments.

By 1500, 21 English towns had waits. Between 1500 and 1642, the outbreak of the English Civil War, 36 more towns established bands. All but the smallest towns hired at least three waits. Larger towns kept four, or even five. No other English town matched London's six. Some towns paid a steady salary; others did not. Some towns provided the instruments that their waits played; in others, the waits had to purchase their own. Most towns allowed their waits to travel and gave visiting waits limited opportunities to play in the city. Resident waits enjoyed a monopoly on the most lucrative private engagements. The combination of shawms and trombones was the most common ensemble at the start of the sixteenth century, but as time went on, waits were expected to play stringed instruments more and more.[52]

The Trombone in Church

The use of wind instruments in the liturgy occurred sporadically as early as the first decade of the sixteenth century, but did not become a common practice until the 1560s. The publication of church music suitable for performance with an instrumental ensemble follows a similar history. Isolated titles came out for several years before there was sufficient demand for significant numbers of publications.

When instruments first began to participate in the liturgy, they alternated with the choir. This practice is especially well documented in the case of the organ. As it seems unlikely that instrumental ensembles had a significantly different role in the liturgy than the organ, the many books written to guide the organist also serve to explain how other instruments were used within the Mass. The organist provided fairly continuous music remaining silent only during the readings from the Epistle and the Gospel and a few other places. The organist joined the choir for all five sections of the Ordinary. For most of the Proper, the choir did not sing at all. The celebrant spoke these prayers while the organ played.

There was opportunity for several extended instrumental compositions within the Mass.

As early as the late fifteenth century, the organ also began to substitute for the choir for certain parts of the Proper. At some point in the sixteenth century, however, it began to play along with the choir instead of alternating with it. An organ book compiled for Santa Maria Maggiore in Bergamo in about 1550 may be among the earliest that could be used as a set of organ accompaniments for chant as opposed to alternation.[53]

Several collections of instrumental church music of the early seventeenth century identify exactly where in the liturgy each piece was intended to be played. For example, Carlo Milanuzzi's *Armonia sacra* (1622) includes a concerto "per l'Introito," a canzona "per l'Epistola" (which must have been played before or after, but not during the reading of the Epistle), a concerto "per l'Offertorio," a concerto "per l'Eleuation," a canzon "per il Post Communio," and a canzon "per il Deo Gratias." This last piece, titled "La Guaralda," for violin, trombone, and organ, was composed by the otherwise unknown P. A. Mariani.[54] That Milanuzzi spent his entire career serving small churches indicates that the use of an instrumental ensemble was not limited to large churches. Milanuzzi's collection also exemplifies a style of monodic music for a small group of singers and instrumentalists, the earliest published example of which is *Cento Concerti Ecclesiastici* by Lodovico Viadana. A number of these pieces call for trombone, as do several small-scale motets by Alessandro Grandi, among others.

The role of the organ and/or instrumental ensemble in Vespers was not significantly different from their participation in the Mass. In addition to whatever they did with the choir, they performed canzonas or similar pieces as a substitute for the antiphons that followed the Magnificat or the Psalms.

Spain and Latin America

Spanish churches were among the earliest to welcome the participation of musical instruments in the liturgy. Spain had more than two dozen important musical centers, each with its own traditions. Whether because of economic conditions or local taste, even some large churches in Spain either did not use instruments at all or used them only on special occasions. At the Escorial, the palace/monastery constructed by Philip II, even polyphony was forbidden in keeping with the king's adherence to the most severe interpretation of the Counter Reformation. Elsewhere, notably Toledo, accompanied music became the norm even for ordinary services.[55]

At first, churches that used instruments hired the town band or the local court band intermittently for special occasions. By the mid-1510s, the cathedral of Seville hired musicians on a fairly regular basis. In 1526, the chapter decided that it would be preferable to establish its own band. Before the end of the century, there were resident wind bands of shawms and trombones in at least nine other cathedrals and some parish churches.[56]

One of the rationales for Spanish conquest of the Americas was to spread the Catholic faith to the new world. Therefore, missionaries assigned to working with the Aztecs arrived in Mexico as early as 1523 and Mex-ico City got its first bishop in 1528. As early as 1554, the cathedral boasted a sizable instrumental ensemble, including trombone, despite the efforts of one archbishop to suppress all instruments except the organ. Smaller parochial churches, even less restrained by the archbishop, used instruments with abandon.

By all accounts, the Aztecs learned to sing and play Spanish music very quickly. Some of them could even make European instruments and compose polyphonic music. In 1561, reports of the extent of the Aztec's musical activities reached Philip II. He disapproved of the cost of supporting a large number of instrumentalists who

Fig. 6.5. Spanish church band. Bronze medallion by Juan Marin and Bautista Vásquez, cast by Bartolomé Morel (1564). Used with permission of Seville Cathedral.

played "trumpets, clarions, shawms, trombones, flutes, cornetts, dulzainas, fifes, viols, rebecs, and other kinds of instruments" and demanded a reduction in the number of Aztec musicians.[57]

The king's decree had only a short-term effect. An ordinance of 1573 authorized the use of vocal and instrumental musicians to induce the natives to congregate in towns. An ordinance of 1618 decreed that in any native town of 100 or more, two or three musicians would be exempt from paying tribute to the crown. Local authorities sometimes managed to increase that number. Recent research has detailed the use of instruments (including the trombone) in the towns of Santafé (in present day Colombia) and La Plata (in present day Bolivia). Both of these towns were established in 1538. The earliest documentation of instruments in the Santafé cathedral comes in a government official's report of 1598. The cathedral of La Plata had instruments no later than 1603. These towns used the same instruments used in Spain, including shawms, flutes, trumpets, trombones, and curtals, well into the seventeenth century. Most of the players appear to be either natives or slaves. Trombones are also attested in the cathedral of Lima in the first half of the seventeenth century and in Cuzco (both in modern Peru) in the late 1670s.[58]

Italy

The earliest reference I have found to the use of instruments in an Italian church is at Santa Maria Maggiore in Bergamo. In 1527, the church's archives discuss payment for "the son of Cispinus the pauper, *cornicine*." The term literally means horn player, but seems to have been used generically for wind player. Later that year, the church hired a *cornicine* on a five-year contract to play at sung Masses and Vespers on all single feast days and at Compline during Lent. In addition to performing, it was his responsibility to instruct four students in the art of wind playing, giving the church a five-piece band.

The archives do not mention wind instruments again until 1540. In that year, Cerbonio Besutio and Antonio Scandello, two members of the newly reconstituted town band, were listed among the instrumentalists who received an Easter bonus. There is nothing to indicate that an Easter bonus for wind players in the church was anything new or unusual, but the fact that these two men were members of the town band makes it likely that the church did not have its own band at the time. The same two players received an Easter bonus in 1541. In August of that year, a third wind player also received payment from the church. Beginning in January 1542, the church began to pay a regular salary of 25 *librae*. The salary was

doubled in February 1543. As generous as that sounds, it was apparently not enough to satisfy Besutio and Scandello. (The *cornicine* had been offered 90 *librae* in 1526.) They wrangled over salary with the church until 1547, when they left town.[59]

Until more archival research is completed at more Italian towns and courts, it will be impossible to be certain how representative Bergamo was. The first appearance of trombonists in the records of other churches is considerably later: Capella Giulia (1546), San Petronio in Bologna (1560), Modena (1562), Padua (1565), and Mantua (1588).[60] These dates may indicate a change in performance practice (trombonists participating in services for the first time) or merely bookkeeping (churches forming their own band rather than relying on freelance musicians or having performance in church part of the ordinary duties of a town or court band).

The circumstances of the first trombonist to join the chapel at the Sienna Cathedral are surely unique. In 1550, the chapel choir consisted of seven boys and 12 adults, a fairly large choir. War broke out in 1552, and the town was under siege from March 1554 to April 1555. By that time, starvation had reduced it to a third of its former size, and it was forced to capitulate to the army of Emperor Charles V.

During the siege, the chapel continued to function as in pre-war days, apparently in the attempt to maintain an air of normality and to foster civic pride. In defeat, however, it became unsustainable. By November 1556, it had only four adults and was temporarily disbanded. The Spanish overlord ordered its reinstatement, but sufficient numbers of singers were not available. The newly reconstituted chapel consisted of two male sopranos, two tenors, one bass, and a trombonist.

Chapel records do not mention the trombonist between 1561 and 1565, but from 1565 through the end of the century, either a trombonist or a singer who could play trombone was a permanent fixture. It appears that, at first, the trombonist was an emergency measure to cover an otherwise missing bass part. But later, this unique performance practice became one way for Sienna to maintain artistic, if not political, independence.[61]

The court was not the only important musical center in Florence. At least four churches regularly performed polyphonic liturgies. As far as the use of the trombone is concerned, the most important appears to be Santi Annunziata. It did not pay monthly salaries to very many musicians, but from about 1576 until the end of 1642, more than two dozen different court musicians performed there for various special occasions. As the instrumentalists were often Franciosini from the church's own orphanage, wind music must have been a prominent feature of festival services there. Some of the same musicians appear in payment records for Santa Maria Novella.[62]

When Guglielmo Gonzaga established the new ducal basilica of Santa Barbara (1562–65) and reconstituted the ducal chapel, he was greatly interested in upholding the reforms of the Council of Trent. During his lifetime, the repertory was probably more austere than at a less reform-minded court and slower to accept new styles and practices.

In 1577, documents indicate that the chapel consisted of 12 musicians, most of whose roles are not identified. In 1580, however, all of the 15 musicians were identified. Instrumentalists were limited to two organists, a harper, and a trombonist. By 1589 when the chapel had grown to 23 members, the trombonist was gone; there were two

string players and an organist. Some of the singers played lute or harp. No other trombonist appears in chapel records until 1604, when a German trombonist and trumpeter named Giovanni Tedesco Srofenaur briefly joined a significant and varied group of instruments. The chapel reached its maximum strength, 30 musicians, in 1621, none of whom were wind players. Antonio Aldovino, one of the singers noted in records in 1612 and 1627–29, may have also played trombone.[63]

Although Monteverdi had no responsibility for church music at Mantua, he published a setting of the Marian Vespers in 1610. This music, while clearly composed with the forces of the court of Mantua in mind, looks outward, showing his familiarity with developments in Rome and Venice. Several movements make use of trombones, notably the "Sonata sopra Sancta Maria," for solo voice and instrumental ensemble. The *Vespers* may

Fig. 6.6. Musical angels, by Bartolomeo Roverio. Detail of the ceiling, S. Marco, Milan, Italy (1617). Photo Credit: Alinari / Art Resource, NY.

have helped Monteverdi obtain the position of chapel master at San Marco in Venice in 1613.

The procurators of San Marco hired cornettist Girolamo dalla Casa in 1568 to form a wind band. Even after this permanent band was established, the basilica regularly hired freelance musicians at least until 1617. The impetus for forming it seems to have been the return of Andrea Gabrieli from Munich, where he had worked under Orlande de Lassus. At first, there could have been no more than three or four wind players, paid out of dalla Casa's pocket. Cornettist Giovanni Bassano was hired directly by the procurators in 1576, beginning a major expansion of the band at San Marco. By 1582, the treasurer had the authority to pay for musicians as needed without getting permission from the procurators. The full-time staff now included six players, augmented by twenty or more others for special occasions. The presence of the band (as well as the two organists) was expected only for festivals, not for the daily celebration of the Mass, but Venice did not observe the Roman rite; it held many more festivals than other churches.[64]

Under dalla Casa, the primary function of the instrumental ensemble appears to have been to reinforce the voices or, if necessary, substitute for an absent singer, but it also presented instrumental concerts. In addition to the traditional motets, the ensemble could draw on a considerable body of canzonas, ricercares, and other kinds of pieces that Venetian publishers issued with increasing frequency. The impetus for this repertoire, however, came more from organists than from wind instrumentalists. When dalla Casa died in 1601, Bassano succeeded him. During the service of these two leaders, the nucleus of the ensemble consisted of cornetts and trombones, but stringed instruments were not absent and must have grown in importance. After Bassano's death in 1617, the next concert-master was a violinist, who kept the position until 1661 and transformed the group into a string-based ensemble.

Venice of the late Renaissance is best known for large-scale polychoral music. Its use in Venice can be traced to a collection of music by Adriano Willaert published in 1550. Although Willaert had established Venice as an important musical center, his polychoral music did not have any immediate impact. Until Giovanni Gabrieli became organist at San Marco in 1585, the only other composer of polychoral music appears to be Andrea Gabrieli. The posthumous publication of his pieces in 1587 opened the floodgates. Although they can be sung *a capella*, the participation of instruments (including trombones on the lowest parts) is necessary for a successful performance of these pieces. The use of high, middle, and low choirs, as described by Praetorius, is evident in Andrea Gabrieli's works.

It is with Giovanni Gabrieli, however, that the Venetian polychoral style reached its pinnacle of compositional virtuosity and emotional range. From his earliest instrumental music, he began to write melodies with an instrumental rather than vocal idiom, demanding not only agility, but virtuosity. Their range and tessitura would be unreasonably difficult for even the best singers, but lie very well for cornetts and trombones.

San Marco was not the only Venetian church to use wind instruments. Francesco Guami served as chapel master at San Marciliano in the 1590s. There would seem to be no reason to appoint an instrumentalist to lead a musical establishment that did not use instruments. Thomas Coryat, an English visitor in 1608, reported having heard trombones not only at San Marco, but also at the parish church of St. Laurence. But he reserved his most rapturous comments for the feast of St. Roche, which probably took place at the Scuola di San Rocco: "Sometimes sixteene played together upon their instruments, ten Sagbuts, foure Cornets, and two Violdegambaes of an extraordinary greatness; sometimes tenne, sixe Sagbuts and foure Cornets; sometimes two, a Cornet and a treble violl."[65]

Bologna's most important church, San Petronio, hired its first trombonist in 1560. He remained the only instrumentalist other than organist on the church's payroll until 1574, when a cornett player joined him. Not until 1593 did San Petronio have a larger instrumental group: three trombones, a cornett, and a violin. By 1610, the ensemble consisted of seven trombones, two cornets, and one violin. In 1614, there were five trombones, a cornett, and two violins.[66]

In 1576, Maria Isabella Trombetta joined the convent of Santi Gervasio e Protasio. Her dowry contract required her to bring her trombone to play the bass, certainly a necessary function in a choir of all women's voices. There is no indication of what social class this woman represented, but the main reason why members of the nobility did not play wind instruments was the concern that their faces would be distorted in the process. Cloistered nuns, invisible to their audience, were not in any position to care about that.[67]

One consequence of the Council of Trent was to minimize the interaction between nuns and the outside world. In fact, in 1580, the Archbishop of Bologna issued a number of decrees that had the effect of making the nuns heard but not seen. Their worship services became very attractive to the public. Although these regulations nominally remained in effect for 180 years, appeals to the Sacred Congregation softened the effect of some of them. Others were ignored. In 1600, the nuns of San Giovanni Battista requested an outside trombone teacher. A teacher identified as Geronimo del Trombone asked for permission to teach in convents on account of the burden of being the father of four daughters. An inventory of nuns' property in Santa Margarita in 1613 includes trombones, along with several other instruments that were nominally forbidden. Since trombones were associated at one time or another with three of the 24 convents in Bologna, they may have been used at some convents in other places.

Early in the seventeenth century, a new style of mass composition developed known as the concerted mass, a mixture of the old-fashioned choral mass and the new monodic style combining voices and instruments. The earliest description comes in Banchieri's *Conclusioni nel suono dell'Organo* (Bologna, 1609). The mass itself is no longer extant, but one of the four choirs was three trombones and one contralto voice. Concerted masses of this type became common not only in Bologna, but all over northern Italy. They constitute almost the only innovative music of the seventeenth century in which trombones commonly participated.[68]

One of the earliest significant composers of the concerted mass, Camillo Cortellini, learned to sing and play trombone and cornett, most likely from his father, and studied counterpoint with the leader of the Concerto Palatino. He became a member of that group in February 1577 as second cornett player. In 1593, he was hired as a singer at San Petronio, with the understanding that he would play trombone as required. After 1600, however, church records mention him exclusively as a trombonist. Meanwhile, his service in the Concerto Palatino continued, and he became its leader in 1611. He kept both jobs for the rest of his life and also worked at other churches.[69]

From 1595 to 1626, Cortellini published eleven collections of sacred music, including psalms, motets, and masses. His *Messe a otto voce* (1617) includes three trombones. His last published collection, *Messe concertante a otto voce* (1626), contains explicit instructions on how the instruments are to be used. The indication of trombone parts occurs in the alto, tenor, and bass partbooks of the second chorus. It is a mistake to conclude that the parts would therefore have been played on alto, tenor, and bass trombones; the alto trombone may have been unknown in Italy. Trombones and the chorus alternate verses. Because the trombone parts do not double voices but replace them, they are independent lines.

Germany and Flanders

Köchel first documented a trombone in the imperial chapel in 1680.[70] The significance of that date is strictly administrative. Before that time, there was little attempt to identify what instrument anyone played. As Maximilian I started the tradition of using wind instruments in the liturgy and Charles V continued it, every subsequent emperor probably heard trombones in sacred services at least on special occasions. The court of Ferdinand II made extensive use of the trombone. As this practice seems to have arisen from the emperor's fascination with Venetian polychoral music, and thus represents a departure from tradition, consideration of the music of his court is reserved for the next chapter.

The Bavarian court at Munich, under the leadership of Orlande de Lassus, boasted at least two excellent trombonists, Francesco Guami and Fileno Cornazzani. Many of Lassus's motets were printed with a rubric that was common in the sixteenth century: "apt for voices and instruments." The cover of his *Missae aliquit quinque vocum* (1589) depicts an instrumental ensemble that includes two trombones.[71] Although the musicians are gathered around a table, as if for a secular performance or for a rehearsal, and not in a choir loft or other obvious church setting, this cover points to the probability that Lassus used similar instruments in church.

The church of Our Lady in Antwerp, ruled by Spain after the abdication of Charles V, was so large that many masses could be sung in various places in the church at the same time without disturbing each other. It contained chapels for six confraternities. Most of the musicians on the church's payroll also served the confraternities. (Two other churches in Antwerp, St. James and St. George, were likewise home to at least one confraternity each.) Nightly services at both Our Lady and St. George included a *lof*, a Marian service held after Vespers that featured the *Salve Regina*. Each of the confraternities sponsored weekly masses. The rotation at Our Lady resulted in one votive mass every day of the week, Monday through Saturday.

Instruments were sometimes used for these votive masses. A statute of 1590 sets the pay scale for singers at four *stuivers* for singing without instruments and five *stuivers* for singing with instruments. The extra pay reflected the extra rehearsal that would have been necessary. The use of instruments began no later than 1508, when a payment was recorded for copying music for the town band. It appears that the *lof* was usually unaccompanied, but that a single instrumentalist, playing either cornett or trombone, joined the singers once or twice a week. In 1531 alone, Susato played trombone for the *lof*

Fig. 6.7. Angelic consort from the high altar at St. Maurice church, Fribourg, by Peter Spring (ca. 1600). *Brass Bulletin* 67 (1989): 55, © by Editions Bim /The Brass Press, www.editions-bim.com.

at Our Lady 19 times. Compared to the courts, churches in towns have not been studied much. Antwerp may or may not be representative. The practice of a single instrumentalist supporting the singers in a votive mass is also attested at 's-Hertogenbosch.[72]

Reformed churches led by Ulrich Zwingli and John Calvin did not use instruments. They even destroyed the organs in their churches. Lutheran churches, on the other hand, chose to reinterpret the traditional worship

service, not replace it. Martin Luther's concept of the priesthood of all believers led him to seek as much lay participation as possible. Therefore, congregational singing became a key element. But Luther also believed that limiting church music to what was simple enough for a musically uneducated congregation to sing would lead not to a sense of participation in a divine mystery, but to boredom and disinterest. Therefore, a trained choir still played an important role in his understanding of worship. (He also rejected the extreme iconoclasm of other reformers. Representational art, such as the altar carving in Fig. 6.7, was not excluded from Lutheran churches.)

In contrast to his enthusiasm for singing, Luther barely mentioned instruments at all. Passing references in some of his informal writings show that he did not disapprove of them, but neither did he consider them necessary. In practice, therefore, Lutheran churches used them the same way Catholic churches did. Not all churches of either denomination used instruments at all. When they did, the choir and organ (with or without other instruments) usually alternated verses of those parts of the service that they performed.[73]

The organ began to accompany the choir, not just alternate with it, in Italian churches around midcentury. Italian practices eventually caught on in Germany, and the use of instruments to accompany the choir must have been adopted in Lutheran churches without much comment. At first, the congregation sang without accompaniment, perhaps after an intonation on the organ. Instruments probably began to accompany the congregation at about the same time they began to accompany the choir.

Throughout the sixteenth century, therefore, whatever profound differences there were in the theological content of the service, the music at a Lutheran church would not have sounded much different from that in a Catholic church. But the Lutherans did not settle into this familiar practice without some interruptions and theological soul searching.

Churches in Nuremberg, for example, completely abandoned polyphonic music, the organ, and other musical instruments in their services in 1524. It took about twenty years to restore these practices. The political situation in Nuremberg made this liturgical experimentation somewhat risky. As a free imperial city, Nuremberg owed a special personal allegiance to the emperors, all of whom were Catholic. They would treat rumors of religious unorthodoxy in Nuremberg (or any other free imperial city) as a particularly serious matter. Therefore, the necessity to appear loyal to the emperor loomed large among the factors that eventually led the city council to adopt a more conservative liturgy than that adopted by many other Lutheran cities of a different status.

By 1589, individual bandsmen were assigned to play at services in specific churches in town, the council's angry response to their neglecting to appear for church services in favor of other musical opportunities. Five men were distributed among four churches. Since ordinarily a minimum of one cornett and one trombone would have been needed for each service, perhaps Nuremberg

followed the practice seen in Italian churches, requiring apprentices to play alongside the salaried musicians without pay. Because of Nuremberg's political situation, its liturgy cannot be considered typical, but since there was so little musical difference between Lutheran and Catholic services, it is at least representative of normal Lutheran use of instruments.[74]

The chorale, that most characteristically Lutheran musical form, did not transform Lutheran music into something truly distinctive until well into the seventeenth century. In the early decades of the century, however, Saxon composers under the influence of Venetian practices, created a body of music that made prominent use of the trombone. These include Praetorius, Schein, and Schütz.

Praetorius was chapel master at the court of Brunswick-Wolfenbüttel, but when the duke died in 1613, he was lent to the elector in Dresden as acting chapel master for the next two and a half years. After that, although still nominally employed at Wolfenbüttel, he traveled extensively until his death in 1621. His importance to the history of the trombone cannot be exaggerated. The second and third books of his *Syntagma musicum* are indispensable primary source material for the study of the music of the early Baroque. His own compositions provide illustrations of many of his performance practice recommendations.

These recommendations, however, were based on his understanding of Italian practice. Nearly every time Praetorius discusses how to use trombones, it is in the context of large-scale polychoral works in the manner of Giovanni Gabrieli. Within such a work, a choir might be made up of voices only, instruments only, or a mixture of voices and instruments. But where Gabrieli often specified instrumentation in his publications, Praetorius presents the music director with an array of possibilities from which to make choices, including a low choir of a single alto voice over three trombones.[75]

Concerning smaller works in the manner of Viadana or Grandi, using one, two, or three concerted voices accompanied only by organ or regal, Praetorius commented that many Germans thought this texture sounded empty. He felt the need to add a four-part choir, which could always sing with trombones or violins, and wrote that he achieved great acclaim for doing so. If one must use an organ alone for accompaniment of such music, the accompaniment must not include diminutions or runs. He thought flute stops playing such a texture will only bore the audience, so the organist is much better off selecting reed stops, which sound more like trombones. After commenting that viols have an advantage over wind instruments, not having to interrupt their sound to take a breath, Praetorius recommended playing one verse on viols, another on trombones, and a third on recorders and bassoons, thus playing this smaller-scale music with something akin to polychoral richness.[76]

Schein began his service in the electoral choir when he was 13, leaving to receive a university education. He spent the last 14 years of his short life as cantor of Thomaskirche in Leipzig. His works include four major collections of church music and some canzonas. The second volume of his *Opella nova* (1626) is especially noteworthy. It consists of 32 sacred concertos for three to six voices and various instruments. Besides several pieces for which the trombone is designated as the bass instrument, there are eight pieces with independent parts for one to three trombones.

Schütz, the first great composer to work in Dresden, studied in Venice under Giovanni Gabrieli from 1609 until 1612. Nominally in the service of the landgrave Moritz of Hessen-Kassel, he was summoned to Dresden to serve the elector Georg I in 1614. He made a second trip to Italy in 1628 and probably met Monteverdi. His *Psalmen Davids* (1619) and Part I of *Symphoniae sacrae* (1629) include important works with one to six trombone parts.[77]

England

The primary institution devoted to sacred music at the English court, the Chapel Royal, consisted entirely of singers. When instrumentalists were wanted, the King's Musick supplied them. There is no evidence that the trombone or any instrument other than the organ participated in the celebration of the mass or other liturgical services in England during the first half of the sixteenth century, even after Henry VIII and his entourage witnessed the French king's trombones at the Field of the Cloth of Gold in 1520. By about 1560, when the practice of using instruments in the liturgy was commonplace at several churches and chapels on the continent, it was still not recorded in England.

Elizabeth's reign saw some important changes. She insisted on such a showy service in her chapel, including the use of cornetts and trombones, that the use of the English language was said to be the only difference between her services and Catholic services at continental courts. The earliest document that explicitly states that instruments participated in the liturgy describes Elizabeth's visit to Worcester Cathedral in 1575, when there was "a grete and solempne (sic) noise of singing of service in the quire both by note and also by playing with cornets and sackbuts." An Italian visitor to Canter-

bury Cathedral in 1589 took note of the trombones and declared that, contrary to the propaganda he had heard about the destruction of culture by English Protestants, the English services sounded and looked as impressive as anything on the continent with the possible exception of the papal choir.[78]

The reorganization of the church under Henry VIII undermined the financial base of most English churches. They often could not afford to keep a full complement of choristers and paid their organists poorly. The great music produced for the Chapel Royal, the principal cathedrals, or university chapels had little impact on the musical experience of the rest of the country. Most churches would have had little opportunity to use instruments. In some larger churches, however, cornetts and trombones began to be used routinely. Whenever the queen visited an important church, the service would be especially lavish and impressive, most likely using her own musicians. The city waits were hired for Christmas in Norwich (1575) and for unspecified services at Chester (1591) and York (1623). In 1598, Canterbury Cathedral became the first English church to hire a permanent band of musicians. Subsequently, cathedrals in Dublin, Durham, and Gloucester added bands to their staffs.[79]

After Elizabeth's death, the use of instruments in English cathedrals increased, especially for major festivals. Other than the organ, trombones and cornetts were the instruments most frequently heard. Any other instruments, such as viols or recorders, appear to have been exceptional. One reason is that stringed instruments could not as easily stay in tune. Charles Butler commented:

> But becaus *Entata* [stringed instruments] ar often out of tun; (which soomtime happeneth in the mids of the Musik, when it is neither good to continue nor to correct the fault) therefore, to avoid all offence, (where the least shoolde not bee givn) in our Chyrch-solemnities onely the Winde-instruments (whose Notes ar constant) bee in use.[80]

It is a matter of conjecture just how they were used. Most likely, they doubled the voices. They may have also substituted for vocal lines. It is possible that they occasionally played accompaniments independent of the singers, although the evidence for this practice is strongest when verse anthems were played in homes, as opposed to during services.

Although Elizabeth and her successors preferred lavish church services, there was a strong undercurrent of a more austere Puritanism, which eventually prevailed. In 1627, the Provost of Trinity College Dublin disapproved of the "pompous service of Christ Church Dublin, which was attended and celebrated with all manner of instrumental music, as organs, sackbuts, cornets, viols, &c, as if it had been at the dedication of Nebuchadnezzar's golden image in the plain of Dura." The senior prebendary at Durham Cathedral used the same imagery in a sermon in 1628. He continued to express his disapproval of high-church worship for years thereafter.[81] Although they had little immediate influence, their ideology became official government policy under the Cromwells.

Mixed Ensembles

The very earliest repertoire of the wind band, in common with all other instrumental performances, included arrangements of the well-known secular songs of the day. As early as 1520, instrumental arrangements of French and Flemish chansons were known in both Italy and Germany as canzonas. By the end of the century, the term also referred to original compositions similar in style to the chanson. The first seems to be "La bella: Canzone di sonar," which concludes Nicolo Vicentino's fifth book of madrigals (1572). The earliest collection of original ensemble canzonas, Florentino Maschera's *Libro primo de canzoni da sonare*, appeared in 1582 and proved popular enough to justify a reprint in 1584. Once composers began to specify the instrumentation of their ensemble music, trombones joined ensembles with stringed instruments in both Italy and England.

Given the traditional importance of the wind band, and the fact that bandsmen had been arranging and distributing arrangements of vocal music for generations, it would be tempting to suppose that the first canzonas were published by and for bandsmen. Maschera, however, was a violinist. Nearly all of the other composers of canzonas were organists.

Because canzonas were primarily composed by church musicians, it would also seem that they were originally intended primarily, if not exclusively, as church music. In fact, by the time Maschera's collection appeared, Venetian publishers had been issuing collections of sacred music that mentioned the use of instruments for decades. The full title of the earliest of these, a collection of motets by Gombert published in 1539, proclaims that the music is suitable for performance with or by *lyris* and *tibijs*, that is, stringed or wind instruments. After about 1562, similar collections appeared frequently.[82]

The term *canzoni da sonare* used by Maschera eventually became *sonata*. After coexisting for a while, the newer term eventually supplanted the older one. During the time the two terms were both current, there is an important distinction between them. Most composers of canzonas were organists; most composers of sonatas were violinists. Most canzonas were written for church occasions. Even though the instrumentation is often unspecified, the choice of instruments was limited to church instruments: violins, cornetts, and trombones. A specified ensemble of violins, cornetts, and trombones is most likely to be a canzona. Sonata composers, on the other hand, explored new instrumental techniques and idioms, different combinations of instruments, indications of dynamics, bowings, and other effects.[83]

A sonata by Biagio Marini ("La Foscarina" from *Affetti musicali*, 1617) illustrates the exploration of new techniques and idioms. It is scored for two violins or cornetts and trombone or bassoon. Certain passages are marked "tremolo con l'arco" (tremolo with the bow) in the violin parts and "tremolo col strumento" (tremolo with the instrument) in the trombone part. In this case, tremolo refers to an imitation of the organ tremolo and was probably achieved by dividing a half note into four eighth notes and playing all of them with the bow moving in the same direction. The wind instruments had to imitate this effect with the breath and tonguing. Similar works by other composers soon followed, including at least one more that specified trombone: Giovanni Battista Riccio's "Canzon la Pichi" from *Il terzo libro delle divine lodi musicali* (1620).[84] It is interesting that this modest expansion of the trombone's technique would originate with a violinist and that no similar innovation seems to have come from a wind player.

Although the composers who played wind instruments seem on the whole not to have been greatly interested in writing and publishing canzonas and sonatas, wind instruments were conspicuous among the instruments named in the title pages and tables of contents of the various collections that appeared between 1597 and about 1630.

The publication of Giovanni Gabrieli's *Sacrae symphoniae* in 1597 marks the first time that ensemble instruments were specified in a printed collection. Sartori's transcription of the table of contents of this collection does not show the names of any instruments, but his notes identify one piece for violin, cornett, and six trombones (the "Sonata, pian e forte"); one for eight cornetts and two trombones with or without organ accompaniment; and one for violin, cornett, and nine trombones.[85] (Actually the latter piece, *Canzon quarti toni*, calls for violin, two cornetts, and twelve trombones.)

According to Sartori, the trombone is specified in 81 pieces in 26 collections of Italian music by 22 different composers through 1630. (See Table 6.1.)

Table 6.1.   Sartori's Specifications for the Trombone

Sartori	Composer	Title	A	B	C	D
1597e	Gabrieli, Giovanni	Sacrae symphoniae	3	3		
1602a	Viadana, Lodovico	Cento concerti ecclesiastici	2	2		
1610d	Cima, Giovanni Paolo	Concerti ecclesiastici	3	1	1	
1611a	Franzoni, Amante	Concerti ecclesiastici	1	1		
1613a	Franzoni, Amante	Apparato musicali	1	1		
1613b	Belli, Giulio	Concerti ecclesiastici	2	2		
1613c	Porta, Ercole	Vagha ghirlanda	2	1		1
1614e	Lapii, Petri	Sacrae melodiae	1			1
1614k	Usper, Francesco	Messa e salmi da concertarsi	1	1		
1615o	Borsaro da Reggio, Archangelo	Odorati fiori	2	2		
1617c	Marini, Biagio	Affetti musicali	15	2	1	
1620b	Riccio, Gio. Battista	Terzo libro delle divine lodi musicali	6	4		
1620h	Banchieri, Adriano	Primo libro delle messe e motetti	1	1		
1621b	Cesare, Giovanni Martino	Musicali melodie	16	8	1	
1621f	Bernardi, Steffano	Madrigaletti a due e tre voci	7			6
1622a	Milanuzzi, Carlo	Armonia sacra	1	1		
1622c	Banchieri, Adriano	L'organo suonarino	6	4		
1624d	Merula, Tarquinio	Primo libro de motetti e sonate	3			1
1625b	Picchi, Giovanni	Canzoni da sonar	16	11		
1626m	Marini, Biagio	Sonate, symphonie . . .	18	6	1	1
1628d	Grandi, Ottaviomaria	Sonate	2	2		
1629b	Grandi, Alessandro	Motetti a una, et due voci . . .	1		1	
1629c	Pietragrua, Gasparo	Concerti, et canzon francese	4			1
1629d	Mont'albano, Bartolomeo	Sinfonie . . .	2	2		
1629e	Castello, Dario	Sonate concertante	9		4	
1629f	Castello, Dario	Sonate concertante, libro 2	13	6		

A = Number of pieces that specify any wind instrument (including when the wind instrument is an alternative)
B = Number of pieces that specify trombone(s) (simply)
C = Number of pieces that specify trombone(s) with another instrument given as alternative
D = Number of pieces that specify some other instrument with trombone given as alternative

Notes: In Porta's *Vagha ghirlanda* (1613c), the piece in Column D has trombone as an optional fifth part to a concerto for unspecified instruments. Porta's *Sacro convito musicale* (1620a, not on table) has 11 part books: 5 voices, 2 violins, 3 trombones, and bass. There are four instrumental pieces (three for two instruments, one for four instruments). The table of contents does not specify the instrumentation of those or any of the vocal pieces. The trombone part books are seven pages, and violin part books six pages. Marini's *Sonate, symphonie . . .* (1626m) also contains pieces for two violins or two cornets and another for two cornets, both with two trombones ad libitum.

To the extent that the biographies in standard reference sources identify them as instrumentalists at all, these composers include eight organists, three violinists, and two wind players: Giovanni Martino Cesare and Dario Castello. *Musicali melodie per voci et instrumenti* (1621) by Cesare, a cornettist and trombonist, includes 28 pieces, 17 of which require instruments. Of these, nine specify trombone, including "La Hieronyma" for trombone or viola solo. Castello's two collections of *Sonate concertate in stil moderno* (1621, 1629) contain 29 sonatas, of which 10 specify either "Trombone or Violeta" or "Trombone or Viola." In each case, the soprano instruments are unspecified. The trombone would most naturally have been paired with cornetts and the violeta or viola with violins. There are, however, enough pieces where the combination of violin and trombone is specified that performance of Castello's music by a mixed ensemble is certainly possible.

Much of this music emphasizes the soprano and bass, with the inner parts relegated to a chordal accompaniment. Newman implies that the only function of the trombone in the Baroque sonata was to play the bass line.[86] There are, however, ample instances of pieces with more than one trombone part and/or pieces where the trombone and violin, viola, or other non-bass instrument are alternatives. Composers used the trombone more flexibly than Newman supposed.

The English developed their own characteristic small ensemble music. The trombone found a place in the broken consort, a usage of the trombone so different from the traditional wind band that it was the provenance of specialists. Praetorius described the English consort as "several people with various instruments, such as harpsichord, large lyra, double harp, lute, theorbo, pandora, penorcon, cither, viol, a small violin, transverse flute or recorder, sometimes also a soft trombone or rackett, play[ing] together quietly and softly, forming a pleasant and harmonious ensemble."[87] Although Praetorius never visited England, he had opportunity to speak with people familiar with the difference between this English practice and the large, loud wind ensemble so prominent in Germany.

Trombone is specified as the bass instrument in some consort pieces by Coperario, Loosemore, and Hingeston. The parts require considerable dexterity, as well as a soft dynamic level. Most consort pieces specified or assumed to be viol pieces have bass lines similar in style, range, and technical agility to these trombone parts. There seems to be no good reason to suppose that any one of them could not or would not have been played on trombone. Court records make a clear distinction between the relatively few specialist trombonists who were capable of playing this music and the larger number who played trombone among other wind instruments and who were probably limited to playing ordinary wind band music. With a mixture of traditional instruments and new imports from the Continent, the English eagerly experimented with various combinations.

The broken consort with a trombone was not a seventeenth-century innovation. In 1569, Queen Elizabeth purchased a trombone for her own use. That almost certainly does not mean that she played it herself. It is quite clear that in England, as elsewhere, the trombone was an instrument played by professionals. It does suggest, however, that she purchased an especially fine specimen to be played as a consort (soft) instrument in her private chamber.

It appears that none of the nobility maintained a chapel for sacred music, but they maintained instruments for all the same purposes that noblemen elsewhere did: "At great feasts, when the earl's service is going to the table, they are to play upon shagbut, cornetts, shawms, and such other instruments going with wind. In meal times to play upon viols, violins, or other broken music. . . ."[88] Broken consorts in at least some noble households must have included trombone. Evidence is found in the inventories of instruments owned by families that employed musicians. The Kytson family of East Anglia owned most of the usual consort instruments, including two trombones. In Lancaster, the Shuttleworths had one trombone and the Heskiths had at least two; their inventory lists "sagbuts" in the plural, but does not specify how many. These documents come from the years 1603, 1612, and 1620.[89] That the Shuttleworths had only one trombone indicates that it was strictly a consort instrument, as that is the only kind of music that used trombones at all but did not require more than one. That the Kytsons and Heskiths owned two trombones, as well as cornetts, indicates that they could listen to wind band music.

New Dramatic Music

Comedy as a theatrical genre disappeared with the collapse of the Roman Empire, but old Latin comedies were revived in Italy in the last half of the fifteenth century and inspired poets to try their hand at writing new comedies. Music had been an integral part of both ancient drama and the liturgical and quasi-liturgical drama of the Middle Ages. It is no surprise, then, that it soon became an important adjunct to the reestablished tradition of comedy. Musical interludes, known as *intermedii*, occurred between the acts.

Written mostly for court performance, comedies frequently took on political significance. By the middle of the sixteenth century, theatrical spectacles had taken the place of the medieval grand entry as a means of projecting the splendor, dignity, and power of the local sovereign. Minor and Mitchell list 30 Italian theatrical productions in 13 different cities between 1471 and 1539 that required music.[90]

The Florentine *intermedii* are by far the best known of these extravaganzas. Materials for two of the productions (1539 and 1589) are preserved in their entirety. Some music from others is still extant. Even when the music has been completely lost, however, it is often possible to reconstruct the instrumentation of individual numbers from official published descriptions. Many of these survive, along with unofficial accounts representing various political viewpoints.

In most if not all productions, the musicians followed certain conventions of instrumentation. A scene could be set in the heavens, in the countryside, in a city, at sea, or in the underworld. Certain instruments or combinations of instruments were considered appropriate to each setting. A scene among the gods on Mount Olympus usually represented the hosts of the event in allegorical garb. Therefore, a large mixed ensemble of instruments played by courtiers (such as lutes, viols, and keyboard instruments) and instruments played on state occasions (trumpets, trombones, cornetts, and shawms) typically accompanied these scenes.

Pastoral scenes belonged to the more plebeian instruments: reeds, flutes, bagpipes, and so forth, although plucked string instruments, viols, and the occasional trombone also participated. Infernal scenes usually relied on organs, viols, and trombones, most often playing in a lower register. Where one trombone was sufficient for most scenes, infernal scenes often used four. Battle scenes most frequently used trumpets and drums, although trombones and cornetts were likewise appropriate. The transverse flute predominated in seascapes, frequently supported by a trombone. Therefore, the trombone was appropriate for nearly every kind of scene.[91]

The most elaborate music for the wedding of Cosimo I and Eleanore of Toledo (1539) came in the *intermedii* to Antonio Landi's play *Il Commodo*. A song scored for alto voice and four trombones was performed after the fifth act. The fourth trombone part descends to $E\flat$, the lowest and most awkward note on a tenor trombone in A. It was probably played on a bass trombone. The evening's finale followed, a four-part number performed by eight singers and eight instrumentalists. Brown supposed that the instruments were divided into a soft and a loud quartet, which probably consisted of violin, cornett, tenor cornett, and trombone.[92]

No music is extant for the 1548 entry of Henry II of France and Catherine de Medici into Lyons. Trombones appeared in two pieces: a four-part piece for SATB singers, three crumhorns and trombone (doubling the bass part) following the second act, and a five-part (SSATB) piece for singers, two cornetts, and three trombones (doubling the lowest three voice parts) following the fourth act. This music marks a turning point of sorts in the history of instrumentation. The earlier *intermedii*, along with more ordinary performances of similar music, had made exclusive use of consorts of like instruments. The Lyons entry featured mixed consorts and used spinets as chordal foundation instruments. Both of these innovations became more important and more prominent in later entertainments, despite the fact that they introduced incompatibilities of tuning that may have sounded very bad at times.[93]

King Henry III of France mounted a landmark entertainment in 1581 for the marriage of one of his favorite courtiers to the queen's half sister. He spared no expense in festivities that lasted for more than two weeks, culminating in one of the most important French theatrical entertainments of the century, *Le balet comique de la royne*. The bride and groom were all but ignored in this presentation. Like any other court spectacle anywhere in Europe, the intent of the presentation was to glorify the power and dignity of the king. Before the dramatic presentation actually began, the assembled dignitaries heard music played by "shawms, cornetts, trombones, and other sweet musical instruments."[95]

This is the only explicit reference to the trombone in the official memorial book that was published the following year. It appears, however, that its author, Balthasar de Beaujoyeulx, was more interested in describing what the audience saw than what it heard. In describing the stage, he mentioned two special areas, Pan's wood and a heavenly vault that included "ten musical consorts, each one different from the others." He may not be a reliable witness when it comes to the instruments he did mention explicitly. At one point, he described eight satyrs, one singing and the other seven playing flutes. The instruments pictured on the facing page, however, are clearly cornetts.[96] If the picture, and not the description, is correct, musicians of the royal Stable participated in the ballet, not just in the instrumental prelude, and so trombones may have been among at least one of the frequent ensembles that Beaujoyeulx simply described as "instruments." If so, however, they probably accompanied dancing, not singing, a very traditional and ordinary role for the loud band.

The wedding of the Florentine duke Ferdinand I and Christine of Lorraine in 1589 included six *intermedii* with a total of 30 separate pieces for Girolamo Bargagli's *La pellegrina*, with music contributed by Cristofano Malvezzi and others. This is the second such festival for which nearly all of the production materials are extant. The second and fifth *intermedii* did not use trombones. Up to four trombones participated along with a variety of other instruments in most of the others. For the same wedding, another play (Giovanni Maria Cecchi's *L'esaltatione della croce*), likewise with six *intermedii*, was also performed. All of the music has been lost, but Cecchi's description indicates that it required a comparably large cast of singers and instrumentalists, including four trombones.[97]

While the practice of interpolating *intermedii* into a comedy performed for a state occasion continued into the seventeenth century, the festivities of 1589 are nearly the last to be studied in any detail by modern scholars. Before the end of the following decade, the new genre of opera emerged and captured the imagination of musicians and audiences alike. Comedies with *intermedii* were no longer the cutting edge of theatrical innovation. The very earliest operas of Peri, Cavalieri, and Caccini did not include a large array of instruments. These composers concerned themselves with devising a new kind of dramatic singing, for which the music of the *intermedii* did not provide any relevant models.

The tradition of lavish instrumentation carried over into some of the earliest operas, however, notably including Monteverdi's *Orfeo* (Mantua, 1607). It was first performed before an aristocratic academy called Accademia degli Invaghiti, whose members included Francesco Gonzaga, son of the reigning duke and who commissioned the opera. Perhaps for this reason, there are no extant drawings of the costumes or sets and no elaborate

Fig. 6.8. Figure of a muse with an alto trombone by Giorgio Vasari, for an *intermedio* performed during wedding festivities for Prince Francesco de' Medici and Joanna of Austria (1566). Pen and ink drawing. Gabinetto dei Disegni e delle Stampe, Uffizi, Florence, Italy. Photo Credit: Scala/Ministero per i Beni e le Attività culturali / Art Resource, NY.

commemorative descriptions, such as exist for many of the Florentine *intermedii*. It is a testament, therefore, to its strictly artistic success that it was performed several more times over the next few years and that the score was printed not once, but twice (in 1609 and 1615).

The instructions in the score make it clear that the opera contains two separate groups of instruments, each associated with one of the two locations in the opera. Acts I, II, and V take place in the countryside, acts III and IV in the underworld. The pastoral scenes are accompanied by a string ensemble, recorders, and continuo (organs, harpsichords, and plucked string instruments). But the instructions at the end of Act II tell this group to be silent while the cornetts and trombones play, along with the regal as the continuo instrument. The reverse instruction is given at the end of Act IV: the cornetts, trombones, and regal cease while the strings and flutes play. Although dramatic considerations dictate that the strings intrude on the winds at certain key points in the third and fourth acts, the winds are never heard during the pastoral scenes.

About 75 musicians for the *intermedii* written to celebrate the wedding of Cosimo de' Medici, future Grand Duke Cosimo II, and Maria Magdelena of Austria in 1608 were divided into two choirs, with three singers

to a part. The 15 instruments in the first choir included two tenor trombones and a bass trombone. The second choir had 15 different instruments, including two trombones.[98]

Monteverdi's second opera, *Arianna* (Mantua, 1608), may have used a large and varied instrumental ensemble, but since nearly all of the music is lost, it is difficult to tell. Writing in 1607, Agazzari asserted that wind instruments were no longer used in "good and pleasing consorts," but only in noisy ones. In general, they did not blend well with the strings. He did, however, state that a trombone could replace the violone in a small consort where *organetti* played the upper octave, provided that it played softly. He also noted on some occasions, presumably those that required more than the usual amount of rehearsal, well-played wind instruments did in fact adorn and beautify an ensemble.[99]

Part of the celebration for the baptism of Prince Friedrich of Württemberg in 1616, the *Ballet of the Twelve Nations* more nearly resembled the English masque than the proto-operas of Italy. Dancers and musicians representing twelve nations emerged from four huge heads and performed appropriate dances for each. It appears that each head contained one dancer and one musician for each of three nations. The third pair from the second head rep-

Fig. 6.9. Ballet of the Twelve Nations, performed following the banquet in honor of the baptism of Prince Friedrich of Württemberg (1616), from Esaias van Hulsen and Matthäus Merian, *Repraesentatio der furstlichen Aufzug und Ritterspil*. Courtesy of Landesbibliothek Stuttgart.

resented Lapps (an aboriginal people of northern Europe, who prefer to be known as Sami), and the dance was done to the accompaniment of a trombone (see Fig. 6.9).[100]

When Wladislaw Sigismund, a Polish prince, visited Florence in 1625, festivities in his honor included performance of a new ballet-opera by Francesca Caccini, *La liberazione di Ruggiero*. Perhaps because this work was the theatrical highlight of a state occasion, it makes use of a large ensemble. One scene calls for four viols, four trombones, organ, and harpsichord. Like many scenes with trombones, it takes place in the underworld. There were other politically significant operas produced both in Florence and elsewhere. It is possible that some of them used trombones. The future of opera, however, was not in state occasions, but in the commercial opera houses, the first of which opened in 1637. Trombones were apparently never heard in any of them until Gluck introduced them in *Orfeo ed Euridice* in 1762.

Notes

1. De la musiche poi per mezo delli instrumenti causate; il simile anchora adiuiene; ciò è che alcune plebee e degne di biasmo; e altre honorate si trouano; e diuerse diuersi affetti commuouano. Plebei e indegni d'un' homo ciuile, son tutti quelli instrumenti, che per l'uso di essi è forza che qualche parte de la persona, ò uero in quel mentre che s'usan, storchino e brutta rendino; ò uero à qualche honorata operatione, rendin men'atta, e per non hauer noi notitia di quelli instrumenti antique, come son Fistole, Tibie, Petadi, Eptagoni, // Samfonie, Sambuci, e simili; accommodandogli io al nostro modo di questi tempi; dico che tali instrumenti uili, e uolgori, i quali ne l'uso di essi rendin qualche parte de la persona uilmente storta, ò à qualche virtuosa operation disadatta; sarien come Trombe, Piffare, Cornamuse, Cornette, Flauti, Tromboni, Tamburi, e simili; de i quali la maggior parte, ò per soffiamento e sforzo di fiato, ò per qualche simil'atto seruile; e forza che aggrauato e sforzato il fiato e lo spirito, renda il uolto brutissimo, e di non son che schisezza, ripieno; e fiaccandosi il petto, uengha la persona à sneruarsite che peggio è, per il conturbamento e concitation de gli spiriti, si rendan manco disposti à la moderation de i costumi. Alessandro Piccolomini, *De la institutione de tutta la vita de l'homo nato nobile e in città libera* (Venice: Hieronymum Scotum, 1542), 50–51.

2. Vincenzo Galilei, *Dialogo di Vincentio Galilei nobile fiorentino della musica antica, et della moderna* (Florence: G. Marescotti, 1581), 141–42; English translation by Claude V. Palisca, *Dialogue on Ancient and Modern Music* (New Haven, Conn.: Yale University Press, 2003), 352–55; Keith McGowan, "The Prince and the Piper: *Haut, bas,* and the Whole Body in Early Modern Europe," *Early Music* 27 (1999): 220, 225.

3. Frank Dobbins, *Music in Renaissance Lyons* (Oxford: Clarendon Press, 1992), 105–6.

4. Edmund A. Bowles, *Musical Ensembles in Festival Books, 1500–1800: An Iconographical & Documentary Survey* (Ann Arbor, Mich.: UMI Research Press, 1989), 27–31.

5. Bowles, *Musical Ensembles in Festival Books*, 37–40.

6. Frances A. Yates, "Dramatic Religious Processions in Paris in the Late Sixteenth Century," *Annales musicologiques* 2 (1954): 215–70.

7. Bowles, *Musical Ensembles in Festival Books*, 157.

8. François Lesure, *Musique et musiciens français du XVIe siècle* (Geneva: Minkoff, 1976), 74, 78, 137.

9. Higinio Anglès, *Hygini Anglés: Scripta musicologica*, ed. Joseph Lopéz-Calo (Rome: Edizione de Storia e Letteratura, 1975–76), 1432.

10. Higinio Anglès, *La música en la corte de Carlos V* (Barcelona: Consejo Superior de Investigaciones Científicas, 1965) 1:10–13.

11. Luis Robledo, "Questions of Performance Practice in Philip III's Chapel," *Early Music* 22 (1994): 199; B. Kenyon de Pascual, "The Wind Instrument Maker, Bartolomé de Selma (†1616), His Family and Workshop," *Galpin Society Journal* 39 (1986): 22, 25.

12. Douglas Kirk, "Churching the Shawms in Renaissance Spain: 'Lerma, Archivo de San Pedro Ms. Mus.1,'" (Ph.D. diss.: McGill University, 1993), 1:31–32.

13. Hellmut Federhofer, "Biographische Beiträge zu Erasmus Lapicida und Stephan Mahu," *Die Musikforschung* 5 (1952): 42–43.

14. Steven Saunders, *Cross, Sword, and Lyre: Sacred Music at the Imperial Court of Ferdinand II of Habsburg (1619–1637)* (Oxford: Clarendon Press, 1995), 19.

15. Walter Senn, *Musik und Theater am Hof Innsbruck: Geschichte der Hofkapelle vom 15. Jahrhundert bis zu deren Auflösung im Jahre 1748* (Innsbruck: Österreichische Verlagsanstalt, 1954), 72, 135, 166.

16. Philip Crabtree, "The Vocal Works of Gioseffo (ca. 1540–1611) and Francesco Guami (ca. 1544–1602)," (Ph.D. diss.: University of Cincinnati, 1971), 1:59–60.

17. Massimo Troiano, *Dialoghi di Massimo Troiano* (Venice, 1569), facs. ed. by Horst Leuchtmann, *Die Münchner Fürstenhochzeit von 1568: Massimo Troiano; Dialoge* (Munich: Katzbichler, 1980), 34, 61–67, 112, 146.

18. Troiano, *Dialoghi*, 44–45.

19. Franz Liessem, "Phileno Agostino Cornazzani, oberster Instrumentalist der herzoglichen Hofkapelle zu München unter Orlando di Lasso," *Die Musikforschung* 24 (1971): 368–85; Michael Praetorius, *Syntagma musicum: Tomus secundus; De organographia* (Wolffenbüttel, 1619; facs. ed., Berlin: Trautwein, 1884), 31. English translation by David Z. Crookes (Oxford: Oxford University Press, 1986), 43.

20. Bowles, *Musical Ensembles in Festival Books*, 73–80, 103, 105.

21. Anthony C. Baines, "Two Cassel Inventories," *Galpin Society Journal* 4 (1951): 30–38; Egon Kenton, *Life and Works of Giovanni Gabrieli* (n.p.: American Institute of Musicology, 1967), 355.

22. Bowles, *Musical Ensembles in Festival Books*, 199–201. See also 143, 167, 188, 213–24 for other festivals.

23. Eric F. Fiedler, *"Zingen, Pumart, Pusaun*: The Manuscript *Regensburg, Bischöfliche Zentralbibliothek, MS A.R. 775-777* as a Source of Information about Wind-Band Performing Practice in Late Sixteenth-Century Southern Germany," in *Festschrift für Winfried Kirsch zum 65. Geburtstag*, ed. Peter Ackermann, Ulrike Kienzle, and Adolf Nowak (Tutzing: Hans Schneider, 1996), 34–48.

24. Kristine K. Forney, "Music, Ritual, and Patronage at the Church of Our Lady, Antwerp," *Early Music History* 7 (1987): 26–27.

25. Kristine K. Forney, "New Insights into the Career and Musical Contributions of Tielman Susato," in *Tielman Susato and the Music of His Time: Print Culture, Compositional Technique, and Instrumental Music in the Renaissance*, ed. Keith Polk (Hillsdale, N.Y.: Pendragon, 2005), 1; Kristine K. Forney, "New Documents of the Life of Tielman Susato, Sixteenth-Century Music Printer and Musician," *Revue belge de musicologie* 36–38 (1982–84): 35.

26. Keith Polk, "Susato and Instrumental Music in Flanders in the 16th Century," in *Tielman Susato and the Music of His Time: Print Culture, Compositional Technique, and Instrumental Music in the Renaissance*, ed. Keith Polk (Hillsdale, N.Y.: Pendragon, 2005), 75–89.

27. Bartlett Russell Butler, "Liturgical Music in Sixteenth-Century Nürnberg: A Socio-Musical Study," (Ph.D. diss.: University of Illinois, 1970), 546, 614–18.

28. Carl Gustav Anthon, "Music and Musicians in Northern Italy during the Sixteenth Century," (Ph.D. diss.: Harvard University, 1943), 238–39.

29. Osvaldo Gambassi, *Il Concerto Palatino della signoria di Bologna: Cinque secoli di vita musical a corte (1250–1797)* (Florence: Olschki, 1989), 11, 28, 34–36, 58–62.

30. Gambassi, *Concerto Palatino*, 64; Robert Stevenson, *Spanish Cathedral Music in the Golden Age* (Berkeley and Los Angeles: University of California Press, 1961), 18.

31. Luigi Nerici, *Storia della musica in Lucca* (Lucca: Tipografia Giusti, 1879; repr., Bologna: Forni, 1969), 186–88.

32. Crabtree, "The Vocal Works of . . . Guami," 1:63–72; Denis Arnold, *Giovanni Gabrieli and the Music of the Venetian High Renaissance* (London: Oxford University Press, 1979), 146, 188.

33. Nerici, *Storia della musica in Lucca*, 194–95.

34. Gary Towne, "Tubatori e Piffari: Civic Wind Players in Medieval and Renaissance Bergamo," *Historic Brass Society Journal* 9 (1997): 175–95.

35. Iain Fenlon, *Music and Patronage in Sixteenth-Century Mantua*, 2 vols. (Cambridge: Cambridge University Press, 1980), vol. 1, passim.

36. Susan Parisi, "Ducal Patronage of Music in Mantua, 1587–1627: An Archival Study" (Ph.D. diss.: University of Illinois, 1989), 472–74.

37. Claudio Monteverdi, *The Letters of Claudio Monteverdi*, trans. Denis Stevens (London: Faber and Faber, 1980), 64–65, 68, 81.

38. Parisi, "Ducal Patronage," 378–82.

39. Howard Mayer Brown, "A Cook's Tour of Ferrara in 1529," *Rivista italiana di musicologia* 16 (1975): 216–41.

40. Anthony Newcomb, *The Madrigal at Ferrara, 1579–1597* (Princeton, N.J.: Princeton University Press, 1980), 1:33–34.

41. Andrew C. Minor and Bonner Mitchell, *A Renaissance Entertainment: Festivities for the Marriage of Cosimo I, Duke of Florence, in 1539* (Columbia: University of Missouri Press, 1968). See also David M. Guion "Theories of Tuning and Ensemble Practice in Italian Dramatic Music of the Early Baroque, or, Oh Where, Oh Where Have the Wind Instruments Gone?" *Historic Brass Society Journal* 12 (2000): 239.

42. *Les fêtes du mariage de Ferdinand de Médicis et de Christine de Lorraine, Florence 1589: I. Musique des intermèdes de "La Pellegrina,"* ed. D. P. Walker (Paris: Centre National de la Recherch Scientifique, 1963), xi–xxii. See also Guion, "Theories of Tuning," 241.

43. Warren Kirkendale, *The Court Musicians in Florence during the Principate of the Medici, with a Reconstruction of the Artistic Establishment* (Florence: Olschki, 1993), 61–67, 107–13, 285–86, 289.

44. Claudio Sartori, *Bibliografia della musica strumentale italiana stampata in Italia fino al 1700* (Florence: Olschki, 1952, 1968) 1:242–44; The publication in question is *Il primo libro delle musiche di Lorenzo Allegri*, Sar. 1618c; Kirkendale, *Court Musicians in Florence*, 290, 300–302.

45. Kirkendale, *Court Musicians in Florence*, 112–13, 383–84, 394–95, 397.

46. Marcello Castellani, "A 1593 Veronese Inventory," *Galpin Society Journal* 26 (1973): 16–17.

47. Trevor Herbert, "The Trombone in Britain before 1800" (Ph.D. diss.: Open University, 1984), 377.

48. David Lasocki, *The Bassanos: Venetian Musicians and Instrument Makers in England, 1531–1665* (Hants, England: Scolar Press, 1995), 143–44, 173–75.

49. Bowles, *Musical Ensembles in Festival Books*, 43; Walter L. Woodfill, *Musicians in English Society from Elizabeth to Charles I* (Princeton, N.J.: Princeton University Press, 1953), 178.

50. Thurston Dart, "The Repertory of the Royal Wind Music," *Galpin Society Journal* 11 (1958): 70–77.

51. Woodfill, *Musicians in English Society*, 33–53; Fiona Kisby, "Royal Minstrels in the City and Suburbs of Early Tudor London: Professional Activities and Private Interests," *Early Music* 25 (1997): 212–23.

52. Lyndesay G. Langwill, "The Waites: A Short Historical Study," *Hinrichsen's Musical Yearbook* 7 (1952): 181; Woodfill, *Musicians in English Society*, 74–108.

53. Stephen Bonta, "The Uses of Sonata da Chiesa," *Journal of the American Musicological Society* 22 (1969): 83; Gary Towne, "Gaspar de Albertis and Music at Santa Maria Maggiore in Bergamo in the Sixteenth Century" (Ph.D. diss.: University of California, Santa Barbara, 1985), 233–35.

54. Sartori, *Bibliografia della musica strumentale*, 1:281–82.

55. Kenneth Kreitner, "Minstrels in Spanish Churches, 1400–1600," *Early Music* 20 (1992): 538; Stevenson, *Spanish Cathedral Music*, 297.

56. David M. Guion, "Wind Bands in Towns, Courts, and Churches: Middle Ages to Baroque," *Journal of Band Research* 42 (Spring 2007): 30–32.

57. Robert Stevenson, *Music in Mexico: A Historical Survey* (New York: Crowell, 1952), 65.

58. Egberto Bermúdez, "The *Ministriles* Tradition in Latin America: Part One: South America 1. The Cases of Santafé (Colombia) and La Plata (Bolivia) in the Seventeenth Century," *Historic Brass Society Journal* 11 (1999): 149–62; Daniel Mendoza de Arce, *Music in Ibero-America to 1850: A Historical Survey* (Lanham, Md.: Scarecrow, 2001), 140–41; Geoffrey Baker, "Music at Corpus Christi in Colonial Cuzco," *Early Music* 32 (2004): 358.

59. Towne, "Gaspar de Albertis," 56–57, 187–91.

60. Frank A. D'Accone, "The Performance of Sacred Music in Italy during Josquin's Time, c. 1475–1525," in *Josquin des Prez*, ed. Edward E. Lowinsky (London: Oxford University Press, 1976), 616.

61. Frank A. D'Accone, "Music at the Siennese Cathedral in the Later 16th Century," *Report of the 14th Congress of the International Musicological Society* (Bologna 1987) (Turin: Edizioni di Torino, 1990), 3:729–31.

62. Kirkendale, *Court Musicians in Florence*, 643, 645, 648–49.

63. Parisi, "Ducal Patronage of Music in Mantua," 27–36, 517.

64. Eleanor Selfridge-Field, *Venetian Instrumental Music from Gabrieli to Vivaldi*, 3rd rev. ed. (New York: Dover, 1994), 15; Arnold, *Giovanni Gabrieli*, 7, 19–21, 35, 128, 137–38.

65. "Early Orchestras: Some Contemporary Accounts," *Galpin Society Journal* 1(1948): 27.

66. Osvaldo Gambassi, *La capella musicale de S. Petronia: Maestri, organisti, cantori e strumentisti dal 1436 al 1920* (Florence: Olschki, 1987), 86–117.

67. Craig A. Monson, "Disembodied Voices: Music in the Nunneries of Bologna in the Midst of the Counter-Reformation," in *The Crannied Wall: Women, Religion, and the Arts in Early Modern Europe*, ed. Craig A. Monson (Ann Arbor: University of Michigan Press, 1992), 200.

68. Anne Schnoebelen, "The Concerted Mass at San Petronio in Bologna ca. 1660–1730: A Documentary and Analytical Study" (Ph.D. diss.: University of Illinois, 1960), 157.

69. Rossana Dalmonte, *Camillo Cortellini: Madrigalista Bolognese* (Florence: Olschki, 1980), 10–19.

70. Ludwig von Köchel, *Die kaiserliche Hof-musikkappelle in Wien von 1543 bis 1867* (Vienna: Beck'sche Universitätsbuchhandlung, 1869), 25.

71. See Tom L. Naylor, *The Trumpet & Trombone in Graphic Arts, 1500–1800* (Nashville, Tenn.: Brass Press, 1979), plate 67.

72. Forney, "Music, Ritual and Patronage," 2–15.

73. Ronald L. Gould, "The Latin Lutheran Mass at Wittenberg, 1523–1545: A Survey of the Early Reformation Mass and the Lutheran Theology of Music. . . " (D.S.M. diss.: Union Theological Seminary, 1970): 18–27.

74. Butler, "Liturgical Music in Sixteenth-Century Nürnberg," 503–5, 524–44, 619–21, 613.

75. Michael Praetorius, *Syntagma musicum: Tomus tertuis; Termini musici* (Wolffenbuttel: Holwein, 1619; facs. ed., Berlin: Trautwein, 1884), 153; English translation by Hans Lampl (n.p.: American Choral Directors Association, 2001), 167.

76. Praetorius, *Termini musici*, 116–17; Lampl, 132–33.

77. See Frederick Staten Miller, "A Comprehensive Performance Project in Trombone Literature with an Essay on the Use of the Trombone in the Music of Heinrich Schütz" (D.M.A. essay: University of Iowa, 1974).

78. Herbert, "Trombone in Britain," 109, 155, 371.

79. Woodfill, *Musicians in English Society*, 135 ff.

80. Charles Butler, *The Principles of Musik, in Singing and Setting: With the Two-Fold Use Thereof (Ecclesiasticall and Civil)* (London: John Haviland, 1636), 103.

81. Herbert, "Trombone in Britain," 227–33.

82. Stephen Bonta, "The Use of Instruments in Sacred Music in Italy, 1560–1700," *Early Music* 18 (1990): 521.

83. Eleanor Selfridge-Field, "Instrumentation and Genre in Italian Music, 1600–1670," *Early Music* 19 (1991): 61–63.

84. Stewart Carter, "The String Tremolo in the 17th Century," *Early Music* 19 (1991): 43–46.

85. Sartori, *Bibliografia della musica strumentale*, 1:96–97.

86. William S. Newman, *The Sonata in the Baroque Era*, 3d ed. (New York: Norton, 1972), 53, 55.

87. Praetorius, *Termini musici*, 5; Lampl, 5.

88. Richard Braithwaite, *Some Rules and Orders for the Government of the Household of an Earle* (London, 1621), quoted in Bowles, *Musical Ensembles in Festival Books*, 125, n. 7.

89. Herbert, "Trombone in Britain," 179, 197, 213, 407.

90. Minor and Mitchell, *A Renaissance Entertainment*, 46.

91. Robert L. Weaver, "Sixteenth-Century Instrumentation," *Musical Quarterly* 47 (1961): 363–78.

92. Howard Mayer Brown, *Sixteenth Century Instrumentation: The Music for the Florentine Intermedii* (s.l.: American Institute of Musicology, 1973), 93.

93. Brown, *Sixteenth Century Instrumentation*, 93–4; Guion, "Theories of Tuning," 236–37.

94. Brown, *Sixteenth Century Instrumentation*, 96–105; Bowles, *Musical Ensembles in Festival Books*, 53–58.

95. hauts-boys, cornets, sacquebouttes, & autres doux instrumens de musique. Balthazar de Beaujoyeulx, *Le balet comique*, facs. ed. with introduction by Margaret M. McGowan (Binghamton, N.Y.: Center for Medieval & Early Renaissance Studies, 1982), fol. 7v.

96. Beaujoyeulx, *Le balet comique*, fol. 5v, 31v, 32r.

97. Brown, *Sixteenth Century Instrumentation*, 107–35.

98. Tim Carter, "A Florentine Wedding of 1608," *Acta musicologica* 55 (1983): 93, 95, 107.

99. Agostino Agazzari, "Of Playing upon a Bass with All Instruments and of Their Use in a Consort," in *Source Readings in Music History*, ed. Oliver Strunk; rev. ed., gen. ed. Leo Treitler (New York: Norton, 1998), 622.

100. Ludwig Krapf and Christian Wagenknecht, eds., *Stuttgarter Hoffeste* (Tübingen: Max Niemeyer, 1979), 6.

CHAPTER SEVEN

~

The Decline and Revival of the Trombone, 1630–1830

Over the course of the seventeenth century, the trombone disappeared completely from some places. It persisted in others (notably German and Italian cities), but usually with reduced significance. The chief exception to this pattern of decline was the Habsburg imperial court, where it took on an importance that it had not had there before. Late in the eighteenth century, Rome, Vienna, and Paris became launching pads for the worldwide revival of the trombone.

The year 1630 makes a convenient date to begin the present chapter, but signs of the decline of wind instruments were evident long before then. This chapter will examine the near extinction and subsequent revival of the trombone, ending chronologically with the music of Beethoven and Schubert, which completed the acceptance of the trombone as a permanent member of the symphony orchestra.

Marginalization of Wind Music

At the same time the role of the trombone and the musical competence of trombonists were growing, attitudes that would ultimately marginalize them developed among the aristocracy. Gentlemen were expected to be music lovers. It was not enough merely to listen to music. They needed also to understand the rules of counterpoint, be able to sing at sight, and play several musical instruments. The standards of acceptable performance were no lower for amateurs than for professionals, but only certain instruments were considered suitable for gentlemen. These included the lute, viol, and keyboard instruments, largely because they enabled the performer to play all the voices of a composition without anyone else's aid. Wind instruments can only play one voice. In

addition, as shown in chapter 6, wind instruments were objectionable because the common people especially liked them. Also, playing them distorted the player's face and took obvious physical energy, which made them unfit for the nobility.

In his chapter on amateur music, Anthon commented on the instruments played by various individuals, both of the nobility and otherwise. Although the flute and cornett occur on some of the lists, the trombone does not. The absence of any explicit reference to it in this context indicates that it was one of the instruments reserved for professional musicians.[1]

This fact would seem to have two important consequences. First, books about music were aimed at amateurs, not professionals. There would have been little interest in detailed descriptions of the trombone; few if any in the target audience would have attempted to play it. That is perhaps why Virdung and his followers had little to say about it. Second, there would be no need to arrange music for trombone comparable to the lute and keyboard intabulations that became common by the end of the sixteenth century.

The trombone was totally absent from the most important early seventeenth-century developments: the birth of the orchestra and of opera as a commercial public spectacle. Where earlier ensembles were based on wind instruments with some participation of stringed instruments, the orchestra as it emerged during the seventeenth century was based on members of the violin family with little participation of wind instruments. The orchestra was often the focus of attention when it played where non-orchestral ensembles were likely to have a more peripheral role. In late seventeenth-century Rome, the ensembles for serenatas, oratorios, and outdoor festivals tended to be more orchestral than those for church music, cantatas, or operas.[2]

Trombones, along with most other wind instruments, were largely excluded from opera. That fact cannot result from any economic troubles left over from the plague of 1630–31. Opera was extravagantly expensive. Its audiences demanded star-caliber singers and elaborate stage machinery. If they had wanted a colorful instrumental accompaniment, it would have been provided. I have not located a single instance of the trombone being used in any commercial opera anywhere in the world from the opening of the first theater in 1637 until Gluck's *Orfeo ed Euridice* in 1762.

At least part of the reason has to do with the interest in tuning systems that started in the late sixteenth century. Agricola espoused the traditional Pythagorean tuning as late as 1545, but shortly thereafter, all other writers explored new ideas. Zarlino developed a new classification of instruments. Writings of Zacconi, Cerone, Praetorius, Bottrigari, and Artusi show its influence. (See chapter 3.) Some of these authors noted that fretted stringed instruments, unfretted stringed instruments, keyboard instruments, and wind instruments all used different tuning systems.

Bottrigari had often been disappointed by performances of music by large mixed ensembles and concluded that it was because of the incompatibility of the tuning systems. The central premise of his entire treatise is that a large mixed ensemble must necessarily play out of tune and therefore cannot sound as pleasing as a homogeneous ensemble; wind instruments cannot play in tune with fretted strings.[3] Artusi was quick to take issue. He said that any wind instrument, not just the trombone, could bend pitches in any direction and therefore in the hands of good players could play in tune with any other instrument. His reasoning was more nearly correct than Bottrigari's, but his work had little influence.

Bottrigari knew very well that the trombone, unlike other wind instruments, could match any tuning system used by any other instrument. In general, however, people of the time did not observe such distinctions. Wind instruments were suitable for the kinds of music they had always played. They were not needed or welcome in the newer kinds of music.

Given that the orchestra and the continuo had eclipsed the earlier consort principle as the basic means of organizing instrumental music, what role could there have been for wind instruments? According to Bottrigari, they could not play in tune with the lutes, which remained the most important group of foundation instruments in the early seventeenth century, or with viols,

which remained the most important consort family. Only the trombone could play well in tune with all other instruments, but the most common trombone was the tenor. The newest textures in Italian music depended on a polarity between treble and bass, with the middle ground being supplied by the foundation instruments. A tenor trombone could and frequently did play the bass line, but it would be less satisfactory in that role than a bass viol.

This discussion of tuning only partially explains why the trombone was excluded from more than a century of operas. Other wind instruments occasionally appeared in even the earliest Venetian operas. By Bottrigari's reasoning, there would be intonation problems between any of them and any fretted continuo instruments, while the trombone could play in any tuning system. For the rest of the answer to the trombone's exclusion not only from opera, but also from most other new genres for most of the Baroque period, it is necessary to return to its social status.

By 1630, it was a very old instrument. With the exception of church music and some very exceptional courtly entertainments, it was locked into an ensemble that had long since been reduced to aural wallpaper: necessary for certain occasions, but with little prestige. The musically more limited trumpet was associated with dignity, nobility, and the glory of war. The flute and other instruments of the old medieval "soft" consort served for the private entertainment of the nobility and not for the ears of the general public. These instruments found a place in opera in scenes where their role resembled how they functioned in real life.

The trombone had no real-life associations with anything that was ever depicted on the operatic stage. Its use in the *intermedii* and the earliest operas symbolized the underworld. Such supernatural scenes and infernal characters as may have appeared in early commercial operas had no help from trombones. Significantly, the occasional trumpet parts in early operas were mostly solos. Flute parts could be either solos or ensembles, but flutes were considered soft instruments. The trombone was not traditionally a solo instrument. A trombone ensemble would have intruded too much on the exciting new monochromatic sound of the string orchestra. Thus, there was no suitable role for it in opera for more than a century.

The Disappearance of the Trombone

In France and England, a single royal court dominated cultural life. Whatever was out of favor at court could not long persist elsewhere. It is comparatively easy to document the disappearance of the trombone from the musical life of these two countries. Elsewhere, it becomes more complicated. The trombone disappeared from courts and many towns in Italy and Germany at various times and for various reasons, but it persisted in others.

France

Throughout the sixteenth century, records of the king's Stable make it clear that its instrumentation included trombones, but it is difficult to find descriptions of any specific events for which it played. I have found only one event of the entire seventeenth century where the trombone is explicitly mentioned: the coronation of Louis XIV in 1654. The division of the royal music into Chapel, Chamber, and Stable continued until the Revolution. The Stable performed for victory ceremonies, celebrations of royal births and weddings, state funerals, and for visiting dignitaries. Isherwood mentions violins and oboes frequently, but trombones, shawms, and cornetts not at all.[4]

A series of documents titled *L'État de la France* appeared sporadically between 1644 and 1789 and served as a semi-official guide to the French court. The 1644 issue listed the names of twelve trumpeters in the Stable, but does not acknowledge any of its other divisions. It became more informative with the 1652 issue. Besides the trumpeters, it lists six other divisions including twelve "players of violins, oboes, sackbuts, and cornetts." Pierre de Houteuille and Nicolas Malois are identified as "sackbut and tenor violin." They were only part-time trombonists. The fact that trombone is listed first probably has more to do with history than with their actual duties. They appear with the same information in lists for 1653 and 1657.[5]

The 1661 list does not name individuals, but contains a general statement of duties: "At the entrances of the king [into the cities of the kingdom], and other solemnities, the trumpets, shawms, fifes, drums, trombones, cornets, etc. serve to render the occasion more festive." Similar language appears in every remaining issue. Beginning in 1697, a new reference to "Twelve grand oboes and violins of the Large Stable, formerly grand shawms, cornets, and trombones" replaced the former "players of violins, oboes, sackbuts, and cornetts." This statement or something like it appears in the summary of Stable

Fig. 7.1. Detail from "Le sacre et couronnement de Louis XIV" by Antoine Lepautre (1654). Tom L. Naylor, *The Trumpet & Trombone in Graphic Arts 1500–1800,* plate 43, © by Editions Bim /The Brass Press, www.editions-bim.com.

personnel through the 1789 issue. Oddly enough, so does the statement printed since 1661 about the function of the Stable when the king entered one of his cities. After a while, the former name of the unit was dropped, but it reappeared in 1789, along with a personnel list that included the names of one part-time trombonist and one part-time cornettist.[6]

By no later than 1670 (even though *L'État* does not reflect it until 1697), the Stable consisted of a large number of oboes and bassoons. The oboe was a new instrument, a refinement of the shawm. The French court had tremendous influence all over Europe. A new French-style oboe band was established at Stuttgart in 1680. Twenty years later, nearly every other German-speaking court and the English court had replaced the traditional wind band of cornetts and trombones with the new oboe band.[7]

Horns were added to this group early in the eighteenth century, beginning in Bohemia. By the middle of the eighteenth century, the clarinet joined the ensemble, sometimes as a companion to the oboe and sometimes as its replacement. So while the rise of the string orchestra in Italy marginalized wind instruments, the rise of the French oboe band determined which wind instruments would first become the core elements of a symphony orchestra.

I am intrigued by the presence of Pietro Chaboud on the personnel lists of San Petronio in Bologna from 1679 to 1684. He appears there as a trombonist, but in other documents as a serpent player or bassoonist.[8] The serpent was important in seventeenth-century French church music, and Chaboud is a French name. One would hardly suppose that a Frenchman moving to Bologna could have won an audition to play an instrument that he did not master at home, so he must have learned all three instruments in France. The trombone probably had a greater presence and role in French music from the Renaissance through the middle Baroque than has so far attracted the attention of scholars, even if it was less than in other places.

England

In England, civil war broke out in 1642 and ended with the beheading of King Charles I in 1649. England had no king until the Restoration in 1660. Oliver Cromwell (r. 1649–58) and his son Richard Cromwell (r. 1658–1660) were Puritans, so the victory of Parliament over the king ended not only the royal musical institutions, but also the use of musical instruments at the various cathedrals in England. In 1660, Parliament deposed Richard Cromwell and invited Charles II to return as king.

The English court before the civil war had two different groups of trombonists. Most of them played a wide variety of wind instruments in the wind band, where a loud and forceful style of playing was needed. Some few other English trombonists, however, specialized in playing trombone to the exclusion of other wind instruments. They participated with string players in performing chamber music, where a soft and delicate style of playing was required.

After the abolition of their court positions, these two groups had different problems in finding employment. Loud players could seek employment as waits or do any of the kinds of freelance work that were available before. The soft players could gain some income in private households or in theaters, but they would have to play more fashionable chamber instruments, especially members of the viol or violin families.

Opportunities for the latter group to play trombone did not disappear entirely. John Coperario, Henry Loosemore, and John Hingeston composed fantasies with trombone parts during the Commonwealth. Much of this music is associated with Cambridge, where several former court musicians were active, including trombonist William Saunders. There is a copy of a 1658 reprint of Dario Castello's *Sonata Concertate in Stil Moderno* in the library of Durham Cathedral.[9] Four of the pieces call for trombone. Depending on when it was purchased, it could represent music available for performance on trombone during the end of the Commonwealth period. It was probably at least attempted by the reconstituted cathedral band after the Restoration.

Nonetheless, trombone specialists had much less to do as trombonists than if they had been able to remain in the royal household. Charles II (r. 1660–85) hired many of his father's musicians for his own court, including some who had been good trombonists. But after 11 years of having to devote most of their energy to other instruments, how capable did they remain? When Saunders petitioned for a place in the household of Charles II, he wrote that he was "allways bredd up in the Art of Musique for Sagbutt and Base Violin . . . [and that if the king would grant him a place] amongst your Band of Violins . . . hee is alsoe willing and ready to doe service on the Sagbutt in you Maties Chappell." His warrant was issued September 2, 1661.[10] It is noteworthy that he mentioned trombone first when he was describing his education and training, but that he no longer considered himself primarily a trombonist. He applied for a position as bass violinist and offered to play trombone if necessary.

At first, the court intended to restore everything to the way it was before the civil war. It reconstituted the loud band, and Matthew Locke's *Music for His Majesty's Sagbutts and Cornetts* may have been composed for the coronation. Trombones were heard again in the cathedrals. And yet the court soon undermined the return of earlier musical practices. On December 12, 1662, John Evelyn noted in his diary that the wind band, which had always accompanied the organ in church, had suddenly been replaced by a consort of 24 violins.[11]

Possibly because the standard of trombone playing was necessarily less than it had been, and certainly because Charles modeled his court after that of France, where the trombone was not heard in any musically significant setting, its use began to decline soon after the Restoration. It continued in the Chapel Royal longer than in other court ensembles, but after its use there was discontinued, it was only a matter of time before it was eventually abandoned elsewhere.

Italy

Italian publishers issued a large quantity of music over the course of the seventeenth century. Table 7.1 shows the rise and fall of the use of the trombone in it. Giovanni Gabrieli's *Sacrae symphoniae*, the first published collection to specify particular instruments for particular parts, requires numerous wind instruments, especially trombones. Until about 1610, few composers specified instruments, but most who did relied heavily on wind instruments. The following decade saw a greater proportion of collections with at least one piece that specified one or more non-keyboard instruments. More of these collections specified stringed instruments than wind instruments, but the number of pieces with trombone parts

increased. The decade from 1621 to 1630 saw a smaller number of new titles, but still more trombone pieces. (See Table 7.2 for Sartori-specific information at the end of Table 7.1.)

Northern Italy suffered a devastating outbreak of the plague in 1630–31. Forty percent of the population of Bergamo died, as did 24% of the population of Bologna. Other towns that suffered devastating loss of life included Brescia (46%), Cremona (46%), Padua (59%), Venice (33%), and hardest hit, Verona (61%).[12] Publication of new music virtually ceased. The number of new titles issued by Italian music publishers did not attain pre-1630 numbers until the 1680s. Although the annual output of new publications eventually recovered, the number of pieces that specified wind instruments did not. The previous table shows the collections that call for trombone through the end of the century.

The trombone had already begun its decline in Italy before the plague. In 1598, Pope Clement VIII took Ferrara from the Este family. It ceased to be a capital city and the remaining Este lacked the resources to patronize music as they had before. The death of Vincenzo II, Duke of Mantua, in 1627 touched off a succession war that forever ended Mantua's cultural significance. These are cases where entire musical traditions suddenly ceased to exist.

In Florence, Antonio Lassagnini, the last of the trombonists hired by Ferdinand I, died in 1634. Cosimo II hired only three wind players, none of whom can be definitely identified as trombonists. Ferdinand II appointed four musicians who appear to have played trombone at least occasionally. None is mentioned as trombonist in

Table 7.1. Rise and Fall of the Use of the Trombone in the Seventeenth Century

Decade	A	B	C	D	E	F
1597–1610	85	9	37	6	1	–
1611–1620	80	26	38	17	2	–
1621–1630	57	35	123	36	12	10
1631–1640	31	24	133*	9	2	–
1641–1650	28	20	36	2	1	3
1651–1660	18	17	13	6	–	–
1661–1670	33	32	17	–	–	–
1671–1680	40	36	10	1	–	–
1681–1690	66	60	4	–	–	–
1691–1700	63	62	–	–	–	–

A: Number of publications. Does not include reprints, the occasional works Sartori cites only on the authority of other bibliographies, or works published in Antwerp or other non-Italian cities.
B: Number of publications that include at least one piece that specifies non-keyboard instruments.
C: Number of pieces that specify wind instruments.
D: Number of pieces that specify trombone (simply).
E: Number of pieces that specify trombone with another instrument given as an alternative.
F: Number of pieces that specify some other instrument with trombone given as an alternative.

* 1638c, Fantini's *Modo per imparare a sonare di tromba*, includes 117 pieces for one or two trumpets. Without this collection, there are 16 pieces that specify wind instruments in the decade 1631–40.

Table 7.2. Additional Sartori Specifications Related to Table 7.1

Sartori	Composer	Title	A	B	C
1636	Buonamente, Gio. Battista	Sonate e canzoni	5	1	1
1637c	Fiamengo, Francesco	Pastorali concenti al prespe	1		1
1637e	Ganasso, Iacobo	Verspertina psalmodia	3	3	
1638i	Molli, Antonio	Motetti e sinfonie	3	3	
1639b	Ucellini, Marco	Sonate, sinfonie, et correnti	1	1	
1640d	Urbano, Gregorio	Sacri armonici concentus	1	1	
1642a	Ucellini, Marco	Sonate, arie et correnti	1	1	
1648	Cazzati, Mauritio	Secondo libro delle sonate	1	1	
1649a	Marini, Biagio	Concerto terzo delle musiche da camera	1		1
1649e	Ferro, Marco Antonio	Sonate . . . Alla sacra cesarea	5		3
1651b	Neri, Massimiliano	Sonate da sonarsi	8	4	
1660d	Ucellini, Marco	Ozio regio	1	1	
1679b	Pasino, Stefano	Sonate	1	1	

A = Number of pieces that specify any wind instrument (including when the wind instrument is an alternative).
B = Number of pieces that specify trombone(s) (simply).
C = Number of pieces that specify trombone(s) with another instrument given as alternative.

Note: The table in chapter 6 has a column D for the number of pieces that specify some other instrument with trombone given as alternative. There are no pieces in that category for this table.

any document later than 1652. By that time, the power and influence of the Medici had declined. The trombone disappeared from Florence mainly because it was no longer fashionable elsewhere.

In Venice, Monteverdi did not promptly fill vacancies after the plague. When opera became a commercial venture in 1637, many musicians, including Monteverdi, found more pleasure and profit from the theaters than from the churches. If the procurators had wanted to maintain San Marco's position as Venice's leading musical institution, they would have had to upgrade salaries and working conditions, but they did not. Its musical establishment regained strength, if not dominance, later in the century. In fact, from the 1680s through 1706, it had four or five trombones.

The death of chapel master Giovanni Legrenzi in 1690 marks the beginning of the final decline of San Marco's orchestra. The procurators imposed a hiring freeze. By 1708, attrition had reduced the orchestra to 18 stringed instruments, one cornett, two trombones, an oboe, and two trumpets. When the freeze was lifted in 1714, the chapel master declared that it was "impossible to find more players of bassoons, trombones and theorboes" and requested permission to substitute different instruments. He eventually hired 12 string players and a trumpeter. The last trombonist died in 1732.[13] The trombone did not disappear from Italy entirely, however. It continued to be used at least in Bologna, Naples, and Rome throughout the seventeenth and eighteenth centuries.

Germany

Germany has so far meant the aggregate of all German-speaking musical centers. Beginning in this chapter, however, Germany is largely Protestant and specifically excludes the Catholic Holy Roman Empire, which, for brevity's sake, will be called Austria. The trombone is named in the score or parts of at least 120 German works in the early seventeenth century, mostly large-scale works written under the influence of Venetian ceremonial music. The most notable composers include Heinrich Schütz, who composed 38 of them, Johann Hermann Schein (34), Michael Praetorius (24), and Samuel Scheidt (7).[14]

Most of the Thirty Years War was fought on German soil, with devastating effect on the artistic and cultural life of the various German states. Saxony was especially hard hit. In 1632, there were 39 musicians serving the Dresden court, but only 10 in 1639.[15] The war did not end until 1648, and economic recovery did not come immediately. As a result of the war, German princes could no longer afford to support large-scale works. Since the trombone had figured prominently in these works, but not in smaller works, the war effectively ended its role in German courts. Once they could again finance a large musical establishment, the Venetian style seemed old fashioned. Newer Italian and French styles, which made no use of the trombone, came into vogue.

The war did not immediately cause the disappearance of the trombone from German courts; there were three trombonists in Dresden as late as 1694, but the chapel was restructured along French lines shortly thereafter. In 1662, trombones were probably heard at ceremonies for the baptism of Prince Maximilian Emanuel von Wittelsbach in Munich, the grandest festival ever presented by the Bavarian court. As late as 1679, the Bavarian musical establishment had 29 instrumentalists, including trombonists. Trombones participated at least in one of the processions when Joseph Clemens, brother of Maximilian Emanuel, became Bishop of Freising in 1690.[16]

Such miscellaneous and sporadic references to the trombone formed most of the entire basis for describing its use in many German courts in the last chapter. There is little research published on the makeup of German musical establishments that allows documentation of either the extent of the use of the trombone or its disappearance. Generally speaking, however, the French-style oboe band replaced the traditional cornett/trombone band as the principal courtly wind ensemble between about 1680 and 1700.

Elsewhere

One of the periodic reviews of staffing at the Spanish court in 1677 noted that there were two places for trombone. One of the players was old and had already been pensioned off. The other did not play well, but the report suggested keeping him until a more suitable replacement could be found. As it turns out, he was never replaced. The only cornett player at court was also old and sick. He was not replaced, either, even though another cornettist petitioned for a post in 1679. Eventually, other cornettists and trombonists must have been hired. At the accession of King Philip V in 1700, a cornettist and a trombonist were pensioned off to make room for a second trumpet player. As late as 1700, the cathedral of Badajoz still had a trombonist in its band, but apparently not by the middle of the eighteenth century.[17]

In America, as in Spain, a vogue for the latest Italian music boosted the popularity of the violin family. Older instruments such as shawms, cornetts, and trombones began to seem old fashioned and slowly disappeared. Trombones were used in Mexico City until about 1760, but may have vanished from other Latin American centers some time earlier.[18]

The activity of publishers in Antwerp indicates that the trombone was used there in midcentury. Nicolaus a Kempis published three collections of sonatas (1644, 1647, 1649). One piece in the second collection and four in the third include parts for a trombone. Two collections of music by Dario Castello, which contain some of the most important and difficult wind music of the entire century, were reprinted in Antwerp in 1656 and 1658.

There must have been good trombonists in Antwerp, and yet apparently nothing appeared any later that uses trombones.

The Persistence of the Trombone

Leipzig and other German Towns

If the trombone had disappeared completely, like the crumhorn, for example, this would be a very different book. Instead of telling the history of a contemporary instrument played by many people worldwide in a variety of contexts, it would be about nothing more than a historical curiosity played only by a few specialists in early music. At least three eighteenth-century German writers commented on the trombone's rarity. Mattheson noted that the trombone was used only in church pieces and solemn music. Nicolai noted that the trombone was uncommon in northern Germany but still used and played well in Austria and Bavaria. Writing in 1784 or 1785, when the revival of the trombone was well underway, Schubart noted that although the trombone was greatly neglected and played only by "wretched cornett players," there were still good players in Saxony and Bohemia.[19]

If Schubart used "Bohemia" to refer to the Holy Roman Empire and Nicolai used "Austria" in the same way, then they are in partial agreement. Significantly, each found trombones in an area that the other was not aware of. Zedler noted that it was used by the *Stadtpfeifer* of Thuringia, a region that had long been ruled by Saxony. Leipzig, where Zedler's encyclopedia was published, was thus both a Thuringian and Saxon city.[20]

Civic wind bands declined because string ensembles seemed more aristocratic, important in a time when class consciousness was still strong, and because new military bands (modeled on the aristocratic oboe bands) could be hired on special occasions for less money than it took to maintain a town band. Declining prestige for the bands made it difficult to recruit good musicians to play in them, which led to a lower level of musical competence, which led to still lower prestige. The decline of German civic bands is displayed dramatically by comparing their ubiquitous use in churches around 1650 with the rarity of any reference to them by 1750. They decined, but they did not disappear entirely.

Leonard has identified 199 pieces of Lutheran church music written in the middle or late seventeenth century by 30 different composers. Especially noteworthy among the composers are Johann Rudolph Ahle (17 pieces), Wolfgang Carl Briegel (21), Andreas Hammerschmidt (48), Sebastian Knüpfer (23), Johann Rosenmüller (at least 18), Johann Schelle (14), and Christian Andreas

Schulze (10). Her list does not include late works of Heinrich Schütz, who used trombones in his *Historia von der Geburt Jesu Christi* (SWV 435, 1664) and *Herr Gott, dich loben wir* (SWV 472, before 1668).[21]

About two thirds of these pieces are large-scale works. Most of the smaller pieces were written before the economy recovered from the Thirty Years War. These pieces most commonly call for three trombones, either TTB (60 pieces) or ATB (35 pieces). Sixteen pieces use two trombones (both tenors) and 22 use only a single tenor trombone. Thus, neither the alto nor the bass trombone appears in music that uses fewer than three trombones. Some pieces require more than three trombones, from 17 for TTTB to two for five tenors and two basses. On the other hand, 33 pieces mention the trombone only as an alternative to some other instrument, usually either a mid-range or bass stringed instrument or bassoon.

The problem of determining whether a part was intended for alto, tenor, or bass trombone was touched on in chapter 1. Leonard looked primarily at the range and tessitura.[22] Only a few of these parts would not have been playable on a tenor trombone in A. How they were actually performed must have depended on the preferences and aptitudes of different performers and the instruments available at different churches.

Leonard identified fourteen different roles for the trombone in this music, from doubler of or substitute for voices or other instruments to independent obbligato instrument. These roles include not only the trombone's relationship to voices and instruments, but also its relationship to the structure of the composition, the text, and the overall mood of the piece. Trombones are used exclusively to double voices in only nine of the works. They are completely independent of voices and other instrumental parts in 26 pieces. Some of the independent parts are solos worthy of comparison with the much better-known Viennese repertoire. Trombones participate in instrumental sinfonias in 139 works and frequently take part in imitative passages, entering either before or after the corresponding vocal part. They also frequently imitate other instruments rather than voices.

The old Venetian-style polychoral writing that had been brought to Germany by Schütz persisted into the latter part of the seventeenth century. Almost 30 percent of the pieces are of this type. Other pieces use the instruments and voices to respond to each other antiphonally in quasi-polychoral sections. The overall mood of most of this music is joyful and exuberant, although these composers did not neglect to take advantage of the trombone's more funereal capabilities. The reason for this jubilation is found in the fact that the overwhelm-

ing number of works with trombone parts were intended for the celebratory seasons of Trinity (48), Easter (36), Christmas (30), Pentecost (26), and Epiphany (22). In all, 162 pieces out of the total of 199 were intended for these seasons. These figures are in line with Mattheson's observations:

> A cheerful disposition is best disposed for devotion, where such is not to be done mechanically or simply in a trance. Only the appropriate discretion and moderation with the joyful sounds of the clarino trumpets, trombones, violins, flutes, etc., must never be lost sight of, nor be to the slightest detriment of the familiar commandment, which says: Be joyous; yet in fear of God.[23]

By the time J. S. Bach began his tenure, the general deterioration of civic music noted earlier had reached Leipzig. Perhaps that is why only fifteen of his extant cantatas use trombones. In thirteen they only double the voices in the choir, and some of these trombone parts appear to have been afterthoughts. BWV118, "O Jesu Christ, mein's Lebens Licht" was originally intended for outdoor performance, and so has wind accompaniment, but as soon as Bach had occasion to play it indoors he replaced the wind parts with a string orchestra.

The oldest Protestant denomination is not the Lutheran church, but a group founded by the followers of Jan Hus in 1457, officially named *Unitas Fratrum*, but commonly known as the Moravian Church. After Protestants lost a key early battle in the Thirty Years War, however, the emperor Ferdinand II forced his Bohemian and Moravian lands to convert to Roman Catholicism. *Unitas Fratrum* went underground. In 1722, surviving Moravian Protestants found refuge in Saxony on the estate of Count Nicholas von Zinzendorf and founded a community called Herrnhut. From there, they soon became very active in world evangelism. In America, they founded communities in present-day Pennsylvania and North Carolina.

The impetus for the distinctive trombone choirs that the Moravians developed came from two directions: the town bands that were commonplace in Saxony and the need for appropriate support for voices in outdoor services. Wind instruments (horns) were used to accompany congregational singing as early as 1729. Trombones are first mentioned in 1731 and appear frequently thereafter, along with various other instruments. In 1764, however, documents begin to mention a trombone choir.[24]

The Herrnhut community (as well as later Moravian groups established all over the world) organized itself in groups called choirs that were divided according to sex, marital status, and age. Short worship services were held daily among these groups, partly for the purpose of learning the chorales that the entire congregation would then sing at evening services. The people sang *a capella* if they had to, but with instruments if they were available.

Music education was part of the basic schooling of Moravian children as early as 1725. From at least 1731, brass groups played at funeral processions and during the burial liturgy. Beginning in 1732, brass choirs played before sunrise and througout the liturgy on Easter morning. By 1740, similar *Aufblasen* announced other church festivals as well, including both those celebrated by all Christians and some peculiar to the Moravian church. Even Holy Communion was announced by chorales from the brass choir rather than the ringing of a bell. (The ordinary term for a German band's performance from a tower, *Abblasen*, literally means to blow down. *Aufblasen*, used in Moravian sources, literally means to blow up. Since Moravian trombone choirs also played from church belfries, its significance could be awakening people, both literally and spiritually. A more common word, *aufspielen*, means to strike up the band.)

A distinctively Moravian practice developed around 1750; at sunset, the brass announced the death of a member by playing two chorales. Hans Leo Hassler's "O Haupt voll Blut und Wunden" ("O Sacred Head Now Wounded") was played twice. In between, another chorale let the community know to which "choir" (Married Men, Single Sisters, etc.) the deceased belonged. This unique system was codified by 1754. Eventually, the community outgrew Hernnhut and began to establish other congregations. By 1790, there were about 15 Moravian trombone choirs in Germany and others in the United States. Morvian communities with trombone choirs were eventually established in Canada, Latin America, and Africa. The Moravians used quartets of soprano, alto, tenor, and bass trombones. The soprano trombone was not unique to the Moravians in the eighteenth century; it was used in Lutheran churches as well. Its use does, however, seem confined to certain areas in Protestant Germany.

Turning to secular music, in the aftermath of the Thirty Years War, the life of musicians was difficult. They had to wander from place to place looking for work. They had a reputation as rude and uncouth, not unlike that of itinerant musicians during the Middle Ages. And like those earlier musicians, they banded together and sought legal protection. In 1653, town musicians of north and central Germany formed a guild and submitted their statutes to Emperor Ferdinand III for his approval.

Leipzig established its town band in 1479. In 1599, a balcony was added to the tower of the newly renovated town hall, and the band began to play brief concerts, called *Abblasen*, from there twice a day—once at 10:00 in the morning when the traditional noon break began and again in the evening. At the end of the Thirty Years War, Leipzig's band consisted of four senior members (the *Stadtpfeifer*) and a group of three journeymen (the *Kunstgeiger*). Membership was by audition, usually with the result that new members were accepted as *Kunstgeiger* and eventually promoted to *Stadtpfeifer*. The Kantor of Thomaskirche in Leipzig was also the director of all musical activities in town, and therefore the band's immediate supervisor. The town band, supplemented by whatever amateurs and students were available, constituted the church orchestra. Leipzig was also home to a number of *collegia musica*. Bandsmen participated in performances of some of these groups.

Because the trombones and cornetts were associated with important ceremonial functions, and violins with dancing and entertainment, the *Stadtpfeifer*, as senior members of the group, played the more prestigious wind instruments. The *Kunstgeiger* played only stringed instruments in public unless they were substituting for a *Stadtpfeifer*. According to the statutes of the musicians' guild, these seven men held a legal monopoly not only regarding the daily concerts and other civic ceremonies, but also in providing music for the largest weddings, funerals, and other private events. This monopoly did not prevent others from attempting to cut into the town musicians' livelihood. Much primary source material about German town bands consists of documents relating to lawsuits. Some cases were the bandsmen's suits against these interlopers, who, regardless of their skills and qualifications, were dismissed as *Bierfiedler*, literally beer-fiddlers. The implication was that they were capable of playing only in taverns or other bottom-of-the-barrel gigs. The use of this derisive term does not necessarily mean that "non-union" musicians were all substandard or incompetent.

The formation of the guild did little to enhance musicians' social standing and reputation, but in 1664, Leipzig's band successfully petitioned to expand their number to eight by hiring another *Kunstgeiger*. The winning candidate, Johann Pezel, was well educated and something of a literary as well as musical figure; the classical and literary allusions in his preface to *Hora decima musicorum Lipsiensium* attest to his erudition. (See Document 1, in the appendix.)

Pezel may not have improved the prestige of the other band members, but he certainly raised the visibility of the band with his publication of *Hora decima* in 1670. He left Leipzig when plague broke out there in 1681 and took a similar position in Bautzen, where he remained until his death in 1694. Another major collection of music, *Fünff-stimmigte blasende Musik* was published in Frankfurt in 1685. Both of these collections were composed expressly for a five-part wind band of two cornetts and three trombones.

Although brass instruments had more prestige than stringed instruments within the community of town musicians, they did not within the wider society. As much as modern brass players claim him as one of their own, the ambitious Pezel appears to have been more interested in publishing string music. In fact, one of his collections of string music, *Supellex sonatarum selectarum* (1674), is nothing more than a reprint from the same plates of *Hora decima musicorum*. Disguised with a different title, different dedication, and the addition of a basso continuo partbook, it was published in Dresden instead of Leipzig. His republication of a wind collection in the guise of string music, his use of Latinized forms of his name on the title pages of all of his published works, and the classical allusions and fancy prose of the dedications may all indicate that he was dissatisfied with his career as a lowly town musician.[25]

Another well-known member of the Leipzig band, Gottfried Reiche, was, like Pezel, a trumpet player whose importance to the history of the trombone consists of compositions for wind band. His *Vier und zwanzig neue Quatricinia*, for one cornett and three trombones, was, like Pezel's wind collections, written to provide new music for the twice-daily band concerts. Leipzig's town band lasted until 1862. It underwent one major reorganization at the beginning of the nineteenth century, and trombone virtuoso Carl Traugott Queisser led it for a while.[26]

Neither Schubart nor Nicolai mentioned the Duchy of Württemburg as a center for excellent trombone playing, but two noteworthy figures lived and worked there. Daniel Speer was a church musician and schoolteacher in Göppingen on and off from 1667 until the end of his life. Before his arrival in Göppingen, he served for a few years as a town musician in Stuttgart. Speer's description of the trombone clearly shows first-hand knowledge of it. Like Pezel, he was exceptionally well educated for a town musician. Besides his compositions and treatise, he wrote three autobiographical novels that give a humorous picture of town musicians.[27]

Johann Georg Christian Störl, a Stuttgart composer and younger contemporary of Speer, wrote six tower sonatas for cornett and three trombones. They are in many ways comparable to the works of Pezel and Reiche, but unlike the two Leipzigers, Störl was not a trumpeter or town musician. He held a position of leadership in the duke's musical establishment, and concurrently as a church organist. The bulk of his output as a composer was sacred choral music.[28]

Bologna and other Italian Towns

Bologna lost nearly a quarter of its population in the plague of 1630. Camillo Cortellini, the leader of the Concerto Palatino's *musici*, perished in that year, as did one trumpet player. Otherwise the entire organization survived intact. Never again, however, did it regain the fame and preeminence that it had before the disaster struck, for if the band continued to operate as before, the mainstream of musical development in Italy eventually went on without it. And even though its members continued to include excellent musicians, its standards as an ensemble may have suffered. The church of San Petronio also used trombones extensively, with different personnel.

Like the Leipzig *Stadtpfeifer*, the Concerto Palatino's duties included twice-daily concerts from the balcony of the palace. Its members included some of the most respected musicians in town. Where early in the seventeenth century, the duties of the *musici* seem limited to playing cornett or trombone, the ability to play other instruments increased in importance. In 1779, because of the difficulty of finding students willing to learn to play cornett, the town council replaced the old instrumentation with a French-style oboe band. None of the members lost their jobs; they were all able to play the new instruments. There were two excellent trombonists among the supernumeraries at the time. Antonio Mariotti chose to leave Bologna. He made his career as a specialist on trombone in Naples, Paris, and London. Giovanni Battista Zoboli, on the other hand, chose to stay. By the time he was able to achieve a promotion to full, salaried membership, he was playing bassoon in the band, but won a position as trombonist at San Petronio the same year.[29]

The abolition of the cornett and trombone ensemble nearly happened a century earlier. Although there had been a close working relationship between San Petronio and the Concerto Palatino for centuries, a rift occurred in 1658. New chapel master Maurizio Cazzati published a document that announced sweeping innovations. Among other things, he decreed that no one employed by the Concerto Palatino could also play in the church orchestra:

> The players of Cornetts, Trombones, and Violones should always appear with their instruments in the solemnities and festivities as well as Saturday evenings for

the Litanie or Motet to the Madonna, and when singing is accompanied by Organs, the players of Violin, Violetta, and others also appear with their instruments. . .

Finally, because we know from experience the little good service that the Church and Music receive from the Musicians of the Mansion and the Musicians of the Palace, the latter many times leaving the service halved, and many times all under pretext of going to the Palace, so that its body of eight voices remains diminished at every turn; and those abandoning their own Chorus in order to serve the Music, and Music in order to go to the Chorus, they cannot serve well in either place. Therefore, I declare that the singer or player who enters the Music of the Mansion or the Palace shall be excluded from all Music of S. Petronio. And all in conformity to the decree of the said Most Illustrious Gentleman President and Vestry drawn up by the undersigned Notary.[30]

That Cazzati chose to exclude so many excellent musicians from service at San Petronio demonstrates not only his boldness and unwillingness to be limited by tradition, but also the amount of talent available to him. He made a lot of enemies and was dismissed for incompetence in 1671, Shortly thereafter, six musicians from San Petronio decided to try to work for the basilica and the town simultaneously. One of them, Guido Maria Borghese, would later join the Concerto Palatino as a trombonist. With three other musicians, they approached the town council with the idea of establishing a town string ensemble. The council jumped at the idea of establishing a new and up-to-date ensemble, which would certainly have enhanced the prestige of the town music and secured a favorable image for the members of the council. Had they summarily dismissed the cornett/trombone band and replaced it with a string ensemble, the trombone probably would have eventually disappeared from Bologna, but the wind band was still a valued part of musical life in Bologna, especially the daily concerts from the balcony of the palace.

One of the peculiarities of the political structure of Bologna was that the members of the council served terms of only two months. They had no authority to appropriate money; that was the prerogative of the senate. On October 29, 1671, near the end of their term, the council decided to establish a string ensemble and pay them from the salaries and bread allowances already appropriated for the wind band. The members of the wind band promptly appealed this decision to the next council. The senate, which might have been persuaded to establish another ensemble had they been consulted first, refused to appropriate more money. The chance for

Bologna to update its civic musical establishment thus passed before the end of the year.[31]

By 1630, the personnel lists at San Petronio had not listed singers and instrumentalists separately since 1614, but it is still possible to determine the role of at least some of the personnel by comparing the 1630 list with the 1614 list. The last clearly identifiable trombonist, Camillo Cortellini, died in that year and does not appear at all. Ercole Gaibara, who would later distinguish himself as both trombonist and violinist, was on the San Petronio payroll, but listed in such a way that he may have been hired as a singer. On the surface, then, it appears that the trombone was on the verge of disappearing from San Petronio even before the plague. In fact, however, it played a very important role in a new style of concerted mass that Bolognese composers wrote in abundance. These composers include Cortellini and three successive chapel masters: Cazzati, Giovanni Paolo Colonna, and Giacomo Antonio Perti.

The term *concerted mass* refers to two or more contrasting musical forces. While it can refer to polychoral music for voices alone, it most often means a mass composed for a combination of voices and instruments. In Bologna, it eventually came to mean specifically a mass with solo voices, choir, and instruments. Because of Bologna's influence on sacred composition in Vienna, Beethoven's *Missa solemnis* is a direct descendant of the northern Italian concerted mass of the seventeenth century.

The archives of the Accademia Filarmonica of Bologna include three pieces that explicitly call for trombones: a "Dixit Dominus" by Giovanni Antonio Manara (1667) for two four-voice choirs, each with its own string ensemble and some additional instruments including bass trombone; a "Domine ad adiuvandum" by Benedetto Sarti (1684) for three four-voice choirs, each with its own instrumental ensemble including a tenor trombone in choirs two and three; and an instrumental canzona by Giacomo Predieri (1688) for two choirs of two cornetts and two trombones.[32] Although composers seeking membership in the academy wrote them as test pieces, Manara's and Sarti's may reflect some of the practices of music actually written for the liturgy. Predieri's is more illustrative of the music of the Concerto Palatino.

Records at San Petronio again began to identify musicians according to what they sang or played beginning in 1658. From then on there were either one or two trombonists on the payroll until 1729 (except for the years 1676, a temporary absence, and 1696–1700, when the church disbanded its entire musical establishment to save money). The basilica hired additional musicians,

Fig. 7.2. Musical angels, detail of the apsidal dome of the Chapel of Sant'Andrea. S. Gregorio Magno, Rome, Italy, by Guido Reni (1575–1642). Photo Credit: Alinari / Art Resource, NY.

including one to eight extra trombonists, for special occasions, especially for the patronal feast on October 4. Beginning in 1761, San Petronio again had a trombonist on its payroll until 1893.

Outside musicians hired for the feast of San Petronio in 1658 included trombonists from Treviso and Cento. Marco Ucellini, who included trombone parts in collections published between 1639 and 1660, worked for the Este court in Modena. How long the trombone persisted in any of these towns is impossible to guess. It did, however, continue to be used without interruption in Naples and Rome.[33]

Austria

Vienna

In 1619, Ferdinand II (r. 1619–37) became Holy Roman Emperor. Earlier, during a journey to Italy as Archduke of Austria, he had attended Vespers at San Marco. Greatly impressed, he had a choirbook of Vene-

tian music copied for him. The musicians he assembled as archduke continued to serve him after he became emperor. He presided over the largest and most opulent court in all of Europe.[34] Venetian polychoral music, and the brilliant wind parts that were so vital to the Venetian ceremonial style, became the core of the chapel's repertoire. Every chapel master who served in his court was Venetian. Other strong and abiding influences on Ferdinand II's court included the courts of Mantua and Munich, where wind music was also prominent.

Praetorius's comments on the polychoral style of Giovanni Gabrieli described not only the older Italian works that held a steady place in the Viennese repertoire, but also many of the large-scale works of court composers such as Giovanni Priuli, chapel master from about 1614 to 1626, and Giovanni Valentini, his successor. Trombones, in other words, played a conspicuous part. Viennese composers of this time also produced numerous smaller works, including the kinds of sonatas in which Italians used trombones extensively until about 1630. According to Newman, Valentini composed seven four- or five-part sonatas for "the familiar and various combinations of violins, violas, cornetts, flutes, trombone, bassoon, and organ bass."[35]

The next three emperors, Ferdinand III (r. 1637–57), Leopold I (r. 1658–1706), and Joseph I (r. 1705–1711), were not only music lovers, but also composers of some merit. Charles VI (r. 1711–70) may have been a composer, although no works attributable to him are extant. Maria Theresa (r. 1745–80) was a gifted singer, and Joseph II (r. 1765–90, co-regent with his mother until 1780) had sufficient knowledge of music theory and keyboard instruments to realize continuo parts.[36]

Eventually, the Venetian polychoral style of music favored by Ferdinand II began to seem old-fashioned. Changes in taste had helped put the trombone out of business in parts of plague-ravaged Italy or war-torn Germany of the 1630s. The Austrian empire, by contrast, found new inspiration in the concerted masses of Bologna. Leopold I had 44 volumes of Bolognese masses prepared for him. His court composers, including Antonio Bertali, Johann Heinrich Schmeltzer, and Antonio Draghi, produced new masses according to the Bolognese model.

Johann Joseph Fux, a court composer from the end of Leopold I's reign through the end of Joseph I's reign, became Charles VI's chapel master in 1715. The combination of an Italian tradition, a new openness to French influence, and the native-born and largely self-taught chapel master laid the groundwork for the later Viennese classical style. Fux and his contemporaries took full advantage of the presence of such renowned virtuoso trombonists as Leopold Christian, father and son, among others. The reign of Charles VI thus represents a golden age for the trombone in terms of both the amount and quality of soloistic music written for it.

Maria Theresa had to endure the War of Austrian Succession before her throne was secure. That put an end to some traditions in which the trombone had taken a conspicuous part. By the end of the century, there were no longer any virtuoso trombone soloists in Vienna, but there were still trombonists and new music being written for them to play.

Trombones accompanied the choir during the celebration of the Mass first in the Venetian manner of Gabrieli, then in the Bolognese manner of Colonna and Perti, and eventually in a uniquely Viennese manner beginning with Fux. They also had conspicuous parts in many of the sonatas typically heard before the Mass, at the Gradual, at the Elevation, and for Post-Communion.

Some indication of the importance of the trombone in Viennese church music comes from examining the works of the emperors themselves. At least one sacred work by Ferdinand III and eight by Leopold I include trombone parts.

By far the trombone's most common role in church music was to double the alto and tenor voices of the choir. Viennese composers did not regularly double the bass part with a trombone. Of far more interest to trombonists, however, many of the solo arias are accompanied by trombone solos, which often require great virtuosity. This practice appears to have begun with Fux and the generation of composers that he led, most notably Antonio Caldara. It is possible to identify nearly 200 of Fux's works that include trombones, representing nearly every genre of sacred music and also some sonatas. Caldara was at least equally prolific. The two generations of composers that followed Fux contain no great masters, but they do include a number of imaginative composers who continued to write for trombone in the manner of Fux and Caldara and laid the groundwork for the flowering of Viennese classicism under Haydn and Mozart.[37]

At midcentury, the most common instruments for obbligato solos were the violin and trombone. After about 1770, however, the younger composers began to write more independent parts for oboe, viola, and cello, and fewer trombone solos. But although the trombone eventually lost its solo role in the mass, it continued to be an important part of the orchestra, and not only as a doubling instrument. One need only consider the places in Mozart's *Waisenhauskirche Mass* and the *Requiem* where the trombones are independent of the chorus, in addition to the solo in "Tuba mirum."

In 1783, Joseph II began to impose sweeping reforms on the church. All churches were forced to curtail the number of musicians that they kept on the payroll. Mass compositions became shorter and less elaborate. By no coincidence, many of the best Viennese composers, Mozart included, turned away from the composition of church music entirely until after Joseph's death. Because the trombone had begun to take a less conspicuous role in the mass even before the Josephine reforms, it never regained the prominence that it had in the first seven or eight decades of the century.

Fux and his followers were able to write such florid trombone parts because great virtuosos like the Leopold Christians (father and son), Andreas Boog, or Ignaz Steinbruckner were available. It is equally true that these and others could become great trombonists because there was a constant supply of music for them to play. Between the changes of style in the 1770s and the political conditions of the 1780s, the role of the trombone diminished to the point where there was no incentive to develop excellence on it. At about the same time, composers were beginning to use trombones in operas but they did not include any kind of solo role for them, or even very continuous playing. That is why there were no trombonists at the end of the century who could be compared with the great virtuosos of earlier generations.

Opera was first performed in Vienna to celebrate Ferdinand II's birthday in 1625. Of the hundreds of dramatic works composed for the entertainment of the emperors and invited guests probably only *Il pomo d'oro* by Antonio Cesti includes trombone parts. Surely one of the longest and most complicated operas ever written, it consists of a prologue and five acts. It required 23 stage designs and 39 machines to produce the various special effects and took some 8 hours to perform. Apparently, no other secular dramatic work included trombones until Gluck's ballet *Don Juan* (1761).

Sacred dramatic works are another matter. Trombones became an important component of the Viennese oratorios and *sepolcri* (plural of *sepolcro*), which were a kind of oratorio performed on Maundy Thursday for the private enjoyment of the emperor, his family, and possibly invited guests. They were not performed in any other setting. The librettos were published, but the music was not. Aside from the fact that the trombone parts resemble those of public oratorios and Viennese liturgical music, much of which was written by the same composers, *sepolcri* had no influence beyond the court. In both oratorios and *sepolcri*, the trombone arias were reserved for moments of dramatic intensity and often specifically associated either with the word of God or his wrath and judgment.

From 1669 until his death in 1699, Antonio Draghi was the leading composer of these dramas. Of his 29 *sepolcri*, only one, *Il libro con sette sigilli*, uses trombones, and that in only one scene. Many eighteenth-century *sepolcri* and oratorios use the trombone as a solo instrument. Marc'Antonio Ziani included seven trombone arias in four of them written between 1704 and 1708. The emperor Joseph I inserted one in an otherwise anonymous *sepolcro* in 1705. From 1716 until 1735, at least one oratorio with at least one trombone aria was written every year. Earlier works were revived in 1736 and 1737, and then new works with trombone arias appeared in 1738 and 1739. After that, the tradition abruptly ceased. Charles VI died in October of 1740 after a long illness, and in the succession war that followed, much of the musical life of the court had to be sacrificed. Never again, in fact, did the imperial court patronize music on the lavish scale seen in the reigns of the emperors from Ferdinand II through Charles VI. [38]

Antonio Caldara, the most prolific composer of trombone arias, composed 43 oratorios altogether; 24 of them were composed after he moved from Italy to Vienna, 11 of which contain trombone arias. He also composed movements that involve several solo singers in succession, each accompanied by a different solo instrument, frequently pairing an alto trombone with an alto singer. Fux included trombone arias in six of his 14 oratorios. [39]

I mentioned earlier that trombones took part in sonatas played during the liturgy. These same works were also suitable for chamber music, that is, music for recreation and entertainment rather than worship. Bertali, Fux, and Franz IgnazTuma, among others, wrote several works for small instrumental ensembles that included one or more trombones. [40]

Georg Wagenseil, one of the leading musicians of his generation at the imperial court, composed a wide variety of music, including what is generally considered the earliest extant concerto for trombone. According to Wigness, it was written some time before 1763 and probably intended for one of the three most outstanding trombonists among the Viennese court: Leopold Christian Jr., Andreas Boog, or Ignaz Steinbruckner. It is a problematical work, with two movements, inviting speculation that it is either incomplete or part of a larger work. There is no extant score, only two sets of parts in different hands, found not in Vienna but Kroměříž. One of them names both Wagenseil and Reiter as composer. Shifrin raises the possibility that the work was written for the consecration of a new Archbishop of Olomouc in 1777, that the intended performer was Thomas Gschlatt, that Wagenseil died before completing the work, and that Georg Reutter finished it. The loss of the original manuscript makes certainty impossible. [41]

Salzburg

From 1278 until the abolition of the empire, Salzburg was ruled by prince-archbishops. It achieved its first musical significance during the reign of Wolf Dietrich (r. 1587–1612), who instituted many of the practices that were still in place in the time of the Mozarts nearly two centuries later. The archdiocese supported four independent ensembles. An adult choir and a boys' choir performed mostly at the cathedral. There was also a group of trumpeters besides the main court music. Additionally, the town and the military both had their own musical establishments. The military band in Mozart's day was the standard *Harmonie* band. The town band probably originated in the late Middle Ages or early Renaissance, just like bands everywhere else and would have been comprised of cornetts (or shawms) and trombones. It still had trombones in Mozart's time. Marpurg noted:

> Finally, three trombonists are also used in the choir, namely to play the alto, tenor, and bass trombones, which the tower master and two of his subordinates must supply for a certain annual income.[42]

A trombonist first appears in court payment records in 1608, although town musicians may have supplied trombonists earlier than that. The practices recommended by Praetorius probably fit the music in Salzburg during this time. As elsewhere in Austria, trombones were among the most commonly used instruments. Composers rarely prescribed instruments in the written music, however. Any given work could be performed very differently from one time to the next, depending on the importance of the occasion.[43]

Musically speaking, the Salzburg court reached its pinnacle under the leadership of Siegmund Christoph, Count of Schrattenbach (r. 1753–71). Not only was he lavish in his support of court music in general, but he was a strong supporter of the Mozarts. When he died, Joseph II appointed Hieronymous, Count of Colloredo (r. 1772–1806). Colloredo's attempts to reform and modernize the archdiocese by secularizing it were no more popular than Joseph II's parallel reforms and just as ruinous for the composition of church music. The bad blood between Colloredo and Wolfgang Mozart is legendary.

Mozart composed at least five works for trombone during Schrattenbach's lifetime. Two are particularly noteworthy: *Die Schuldigkeit des ersten Gebots* (K.V. 35, 1767), which he wrote as a child of 11 when Schrattenbach locked him up to find out if he could really compose music without help from his father, and the *Missa solemnis: "Waisenhaukirche Mass"* (K.V. 47a (139), 1768). Before Colloredo literally had him kicked out of the court in 1781, Mozart wrote nine other sacred works (including three masses) that included trombone parts. The "Waisenhaukirche Mass" was composed not for Salzburg, but for the consecration of an orphanage church in Vienna. Figure 7.3 shows the interior of this church.

The most important figure in Salzburg as far as the trombone is concerned, however, is not Mozart but the trombone virtuoso Thomas Gschlatt, who served there as solo trombonist from 1756 to 1769.[44] Marpurg wrote, "Mr. Thomas Gschlatt of Stockerau in Lower Austria is a great master on his instrument, which very few will do as well. He also plays a good violin and violoncello and blows the horn no less well."[45]

In addition to the first Mozart piece mentioned above, the solo works written for Gschlatt included movements in at least five works by Johann Ernst Eberlin, apparently several by Anton Adlgasser, at least one serenade by Leopold Mozart, and several pieces by Michael Haydn, including a "Larghetto à Trombone Conc^{to}," a divertimento, and "Adagio e Allegro molto" for horn and trombone.[46] Marpurg's comments indicate that Gschlatt was not exclusively a trombonist. There was evidently not enough music with solo trombone parts to keep him busy, and he was not part of the town band. He left the court of Salzburg to become the tower master in the Moravian town of Olomouc in 1769. After his departure, there were no more opportunities to compose soloistic trombone parts in Salzburg.

Kroměříž and Olomouc

Up until just before the Thirty Years War, Bohemia and Moravia had a strong Protestant movement. The war, in fact, began with Ferdinand II's decision to crush Protestantism and compel the people to return to obedience to Rome. This process was completed by 1626. Ferdinand then promoted certain ecclesiastics to the title of prince-bishop. Moravia was ruled by the Prince-Bishop of Olomouc, who resided in a castle in the nearby town of Kroměříž. Karl Liechtenstein-Castelcorno served as prince-bishop from 1664 to 1695. Like many other nobles in the empire, he was an art and music lover with his own musical household. He was especially interested in native musicians and in instrumental virtuosity. Some 1400 pieces of music were either composed or copied for his court, and more than a thousand of them still survive.

Most of the music in the archive was composed for religious services, either for the prince-bishop's private chapel, the cathedral in Olomouc, or the collegiate church of St. Mauritius in Kroměříž. Although Liechtenstein's musical establishment was smaller than the imperial court, it was comparable in quality of both the composers and the performers at his disposal. It was one of the places that Leopold I loved to visit. Outstanding resident composers included Philipp Jakob Rittler, Pavel Vejvanovský, and Heinrich Biber.[47]

Vejvanovský, trumpet virtuoso, leader of the castle wind band, and choir director at St. Mauritius, is a prime example of Liechtenstein's interest in promoting local musicians. The archive includes 142 of his pieces. His more soloistic trombone parts display a lyrical style that demands a wide range and great technical facility. Biber was Leichtenstein's first chapel master, but left Kroměříž for Salzburg after only four years of service. A sonata that he wrote in Kroměříž for two violins, trombone, and

Fig. 7.3. Interior of the Waisenhauskirche in Vienna. Photo Credit: Erich Lessing / Art Resource, NY.

continuo has been published and recorded in the twentieth century. It contains a brief solo for each instrument. Although Biber is best known today as a composer of violin sonatas, the trombone solo in this piece shows that he understood the character and technical possibilities of the trombone very well.

According to an inventory taken in 1760, there were three anonymous trombone concertos in the prince-bishop's library. In other words, even if the Wagenseil concerto was composed before 1763, it is not the first ever written for trombone, merely the earliest still extant. That a virtuoso like Gschlatt would find it attractive to leave Salzburg for Olomouc indicates that the tradition of excellent trombone playing continued well into the eighteenth century. Copies of many works with soloistic trombone parts exist in multiple collections, indicating that the tradition in Bohemia was not limited to a few major cultural centers. In fact, it lasted longer in Bohemia than in either Vienna or Salzburg. Frantisek Navratil, Alois Nanke, and Jan August Vitasek, all of whom lived into the nineteenth century, wrote works with soloistic trombone parts. Manuscript copies of some works with prominent trombone parts were made, presumably for performance, as late as 1889.[48]

Melk and other Austrian Centers

The abbey of Melk stands on the Danube River west of Vienna. In the eighteenth century, it was about a day's travel, which made it a very convenient stopping point for travelers to and from Vienna. Entertaining distinguished visitors such as members of the imperial court was an important aspect of life at Melk. Therefore an excellent musical establishment was essential. Melk's wind band traced its lineage back to the Middle Ages. Its leader was identified by a variety of titles, among them tower master, although by the eighteenth century the band apparently no longer played from towers. That Johann Jacob Christian, tower master from 1663 to 1673, was the father and therefore presumably the teacher of the renowned trombone virtuoso Leopold Christian Sr. is sufficient evidence that Melk enjoyed excellent wind music in the seventeenth century.[49]

The band played for the same kinds of occasions as most other similar bands: church services, carnival celebrations, ceremonies and entertainment for visiting dignitaries, various processions, and in the theater orchestras as needed. Trombones would probably have been routinely included in all of these kinds of performance except in the theater. One standard occasion for wind music, if not unique, seems unusual. Austrian abbeys had times set aside twice a year for bloodletting as a health measure. At Melk, this was done for three days in May and three days in September. These occasions were counted as rest days, with special care taken in planning both special meals and special music, including performances by the wind band.

A number of important musicians had ties to Melk. Notable trombonists included Johann Anton Bachschmidt and Roman Korner. Johann Georg Albrechtsberger became organist at Melk in 1759 and remained there until 1765, composing prolifically. His "Alma Redemptoris Mater" (1761) contains soloistic parts for both alto and tenor trombones. He was living in Vienna at the time he composed his trombone concerto in 1769.

Joseph II's reforms hit Melk hard. By the time he died, there were only 15 monks in residence. It had lost its seminary, gymnasium, and boys' choir. During this disruption, a collection of instruments was lost, as was the cataloging system for organizing the music library. Enough music survived to make it worthwhile to try to recatalog it later, but in the meantime, some of it was apparently used for scrap paper or otherwise destroyed.

Franz Schneider moved to Melk as a young man to study organ and composition with Albrechtsberger. The reforms caused so much disruption that he became the abbey's music director, the first lay person ever to hold this position. He devoted the rest of his career to church music. Of his nearly 200 extant works, 48 include parts for trombone, usually alto and tenor. One of his masses, no. 2 in Freeman's catalog, reflects the effects of Joseph's reforms. It was first composed in 1782, before the loss of the schools, and calls for chorus and an orchestra that did not include trombones. In order to use this mass later, Schneider had to rescore it. He had no orchestra, so he replaced it with an organ. The choir apparently needed help, so he augmented it with trombones.[50]

Music at Melk did not begin to recover until 1811, when a new abbot reestablished a boys' school and choir. Rejuvenation of the abbey's musical life came swiftly after that. Musical receipts from 1817 indicate that several major works were acquired and performed in that year, including at least three with trombone parts: Haydn's *Creation*, *Seasons*, and *Seven Last Words*. The receipts also indicate that two trombones were among the instruments repaired in that year.[51]

So far this section has examined the use of the trombone at the imperial court, the courts of two prince-bishoprics, and an important abbey. Music with parts for trombone, including virtuosic solo parts, has been found at at least four other abbeys (Göttweig, Klosterneuberg, Kremsmunster, and Lambach) and at at least one parish church in Vienna (Schottenstift). The town of Linz had two special traditions that used a trombone ensemble. One was to play equali for funerals. It is not clear when this tradition started, but the use of the term *equale* to refer to a short, chordal piece for trombone ensemble seems to have originated with Franz Xaver Glöggl, who persuaded Beethoven to compose his equali. The other was to play music from the tower of the town hall on All Souls' Day.[52]

The Revival of the Trombone

Italy and England, Part One

Interested musicians have long known that the trombone was conspicuously used in certain German-speaking areas throughout the eighteenth century. It has been assumed that somehow its worldwide revival came about because composers like Gluck and Mozart found new uses for it. But in fact, the headwaters of this revival are found in Rome.

In 1650, the trombone was confined to the very traditional music provided by the town band and the pope's

Fig. 7.4. The Benedictine Abbey of Melk, seen from the Danube River, by Jakob Prandtauer (1656–1728). Built 1700–1739. Abbey, Melk, Austria. Photo Credit: Erich Lessing / Art Resource, NY.

band. Kircher published a very perfunctory description of it, apparently not considering either the instrument or the ensemble it played in very interesting. Fifteen years later, it began to find new roles when Alessandro Stradella used one in his *Accademia d'Amore*. Only a handful of works over the next several decades are known to have called for trombone, but these include *La Resurrezione* by George Frideric Handel (1708).[53] Handel had heard traditional German wind band music growing up in Germany. He must have heard not only traditional Italian wind band music in Rome, but also in newer concertos, symphonies, and oratorios. The trombone's role in all of this music may have been nothing more than doubling the bass line in the manner of the Bolognese concerted mass, but it was new and fresh enough that when trombones became available in England, Handel took full advantage.

The only well-documented use of the trombone in England between the time of Charles II and 1784 are certain performances of two of Handel's oratorios, *Saul* and *Israel in Egypt*. Both were composed in 1738 and first performed in 1739. No trombonists lived and worked in England at the time. Whoever played these parts must have been traveling foreigners. German or Italian players seem equally plausible.

Handel planned to use trombones in at least two other oratorios. In the "Dead March" in the third act of *Samson* (composed 1741, performed 1742), two trombones double the violins and violas. The already beloved march from *Saul*, reorchestrated to replace the trombones, was quickly substituted for the original march, however, which perhaps was never played at all. Handel also composed another march for trombones and timpani, which was recently noticed among the sketches for *Samson*, although apparently not intended for the oratorio and certainly never performed. In the autograph score of *Hercules* (1744), Handel wrote, then deleted, parts for two trombones in a triumphal march in the first act. Evidently, he hoped that the trombonists who played for *Saul* and *Israel in Egypt* would be available for *Samson* and *Hercules*, but found that they were not.[54]

In the two works where Handel did use trombones, he used them extensively and imaginatively. *Saul* calls for trombones in four choruses and four instrumental movements. *Israel in Egypt* uses them in ten choruses. Unless there are similar parts in the music he heard in Italy, which seems unlikely, his trombone parts are without precedent. Handel was the first composer to use trombones in purely instrumental movements of vocal music. In choral movements, he used them to double other instruments as often as he used them to double the

choir. He also introduced two new kinds of doubling: modified doubling, in which the trombone part is somewhat different from the part being doubled, and autonomous doubling, in which the trombone parts are derived from more than one other part. Handel even wrote some trombone parts that cannot easily be described as any kind of doubling, but they are not at all soloistic.[55]

Perhaps the use of trombones in theater music would have met a dead end after Handel no longer had trombonists to write for, except for Gluck's presence in London. It does not seem possible that Gluck actually heard any of Handel's trombone parts, but he must have acquired printed scores of Handel's music to study. The large choral funeral scene in *Orfeo ed Euridice* is modeled on the large choral funeral scene in *Saul*.[56] That is, one of the only two scenes with trombone parts in Gluck's work is modeled after the scene that contains Handel's most famous piece with trombones.

Once Naples became an important center for the performance and composition of operas, the trombone must have at least occasionally been heard at San Carlo, the royal theater. It was more than an opera theater. At certain times of the year, it became a dance hall, and the orchestra played minuets and contredances. A pay register for 1783–84 shows that there were 80 instruments in the orchestra, including 53 violins (a number that probably includes violas and cellos), six oboes, four clarinets, eight horns, eight basses, and one trombone, played by Antonio Mariotti.[57] Many years later, his friend and compatriot Giacomo Ferrari described how he got that position. (See Document 3, in the appendix.)

It will be forever impossible to document the history and development of the orchestra in Naples. The state archives were destroyed during the Second World War. Some fragments of various archives still exist, however, including documents relating to the years 1781–86. Beginning in 1782, the *tromba spezzata* (trombone) joined the orchestra. The trombonist, Mariotti, earned a higher salary than the trumpeters, so he was clearly a full participant in the orchestra and not an occasional extra. He probably remained in Naples until 1789. In that year, his performance on trombone was a revelation to musicians and audiences in Paris.[58]

A few works produced in Naples that call for trombone can be identified. The "Sinfonia bellica" of Alessandro Scarlatti's oratorio *La Giuditta* (1693) expressly requires "basso di violini e tromboni," that is, more than one trombone to join the basses. The first aria (and only that aria) in Giovanni Paisiello's opera *Olimpiade* (1786) calls for trombone. *Olimpiade* was the first opera Paisiello wrote for San Carlo after a long absence. Mariotti probably played the trombone part. There must have been other trombonists in Naples, however. Mariotti was gone by 1793 when Paisiello revived *Olimpiade* with a new overture that calls for a trombone. Other Paisiello operas that call for trombone include *Proserpine* (Paris, 1803) and *I Pittagorici* (Naples, 1808).[59]

Paisiello was not the only Neapolitan composer who used trombones in operas produced in Paris. So did Antonio Sacchini and Nicolò Piccini. The writing for trombone in Piccini's first Parisian opera, *Roland* (1778), while limited, shows good understanding of its dramatic possibilities. He must have already learned how to use it in works that he composed in Naples.

It is noteworthy that the specific works with trombone that I have identified in Rome and Naples were written for the theater and that all of the uses of the trombone mentioned in Bologna were either for the traditional town band or for the church. A complete picture of the use of the trombone in any of these cities is not yet possible. No work on Bolognese opera as thorough as Schnoebelen's study of masses at San Petronio or archival research on the personnel of Bolognese theaters comparable to Gambassi's works on Concerto Palatino or San Petronio has yet been published. Neither has church music in Naples attracted nearly as much scholarly attention as opera. Scholarly treatments of church music that include consideration of the constitution and use of the orchestra are rare indeed. It seems reasonable to expect that if a complete picture ever becomes available, trombones would be found most commonly in town or church bands and only sporadically in the theater or other settings until at least the 1780s. By that time, the influence of Gluck's operas was paramount, and trombone parts in operas probably became more common all over Italy.

Opera and Other Novelties in Austria

In 1761, Gluck called for a single trombone in the final movement of his ballet *Don Juan*. It marks an important turning point. After using the trombone in *Orfeo ed Euridice* and *Alceste*, Gluck wrote, or rewrote, five operas for Paris that used trombones. Other composers soon followed. The revival of the trombone was underway. The Viennese classical style is an amalgam of elements from earlier French, German, and Italian styles. Perhaps because musicians in any of those other countries could find much that was comfortable and familiar as well as much that was novel, the Viennese style became not only popular but almost dominant worldwide. Most of the developments that will be considered for the rest of this chapter can be traced either directly or indirectly to

new Viennese practices, which in turn can be traced to Handel's novel use of the trombone.

Mozart used trombones in three operas: *Idomeneo* (1781), *Don Giovanni* (1787), and *Die Zauberflöte* (1791). These are the only operas that he wrote that have important supernatural or religious elements. As in Gluck's operas, Mozart used the trombones only to reinforce those elements. *Idomeneo* was performed only twice during Mozart's lifetime and probably had no influence on other composers. The other two operas, on the other hand, immediately became international favorites. His first work for the theater that used trombones, however, was little-known incidental music, composed in Salzburg, for *Thamos, König von Ägypten* (1773?).

Until some large-scale study of opera performances in Vienna is published, it will not be clear how many operas by Mozart's contemporaries used trombones. There were probably not very many. In Paris, Salieri used trombones to excellent dramatic effect in *Tarare*, but when he revised it for Vienna as *Axur, re d'Ormus*, he eventually deleted them. There were no trombonists on the regular payroll at the Burgtheater, so requiring them would have involved extra expense. It appears that three trombones were used for the first seven performances, but not later ones.[60]

Edge has reconstructed the various Viennese orchestras known to have performed Mozart's operas. None of them regularly included trombonists. Along with harpists and mandolin players, trombonists were hired only if they were needed for particular works. It appears that, as a cost-cutting move, trombones were omitted from performances of *Don Giovanni* during the 1788–89 season. Even though *Die Zauberflöte* was given its premiere at a much smaller theater, trombones were added to the orchestra for that performance, if not necessarily subsequent ones. The personnel records are no longer extant.[61]

Mozart used trombones in only one concert work, the oratorio *Davidde penitente*, which was performed by the Tonkünstler-Societät in 1785. Two trombonists appear on the orchestra list for that concert, but not on other lists. Edge summarizes only the three extant lists from concerts that included Mozart's music, so it is possible that other composers occasionally wrote concert works with trombone parts. Since the trombones were so clearly hired as extras and were not regular members of the orchestra, the number of such works cannot be large.

Joseph Haydn's first use of the trombone occurs in the 1784 revision of his oratorio *Il ritorno di Tobia*, originally composed nine years earlier. He made extensive cuts, but also added two new choruses. The second, "Svanisce in un momento," requires two trombones. The use of two alto trombones instead of a trio of alto, tenor, and bass marks the only resemblance to the traditional Viennese manner of writing trombone parts. Otherwise, his rather tentative scoring for trombone clearly shows his familiarity with Handel's trombone parts.

Beginning with the *Seven Last Words*, however, Haydn wrote trombone parts with assurance and boldness. Later works with trombones include *The Creation*, *The Seasons*, and *Te Deum*. All of Haydn's trombone parts show a greater resemblance to Handel's practice than to the traditional Viennese manner. Haydn is the only important Austrian composer of church music who never scored for the trombone in any of his masses.

In Beethoven's music, the revival of the trombone is complete. Although his Fifth Symphony is not the first symphonic use of the trombone, he was the first internationally known composer to introduce trombones into a symphony, and his music is the earliest symphonic music with trombone parts that has ever been performed with any regularity. He used the trombone in the following works: the Fifth Symphony (op. 67, 1807–08), Sixth Symphony (op. 68, 1808), a march for military band (WoO, 1809), the opera *Fidelio* and the last three of its overtures (op. 72, 1804–14), the oratorio *Christus am Oelberg* (op. 85, 1811), *Drei Equali* for four trombones (WoO 30, 1812), *Wellington's Victory* (op. 91, 1813), a march in *Die Ruinen von Athen* (op. 114, 1811), *Missa solemnis* (op. 123, 1819–23), the overture to *Die Weihe des Hauses* (op. 124, 1822), and the Ninth Symphony (op. 125, 1822–24).

Albrecht has identified the brass players available to Beethoven, along with his professional relationships with some of them. It is evident that among Viennese orchestras, only the Theater auf der Wieden, which premiered his Fifth and Sixth symphonies, had a permanent trombone section. Although the alto trombone player must have had a very secure high register, none of these players was a specialist on trombone. That fact may partly account for Beethoven's basically tentative and unadventurous trombone parts.[62]

His trombone writing more nearly resembles the French operatic style than anything that had ever been composed in Vienna. Although there had long been expert trombonists available in Vienna, the ones in France were not very good. Trombone parts there were limited to the least interesting of the instrument's capabilities: simplified doubling, harmonic filler, rhythmic punctuation, and making loud sounds. Besides demanding a much wider range than Parisian trombonists were capable of playing, Beethoven did not explore what else

a section of trombones could add to his orchestration. Alone among wind instruments, the trombone never got a solo role in Beethoven's orchestra. He did not quite integrate the trombones with the trumpets and horns to form a unified brass choir, although that is one area where his successors finished what he started.

In the choral works with trombone parts (*Christus am Oelberge*, *Missa Solemnis*, and the Ninth Symphony), Beethoven added doubling the chorus to the trombones' roles. He had learned from Haydn (and possibly from Handel) that it is not necessary for the trombones to double the chorus exactly. Such was his influence on future generations that until past midcentury critics scolded composers who went very far beyond his practice in writing for trombone.

Of all the great composers who lived and worked in Vienna (composers of light music excepted), only Franz Schubert was actually born and raised there. At the age of 11, he obtained a place in the imperial choir, which admitted him to study at the *kaiserlich-königliches Stadtkonvikt* (Imperial/Royal/City Seminary). He received a much more well-rounded education there than he could have under any other circumstances, being from a poor family. He also played in, and sometimes conducted, the seminary orchestra, which played several of his student works.[63]

Schubert may have had the opportunity to hear and perhaps perform some of the older church music written when the trombone was at its most prominent. Even though the trombone was no longer the important soloist that it had been, the tradition of using trombones in sacred music was still alive and well. To name just one example, Salieri wrote a mass in 1809 that used two trombones, notated in alto and tenor clefs. At first glance, this appears to follow Fux's example from a century earlier. But where Fux used the trombones to double the alto and tenor voices in the choir colla parte, Salieri used them in the more flexible manner of Handel, Gluck, and Haydn. The trombones in this mass sometimes play with the chorus, more likely using a modified or autonomous doubling than strict doubling. At other times, the trombones play figures similar to those of other wind instruments, which do not resemble the choral parts at all.[64]

By the time Schubert left school in 1813, he had used trombones in an overture in D (D. 26), a nonette in E♭ (D. 79), and in two different versions of a *Singspiel* called *Der Teufels Lustschloss* (D. 84). Before any of these, however, unfinished fragments of an overture (D. 2A), a symphony (D. 2B), and a mass (D. 24E), started when he was 13 or 14, likewise call for trombones. In these pieces and fragments, Schubert called for two, three, or even four trombones.[65] In his maturity, Schubert used trombones extensively in sacred music (including masses in A♭ and E♭), music for the theater (including the opera *Alfonso und Estrella* and incidental music to *Rosamunde*), and in his last two symphonies, as well as numerous unfinished works in all of these categories.

Like Beethoven, Schubert did not write trombone solos, but he gave the trombones special prominence, with exposed, thematically significant parts. He did not limit the trombones to tutti passages as so many earlier composers had. Instead, they are likely to be heard, with or without other brass instruments, even in very lightly scored passages. His late symphonies surely would have been a revelation to his contemporaries had they been readily available. But while Schubert's songs, piano music, and chamber music were widely familiar in his lifetime, his large-scale compositions were not known at all until about midcentury.

Paris

In a letter to the Comte de Billy dated February 11, 1749, the Comte de Clermont mentioned that he had a trombone in his private orchestra.[66] This letter is the earliest record of the use of the trombone in eighteenth-century France. Clermont's orchestra is not well documented, however. It is not clear whether it had any influence on later developments.

The private orchestra of La Riche de Pouplinière is more important in French musical history. According to François-Joseph Gossec, who joined the orchestra in 1751 and served as its leader from 1756 until Pouplinière's death in 1762, Pouplinière imported three German trombonists for his orchestra. In Gossec's *Messe des morts*, composed in 1760 and performed by Pouplinière's orchestra, an off-stage band used in the "Tuba mirum" movement consists of one clarinet, two trumpets or horns, and three trombones.[67]

Gossec also claimed to be the first composer to use trombones in a French opera, but it is Gluck more than anyone else who introduced the trombone to France. His first opera composed for a French audience, *Iphigénie en Aulide* (1774), used only one trombone. He produced four other operas in Paris that call for three trombones: *Orphée et Euridice* (1774), *Alceste* (1776), *Iphigénie en Tauride* (1779), and *Echo et Narcisse* (1779).

Gluck exercised enormous influence on other composers who composed operas for the Parisian stage. Before the Revolution, nearly all of the operas with trombone parts used three trombones, concerned mythological subjects, and used the trombones only in scenes that are associated with either the supernatural or death. Note values are usually a quarter note or longer. The trombones hardly ever have moving parts against sustained notes in other instruments. The trombones are usually limited to tutti or near tutti passages and usually play at a very loud dynamic. Their parts have little or no thematic significance, but merely provide harmonic filler, rhythmic punctuation, and volume. There are two ways in which other composers did not follow Gluck's example: the upper range of all other trombone parts is significantly lower than his and no other composer used trombones to double the voices in choruses.[68]

Even though trombones were used in several operas produced in the 1770s and 1780s, they did not become commonplace until the 1790s. In 1789, two opera theaters, the Opéra and the Théâtre de la rue Feydeau, as well as the Concert Spirituel, all hired permanent trombonists for the first time. One is also attested at the royal court in that year. The Opéra had hired trombonists when needed on a freelance basis since the 1774 premiere of Gluck's *Iphigénie en Aulide*. There were four trombonists altogether who played there during this time. First names are not recorded, but the last names are Braun l'aîné (the elder of two brass musicians named Braun, and very likely André Braun, who later wrote a method book for trombone), Mozer, Sieber, and Nau.[69]

The first permanent trombonist at both the Concert Spirituel and the Théâtre de la rue Feydeau was Antonio Mariotti. Where the others mentioned were all horn and/or trumpet players who played trombone occasionally, Mariotti was the first specialist on trombone that French audiences had ever heard. The *Almanach général* of 1791 declared that he was "astonishing for his precision on this instrument, the pleasing effect of which was formerly unknown in France." The year 1789 also marks the beginning of the French Revolution. By 1791, Mariotti evidently felt that Paris was no longer a safe place for him and moved to London, unfortunately for the development of trombone technique in France. Perhaps because of the memory of Mariotti's mastery, Choron declared that the trombone had been invented in Italy forty years earlier and introduced into France thirty years earlier (ca. 1773 and 1783).[70]

The French constitution of 1791 provided for major public festivals every year to commemorate the fall of the Bastille, the overthrow of the monarchy, the execution of the king, and similar events. As the Revolution continued, the more radical factions proposed to destroy everything associated with the old order. That included replacing Christianity with a new man-made religion. By 1794, the government planned lesser public festivals every ten days (the concept of weeks being abolished) as sort of an ersatz church service to honor nature, agriculture, youth, old age, political martyrs, the "Supreme Being," and so forth. Such ceremonies required not only music, but new music based on new political principles.

The standard military band, pairs of oboes, clarinets, bassoons, and horns, would remind everyone of the displaced royalty. A string orchestra likewise had unwanted aristocratic connotations. The ideals that had displaced that aristocracy demanded a fresh, new sound. For ideological reasons, the government planned to hold its festivals outside under the heavens, which brought up certain practical considerations. The standard military band could not produce enough sound to be heard by large crowds, and a string-based orchestra could not stay in tune in those playing conditions. Therefore, a wind band as large as a string orchestra was the logical solution. Bernard Sarrette, a captain in the national guard in charge of training military musicians, formed a wind band of unprecedented size: 78 musicians in 1789, reduced to 54 in 1792, but still vastly larger than any other wind band in the world.[71]

Although not all of the festivals mandated by the government actually took place, new music was composed for at least 40 festivals between 1790 and 1799. Whitwell has documented 158 different pieces, at least 71 of which require trombones. Some of the pieces have three trombone parts, but most have only one. It appears that no matter how large the band was, there were no more than three trombonists available to play in it. At its largest, all three would have had to double on one part just to be heard. Initially, at least, these festivals appealed to the popular imagination. The style of trombone playing that was necessary for the festivals soon found its way into the operatic orchestra. There are also a few pieces of orchestral music with one trombone part that most likely also owe much to the style of the band music.[72]

The Revolution had as profound an effect on the use of the trombone in opera as it did on everything else in France. In pre-Revolutionary opera the use of the trombone had been sporadic but the sound of the trombone had a special significance to the setting and mood of the operas in which it was heard. Because of the violent fervor with which various successive governments pressed their anti-aristocratic agendas, the kinds of mythological subjects that had been standard fare gave way to more contemporary and democratic ones.

So-called rescue operas, in which beleaguered heroes were saved from certain death at the hands of oppressors in the final act, are typical of what Parisian audiences expected from operas at this time. Occasionally, the sound of the trombone in the orchestra coincided with the appearance of soldiers on stage, a tribute to its new role as a military instrument. More often, however, it was just another instrumental resource, with no significance for the plot or setting.

All of the pre-Revolutionary operas that used trombones were produced at the Opéra. That theater continued to use three trombones as the Revolution progressed, but most operas with trombone parts were produced at other, smaller theaters and used only one trombone, invariably a bass trombone in B♭.

Lajarte and Cucuel both claim that nearly every opera written after 1791 included trombone parts. My own survey found trombone parts in only 40 of 86 scores available to me, but published scores of the time are notoriously unreliable.[73] The trombone parts doubled the bass line. Their part was modified to omit all embellishments and rhythmic interest. They played in all loud tutti passages and only rarely in either softer or more lightly scored passages. Only one of these parts goes too low for a B♭ trombone. Given the combination of low tessitura, narrow bore instrument, loud dynamics, and hard articulation, the sound must have been coarse, blaring, and to the standards of any other place and time, unpleasant and unmusical. And yet French composers must have thought that they were doing something fresh and original in writing for a seemingly new instrument.

England, Part Two

The revival of the trombone in England began precisely with the Handel Commemoration of 1784. Performances on that occasion were the first to use trombones on English soil since the early 1740s. The organizers desired to assemble a larger orchestra than had ever been heard before. They sought to assemble all of the resources that Handel had used and not to rely on the expedient of omitting or substituting for any of his instrumentation. Finding trombones caused some trouble, as Burney related:

> In order to render the band as powerful and complete as possible, it was determined to employ every species of instrument that was capable of producing grand effects in a great orchestra, and spacious building. Among these, the sacbut, or double trumpet, was sought; but so many years had elapsed since it had been used in this kingdom, that, neither the instrument, nor a performer on it, could easily be found. It was, however, discovered, after much useless enquiry, not only here, but by letter, on the continent, that in his Majesty's military band there were six musicians who played the three several species of sacbut; tenor, base, and double base. The

names of these performers will be found in the general list of the band.

A comparison of the names of trombonists with the lists of players of other instruments shows what instrument(s) they played besides trombone.

> Tromboni, or sacbuts. Mr. Karst [2nd oboe? spelled Karist in that list], Mr. Kneller [1st oboe and/or bassoon], Mr. Moeller [horn], Mr. Neibour [double bass], Mr. Pick [tenor (=viola?)], Mr. Zink [bassoon]. These performers played on other instruments when the sacbuts were not wanted.[74]

It is possible to identify some of these trombonists more specifically. Karst (Karist) was almost certainly Johann George Karst, who was rejected for membership in the Royal Society of Musicians in 1785 by a vote of 23–1. Pick is probably Henry Pick, who usually played violin. Neibour is the double bass player John Christopher Henry Neibour, who was evidently admitted to the Royal Society of Musicians under the name Henry Neighbor.[75]

The novelty of the instrument itself is apparent in the recollections the Earl of Mount-Edgcumbe: "To give force and fullness to the orchestra, larger instruments were also invented and made expressly for this occasion; double kettle drums, bass trumpets, trombones, and even *double* double basses, all of which added surprisingly to the harmony, and were indeed necessary to make the bass sufficiently powerful to counter balance so vast a band of violins."[76]

Before the concert, music accompanied the entrance of the royal family. John Marsh noted in his diary that trombones were among the instruments that "produced an amazingly grand effect." Once they were seated, the concert began with the Coronation Anthem. Marsh wrote, "This symphony with its beautiful modulation having continued some time at length the whole force of the orchestra with all the voices, full organ, trumpets, trombones, double drums etc. burst upon us all at once, in the words 'Zadoc the Priest' etc. the force & effect of w'ch almost took me off my legs & caused the blood to forsake my cheeks."[77]

Burney mentioned trombones in two places in his description. On the opening night, the Overture and the Dead March from *Saul* opened the second half. These were followed by an anthem that had been played for the funeral of Queen Caroline in 1737. Burney remarked, "This elegant, mild, and sorrowing strain, after all the riotous clangor of jubilation in the *Te Deum* [which closed the first half], and powerful percussion of drums, and tuneful blasts of trumpets and sacbuts, in the Dead March, was soothing and comforting to the ear."[78]

After the three performances originally scheduled, the king commanded that some of the music be repeated in two more concerts. Commenting on the repetition of *Messiah*, Burney noted that there were some significant differences: "Another new and grand effect was produced to-day in the Hallelujah, and last Chorus, 'Worthy is the Lamb,' by the introduction of the *tromboni*, which were not used in these Choruses, on the former occasion."[79]

That the first two pieces Marsh heard both had added trombone parts may indicate that they were used liberally. It is clear from Burney's official account, however, that trombones were used little enough that the players were expected to play other instruments as well. But however much or little trombone parts were added to Handel's music for the commemoration, it seems to have started a trend. Samuel Arnold's oratorios *Redemption* (1787) and *The Triumph of Truth* (1789), compiled from Handel's music, both use four trombones. Figure 7.5 shows just one of many advertisements published in the *Times* as late as March 1800 that refers back to the trombones used at the Handel Commemoration.

Burney may not be accurate in his enumeration of personnel. Other sources record only three trombonists: Zink, Miller, and Niebuher (close enough to Burney's Moeller and Neibour). His claim that six players were found in the king's military band cannot be taken at face value, either. The players may or may not have been found in that band, but they certainly did not play trombone there. As they were apparently all German, they were probably trained as *Stadtpfeifer* and played trombone, among other instruments, before moving to England. Handel's trombone parts (along with the new ones added for the occasion) are not technically difficult, so it was not necessary for any of these men to have been excellent players to produce a good effect, provided that they were musically sensitive. In 1794, a directory of musicians named six trombonists:

> 1) Dressler, John: double-bass and trombone. Drury Lane Theatre, the Abbey, & c. 2) Franks: trombone at the Abbey and Ranelagh. 3) Mariotti: trombone at the Oxford Meeting, 1793. 4) Schubert, Geo. Fredk.: trombone and bassoon. Drury Lane Oratorios and at the Abbey. 5) Zinck: trombone in the Queen's Band, and at the Abbey. 6) Zwingman, John: violin and trombone, of the Guards Second Regiment.

Two others known to have played trombone, John Caspar Flack and his son John Flack, appear in the directory as hornists.[80]

This modest list indicates that ten years after the Handel Commemoration, trombones were once again

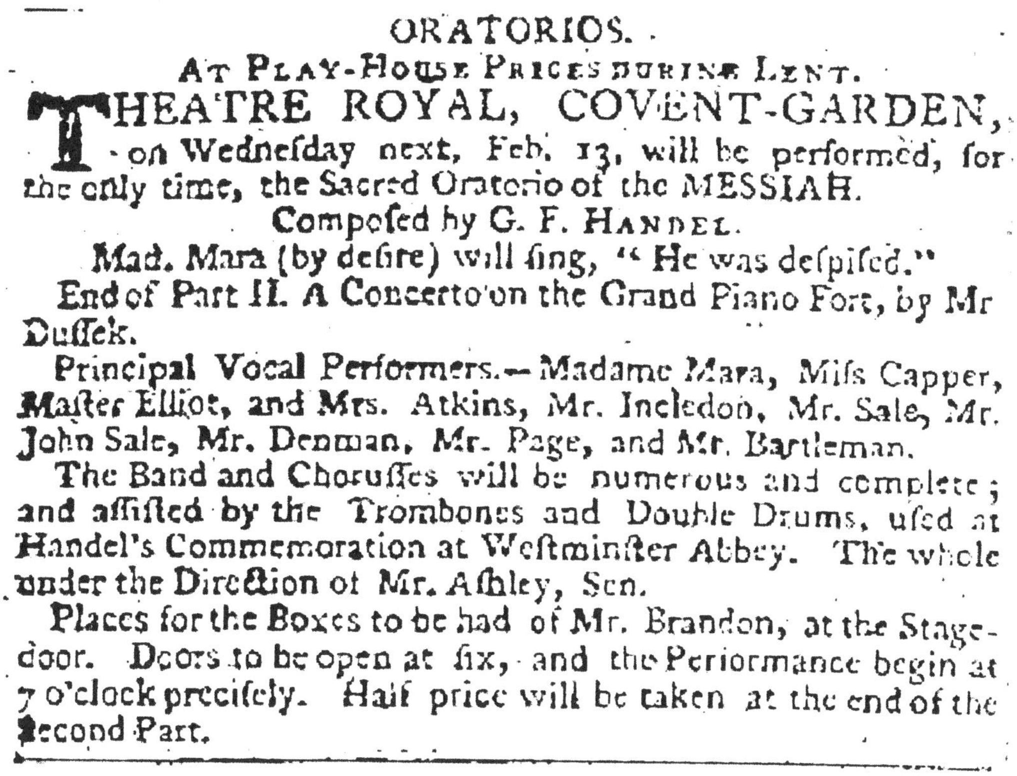

ORATORIOS.

AT PLAY-HOUSE PRICES DURING LENT.

THEATRE ROYAL, COVENT-GARDEN, on Wednesday next, Feb. 13, will be performed, for the only time, the Sacred Oratorio of the MESSIAH.

Composed by G. F. HANDEL.

Mad. Mara (by desire) will sing, "He was despised."

End of Part II. A Concerto on the Grand Piano Forte, by Mr Dussek.

Principal Vocal Performers.—Madame Mara, Miss Capper, Master Elliot, and Mrs. Atkins, Mr. Incledon, Mr. Sale, Mr. John Sale, Mr. Denman, Mr. Page, and Mr. Bartleman.

The Band and Chorusses will be numerous and complete; and assisted by the Trombones and Double Drums, used at Handel's Commemoration at Westminster Abbey. The whole under the Direction of Mr. Ashley, Sen.

Places for the Boxes to be had of Mr. Brandon, at the Stage-door. Doors to be open at six, and the Performance begin at 7 o'clock precisely. Half price will be taken at the end of the second Part.

Fig. 7.5. Advertisement from the *Times* for a performance of Handel's *Messiah,* with trombones, February 13, 1799.

found in the royal household, the theater, the church, and also in the military. Zinck is probably the same as the Zink already mentioned, and therefore the only one on the list who had played for the Handel Commemoration. The directory does not constitute a complete listing of all of London's professional instrumentalists, and some or all of the other trombonists who played for the Handel Commemoration may have still been active. Certainly the most important name on this list is Mariotti. The trombone must have been a minor part of the professional activities of most of the German-trained musicians in London. Mariotti, on the other hand, was a specialist on trombone even though he could probably play other instruments as well. He quickly became England's leading trombonist.

In 1805, Mariotti, Zwingman, and one of the Flacks played trombone for a music festival in Liverpool. In 1818, Mariotti and I. Hatton played for one in Oxford. Throughout the lifetime of the *Harmonicon*, an English musical journal that appeared between 1823 and 1833, Mariotti appears at the head of the trombones in nearly every list of orchestral personnel. These lists are frequently prefaced with a statement that the orchestra consisted of the finest musicians in England. Most of-

ten, Mariotti was identified as the principal trombonist, which at that time was the bass trombonist. In printing the anecdote about Mariotti's audition before the king of Naples (see Document 3, in the appendix), the *Harmonicon* mentioned that he had lately been driven from his post at the King's Theatre "by disgraceful intrigues."[81]

Public subscription concerts began in the late 1750s. One series, the Professional Concert, began in 1785. It engaged Ignaz Pleyel as its resident composer for the 1792 season to counter the success of a newer concert series led by Johann Peter Salomon, who had engaged Joseph Haydn in that capacity the previous year and had managed to bring him back. The Professional Concert engaged a trombonist, one of the Flacks, for the 1792 season, the only time over the entire existence of that series that a trombone was called for.[82] Four of Pleyel's pieces include trombone: three symphonies and a sinfonia concertante. There can be no doubt that the *Sinfonia concertante in F major* (Ben. 113) was performed in London. It received excellent reviews.[83] It is less clear which symphonies were performed. The programs and other available evidence are silent as to the keys of the works performed. Pleyel arrived with a trunkload of music, but also, according to advertisements, composed new works for each concert. In Pleyel's obituary, Fétis wrote:

> The first concert under his conductorship was given on the 13th of February, 1792; the success of his music was prodigious; he surpassed himself, and showed that he was worthy to contest the palm even with his illustrious master. He wrote three symphonies, of which one in E♭ was particularly admired as an excellent composition. Unfortunately, the "Professional Concert" was discontinued a few years after, and by the dispersion of its library Pleyel's symphonies, of which he had not preserved any copies, were lost to the world. . . .
>
> Truth, however, obliges us to remark that Pleyel did not, in the opinion of his English hearers, approach at all near to Haydn; on the contrary, his inferiority was universally felt and acknowledged, even by those who relied upon the support of his talents. In two seasons more, Salomon, supported by Haydn, drove his rivals out of the field.[84]

The symphonies were not lost after all. Autograph manuscripts of the scores of three symphonies (Ben. 150A in B♭ major, Ben. 152 in E♭ major, and Ben 155 in A major) that include a part for trombone exist both in London and Paris. Benton's catalog gives dates of 1800, 1801, and 1803 respectively. I was her graduate assistant at the time the catalog appeared. When she lent me microfilms of the three symphonies to study for my dissertation, she told me that she thought her dating in the catalog was incorrect, that the symphonies were probably the same ones that Fétis thought had been lost. As she died within two years of that conversation, it is no longer possible to determine when she changed her mind, or what her evidence and reasoning were for either date, but there are problems with either view.

Favoring the later date, Benton presented Ben 150A as a later reworking of Ben 150. This latter symphony was published in 1799 by Pleyel's own publishing firm (and three others). A review quoted in Benton's catalog says that it was Pleyel's first new symphony in eight years. Since the date of Ben 150 is so well established, any reworking of it must have been done later. On the other hand, favoring an earlier date, an arrangement of Ben 155 for piano trio was published by the London publisher Lavenu & Mitchell in 1803. The title page reads, "Pleyel's Celebrated Overture in A N⁰ 1 Composed for the Professional Concert . . . ." It seems unlikely that anyone would issue an arrangement of a new (and unpublished) work and then advertise it as one performed on a well-known occasion 11 years earlier.

Not only are these three symphonies the only ones of Pleyel that have a trombone part, they are also his only three symphonies for which an autograph manuscript is preserved in London. Pleyel was in London during the only season for which the orchestra of the Professional Concert included a trombonist. Therefore, it seems most likely that they were all composed in London for the Professional Concert. In that case, Ben 150 must have been derived from Ben 150A and not the other way around.[85]

Although Pleyel's music was well received by most accounts, Haydn's music vastly overshadowed it. None of Haydn's music that was heard in London includes trombone parts. His opera *L'anima del filosofo*, which includes parts for two trombones, was written for London's Haymarket Theatre but was never performed there or anywhere else during his lifetime. It is ironic that Haydn, who had used trombones in only one piece before his journey to England despite living in an area with a long tradition of trombone music, would introduce them in an opera written for London, where the trombonists could not have been anywhere near as proficient as the ones in Austria. Both trombone parts are extremely high. The English trombonists would have had trouble with them and perhaps declared them impossible.

By the 1790s English theater music had reached such a low point that the resident composer of the Drury Lane Theatre, Michael Kelly, was musically illiterate. He made up melodies and hummed them to one Ferdinand Mazzanti, who wrote them down and provided the harmonies and orchestration. It appears that their 1798 production, *Blue Beard*, was the first opera by an English composer to use trombone. Kelly's incidental music to Sheridan's play *Pizarro* likewise uses a trombone.[86]

Writing in about 1807, Marsh observed that the bass trombone played the simplest part that could be derived from the general bass, and that other trombone parts, if used at all, were similarly simple. Since the trombone was still not in general use, composers seldom included parts for them in their scores. If trombones were available, anyone could provide suitable parts for them to play. In the better orchestras, the trombonist could devise a part directly from the double bass part.[87] Therefore, potentially any piece played by an English orchestra could have been performed with a trombone on some occasions, such as the frequent festivals for which Mariotti was engaged, and not on others. Later in the nineteenth century, it became commonplace to add new trombone parts to pieces by Handel, Mozart, Beethoven, and other composers who had not provided them in the first place.

Elsewhere

Although little has been said about Sweden in previous chapters, it is likely that the trombone played the same role in Swedish society as elsewhere. It is not clear whether the trombone reappeared in Sweden in the eighteenth century or whether its use had persisted. In either case, the orchestra of the Swedish royal court had three trombonists on its payroll as early as 1790, making it one of the first orchestras in Europe to have such a large trombone section.

Numerous composers in Sweden wrote music with trombone parts in the late eighteenth century, including both operas and symphonic works. For the history of the trombone, the most interesting of these is the Third Symphony of Johann Nikolas Eggert. If Beethoven's Fifth Symphony (first performed December 22, 1808) is the earliest symphonic work in the standard repertoire that includes trombone parts, Eggert's may be the earliest one that would be welcome on modern concerts. He selected it as one of the works for his debut as a conductor on May 14, 1807. This well-documented date may or may not be the first performance of the symphony.[88]

Russian culture had little contact with Western Europe until the end of the sixteenth century, but in the seventeenth century, the imperial court began to open itself to Western influences. Polyphonic choral music made its first appearance in the worship services of the Russian Orthodox Church, and, at least at court and in the homes of noble families, an interest in instrumental music began to grow. Both of these trends attracted foreign musicians. At first, the most common instruments were native folk instruments. Eventually, the court ordered the hiring of foreigners to play Western instruments. In August of 1672, the tsar's agent hired four German musicians who played a variety of instruments, including trombone.[89] It is not clear at this time whether this hiring marks the beginning of the permanent presence of the trombone in Russia or a temporary appearance that lasted no longer than the service of one group of musicians.

The first opera published in full score in Russia was *Nachal'noe upravlenie Olega*. Jointly composed by Giuseppe Sarti, Carlo Canobbio, and Vasily Pashkeevich to a libretto by the empress Catherine the Great, it appeared in 1791. It calls for a very large orchestra, including two trombones. By this time, the Russian court sought to become a European power. Western culture seems not yet to have taken root anywhere outside of the court and nobility, but there was a fairly constant stream of foreign composers of operas. Boieldieu, for example, conducted two of his operas in St. Petersburg, *Ma tante*

Aurore and *La jeune femme colère*, which, according to scores published in Paris, require trombones. At the same time, there also appears to be some use of the trombone in military music.

The trombone was introduced to English colonies in America by the Moravian church. Their first settlement, at Savannah, Georgia, in 1735, was disbanded in 1740, having sold its trumpets and horns to General James Oglethorpe. Although it appears that this colony did not have trombones, it did have what was probably the first brass ensemble in the New World.[90]

Bethlehem, Pennsylvania, founded in 1741, became an important center from which other Moravian towns such as Nazareth, Pennsylvania; Lititz, Pennsylvania; and Hope, New Jersey, were established. As early as May 1744, Bethlehem had an ensemble of trumpets and horns. The first slide trombones, a quartet of soprano, alto, tenor, and bass, arrived in 1754. By the end of the century, Bethlehem and Lititz each had two trombone quartets, and Nazareth and Hope each had one. The Hope community disbanded in 1808, and Bethlehem obtained its trombones, making three quartets of trombones available there. The small town of Emmaus, Pennsylvania, established its trombone choir in 1820.[91]

A third Moravian colony was established at Bethabara, North Carolina, in 1753. It had trombones by 1768 and like Bethlehem was successful enough to establish another town, Salem, in 1766. Salem had its own band by 1771 and soon overshadowed Bethabara in importance. It obtained Bethabara's trombones in 1772. (Bethabara received another set in 1785.)[92]

The Moravians believed that music was a gift from God and a necessary spiritual pursuit, but they did not believe that it was a worthy profession. With very few exceptions, all of its musicians, including the trombonists, were amateurs, however skilled and dedicated. Until at least the 1820s, they and their coreligionists in Germany were the only significant body of amateur trombonists in the world.

Notes

1. Carl Gustav Anthon, "Music and Musicians in Northern Italy during the Sixteenth Century," (Ph.D. diss.: Harvard University, 1943), 35–59.

2. See Neal Zaslaw, "When Is an Orchestra Not an Orchestra?" *Early Music* 16 (1988): 484–87; John Spitzer, "The Birth of the Orchestra in Rome: An Iconographic Study," *Early Music* 19 (1991): 19–20.

3. For a more detailed look at these issues, see David M. Guion, "Theories of Tuning and Ensemble Practice in Italian

Dramatic Music of the Early Baroque, or, Oh Where, Oh Where Have the Wind Instruments Gone?" *Historic Brass Society Journal* 12 (2000): 230–243.

4. Robert M. Isherwood, *Music in the Service of the King: France in the Seventeenth Century* (Ithaca, N.Y.: Cornell University Press, 1973), 281–305.

5. "Ioüers de violons, haut-bois, saqueboutes & cornets"; "saqueboute & taille(s) de violon," *États de la France (1644–1789): La musique*; Recherches sur la musique française classique 30: *La vie musicale en France sous les rois Bourbons* (Paris: Picard, 2003), 80.

6. "A ces Entreés des Rois, & autres solemnitez, il fait servir les Trompettes, Hautbois, Violons, Fifres, Tabourins, Saqueboutes & Cornets, &c. pour rendre la Feste plus celebre"; "Douze Grands Haut-bois & Violons de la Grande Ecurie, anciennement apelés Grands Haut-bois, Cornets & Saqueboutes," *États de la France*, 99, 221, 370–71.

7. David Whitwell, *The History and Literature of the Wind Band and Wind Ensemble*, vol. 3, *The Baroque Wind Band and Wind Ensemble* (Northridge, Calif.: Winds, 1983), 4–11.

8. Osvaldo Gambassi, *La capella musicale de S. Petronia: Maestri, organisti, cantori e strumentisti dal 1436 al 1920* (Florence: Olschki, 1987), 146–49; Anne Schnoebelen, "The Concerted Mass at San Petronio in Bologna, ca. 1660–1730: A Documentary and Analytical Study," (Ph.D. diss.: University of Illinois, 1966), 321.

9. Claudio Sartori, *Bibliografia della musica strumentale italiana stampata in Italia fino al 1700* (Florence: Olschki, 1952, 1968), 2:130.

10. Andrew Ashbee and David Lasocki, *A Biographical Dictionary of English Court Musicians 1485–1714* (Aldershot, England: Ashgate, 1998), 985.

11. Quoted in Whitwell, *Baroque Wind Band*, 197–98.

12. Carlo M. Cipolla, *Fighting the Plague in Seventeenth-Century Italy* (Madison: University of Wisconsin Press, 1981), 100.

13. Eleanor Selfridge-Field, *Venetian Instrumental Music from Gabrieli to Vivaldi*, 3rd rev. ed. (New York: Dover, 1994), 18–20, 341, 348; Denis Arnold, "Orchestras in Eighteenth-Century Venice," *Galpin Society Journal* 19 (1966): 5–6.

14. Charlotte A. Leonard, "The Role of the Trombone and Its *Affekt* in the Lutheran Church Music of Seventeenth-Century Saxony and Thuringia: The Early Seventeenth Century," *Historic Brass Society Journal* 10 (1998): 57–91.

15. Gina Spagnoli, *Letters and Documents of Heinrich Schütz, 1656–1672: An Annotated Translation* (Ann Arbor, Mich.: UMI Research Press, 1990): 5.

16. Spagnoli, *Letters and Documents*, 93; Ortrun Landmann, "The Dresden Hofkapelle during the Lifetime of Johann Sebastian Bach," *Early Music* 17 (1989): 19–21; Bowles, *Musical Ensembles*, 308 n.5, 357, 383–84.

17. Beryl Kenyon de Pascal, "Brass Instruments and Instrumentalists in the Spanish Royal Chapel from the Late Seventeenth to Mid-Eighteenth Centuries," in *Brass Music at the Cross Roads of Europe*, ed. Keith Polk (Utrecht: Foundation for Historical Performance Practice, 2005), 69, 73; Beryl Kenyon de Pascal, "A Brief Survey of the Late Spanish Bajón," *Galpin Society Journal* 37 (1984): 73.

18. Daniel Mendoza de Arce, *Music in Ibero-America to 1850: A Historical Survey* (Lanham, Md.: Scarecrow, 2001), 114, 267.

19. Johann Mattheson, *Das neu-eröffnete Orchestre* (Hamburg: Self-Published, 1713), 266–67; quoted with English translation in David M. Guion, *The Trombone: Its History and Music, 1697–1811* (New York: Gordon and Breach, 1988), 25; Friedrich Nicolai, *Beschreibung einer Reise durch Deutchland und die Schweitz, im Jahre 1781* (Berlin and Stettin, 1784), 4:545; Christian Friedrich Daniel Schubart, *Ideen zu einer Aesthetik der Tonkunst*, ed. Ludwig Schubart (Vienna: Degen, 1806), 317; quoted with English translation in Guion, *Trombone*, 86.

20. Johann Heinrich Zedler, *Grosses vollständiges Universal-Lexicon* (Leipzig: Zedler, 1732–1750), vol. 28, col. 1696; quoted with English translation in Guion, *Trombone*, 48.

21. Unless otherwise noted, information in this section is from Charlotte A. Leonard, "The Role of the Trombone and Its *Affekt* in the Lutheran Church Music of Seventeenth-Century Saxony and Thuringia: The Mid- and Late Seventeenth Century," *Historic Brass Society Journal* 12 (2000): 161–209; Frederick Staten Miller, "A Comprehensive Performance Project in Trombone Literature with an Essay of the Use of the Trombone in the Music of Heinrich Schütz" (D.M.A. essay: University of Iowa, 1974), 135–36, 138–39, 145–46.

22. Leonard, "The Role of the Trombone," 205, notes 22–24.

23. Ein aufgeräumtes Gemüth reimet sich am schönsten zur Andacht; wo diese nicht im Schlummer oder gar im Traum verrichtet werden soll. Nur muß die nöthige Bescheidenheit un Mäßigung bey dem freudigen Klange der Clarinen, Posaunen, Geigen, Flöten u. niemals aus den Augen gesetzet werden, noch der bekannte Befehl den geringsten Abbruch leiden, da es heißt: Sey frölich; doch in Gottes Furcht. Johann Mattheson, *Der vollkommene Capellmeister* (Hamburg: Christian Herold, 1739), 83; English translation by Ernest C. Harriss, *Johann Mattheson's "Der vollkommene Capellmeister": A Revised Translation with Critical Commentary* (Ann Arbor, Mich.: UMI Research Press, 1981), 209.

24. Ben van den Bosch, *The Origin and Development of the Trombone-Work of the Moravian Churches in Germany and All the World*, trans. C. Daniel Crews (Winston-Salem, N.C.: Moravian Music Foundation, 1990), 4–7; See also Ken Shifrin, "The Moravian Brotherhood Trombone Choirs: Neither Moravian nor Choirs," *Brass Bulletin* 121 (2003): 56–64, and Paul Peucker, "The Role and Development of Brass Music in the Moravian Church," in *The Music of the Moravian Church in America*, ed. Nola Reed Knouse (Rochester, N.Y.: University of Rochester Press, 2008), 169–73.

25. Elwyn A. Wienandt, *Johann Pezel (1639–1694): A Thematic Catalogue of His Instrumental Works* (New York: Pendragon, 1983): xi–xiii, xxiii–xxv.

26. David M. Guion, "Wind Bands in Towns, Courts, and Churches: Middle Ages to Baroque," *Journal of Band Research* 42 (Spring 2007): 46–49.

27. Henry Howey, "The Lives of *Hoftrompeter* and *Stadtpfeiffer* as Portrayed in Three Novels of Daniel Speer," *Historic Brass Society Journal* 3 (1991): 65–78.

28. William R. Lee. "Wind Music of the Baroque: J. G. C. Stoerl and His Tower Sonatas," *Journal of Band Research* 20 (Fall 1984): 2–8.

29. David M. Guion, "The Missing Link: The Trombone in Italy in the 17th and 18th Centuries," *Early Music* 34 (2006): 227–230.

30. I sonatori di Cornetti, Tromboni, e Violoni sempre compariscano con i loro instrumenti cosi nelle solennità, e feste, come ne' Sabbati la sera per le Litanie, ò Mottetto alla Modonna [sic], e quando si canterà sù gli Organi, compariscano ancora i sonatori di Violino, Violette, Tiorbe, & altri con i loro instrumenti. . . .

Finalmente perche si è conosciuto dall'esperienza il poco buon seruitio, che riceue la Chiesa, e Musica da Mansionarij Musici, e da Musici di Palazzo, lasciando questi i molte volte il seruitio ammezzato, e molte volte in tutto sotto pretesto d'andare à Palazzo, per lo che resta sminuito ogni volta il corpo di essa d'otto voci; E quelli abbandonando il proprio Coro per seruire alla Musica, e la Musica per andare al Coro, non ponno ben seruire ne all'vno, ne all'altra; Però dichiarasi, che quel Cantore, ò Sonatore, che entrarà Mansionario, ò Musico di Palazzo subito sia escluso affatto dalla Musica di S. Petronio. Et il tutto in conformità del decreto di detti Illustrissimi Signori Presidente, e Fabbricieri rogato per l'infrascritto Notaro di essa. Maurizio Cazzati, *Ordini per la musica dell'insigne collegiate di S. Petronio, Reformati d'ordine de gl'illustrissimi presidente, e fabbricieri della reverenda fabbrica di essa. L'anno 1658*, 6, 11–12; facsim. in Osvaldo Gambassi, *La capella musicale de S. Petronio: Maestri, organisti, cantori e strumentisti dal 1436 al 1920* (Florence: Olschki, 1987), 357–89.

31. Osvaldo Gambassi, *Il Concerto Palatino della signoria di Bologna: Cinque secoli di vita musical a corte (1250–1797)* (Florence: Olschki, 1989), 16–18, 265–69 (docs. 567–69).

32. Osvaldo Gambassi, *L'Accademia Filarmonico di Bologna: Fonddazione, statuti e aggregazioni* (Florence: Olschki, 1992), 114, 117, 118.

33. Guion, "Missing Link," 226–27. On the pope's band at Castel Sant'Angelo, see James Wesley Herbert, "The Wind Band of Nineteenth-Century Italy: Its Origins and Transformation from the Late 1700's to Mid-Century" (D.E. diss.: Teachers College, Columbia University, 1986), 34–40.

34. Steven Saunders, *Cross, Sword, and Lyre: Sacred Music at the Imperial Court of Ferdinand II of Habsburg (1619–1637)* (Oxford: Clarendon Press, 1995), 19.

35. William S. Newman, *The Sonata in the Baroque Era*, 3rd ed. (New York: Norton, 1972), 204–05.

36. H. V. F. Somerset, "The Habsburg Emperors as Musicians," *Music & Letters* 30 (1949): 204–15.

37. See Bruce C. MacIntyre, *The Viennese Concerted Mass of the Early Classical Period* (Ann Arbor, Mich.: UMI Research Press, 1986), 9 for a list of 28 composers of masses, and 57–92 for biographical information. The composers named used trombone in at least one of the 72 masses in the thematic catalog, 581–72.

38. Carl B. Schmidt, "Antonio Cesti's *Il pomo d'oro*: A Reexamination of a Famous Hapsburg Court Spectacle," *Journal of the American Musicological Society* 29 (1976): 381–412; Stewart Carter, "Trombone Obbligatos in Viennese Oratorios of the Baroque," *Historic Brass Society Journal* 2 (1990): 55.

39. Eleanor Selfridge-Field, "The Viennese Court Orchestra in the Time of Caldara," in *Antonio Caldara: Essays on His Life and Times*, ed. Brian Pritchard (Aldershot, England: Scolar Press, 1987), 134.

40. Michael Grant Vaillancourt, "Instrumental Ensemble Music at the Court of Leopold I (1658–1705)" (Ph.D. diss.: University of Illinois, Urbana-Champaign, 1991), 77–102; Niels Martin Jensen, "The Instrumental Music for Small Ensemble of Antonio Bertali: The Sources," *Dansk aarbog for musikforkning* 20 (1992): 33ff; Klaus Winkler, "Die Bedeutung der Posaune im Schaffen von Johann Joseph Fux," in *Johann Joseph Fux und die barocke Bläsertradition*, ed. Bernhard Habla (Tutzing: Hans Schneider, 1987), 178–82; C. Robert Wigness, *The Soloistic Use of the Trombone in Eighteenth-Century Vienna* (Nashville, Tenn.: Brass Press, 1978), 9–19.

41. Wigness, "Soloistic Use," 19, citing an article in *Die Musik im Geschichte und Gegenwart*; Ken Shifrin, "The Solo Trombone of the Bohemian Baroque, Part Two," *Brass Bulletin* 120 (2002): 48–54.

42. "Endlich gebraucht man auch zum Chor 3 Posaunisten. Nähmlich die Alt- Tenor- und Basstrombone zu blasen, welches der Stadtthürmermeister mit zweenen seiner Untergebenen, gegen einem gewissen jährlichen Gehalt, versehen muss." Friedrich Wilhelm Marpurg, *Historisch-Kritische Beyträge zur Aufnahme der Musik* (Berlin: Gottlieb August Lange, 1757), 3:195.

43. Eric Thomas Chafe, *The Church Music of Heinrich Biber* (Ann Arbor, Mich.: UMI Research Press, 1987), 37, 54. Beginning on p. 233, Chafe presents a catalog of 147 musical works of Biber. Six of the eight masses include trombone parts, as do 34 other sacred works. A sonata for two violins, trombone, and continuo, preserved in the Kroměříž archive, does not appear in this catalog.

44. The most extensive study of Gschlatt is J. Richard Raum, "An Historic Perspective of an 18th-Century Trombonist," *Brass Bulletin* 87 (1994): 10–29; 88 (1994): 18–35; 89 (1995): 31–49, which is unfortunately a fictionalized account. Although Raum bases the three-part article on both primary and secondary sources, much of the material is more speculative and imaginative than factual.

45. "Hr. Thomas Gschlatt, aus Stockerau in Unteröstereich. Ist ein grosser Meister auf seinem Instrumente, dem es sehr wenig gleich thun werden. Er spielt auch eine gute Violin und

das Violoncell, bläset nicht weniger ein seines Waldhorn." Marpurg, *Historisch-Kritische Beyträge*, 3:189.

46. Wigness, *Soloistic Use*, 24–25; T. Donley Thomas, "Michael Haydn's Trombone Symphony," *Brass Quarterly* 6 (1962): 3–8.

47. See Stephen C. Anderson, "Selected Works from the 17th-Century Music Collection of Prince-Bishop Karl Liechtenstein-Kastelkorn: A Study of the Soloistic Use of the Trombone," *ITA Journal* 11 (Jan. 1983): 17–20; 11 (Apr. 1983): 35–38; 11 (July 1983): 29–32; 11 (Oct. 1983): 20–22; 12 (Jan. 1984): 33–37.

48. Jiři Sehnal, "Das Musikinventar des Olmützer Bischofs Leopold Egk aus dem Jahre 1760 als Quelle vorklassischer Instrumentalmusik," *Archiv für Musikwissenschaft* 29 (1972): 315; Ken Shifrin, "The Solo Trombone of the Bohemian Baroque, Part One," *Brass Bulletin* 119 (2002): 65–66.

49. Robert N. Freeman, "The Fux Tradition and the Mystery of the Music Archive at Melk Abbey," in *Johann Joseph Fux and the Music of the Austro-Italian Baroque*, ed. Harry White (Aldershot, England: Scolar Press, 1992), 19; Robert N. Freeman, *The Practice of Music at Melk Abbey, Based upon the Documents, 1681–1826* (Vienna: Österreichischen Akademie der Wissenschaften, 1989), 106.

50. Robert N. Freeman, *Franz Schneider (1737–1812): A Thematic Catalogue of His Works* (New York: Pendragon, 1979), 4–8.

51. Freeman, *Practice of Music*, 350–51.

52. J. Richard Raum, "Extending the Solo and Chamber Repertoire for the Alto Trombone," *ITA Journal* 16 (Spring 1988): 11–23; Howard Weiner, "Beethoven's *Equali* (WoO 30): A New Perspective," *Historic Brass Society Journal* 14 (2002): 227–28.

53. Guion, "Missing Link," 226–27.

54. Donald Burrows, "Handel, the Dead March, and a Newly Identified Trombone Movement," *Early Music* 18 (1990): 408; Winton Dean, *Handel's Dramatic Oratorios and Masques* (London: Oxford University Press, 1959), 429.

55. David M. Guion, "What Handel Taught the Viennese about the Trombone," *Historic Brass Society Journal* 15 (2003): 291–97.

56. Walther Siegmund-Schultze, "Georg Friedrich Händel als ein Wegbereiter der Wiener Klassik," *Händel-Jahrbuch* 27 (1981): 33–34; Guion, "What Handel Taught," 298–305.

57. Anthony DelDonna, "Production Practices at the Teatro di San Carlo, Naples, in the Late 18th Century," *Early Music* 20 (2002): 440.

58. Anthony DelDonna, "Behind the Scenes: The Musical Life and Organizational Structure of the San Carlo Opera Orchestra in Late-18th Century Naples," in *Fonti d'archivio per la storia della musica e dello spettacolo a Napoli tra XVI e XVIII secolo*, ed. Paologiovanni Maione (Naples: Editorial Scientifica, 2001), 428, 437–38.

59. Introduction to *Arcangelo Corelli: Historisch-kritische Gesamtausgabe der musikalischen Werke*, vol. 5, *Werke ohne Opuszahl*, ed. Hans Joachim Marx (Cologne: Arno Volk, 1976), 23;

Michael F. Robinson, *Giovanni Paisiello: A Thematic Catalogue of His Works*, vol. 1, *Dramatic Works* (Stuyvesant, N.Y.: Pendragon, 1991): 365, 371, 548, 564.

60. John A. Rice, *Antonio Salieri and Viennese Opera* (Chicago: University of Chicago Press, 1998), 412–15.

61. Dexter Edge, "Mozart's Viennese Orchestras," *Early Music* 20 (1992): 76–77.

62. Theodore Albrecht, "Beethoven's Brass Players: New Discoveries in Composer-Performer Relations," *Historic Brass Society Journal* 18 (2006): 52–56.

63. Maurice J. E. Brown, *Schubert: A Critical Biography* (London: Macmillan, 1958), 13–15.

64. Antonio Salieri, *Messe in B-dur (1809)*, ed. Jane Schatkin Hettrick, *Denkmäler der Tonkunst in Österreich*, v. 146 (Graz: Akademische Druck u. Verlagsanstalt, 1988).

65. Otto Erich Deutsch, *Franz Schubert Thematisches Verzeichnis seiner Werke in chronologischer Folge*, new ed. by Werner Aderhold (Kassel: Bärenreiter, 1978).

66. Quoted in Georges Cucuel, *Études sur un orchestre au 18me siècle* (Paris: Fischbacher, 1913), 15.

67. Guion, *Trombone*, 168–70; François-Joseph Gossec, "Notice sur l'introduction des cors, des clarinettes et des trombones dans les orchestres français, extraite des manuscrits autographes de Gossec," *Revue musicale* 5 (1829): 219, 221, 222.

68. Guion, *Trombone*, 174–78. The chart listing individual operas on p. 175 is printed poorly. Several works do not line up with the right composer. See David M. Guion, "The Instrumentation of Operas Published in France in the 18th Century," *Journal of Musicological Research* 4 (1982): 134–41, for clarification.

69. *États de la France*, 370–71; Jan LaRue and Howard Brofsky, "Parisian Brass Players, 1751–1793," *Brass Quarterly* 3 (1960): 133–40.

70. "étonnant pour sa précision sur cet instrument, dont le bel effet était inconnu en France." Quoted in Guion, *Trombone*, 162–63; Louis-Joseph Francoeur, *Traité général des voix et des instruments d'orchestre: Nouvelle édition revue et augmentée des instruments modernes*, ed. Alexandre Choron (Paris: Aux adresses ordinaires de musique, 1813), 72.

71. Constant Pierre, *Le Conservatoire Nationale de Musique et de Déclamation: Documents historiques et administratifs, recueillis ou reconstitués* (Paris: Imprimérie National, 1900), 103.

72. David Whitwell, *Band Music of the French Revolution* (Tutzing: Hans Schneider, 1979), 101–201; Guion, *Trombone*, 186–87.

73. Théodore de Lajarte, "Introduction du trombone dans l'orchestre de l'Opéra," *La chronique musicale* 6 (Oct.–Dec. 1874): 78; Cucuel, *Études sur un orchestre*, 35; Guion, "Instrumentation," 119, 143.

74. Charles Burney, *An Account of the Musical Performances in Westminster-Abbey, and the Pantheon, May 26th, 27th, 29th; and June the 3d, and 5th, 1784: In Commemoration of Handel* (London: T. Payne, 1785), 7, 19 of the second sequence of pagination. The instruments in square brackets indicate which

other instrument(s) each man played according to the listing on 17–19.

75. Philip H. Highfill Jr., Kalman A. Burnim, and Edward A. Langhans, *A Biographical Dictionary of Actors, Actresses, Musicians, Dancers, Managers & Other Stage Personnel in London, 1660–1800* (Carbondale and Edwardsville: Southern Illinois University Press, 1973–93). There are entries for Kneller, Moeller, and Zink as well, but these add no details to what has already been said.

76. Richard Mount Edgcumbe, *Musical Reminiscences of the Earl of Mount Edgcumbe: Containing an Account of the Italian Opera in England from 1773 to 1834*, 4th ed. (London: John Andrews and F. H. Wall, 1834; repr., New York: Da Capo, 1973), 48.

77. *The John Marsh Journals: The Life and Times of a Gentleman Composer (1752–1828)*, ed. Brian Robins (Stuyvesant, N.Y.: Pendragon Press, 1998), 317–18.

78. Burney, *Account*, 33 of second sequence. Burney disliked the sound of the trombone and said so very explicitly. See Guion, *Trombone*, 92.

79. Burney, *Account*, 112 of second sequence.

80. Lyndesay G. Langwill, "Two Rare Eighteenth-Century London Directories," *Music & Letters* 30 (1949): 41.

81. *Times* (Feb. 25, 1805): 1; (May 11, 1818): 2; *Harmonicon* 8 (1830): 372.

82. Simon McVeigh, "The Professional Concert and Rival Subscription Series in London, 1783–1793," *Research Chronicle* [of The Royal Musical Association] 22 (1989): 12, 103.

83. Rita Benton, *Ignace Pleyel: A Thematic Catalogue of His Compositions* (New York: Pendragon, 1977), 19.

84. Le premier concert eut lieu le 13 février 1792; le succés de la musique de Pleyel fut prodigieux. Il s'était surpassé et s'était montré digne de lutter avec son illustre maître. Les symphonies étaient au nombre de trois; il s'en t rouvait une en *mi* bémol qui a été surtout signalée comm un ouvrage excellent. Malherueusement le *Professional concert* fut dissous quelques années après, la bibliothèque dispersée, et les symphonies, dont Pleyel n'avait point gardé de copies, furent perdues pour toujours. François Fétis, "Notice sur Ignace Pleyel," *La revue musicale* 5 (Dec. 3, 1831): 364; English translation with editorial footnote, *Harmonicon* 10 (1832): 26.

85. See also Arthur Searle, "Pleyel's 'London' Symphonies," *Early Music* 36 (2008): 231–44.

86. Guion, *Trombone*, 147.

87. John Marsh, *Hints to Young Composers of Instrumental Music* (London: Clementi, Banger, Hyde, Collard, & Davis, ca. 1807), quoted in Guion, *Trombone*, 86.

88. Avishai Kallai, "Joachim Eggert: Authenticating the Premiere Performance of His E-Flat Symphony," *STM Online* 4 (2001): www.musik.uu.se/ssm/stmonline/vol_4/kallai/index.html

89. Miloš Velimirovi , "Warsaw, Moscow and St Petersburg," in *The Late Baroque Era: From the 1680s to 1740*, ed. George J. Buelow (Englewood Cliffs, N.J.: Prentice Hall, 1994), 458.

90. Harry H. Hall, "Early Sounds of Moravian Brass Music in America: A Cultural Note from Colonial Georgia," *Brass Quarterly* 7 (1964): 118–20.

91. Peucker, "Role and Development," 173–77; Harry H. Hall, "The Moravian Wind Ensemble: Distinctive Chapter in America's Music" (Ph.D. diss.: George Peabody College for Teachers, 1967), 136–38, 159, 179.

92. Hall, "Moravian Wind Ensemble," 43–45, 282–83; Thomas Jerome Anderson, "The Collegium Musicum Salem, 1780–1790: Origins and Repertoire" (Ph.D. diss.: Florida State University, 1976), 78–87.

CHAPTER EIGHT

~

The Modern Trombone, 1830–2000

Early in the nineteenth century, a distinction arose between "high culture" and "vernacular" music.[1] The arguments in the early nineteenth century took place among the aristocracy and upper reaches of the middle class. Low-status concerts offered some of the same music as high-status concerts, but to a less affluent audience. Social structure has changed greatly since then, but some of the artistic distinctions have persisted.

Once the lines were drawn, the trombone had such different roles in the two kinds of music that it will be necessary to consider them separately in this chapter. The term *high culture* cannot be comfortably applied to the very different social structure after the middle of the nineteenth century, much less the twentieth century, so I will use *art music* instead. *Vernacular* seems a usable term throughout the period, although the specific meaning of vernacular music changes over time.

The trombone was a late and not always welcome addition to high culture. A writer in the *Allgemeine musikalische Zeitung* observed,

> Good trombones are wishful thinking. The importance and beauty of this instrument have generally not yet been appreciated enough. The trombone's tone can have the most splendid effect, but a single note from a trombone can also ruin everything. In operas like *Don Giovanni*, *Jacob und seine Söhne* and *Fidelio* the misery is quite perceptible, and the listener is glad when the lights at the trombone desk are extinguished again.[2]

With some exceptions noted in earlier chapters, it had been rejected for the private entertainment of the nobility since the middle of the sixteenth century, but had remained a part of the more public culture that appealed to the lower social classes through the last of the old

alta-type bands in such places as Leipzig and Bologna. That helps to explain why it was more easily accepted in vernacular music.

The distinction between art music and vernacular music is a convenient organizational device, but not a procrustean bed into which everything can be made to fit. While much of the activity of solo trombonists has been on the vernacular side, some of them—especially in the twentieth century—have aspired to the status of art. Neither does the role of the trombone in church music fit on either side of the cultural divide.

In much of the nineteenth century, *trombone* did not necessarily mean slide trombone. The valve trombone temporarily supplanted the slide trombone throughout the Austrian empire and Italy. In England, France, and the United States, slide and valve trombones coexisted. Contemporary writers seldom specified which form they meant. (See page 60 in the appendix, for a description of a contrabass trombone that is only implicitly a valve trombone.)

The Trombone in Art Music

Development of the Orchestra

Early in the nineteenth century, most orchestras were theater orchestras, although many of them gave concerts. Once concert orchestras became common, they were more gatherings of freelance artists than permanent orchestras in the modern sense. Theater orchestras were probably more stable ensembles, but the seasons were not long. No one could make a living simply playing in an orchestra. Some orchestras had excellent trombonists, but others could not find competent players at all. It would have been possible for orchestras to function quite well without trombones, except that some few pieces that audiences expected to hear required them. These included Beethoven's Fifth, Sixth, and Ninth symphonies, Haydn's *Creation*, Mozart's *Requiem*, and his reorchestration of Handel's *Messiah*. Therefore, every orchestra had the incentive to recruit and develop proficient trombonists, even if not everyone liked the sound.

Some conductors added trombone parts to compositions that originally had none in order to make a grander effect. Trombones were added to Mozart's Fortieth Symphony, Gluck's *Iphigenie en Aulide*, and Beethoven's Second Symphony at a music festival in Halle and to Mozart's *Marriage of Figaro* at the Royal Italian Opera. Performances of Handel's music at the Birmingham Festival used not only the trombone parts that Mozart added, but more added by someone else as well as two serpents and an ophicleide, for *Messiah* and even more additional instruments for *Acis and Galatea*. Critical opinion nearly always opposed the practice, but that did not keep promoters from advertising the presence of trombones, as for example W. B. Healy and W. F. Young were announced on trombone and euphonium respectively for a performance of Handel's *Acis and Galatea*. It continued at least into the 1870s.[3]

By the beginning of the twentieth century, every orchestra had trombones, and even small-town professional orchestras could count on good musicians in every seat. Therefore, this section will be mostly about how the trombone became a standard member of the orchestra in the nineteenth century.

Europe

The Gewandhaus, which opened in Leipzig in 1781, was the first dedicated concert hall in Europe. The orchestra established to perform there was the first orchestra that specialized in concert music; the theater in Leipzig had its own orchestra. Unlike most major German cultural centers, Leipzig had no court. It was a solidly middle-class town with a long and proud heritage of music-making. Although no review of the 1796 performance of Mozart's *Requiem* is extant, it must have made a tremendous impact. After that time, it was played regularly in Leipzig, but without trombones until April 1805, when the performance

> distinguished itself from earlier ones because the trombones were not omitted, as a result of which several passages—such as the Et lux perpetua, and similar ones in the Benedictus, Dies irae, and Oro supplex—for the first time came to the fore with their whole wealth and power. Earlier, one could not risk using these instruments, be-

cause Mozart wrote very difficult parts (sometimes unreasonably so), and we had no trombonists who could perform them reliably. But now a trombone section that can already be called excellent has been formed from among the young men who, after the improved organization of the town musicians, study instrumental music here, and showed themselves to best advantage in this and other concert and theatrical productions.[4]

The orchestra had no permanent trombonists until the 1842–43 season. Before that, it hired them only for the few concerts that required them.

Berlin had competent trombones at least as early as Leipzig did. A review of a performance of Mozart's *Requiem* in 1805 says that it was "perfectly in accord with the wishes of the composer" except for substituting clarinets for the basset horn parts. At the time, it appears that most performances used bassoon or other substitute for the trombone solo in the *Tuba mirum*. On this occasion, it was "sung, with the not half bad trombone, most beautifully and expressively by Mr. Gern"; in the *Benedictus*, "the trombones made a splendid effect."[5] Later in the century, Friedrich Auguste Belcke, one of the most renowned trombonists of his generation, spent most of his career in Berlin as royal chamber musician.

One noteworthy feature of German musical life is the number of orchestras. Not all of them were good, and the trombonists were not always among the better players. In fact, Sundelin had such low regard for them that he recommended against having the trombones play at the very beginning because they would have no way to find their pitch.[6] German orchestras used a trio of alto, tenor, and bass slide trombones, at least according to available books. In some, but not all cases, all three may have been in B♭. From Sattler's invention of the tenor-bass trombone onward, if not earlier, German trombones had a larger bore than those in most of the rest of the world at least until after the Second World War.

Austria was deeply affected by the French Revolution and the Napoleonic wars. Its orchestras were excellent up until about 1790, after which their standards deteriorated. During most of Beethoven's lifetime, they did not play well at all. In his discussion of the size of various Viennese orchestras, Clive Brown frequently gives the numbers of string players, followed by phrases like "the usual wind instruments." Gluck and Mozart both used trombones in their operas, but until more research is done on the many Viennese operas that are no longer performed, it will remain uncertain how early trombones could be included in that description. Nearly 600 performers, including nine trombonists, performed Mozart's orchestration of Handel's *Alexander's Feast* in 1812. Trombones are documented in the *Concert Spirituel* in 1825. Andreas Nemetz played trombone in the Kärntnerthor orchestra from 1823–1828.[7]

Vienna had no concert hall until 1831, when the *Gesellschaft für Musikfreunde* built a small one with a maximum capacity of 600. Earlier, concerts had to be given in one of the theaters, a ballroom, or some other space that was intended and extensively used for some other purpose. Otto Nicolai founded the *Philharmonische Concerte* in 1842. This series flourished under his leadership for five years and then languished under his successors. But after a temporary hiatus, it was reestablished in 1854.[8] From that time on, the Vienna Philharmonic Orchestra has remained one of the best orchestras in the world.

Some time in the 1830s, the court theater orchestra in Vienna purchased a valve trombone from local maker Uhlmann. By the 1850s, all Viennese orchestras used valve trombones with a narrow bore. Soon afterward, Červený began to build and popularize large-bore instruments with rotary valves, but in 1883 a new director of the orchestra decided to replace valve trombones with large-bore German slide trombones manufactured in Leipzig by Sattler's successor, Penzel. One was equipped with the trigger that Sattler had invented. In Prague, as elsewhere in the Austrian empire, valve trombones predominated throughout most of the nineteenth century.[9]

Early in the nineteenth century, three opera theaters, the Opéra, Opéra Comique, and Théâtre Italien, were the most important musical institutions in Paris, along with numerous smaller theaters, an imperial court orchestra, and the Paris Conservatory. All of these drew their personnel from the same pool of players. Most operas presented at the Opéra used three trombones, and operas presented at the other theaters usually used only one. This practice changed under Rossini's influence; there were three trombonists in the orchestra of the Opéra Comique from 1827 onward.[10]

The chaos of the Revolution temporarily ended public concerts. In 1828, the Société des Concerts du Conservatoire presented its first concert. Among the 93 founding members were trombonists Jules Barbier, René Bénard, and Devise (first name unknown). The concert caused a sensation. After the orchestra survived early political and financial threats to its existence, it revived not only Parisian concert life, but the once-moribund Conservatory itself. The orchestra rehearsed more rigorously than any other, so it soon became widely known as the most polished in Europe.

The trombones must have been the weakest section in the early years of the orchestra. Although Barbier remained with the orchestra until his death in 1840, Bénard and Devise were forced to resign before the 1835 season, the first dismissals of members in good standing. Antoine Dieppo joined the orchestra in 1838. From then on, the trombones were well respected. Dieppo remained as principal trombonist, and the most influential trombonist in France, until his retirement in 1867. His colleagues were Antoine Simon and Edouard Dantonnet.[11]

Early on, French orchestras abandoned alto and bass trombones in favor of a section of three tenor trombones. Later, some French and Belgian orchestras tried out Sax's independent-valve system, but it never caught on. Narrow-bore slide trombones persisted until André Lafosse retired from the Conservatoire in 1960. After that time, French trombonists adopted large-bore American instruments with enthusiasm.

Until well into the twentieth century, all Italian orchestras were theater orchestras. They had a very poor reputation among travelers from other countries, especially in Rome. The largest theaters in Italy included La Scala in Milan, San Carlo in Naples, and Fenice in Venice. Among the various orchestras in Emilia-Romagna, Bologna's theater had one trombonist in 1817 and three by 1835. Parma had one in 1822 and three by 1831. Carpi had three trombones in 1828, making it the first of these orchestras with that many. Faenza had only one as late as 1836. All the others had at least two by that date.[12]

A correspondent for the *Allgemeine musikalische Zeitung*, reporting on the coronation of Joseph Napoleon as King of Naples, wrote that all the musicians in the orchestra were local professionals except the trombones, who were French. He claimed, erroneously, "Trombones have been so long unused here that they have become entirely unknown, and a few people think they are a recent French invention." In 1830, a traveling French student claimed that the only good instruments in the Naples orchestra were "the double bass, the trombone and the keyed trumpets." It appears, then, that there was only one trombone in a 50-piece orchestra. Not much later, Bonifazio Asioli wrote that only the largest orchestras should have even one trombone and that using two trombones in harmony was a common abuse. By that time Rossini routinely called for three trombones in his operas. Other Italian composers quickly followed his example.[13]

Rossini's trombone parts were so much more difficult than earlier music that Italian orchestras abandoned slide trombones for valve trombones as soon as they became available. Much of Italy was under Austrian rule, which may also have influenced the adoption of valves.

That change was not universally admired, however. A proposal to a musical congress in 1881 to restore the slide trombone was not acted on. A writer in 1889 expressed a desire to send valve trombones back wherever they came from. In addition to the orchestra, Italian operas regularly featured a band on stage, although Italian composers were not the first to do so. Composers rarely orchestrated the stage band parts. Instrumentation depended on what players were available wherever such a band was needed.[14]

Beginning with the Handel Commemoration of 1784, there was a tradition of using three trombones for the performance of English oratorios. Otherwise, orchestras were slow to require them. London had three principal theaters: the King's Theatre (or under Queen Victoria [r. 1837–1901], Her Majesty's Theatre), Covent Garden, and Drury Lane. The orchestra at the King's Theatre was fairly large and, with the exception of hard times in the late 1820s, staffed with London's best players. If a trombone was needed, Mariotti was hired as bass trombonist. By the early 1820s, the operatic repertoire frequently required three trombonists: John Smithies (or Smithers, generally designated as alto trombone), Schoengen (tenor), and Mariotti (bass). Two of Smithies's sons (James and John Jr.) also played trombone. Not uncommonly, one or the other of the sons joined the father. When Mariotti retired, Albrecht, of the Royal Household Band, took his place. The other two orchestras were smaller until 1847, when conductor Michael Costa broke with Her Majesty's Theatre. He took control of the Covent Garden Theatre, which became known as the Royal Italian Opera. An advertisement for that year identifies the trombonists as Cioffi, Smithies, and Healey.[15]

The two most important concert societies were the Concert of Ancient Music (1776–1848) and the Philharmonic Society (founded in 1813). The Concert of Ancient Music presented mostly vocal music, but it always had an orchestra. It performed only music that was at least 20 years old. Most of its repertoire was from Handel's time or earlier. Hardly any music with authentic trombone parts existed within these limits, but Carse reported that W. Greatorex, its secretary and librarian, "an incorrigible arranger and adder of accompaniments, was kept fairly busy gilding lilies." The orchestra regularly included clarinets, four horns, and three trombones.[16]

Where the Concert of Ancient Music primarily performed vocal music with some instrumental pieces to provide contrast, the Philharmonic Society was primarily an instrumental institution that occasionally performed vocal music. Membership in the society was a privilege rather than a job, as members were not paid. Hardly any of the members played wind instruments, however, so wind players were engaged and paid a fee for whatever concerts required their services. For trombones, the society hired two Smithies and Mariotti, or after his retirement, Albrecht. Even with established orchestras, pickup orchestras played a significant role in London's concert life. For example, an advertisement for a series of Wednesday Evening Concerts announced that the 70-piece orchestra had been "selected from the Royal Italian Opera, the Philharmonic, and Her Majesty's private bands."[17]

Other English towns lacked the variety of London's concert life, but many of them mounted annual musical festivals, often with much larger orchestras than would be heard in London. While they must have used local musicians, they could not have succeeded without the participation of London's leading professionals. The Yorkshire Grand Music Festival of 1823 featured Handel's *Messiah*, the first part of Haydn's *Creation*, and music by Mozart and Beethoven, performed by a combined orchestra and chorus of 450 performers, including nine trombonists. Characteristically, the bass trombonists are listed first.[18]

Nine trombonists were also named for the 1826 Birmingham Musical Festival, of whom at least Albrecht and Smithies are recognizably Londoners. The 1845 Worcester Musical Festival used a more normal-sized orchestra, but the three trombonists (two Smithies and Healey) were all Londoners. In 1857 Charles Hallé established a professional orchestra in Manchester, the first permanent provincial orchestra.[19]

Until after the Second World War, British orchestras used alto, tenor, and bass slide trombones of narrow bore. Unlike any continental country, they used bass trombones in G. Some of the leading British trombonists began to be dissatisfied with their equipment as early as the 1930s. Maxted experienced frustration from his first season in a symphony orchestra, when he could not produce a large enough sound to play Sibelius's Seventh Symphony. Wick compared the sound of small-bore trombones at loud dynamic levels to the tearing of canvas. Both of them, and many others, adopted large-bore American-made trombones as soon as they became available in the 1950s.[20]

It is difficult to find much information on the formation of orchestras in other European countries. It stands to reason that use of the trombone persisted in any musical center that had them at the end of the eighteenth century. It also stands to reason that they would have been kept busy in theater orchestras long before there were any concert orchestras.

St. Petersburg, where trombones were required for an opera on a libretto by the empress, must have had trombones early in the nineteenth century. There was an Italian theater in Odessa, where a Frenchman named Demin was reported as a trombonist of considerable talent. Several pieces that required up to three trombones were composed in Stockholm from 1782 into the nineteenth century, including a symphony by Johann Nikolas Eggert (1807). There was a Philharmonic Society in Ljubljana, Slovenia, before the end of eighteenth century, which attempted to establish a school to train wind players, including trombonists, in 1822.[21]

United States and Canada

Sacred music societies played a greater role in the development of American musical life than they did in Europe, but the earliest ones did not have trombones. It is not always possible to determine when trombones became available or who the first trombonists were in a given city. The Handel and Haydn Society of Boston, the oldest musical organization in the United States, was founded in 1815. In 1819 it presented the first complete American performance of Haydn's *Creation*, but it is not possible to document trombones in its orchestra until 1828. Another early performance of *Creation* took place in Philadelphia in 1822, which had no resident trombonists. Three Moravian trombonists from Bethlehem performed on that occasion.[22]

Like European cities, most American cities had theater orchestras before they had concert orchestras. The earliest ones did not use trombones. A "gentleman from Boston" played the trombone in an oratorio performance in New York in 1816, which featured a chorus of nearly 200 and an orchestra of more than 70. As late as 1825, a New York writer complained that a concert orchestra had no oboes or trombones and not enough strings. Yet in 1828 two different visiting Europeans mentioned trombones in New York orchestras. One named four theaters and observed that every orchestra had a trombone, which played the cello part or even violin part instead of the trombone part. The other noted that with conductors using trombones to make up for lack of other instruments, the orchestras produced a deafening crash.[23]

By the time these articles appeared, four trombonists were working in New York. In order of their appearance in city directories, they were William Plain (1827), Felippe Cioffi (1828), Alexander Kyle (1828), and Thomas Dodworth (1829).[24] Dodworth may have been in New York by 1825 and Cioffi by 1826. Of these, Cioffi, a popular soloist, was the best known and most often mentioned in the press.

Besides the theaters, there were various unsuccessful attempts to establish a sacred music society, an Italian opera company, and a concert orchestra. During the summer, Niblo's Garden offered a variety of musical entertainments. There were also professional opportunities in military bands, dance orchestras, and other musical activities not covered by the press. Musicians did not necessarily make all of their living from music. Cioffi was a distiller for a while.

At the same time New York's early Italian opera companies all failed, New Orleans was able to support competing opera theaters. The first documented performance of an opera there took place in 1796, when the city was still ruled by France. Several attempts to establish an opera company failed financially. John Davis finally established a successful company that appealed to the French population at the Orleans Street Theater in 1819. James H. Caldwell arrived in New Orleans in 1820 and began to manage an American opera company.

One key to the survival of the Orleans Street Theater was that Davis took his company on a tour of northern cities, including New York, during six summers. Both the musical quality and the comparative financial stability of the company were a revelation to musicians there, so when Caldwell sent a representative to New York to recruit players for his St. Charles Street Theater, many of New York's most prominent musicians, including Cioffi, moved south.[25]

Cioffi was not the first trombonist in New Orleans. A member of the Camp Street Theater played a trombone solo in 1832, and a member of the Orleans Street Theater played one in 1834. There must have been orchestral trombonists long before any of them attempted a solo. There was probably at least one trombonist in town before there was a financially stable theater.

Boston, with its Puritan heritage, was perhaps the last major city on the Atlantic coast to have an important theater. The Tremont Theatre was founded in 1827 with the intention that its orchestra would be a major part of the attraction for customers. Its 24-piece orchestra, the largest in Boston up to that time, included one trombone. In 1829, it was hired to accompany the Handel and Haydn Society. Because the earliest sources of the names of Boston's professional musicians usually do not mention what instruments they played, it is impossible to determine when the trombone was first heard there. Since a Bostonian played trombone for an oratorio performance in New York, it was certainly no later than 1816. Lemuel Clark, who played violin, viola, and trombone between 1826 and 1841, is the earliest named trombonist.[26]

It took longer to establish concert orchestras than theater orchestras. Lacking theaters, Boston took the lead, although through 1821, every attempt to establish regular orchestral concerts in Boston failed for lack of public support. The Boston Music Academy, founded in 1833 as a sacred music society, aimed to improve public taste. It soon changed its tactics, and by 1840 it was so successful as a concert orchestra that it virtually dissolved its chorus. In its 1841 season, it boasted the largest orchestra yet heard in Boston: eight violins, two each of the other stringed instruments, pairs of woodwinds, four horns, two trumpets, two trombones, and timpani. Aside from the lack of a third trombone, it had complete instrumentation for a symphony orchestra, although there were hardly enough strings to balance such a full wind section.

Despite this deficiency, the Academy's concerts were so successful that a new organization, the Philharmonic Society, was founded in 1843 to take advantage of the new vogue for symphonic music. Since elevating public taste was not part of its mission, it played lighter, more popular fare. In 1845, it was comparable to the Academy's 1841 orchestra, with more violins and a third trombone, but still weak in the lower strings. Boston could not yet support two rival concert orchestras, and both of them failed before the end of the century. The present Boston Symphony Orchestra was established in 1881.

The earliest financially successful symphonic orchestra in the United States was established in New York. There have been four philharmonic societies in New York among other orchestras. The third, which started in 1824 and folded in 1827, was the earliest New York orchestra that attempted to be primarily a concert-giving organization. Among other problems, it had too few strings and lacked oboes and trombones. The current New York Philharmonic Orchestra, established in 1842, had full instrumentation from the beginning. The trombonists were Dodworth, Plain, and Schutz (or Schultz). Surely all later American symphony orchestras began their lives with three trombones. In the nineteenth century, American orchestras used tenor slide trombones. The lack of alto and bass trombones created the same problems as in France.[27]

Most major American orchestras were founded during the first half of the twentieth century. Before that, professional trombonists regarded the major touring bands as their most important employers. As the number of important orchestras increased, the number of professional wind bands decreased. The professional prestige of the orchestra also increased at the expense of the bands. By the 1920s, many orchestral trombonists sought to mini-

mize the significance of their previous activities with the bands. Gardell Simons, for example, toured with Sousa, but became principal trombonist of the Philadelphia Orchestra in 1915. Ten years later, his entry in a book commemorating the twenty-fifth anniversary of the orchestra credits him as the originator of the modern school of trombone playing. It does not mention his association with Sousa.[28]

Perhaps partly for this reason, Simons began to play a large-bore trombone with a trigger within five years of joining the orchestra. After Simons, Charles Gusikoff and Gordon Pulis also played large-bore instruments. The Philadelphia Orchestra seems to be among the first orchestras to move to large-bore instruments. The San Francisco Symphony Orchestra also adopted them fairly early. When Pulis became principal trombonist with the New York Philharmonic in 1946, he introduced large-bore trombones there. Shortly afterward, not only had most American orchestras changed to larger equipment, so had many other orchestras all over the world. By 1970, the Englishman George Maxted noted that American-made large-bore trombones were used "in practically all orchestras in this country, America and many Continental orchestras."[29]

In Canada, French-speaking areas developed operatic and symphonic performances before the English-speaking areas did. The first operatic performance took place in Quebec City in 1783. Subscription concerts started in about 1790. These early orchestras probably did not have trombones. There was a hiatus in operatic performance during the 1830s, but in 1834 a 60-piece orchestra, including trombone, presented a concert of sacred music. Therefore, when operatic performances started again in the 1840s, with the music of Rossini and Verdi, it is likely that at least one trombone would have been available for the orchestra.

The first serious attempts to form symphony orchestras did not occur until the 1860s. Orchestras were started in Montreal (1868), Toronto (after 1877), Montreal again (1878), and Victoria and Winnipeg (both in the 1880s), but without lasting success. Longer-lived orchestras were established in various cities in the 1890s, but only those in Quebec City and Ottawa survived the First World War. Most major Canadian orchestras were established after the Second World War.[30]

Elsewhere

European art music is now performed all over the world. One major cause of its spread was European colonialism. Spaniards took the trombone to Latin America in the sixteenth century, but it had disappeared by

Fig. 8.1.   Boston Symphony Orchestra brass players, 1925. Trombonists from left to right are LeRoy Kenfield (bass), Eugene Adams (assistant), Lucien Hansotte (second), and Johannes Rochut (principle). Boston Symphony Orchestra Archives.

Fig. 8.2.   Some of the Boston Symphony Orchestra brass players, some time between 1952 and 1966. Trombonists are, from left to right, Kauko Kahila (bass) and William Moyer (second). Boston Symphony Orchestra Archives.

the middle of the eighteenth century. Rossini's operas became popular in Latin America as elsewhere by the 1820s, but the standards of performance were low. Early theater orchestras probably lacked trombones, but probably had them by the time Verdi's operas became popular the 1840s. As elsewhere, concert orchestras gained a foothold with more difficulty. From 1827 to 1853, five philharmonic societies started and failed in Uruguay. A school orchestra there had trombones in the 1830s.[31]

Because so much of the standard European operatic and symphonic repertoire routinely called for trombones by about 1840, it seems likely that orchestras founded anywhere in the world after that time included them. Table 8.1[32] shows the founding dates of some orchestras around the world: the earliest one of the existing professional orchestras per country. It also shows in some cases the date of the earliest known orchestral concert, which was often presented by amateurs. In many cases, theater orchestras and military bands existed earlier than the first concert orchestra. In other places, like Egypt, opera and concerts may have started about the same time. The Cairo Opera House opened in 1869 and presented Italian opera, ballet, and symphonic music for more than a century until it burned down. The premiere of Verdi's *Aida*, which requires three trombones, took place there in 1871.

The Symphonic and Operatic Repertoire

The shadow of Beethoven hung over most of the nineteenth century. The better of the next generations of composers, from Mendelssohn and Schumann to Brahms, were as much intimidated as inspired by his achievements. Instead of leading into the future, therefore, the example of Beethoven seems to have set limits beyond which his followers were reluctant to explore. A contemporary, however, did suggest some new directions. Carl Maria von Weber carefully worked out new combinations of instruments to create a particular atmosphere in his operas. In the Wolf's Glen scene in *Der Freischutz*, seven bullets are cast, each with a different scenic effect and its own orchestration. The horns, bassoons, and trombones make a gruesome sound at the appearance of shadowy hunters. Weber's approach to orchestral color exerted a tremendous influence on later composers.

That later generations of composers treated the trombone with greater confidence and boldness than Beethoven can be attributed to at least four other influences: Schubert (eventually), military bands, popular dance orchestras (both covered later in this chapter), and Rossini. Rossini was the son of a military musician; both father and son were skilled horn players. Therefore Rossini understood brass instruments and their technical and expressive capacities more than any other composer of his time. He did not hesitate to allow trombones to

Table 8.1. Dates for Some of the Earliest Orchestras around the World

Orchestra	City	Founded	Earliest
Cape Town SO	Cape Town, South Africa	1914	1811
El Salvador SO	San Salvador, El Salvador	1922	1859
Nippon Hoso Kuokai SO	Tokyo, Japan	1926	1887
National SO of Costa Rica	San José, Costa Rica	1926	
SODRE SO	Montevideo, Uruguay	1930	1827
Israel PO	Tel Aviv, Israel	1936	
SO of Brazil	Rio de Janeiro, Brazil	1940	1880s
PO of Guatemala	Guatemala City, Guatemala	1944	1934
Buenos Aires SO	Buenos Aires, Argentina	1946	
Hong Kong PO	Hong Kong, China	1947	1895
New Zealand SO	Wellington, New Zealand	1947	1860s
National Symphony of Mexico	Mexico City, Mexico	1947	
Seoul PO	Seoul, South Korea	1948	1920s
Iraqi National SO	Baghdad, Iraq	1948	
Melbourne SO	Melbourne, Australia	1950	1860s
Cairo SO	Cairo, Egypt	1956	1869
Central PO	Beijing, China	1956	1879
National SO of Ghana	Accra, Ghana	1959	
Taipei City SO	Taipei, Taiwan	1969	
Singapore SO	Singapore	1979	

PO = Philharmonic Orchestra
SO = Symphony Orchestra

Note: The "earliest" column refers to the earliest concert orchestra in the country (including amateur and semiprofessional orchestras) mentioned in the sources. Theater orchestras with trombones and military bands may have existed earlier.

double rapid chromatic passages in the cellos and bassoons. He first called for a single trombone in *Il turco in Italia* (1814). He used three for the first time in *Otello* (1816) and invariably required three after *Erminone* (1819).

His orchestration was more brilliant than any of his predecessors' and most of his contemporaries. For that he was both widely imitated and widely reviled. A writer in the *Revue musicale* in 1832 declared that there were only two kinds of musicians: classicists and Rossinists. The Earl of Mount-Edgcumbe complained, "It is really distressing to hear the leading voices strained almost to cracking, in order to be audible over a full chorus and full orchestra, strengthened often by trumpets, trombones kettle-drums, and all the noisiest instruments." He singled out Rossini as a composer of undeniable genius but no taste, so prolific that he plagiarized himself. The earl represents those who disapproved of opera's turn from an aristocratic spectacle to mass entertainment.[33]

Not only those trying to hang on to a dying aesthetic criticized Rossini, however. Berlioz railed at his fondness for three trombones, complaining that it robbed the instrument of its dramatic power. He fumed,

> At the Opéra Comique an old chap is upset at losing his snuffbox—three trombones! He rejoices when he finds it—three trombones! A blind man drinks a glass of cheap wine—three trombones! A stable lad tightens some layabout's belt—three trombones! Every time! . . . It is the present leader of the so-called School of Melody whom we have to blame for this horrible instrumental abuse, while Beethoven and Weber, the leaders of the rival school regarded as a School of Violence and Noise, were alone in upholding the principle of moderation and the intelligent use of instruments.[34]

Fétis could be equally scathing in his assessment of Rossini's music, but also provided a more balanced summary:

> His compositions present the first examples of four violin parts, the formidable union of four horns, common trumpets, keyed trumpets, trombones, ophycleides, &c., all united for the accompaniment of various movements. The varied forms of design and harmony drawn from these instruments, would appear but little appropriate, and still less the constant employment of the double drum, cymbals and triangles. And yet the admirable effects he has drawn from the abuse of means, have in a great measure justified his temerity; and nothing can be a better proof of his genius than his having caused all this noise to be received by a people who before had an aversion for all strong accompaniments.[35]

Although I have not found any contemporary writer who was not severely critical of Rossini's use of the trombones, it certainly influenced other composers, especially Meyerbeer and Spontini, to mention two more who were much better liked by the general public than by the high-culture critics. Indeed, when Rossini provides quick, exposed passages, such as the *William Tell* overture, they generate a certain excitement, but much of the time, the trombones play only chords in closed harmony, or worse yet, rhythmic punctuation in unison, with no particular thematic significance. It is very difficult to keep these kinds of passages in the background and very easy for them to intrude on the melodies being sung or played on other, usually softer instruments. When critics complained that the trombones were too loud, one reason is probably that their parts were so often mere harmonic and rhythmic filler, inserted to increase the overall volume of the orchestra.

Berlioz's criticism of Rossini and his imitators was not that they overused the trombone, but that they trivialized it. His own music demonstrates acute sensitivity to how orchestral color could enhance the dramatic impact of purely instrumental music. He took full advantage of the technical flexibility offered by the invention of valves, while recognizing the tonal superiority of the slide trombone. He appreciated the power available in having trombones present thematic material in unison and used the brass choir both with the full orchestra and independently. Among his more novel effects is Hostias of the *Grand messe des morts*, in which three flutes play high chords accompanied only by eight trombones playing low notes, mostly pedals, in unison. It is still to this day a controversial passage.[36]

While many critics who despised Berlioz's music at least admired his orchestration, he, too, was often rebuked for excessive noise. Commenting on the overture to the *Francs-juges*, one critic wrote,

> I don't believe that even the trumpets of the last judgment will produce an effect more incisive than the one produced here by those thunderous trombones; nevertheless this kind of instrumentation, beautiful and striking though it is, is perhaps a little too melodramatic in character.[37]

The caption to one of the best-known caricatures of Berlioz says, "Fortunately the room is solid. It still stands." (See Fig. 8.3.)

Mendelssohn seems to have been regarded as something of an anti-Rossini or anti-Berlioz. One writer

Fig. 8.3.   Berlioz conducting orchestra with a cannon, caricature by Andreas Geiger.

observed that Mendelssohn's discriminating manner of using trombones "strikes the attention of the intelligent hearer." Another review, implicitly scolding Rossini, Berlioz, and others, noted that even composers who cannot match the freshness and beauty of Mendelssohn's ideas could at least learn from his orchestration,

> how much greater effect is to be produced by the judicious use than by the lavish abuse of trombones and

other powerful instruments. Mendelssohn has not very often recourse to these brazen auxiliaries in his orchestral works, but when he does employ them it is with manifest purpose and legitimate effect.[38]

Among works by the first generation of American symphonists, the first and third movements of George Frederick Bristow's Symphony no. 2 (*Jullien*) have trombone solos (Fig. 8.4). Composed in 1853, it is surely the

Adagio

Fig. 8.4. Trombone solo from the third movement of George Bristow's Second Symphony "Jullien."

first symphony to use the trombone as soloist, and it is not clear what inspired it. Perhaps Bristow remembered the sensation caused by Cioffi's solo performances in New York 20 years earlier. Perhaps he even thought Cioffi would be in New York for the occasion, but it was Winterbottom who made the trip. Jullien's orchestra performed it several times, both in New York and London.

William Weber's distinction between high culture and high-status popular music is valid only until about the midcentury, when the tastes of the formerly warring factions began to move closer together. The popular virtuosos impelled concert orchestras to improve their technical standards, but audiences for popular music got tired of the commercial manipulation and musical emptiness that characterized so many of them.

A letter from one of Liszt's fans to a Viennese newspaper in 1846 challenged him to play more Beethoven, which he then began to do.[39] As he and other popular virtuosos began to play the classical literature and morph into concert artists, the trombone, which had no classical literature, disappeared from symphonic concerts as a solo instrument. On the other hand, Rossini's overtures and other excerpts from popular operas found a place on concert programs. The conspicuous trombone parts that the purists had condemned gradually became acceptable.

Another broadening of the classical concert repertoire began in 1829, when Mendelssohn mounted his performance of Bach's *St. Matthew Passion*. By the end of the nineteenth century, Bach cantatas with trombone parts and Schütz's "Fili mi Absalon" found their way on to symphonic programs. The emergence of a new critical attitude toward the trombone is evident in a review of a performance of Berlioz's *Harold in Italy*:

The art has made vast strides in the direction of realism and graphic characterization during the last quarter of a century, and what sounded strange and eccentric in 1837 and even in 1855 may appear comparatively tame to our more experienced ears. We have become used to large orchestras, and three trombones and two "tambours de Basque" are no longer able to shatter our nerves.

Even at this late date, critical opinion was not unanimous. Not four months later another review in the same paper found fault with the orchestration of Schubert's *Mass in E♭*, "the excessive use of the trombones in the contrapuntal passages being especially reprehensible."[40]

Early in the century, orchestras had grown by adding new instruments, such as the trombone. Later, orchestras grew by augmenting the string choir. In 1811, Beethoven requested a string section of 16 performers (4 first violins, 4 second violins, 4 violas, 2 cellos, and 2 basses) to play such works as his Fifth Symphony, which has 17 wind parts and timpani. The Gewandhaus Orchestra, during Mendelssohn's tenure, had 9 first violins, 8 seconds, 5 violas, 5 cellos, and 4 basses and about the same size wind section. Wagner's orchestra at Bayreuth in 1876 had 64 string players, although his wind section was also larger than what Beethoven used. Koury's tables showing the makeup of particular orchestras over time makes it clear that this growth of the orchestra was not a smooth progression by any means, and the proportion of strings to winds varied widely from place to place throughout the nineteenth century. But it does seem safe to say that, in general, the growth of string sections occurred some time after three trombones and four horns became common.[41]

Wagner dominated the last half of the nineteenth century much as Rossini dominated the first half. Richard Strauss mentioned three important technical aspects of Wagner's music: careful attention to melodic independence of the inner parts, accomplishment of polyphony in the brasses through the use of valved instruments, and requiring the virtuoso technique of soloists from all of the members of the orchestra. For these reasons, he considered Wagner's music "the only important progress in the art of instrumentation since Berlioz."[42]

Wagner's basic organizing principle, the Leitmotiv, often includes not only melodic and harmonic ideas, but orchestral color. He approached brass instruments not so much as a brass choir, but as separate choirs of trumpets (including bass trumpet), horns, trombones (including contrabass trombone in the Ring cycle), and even tubas. Wagner expected "tenor-bass" trombones (that is, large-bore tenors) for the upper parts and a bass trombone for the third part. The fourth part is intended for contrabass trombone when it is the bottom voice of the trombone section. When a tuba is used under the trombones, the fourth trombone part is intended for bass trombone.[43] Parts for trombones, like every other member of Wagner's orchestra, are thematically significant. He did not write Rossini-like filler. He could write a heroic melody for the trombones to play in unison, as in the Prelude to Act III of *Lohengrin* or the "Ride of the Valkyries" or soft chordal passages to underline a variety of moods.

Bruckner, who fell under Wagner's influence more than any other symphonist, likewise gave thematically significant passages to the trombones. There has been no detailed analysis of his orchestration. It is certainly more than an imitation of Wagner's practice, as was frequently assumed early in the twentieth century, but the common later view that it closely resembles the way an organist approaches registration is likewise oversimplified.[44]

Brahms, on the other hand, resisted Wagner's influence more than any other symphonist. His insistence on following the symphonic path laid out by Beethoven and Schumann caused him to reject much of Wagner's style, including his coloristic orchestration. It did not prevent him from writing important and exposed chorale passages for trombones in his symphonies.

Major symphonic and operatic works whose trombone parts are mere filler and not thematically significant became the exception rather than the rule, and not only in German music. Trombones have prominent roles in Verdi's operas.[45] Russian composers from Glinka onward, with their love of orchestral color, wrote prominent trombone parts in music with a literary program, such as Rimsky-Korsakov's Second Symphony (*Antar*), and in music with no program, such as Borodin's First Symphony.

In fact, the orchestra continued to grow larger, including at least four trombones with increasing frequency. Mahler is especially well-known for assembling large orchestras. Schoenberg's *Gurrelieder* represents perhaps the greatest extreme of orchestra size. Its brass section (10 horns, 7 trumpets, 7 trombones, and tuba) is larger than Haydn's entire orchestra at Esterháza. Composers generally did not require orchestras of this size for volume, but rather for variety of color. Only in rare passages does the entire orchestra play at once.

A significant number of symphonic and operatic works of this time and somewhat later include trombone solos, including *Hamlet* and *Le comte de Carmagnola*, both for valve trombone, by Ambroise Thomas, *Marche héroïque* by Saint-Saëns, the Third Symphony of Tchaikovsky, the Seventh Symphony of Sibelius, and especially the Third Symphony of Mahler. The mammoth first movement of the latter work includes three extended trombone solos, limited to the middle and lower registers of the instrument. *Der Bürger als Edelmann* by Richard Strauss includes solo bass trombone.

In the early twentieth century, both economic conditions and aesthetic preferences dictated that composers return to using smaller orchestras, but none of the instruments that had been added to the Romantic orchestra were abandoned in the twentieth century. In fact, trombone parts grew more exposed. Short solo passages became commonplace, and longer ones not unusual. An outstanding example is the one in Ravel's *Bolero*. Shorter and less difficult, a solo passage in Stravinsky's *Symphony of Psalms* still manages to violate the prescriptions of every orchestration textbook he could have ever seen. It does not proceed scale-wise nor follow the overtone series in its wide skips.

In general, there was less reliance in twentieth-century music on a single melody with chordal accompaniment. With more different layers in the texture, trombone parts could have their own rhythmic profile and thus be heard as a distinct voice, while at the same time being less likely to overpower the rest of the orchestra. Partly because orchestral playing became the members' primary job and players could devote major time to ensemble precision, trombone parts became more technically demanding. Under the influence of jazz, glissandos, rips, growls, and smears appeared in orchestral trombone parts. Other new techniques include flutter tonguing and the use of a wide variety of mutes, with the straight mute being by far the most common.[46]

Occasionally, twentieth-century composers reached for an instrumental effect that is nearly unplayable as written. Bartók required a glissando from BB to F in both *The Miraculous Mandarin* and *Concerto for Orchestra*. That figure is playable only on a bass trombone in F. He might have encountered it in Hungary and thought it was the standard bass trombone. In fact, hardly anyone had access to one until very late in the century.[47]

Another stylistic revolution near the end of the twentieth century introduced so-called minimalist music. The trombone parts in works such as *A Short Ride in a Fast Machine* by John Adams often consist of alternation between two pitches or other repetitive patterns, but it is not mere filler. The entire work is built from repetition of simple motives, so the trombone parts are not significantly different in that regard from what any other instrument plays. While styles of orchestral music have come and gone, there has been continuity in the institution of the orchestra itself. From Wagner onward, composers have treated trombones as equal members of the orchestra, not merely, as in Mendelssohn's day, as "brazen auxiliaries."

The Trombone in Vernacular Music

While high-status popular music (Italian opera, French grand opera, and the kinds of dazzling virtuosity displayed in private salons and in "benefit" concerts) essentially merged with classical music by the middle of the nineteenth century, low-status music remained distinct. Because of the multiple meanings of the word "popular," I have chosen to use the term "vernacular" to cover whatever is left out of the definition of "high culture" or "art music." As far as the trombone is concerned, it is convenient to discuss vernacular music according to the kind of ensemble that included it. This section includes popular orchestras, wind and brass bands, jazz, salsa, and, for want of a better term, "world music."

While it is necessary to make distinctions between art music and vernacular music, it would be a mistake to see a sharp division. Johann Strauss Jr., for example, played Wagner's music on his concerts years before any of Wagner's operas were produced in Vienna.[48] In both the nineteenth and twentieth centuries it was not at all unusual for professional musicians to play in all sorts of ensembles (for example, symphony orchestra and military band) and styles over the course of their careers, or indeed over the course of a single year. It was not until the twentieth century that it became possible to make a living from performing in any one ensemble, and very few musicians have ever done so. Also in the twentieth

century, wind bands, brass bands, and jazz have in various ways aspired to be considered art rather than entertainment.

There was inevitably cross-fertilization between art music and vernacular music. Trombone parts in symphonic music became more prominent, more thematically significant, and more technically difficult over the course of the nineteenth century. Some concert works even included trombone solos. Each of these advances happened in vernacular music first. On the other hand, vernacular concerts often included art music. This mutual influence continued throughout the twentieth century, too, as can be seen in the influence of jazz rhythms, harmonies, and instrumental techniques on the composition of orchestral music and in the number of classical tunes that became popular songs.

Popular Orchestras

The nineteenth century saw the beginning of the concept of music as a business. The more entrepreneurial orchestras of the time appealed to a public that included the lower middle class and the working class, which could not afford to attend high-culture concerts and were not welcome in the salons and other high-status venues. The best of these low-status orchestras were critically acclaimed as excellent ensembles. In addition to dance music and other light fare, many of them played symphonic music.

In Vienna, Joseph Lanner and Johann Strauss Sr., first as partners and later as rivals, were among the earliest entrepreneurs to become internationally famous in the dance orchestra business. Earlier waltz composers had used a group of no more than a dozen players, and the wind instruments (one each of flute, clarinet, and trumpet, plus two horns) had a very subordinate role. Lanner and Strauss enlarged the string section, added a second flute, clarinet, and trumpet, and eventually oboes, bassoons, and a trombone. Their customers demanded a steady stream of new dance music, and each of these two men composed hundreds of works in their brief lifetimes. Strauss shared the duties of orchestrating the new music with an associate, Philipp Fahrbach, who supplied the trombone parts, along with other winds.[49]

Strauss was among the first conductors to take his orchestra on an international tour. His visit to Paris in 1837 is important for a number of reasons, not the least of which was his subsequent introduction of Parisian-style promenade concerts to Viennese audiences. More important for the history of the trombone, Strauss's orchestra made a tremendous impact on Hector Berlioz, who had never heard a bass trombone before and had not realized how different Germanic orchestral practice was from French practice.

Strauss Jr. used only a single trombone in his earliest works. Frequently, although not in every work, the trombone plays melodies doubling the trumpet line an octave lower. Most often, however, its part doubles the bass line in the cellos and bassoons. In this way it can be prominent without being overpowering. After he started using three trombones, melodies in octaves with a trumpet remain as common as before, but are nearly always played by the third trombonist.

In Paris, Philippe Musard established himself as the leading dance orchestra conductor during the 1830s and '40s. When he conducted balls at the Opéra, his orchestra included 14 cornets and 12 trombones. In 1833, he instituted a widely imitated series of informal concerts he called promenade concerts. In the previous century that was the name of concerts at which aristocrats promenaded in fashionable parks, but Musard's concerts were inexpensive enough to attract an audience that included the lower middle and working classes. They were informal concerts, at which the audience could eat, drink, dance, and otherwise move around. They featured quadrilles, waltzes, and other dance music, but also included classical music.[50]

Jules Rivière recalled, "In addition to being a composer of light music Musard was a very sound musician. He had studied harmony at the Conservatoire in Paris, where he obtained the first prize in 1831" and, "These concerts were popular for a number of years, and deservedly so, for Musard was a very able conductor besides being also a prolific composer." In 1837, Musard's trombonists were Dieppo (also principal trombone in the Société des Concerts du Conservatoire and professor of trombone at the Paris Conservatory), Simon, and Vobaron. As a composer, Musard was the first to entrust the melody to trombones.[51]

Promenade concerts on Musard's model took place at least in New York, Vienna, and London. The London promenades began in 1838, and an 1839 advertisement promised that Mr. Bean would play a trombone solo.[52] The first important conductor of promenade concerts in England was Jullien, who first produced dance entertainments in Paris from 1836–38 and took up permanent residence in London in 1840.

Jullien's showmanship and histrionics are legendary. Nevertheless, his orchestras played with great precision and taste. Jullien did not hesitate to present his audiences with complete symphonies of Mozart and Beethoven, along with the usual dance music. It was a common

practice of conductors of the time to reorchestrate some of the older music that they played, adding new parts for trombone, among other instruments. But a reviewer of a concert on which Jullien had programmed two Mozart symphonies and the overture to *Die Zauberflöte* wrote:

> It was consoling to find that music, in order to be relished by a modern audience, is not obliged, as a matter of necessity, to be boisterous and overpowering, full of violent contrasts, fantastic, exaggerated, and so forth. In the two symphonies there are no loud instruments—no trombones or ophicleides. In the second, the immortal *"Jupiter"* (so called, not by the unassuming Mozart, but by his admirers)—there are not even clarionets. M. Jullien, with real artistic feeling, refrained from interference with the original scores, simply adding a third bassoon in the last-named symphony.[53]

On the other hand, Jullien presented a number of "monster concerts," including on several of them selections from Bellini's *I puritani* performed by 20 each of trumpets, cornets, trombones, ophicleides, and serpents. An advertisement promising a repeat of the piece boasted that it was "received at the last Concert Monstre with applause unprecedented in the annals of instrumental performances."[54] Jullien maintained a large stable of soloists. The earliest trombonists to play on his concerts were Frenchmen: Faivre, Dieppo, and Dantonnet. Once Cioffi moved to England from New Orleans in 1846, he became Jullien's principal trombone soloist and remained in that capacity until 1855.

After Musard's death, Rivière formed an orchestra to play garden concerts in Paris. He later wrote,

> Chatting with Dieppo one day, I learnt he had arranged some trombone quartetts, and it occurred to me that I might make something of a sensation by introducing them at my concerts with three players to each part, making twelve in all. And as, for such a scheme, I needed good performers, I engaged only those who had obtained a first prize in Dieppo's class at the Conservatoire. My plan delighted the handsome Dane, and it was arranged that he should himself conduct on this occasion. The three pieces selected were the septuor from *Lucie*, the Fisherman's Prayer from *Masaniello*, and Johann Strauss's valse *Philomelen*. Playing a valse on a trombone was certainly a *tour de force*, but it was most successfully accomplished, and the performance was a triumph. . . . Many years after, I repeated this performance at the Alhambra, on the occasion of one of my annual benefits, but I did not again venture upon a valse. I replaced it by the quartett from *Rigoletto*.[55]

Rivière later moved to London, where he revived the promenade concerts that had been started by Jullien. In the nineteenth century, promenade concerts did not long survive the death of their founding conductor. Henry Wood began a series in 1895 and conducted it for nearly half a century. It continues, named for him after his death in 1944, to this day.

The Boston Symphony Orchestra established a series of off-season promenade concerts in 1885, now known as the Boston Pops, to prevent players from going back to Europe at the end of the season and perhaps not returning for the next season. When a major symphonic orchestra sponsors promenade concerts, it can thereby offer its members a year-long contract. A similar relationship exists in Cincinnati.

Music for the popular theater (and later for films) also required an orchestra in which the trombone often played a conspicuous role. Johann Strauss Jr. composed *Die Fledermaus* and other light operatic fare in which the general style and orchestration are very much like his dance music, including occasional melodic passages for trombone. The operettas of his contemporaries (including Franz von Suppé, Jacques Offenbach, and Arthur Sullivan) and the next generation (including Franz Lehár and Victor Herbert) also have trombones in the orchestra.

Operettas are part of the ancestry of the American musical, but composers of musicals have rarely done their own orchestration. Robert Russell Bennett orchestrated most of the musicals of Rodgers and Hammerstein or Lerner and Loewe among others.[56] As the twentieth century progressed, scoring began to move away from the traditional orchestra. Not all musicals require strings. Because the composers do not prepare their own orchestration, there is no definitive version of any musical. (That is nothing new; there was never really a definitive version of a Rossini opera, either.) The knowledge that a particular orchestra has excellent players on some instruments and not others has always influenced composers, but orchestrators of musicals must also contend with shifting union contracts and the pressures to cut costs. A show presented for the first time with three trombones might later be reorchestrated to include only one. Just as audiences for the earliest operas did not care about orchestral color, modern audiences are interested in the spectacle on stage, but not necessarily in who is in the pit.

But new entertainment technologies have also presented new opportunities for musicians, including film sound tracks, radio, and television. Trombonists have been seen in the studio bands of late night talk shows and heard on commercials. Arrangers of this music frequently make use of non-traditional sounds, including various so-called extended techniques.

Wind Bands and Brass Bands

Bands are important for a number of reasons. In the nineteenth century, for the first time in history, amateur musicians began playing brass instruments in large numbers. Most of them joined some kind of band. There were more bands than orchestras, and more people heard band music than orchestra music. In fact, many people heard symphonic and operatic music played in band transcriptions before they had a chance to hear it with the original orchestration, if ever. Selections from *La forza del destino* constituted the test piece for a brass band contest at the Crystal Palace in 1863, five years before the opera received its English premiere.[57]

Some orchestral trombonists also played in bands. William Winterbottom, who was an active soloist and played in a variety of orchestras, was also part of the First Life Guards Band and served as bandmaster for at least three other military bands. By the end of the century, Parès recommended that, in both infantry and cavalry bands, the (slide) trombones play not only the trombone parts of orchestra music, but also take on some roles of the bassoons, horns and tuba. His recommendations appear to be more a description of standard practice than a prescription for innovation. They would give the trombones more technically challenging parts than what was generally recommended in standard orchestration treatises.[58]

At least in the first half of the nineteenth century, the military led the evolution of the wind band and brass band in Europe (but not in the United States). Even early in the century, however, there were numerous civic militia bands, which were neither true military bands nor traditional town bands (which were vestiges of the ancient *alta* tradition). Their instrumentation approximated military bands, but their members were civilian amateurs. By the end of the century, there were thousands of bands. The number of military bands had probably grown some. The number of amateur civilian bands had grown exponentially. In Italy alone there were 1,494 civilian wind bands, 78 military wind bands, 113 civilian brass bands, and 40 military brass bands in 1872, involving a total of more than 46,000 players.[59] The following account will concentrate on the development of various kinds of bands and how the trombone came to be a part of them. The narrative will be taken into the twentieth century only in the case of novel developments.

Sundelin's manual for the instrumentation of military music speaks of three kinds of bands: infantry, *Jäger* (light infantry), and cavalry. Infantry bands consisted of mixed woodwind, brass, and percussion. *Jäger* bands (also known as *Hornenmusik*) were all brass. Cavalry bands (also known as *Trompetenmusik*) were slightly larger ensembles, all brass with the addition of timpani. At least one cavalry unit had three trombones as early as 1805, but Prussian infantry bands had no trombones until 1816. Little by little, all the kinds of bands grew both in numbers of players and different instruments. In the late 1820s, Holmes observed, "One distinguishing characteristic of the excellence of this country [Germany] in music is the skill of the wind-instrument bands, and the nicety of tune with which they play pieces containing the most learned modulation."[60]

When Wilhelm Wieprecht heard a military band for the first time (in about 1825) and decided to make military music his career, he left a position in the court orchestra in Berlin to do so, even though it was one of the most prestigious in Europe. Because most established military musicians preferred infantry bands, cavalry bands seemed the best opportunity for an outsider. Wieprecht composed six marches for one cavalry regiment. The limitations imposed by natural trumpets did not allow much harmonic variety, so he persuaded the commander to purchase chromatic instruments, resulting in 11 players of six different sizes of valved and keyed trumpets plus two bass trombones. This instrumentation allowed him to modulate freely. Soon he was asked by other cavalry bands to select new instruments for them. His activity came to the attention the king, who named him Inspector of Army Bands in 1838. In this capacity, he standardized the instrumentation of military bands. Under his leadership, the typical Prussian infantry regiment had 43–47 wind players, including four trombones (alto, tenor, and two basses). Cavalry and *Jäger* bands had three trombones (alto, tenor, and bass).

Most other German states also updated their bands over the course of the nineteenth century. In Munich, Mason observed, "Military music abounds here, and is very fine. One of the best bands I have heard (but not better than the one in Berlin) . . . plays daily at eleven o'clock; say an overture first, and then one or two pieces of lighter music." He also noted Prussian, Bavarian, and Austrian bands in Frankfurt, each trying to surpass the others in daily concerts.[61]

Civic militias and associated bands existed early in the century. One started in Leipzig in 1830, with Queisser as leader of its two bands. After the revolutionary strife of 1848 civic militias were outlawed, but in 1851 new laws allowed the formation of bands as civic clubs. Stripped of the functional obligations of the old bands, the new ones existed strictly for entertainment. There may have been amateur bands with no quasi-military purpose even earlier. In 1837, Mason visited Hamburg and noted, "I passed a very good band in the street—playing at the Doors of gentlemen's houses—there were four clarinets—two Horns—Trombone and Drums."[62]

Austrian military units boasted large groups of mixed brass and woodwind instruments from the very beginning of the nineteenth century. By 1822, various commanders competed with each other for prestige and magnificence to the extent that some of them had bands of 50 players or more. In that year, Emperor Francis I (r. 1792–1835) ordered that no infantry band have more than 34 members. These bands must have been quite good. Just as Wieprecht left a court orchestra to pursue a career as a military musician, Nemetz relinquished a post as trombonist in the Kärntnerthor theater orchestra to become the leader of an infantry band in 1828.[63]

Writing in Austrian-ruled Milan in 1846 about the organization of bands, Joseph Fahrbach listed 25 woodwinds and 26 brass. The three trombones, used for both melody and accompaniment, were almost exclusively valve trombones.[64] Andreas Leonhardt, Austria's first director of military music, reorganized and standardized the various military bands in 1851.

Although Napoleon (r. 1799–1815) allowed the infantry bands of the revolutionary period to languish, he cared about developing trumpet signals for troop movements. His cavalry bandmaster, David Buhl, published 16 fanfares for 4 trumpets, 2 horns, and trombone. When these parts were doubled, the full ensemble consisted of 16 trumpets, 6 horns, and 3 trombones. The brilliant sound of this ensemble had a profound influence on other cavalry bands. Infantry bands remained small; the government declined to support more than nine players for each regiment. Officers hired extra players at their own expense, however, so by 1825 it was not unusual for a regimental band to have more than 30 players, including two trombonists.

By 1845, the French government was concerned about the low standards of its military music. Michele Carafa and Adolphe Sax submitted rival plans for reform. A contest between them, along with several regimental bands, took place on 22 April 1845. All of the bands included three to six trombones. Carafa's included three slide trombones. Sax's included two slide trombones and two valve trombones. A government commission recommended Sax's plan, but because it included instruments for which he owned the patents, it attracted fierce opposition from other manufacturers. With its official adoption in 1854, France became the third country in which one person's vision led to standardization of military instrumentation. It would not happen again for the rest of the century. Rivière, trombonist in an infantry band before launching his career, described what life was like for a French military musician in his memoir.[65]

Not much information about civilian bands in France is available before midcentury. After the revolutionary year of 1848, the number and size of bands began to grow. By the end of the nineteenth century there were 1711 mixed wind bands and more than 4000 brass bands. Some of the largest had more than 100 members.[66]

Much of Italy was dominated or even directly ruled by foreign powers: France until 1815 and Austria thereafter. After Napoleon's defeat, the Austrians and the Kingdom of Sardinia-Piedmont divided the north. The Papal States took up the middle of the peninsula, and the House of Bourbon, with dynastic ties to Spain, ruled the Kingdom of Naples in the south. In 1861, Sardinia-Piedmont expelled the Austrians and Bourbons and became the Kingdom of Italy, adding the Papal States to its territory in 1870.

As a result of the Napoleonic occupation, many ancient town bands, including Rome's official *piffari*, were abolished. The pope also lost his ability to maintain the traditional *piffari* at Castel Sant'Angelo. A new town band known as the Banda Capitolina was formed in 1818. Its instrumentation was piccolo, two small clarinets, six clarinets, four horns, a trumpet, a trombone, a bassoon, a triangle, and a set of bells.[67]

Military bands of Sardinia-Piedmont likewise had to start over after Napoleon withdrew. At first, they were small and poorly funded, but larger bands were formed as part of a reorganization of the army on the accession of King Carlo Alberto (r. 1831–49). By that time, the bands included trombones. There were no true regimental bands in the south, but every company had three *piffari* and three drummers. The king had his own band.

By 1830, Neapolitan military bands had been reorganized and typically consisted of a piccolo, an oboe, 20 clarinets, 4 bassoons, 4 keyed trumpets, 6 horns, 5 or 6 trombones, and three ophicleides.[68]

Various proposals made for reorganizing Italian military music beginning in 1863, two years after the proclamation of the Kingdom of Italy, culminated in standardization of infantry and cavalry bands in 1865, clearly influenced by Austrian bands. Each type included three tenor valve trombones. Reforms undertaken in 1901 included the addition of a bass trombone.

Although Napoleon abolished the official bands of the cities he conquered, that does not mean the music stopped. When Sienna's town band was reorganized in 1815, it included a *tromba duttile*, which was probably more a survival of an obsolete instrument than a forward-looking innovation. This band was apparently professional, but many strictly amateur bands formed all over Italy at about the same time. Cortemaggiore formed both a band (with two trombones) and an orchestra in 1822.[69]

Although there were about 1700 bands in Italy shortly after the unification was complete, there was no standard instrumentation beyond what was attempted for military bands. Therefore, when operas required stage bands (*banda sul palco*), composers never orchestrated them, but instead depended on whatever bands were available locally.

Under the British king George III (r. 1760–1820), the so-called King's Band was filled with people with no musical training. On rare occasions when the band had to play, members hired deputies. The music-loving future George IV (r. 1820–30), on the other hand, formed his own band in 1795. Its personnel included the best available wind players from all over the world. In 1818 it consisted of 34 players including soprano, alto, tenor, and bass trombones. By his death it had grown to 42 players, including six trombones (alto, tenor, and four basses).[70]

As the century began, the government did not support military music at all. Officers could raise bands at

Fig. 8.5. Fodens Motor Works Band (1910), from *Internet Bandsman's Everything Within: Vintage Brass Band Pictures*, www.ibew.co.uk/.

their own expense provided that their bandsmen were all capable of combat. Even so, the Royal Artillery Band had 26 musicians, including three trombones, in 1805. Cavalry bands began to include trombones according to the French model during the Napoleonic years. The bands' conductors were usually foreign-born civilians, who did not go to war.

No one arose in Britain comparable to Wieprecht, Leonhardt, or Sax to take charge of military music, and so there were no national standards of any kind. In 1854, someone thought it would be a good idea for all of the bands of the British Army to play the national anthem at a review in honor of Queen Victoria's birthday. Unfortunately, with no standard arrangement, each band played its own, not all of them in the same key. Meanwhile, the French-massed band that played on the same occasion was excellent. A proposal to establish a school to train British military bandsmen soon followed.[71]

Some sort of standardization of British bands eventually occurred because of the publication of journals devoted to military music. *Jullien's Journal* started in 1844, but the longest lasting was *Boosé's Military Journal*, which began publication in 1846 and continued with some title changes until 1982. Because each journal used basically the same instrumentation in each issue, subscribing bands had incentive to conform. The various journals all required three trombones, usually two tenors and a bass. While the bass trombone in F persisted past midcentury, the preferred British bass was in G, with no trigger. The British did not begin to adopt the B-flat bass trombone with trigger(s) until after the Second World War.[72]

Bands of amateurs attached to militia units or volunteer corps often had trombones as early as the 1790s. Two important kinds of civilian organizations originated in Britain: the circus band and the brass band movement. As traveling musicians, circus bands helped to spread common tastes in popular entertainment. In the early years of the nineteenth century, various businesses formed bands in the villages near where their factories were located. The Clegg family of cotton manufacturers formed a 12-piece band in 1818 in the village of Besses o' th' Barn. The original instrumentation of this band, forerunner of the Besses o' th' Barn Brass Band, was keyed bugle, three clarinets, a piccolo, a trumpet, two horns, a trombone, two bass horns, and a bass drum.[73]

It is impossible to document which was the first brass band, but there were several by the end of the 1830s. Welsh industrialist Robert Thompson Crayshaw established one of the most important, the Cyfarthfa Band, in 1838 as his private band, much the way landed gentry had long patronized music. He used some local players,

but also recruited established professionals to play the most critical parts. It appears that he did not pay them directly for their musical services, but promised them good jobs in his factory. There were other private bands, but more often bands were financed either by local subscription or direct patronage of a manufacturing concern. John Foster, owner of the Black Dyke Mills, established a company band in 1855, partly to provide recreational opportunity for his workers. He provided instruments, a rehearsal room, a bandmaster, and uniforms. While not all brass bands had ties to a manufacturing company, most of their members were part of the working class, something unparalleled on the continent.

Uniquely British brass band contests took place as early as the 1840s but began to occur regularly in the 1860s. Even excluding now-defunct bands, the winners of national championships are too numerous to list here. The rules eventually led to the standardization of instrumentation. While there have been changes to the standards over the years, the trombone section has consistently been two tenor trombones and one bass trombone (in G until after the Second World War). They could be either valve trombones (which first became common in the 1840s) or slide trombones until 1873, after which valve trombones were forbidden.[74]

While earlier bands (and certainly many bands on the continent) essentially provided background music for religious, ceremonial, or social events, contesting encouraged bandsmen and audiences alike to focus attention on the music itself for its own sake and to strive for excellence in performance. Success at contests could significantly enhance a band's budget.

In the United States, officers recruited and paid for most of the earliest regimental bands. In 1834, the government issued regulations that officially recognized army bands for the first time. These regulations in effect limited the size of the bands. Any resemblance between the development of bands in the United States and Europe practically ends there. European military bands were numerous, ubiquitous, and often highly centralized. Civilian bands (British brass bands being the most notable exception) followed the military model. But in the first several decades after independence Congress was reluctant to maintain more than a minimal standing army. American military bands could not exert nearly as much influence as European military bands on the development of other bands.

The United States Marine Band, established by act of Congress in 1798, did not have trombones until some time in the nineteenth century. It appears to have been mediocre at best until John Philip Sousa became its

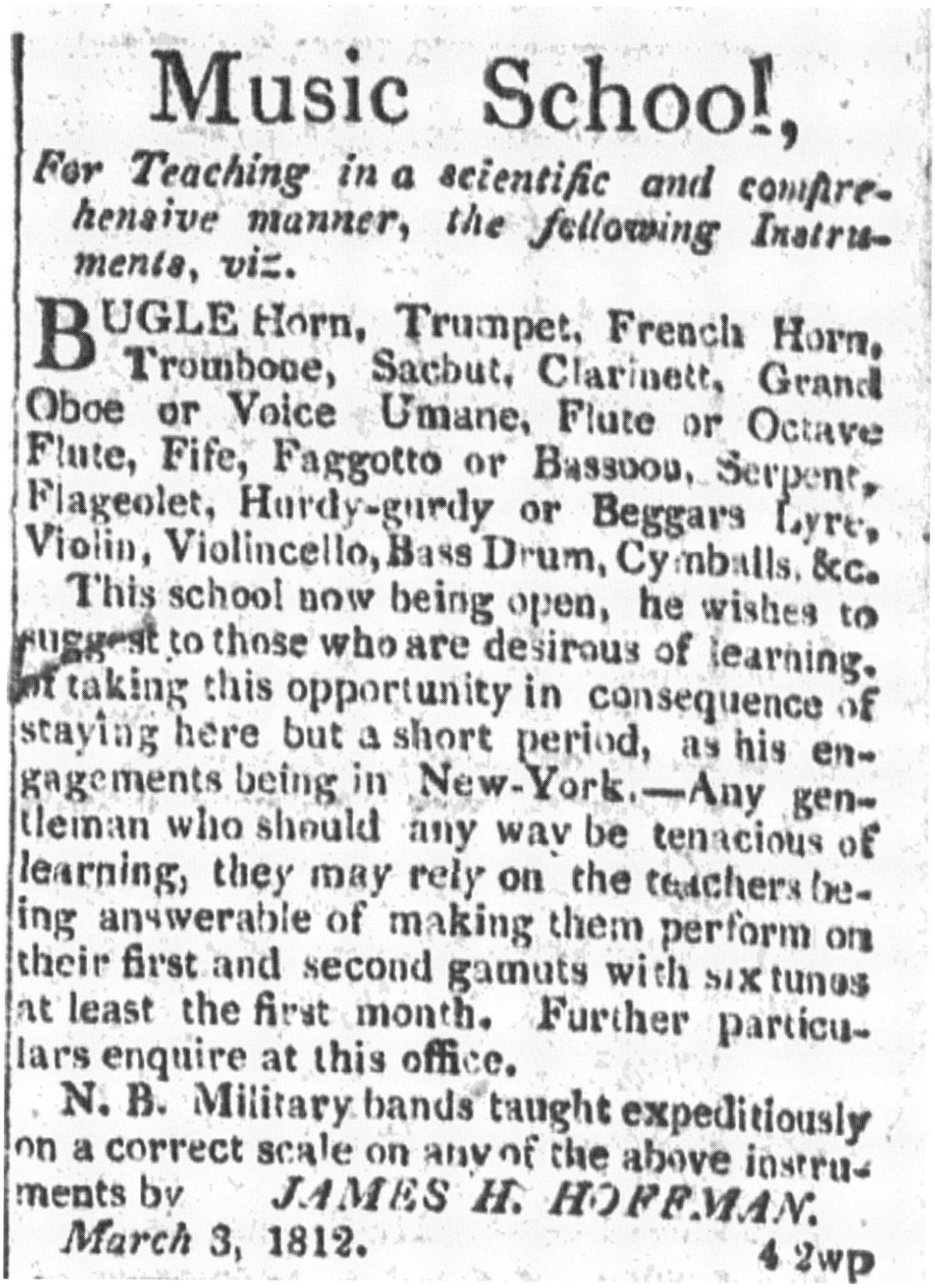

Music School,

For Teaching in a scientific and comprehensive manner, the following Instruments, viz.

BUGLE Horn, Trumpet, French Horn, Tromboue, Sacbut, Clarinett, Grand Oboe or Voice Umane, Flute or Octave Flute, Fife, Faggotto or Bassoou, Serpent, Flageolet, Hurdy-gurdy or Beggars Lyre, Violin, Violincello, Bass Drum, Cymballs, &c.

This school now being open, he wishes to suggest to those who are desirous of learning, of taking this opportunity in consequence of staying here but a short period, as his engagements being in New-York.—Any gentleman who should any way be tenacious of learning, they may rely on the teachers being answerable of making them perform on their first and second gamuts with six tunes at least the first month. Further particulars enquire at this office.

N. B. Military bands taught expeditiously on a correct scale on any of the above instruments by *JAMES H. HOFFMAN.*

March 3, 1812. 4 2wp

Fig. 8.6. One of Hoffman's advertisements, from the *Sentinel of Freedom* (Newark, New Jersey), March 3, 1812. From *Early American Newspapers*, an Archive of Americana Collection, published by Readex (Readex.com), a division of NewsBank, and in cooperation with the American Antiquarian Society.

leader in 1880. The other major service bands were not established until the twentieth century. The military academy at West Point had a band beginning in 1815. There was one trombone by 1821.[75]

Militias controlled by state governments bore the primary responsibility for the national defense. Their members were part-time soldiers, and their bands were essentially civilian bands with some military obligations. Being regulated by the states rather than the federal government, the bands had no incentive to standardize. The earliest bands consisted mostly of woodwinds with a few brass instruments, which may or may not have included one or more trombones. Perhaps the earliest music with a trombone part printed in America was the "Kennebec March" (printed in 1819 in *The Instrumental Director* by Ezekial Goodale) for two clarinets or oboes, F clarinet, three flutes, two horns, trumpet, trombone, bassoon, and serpent. Until the 1850s, most band music was published as piano music and arranged by bandmasters for whatever instrumentation they had available.[76]

The number of itinerant music teachers in the early part of the century testifies to the difficulty in making a living from music outside the major cities. James H. Hoffman advertised his services in numerous small-town newspapers. Some ads explicitly said that his academy would be available only for a short time, but he promised to teach a certain minimum number of tunes on a variety of instruments, often including both trombone and sackbut! The ads typically claim that military bands will be taught accurately on any of the instruments.[77]

In superficial resemblance to developments in Britain, most bands began to adopt all-brass instrumentation some time in the 1830s. These bands were not necessarily very big. The earliest published music for an all-brass ensemble was *Series of Music for Two Bugles and Trombone* by John Friedheim. By the time saxhorns became widely available, brass bands did not necessarily contain trombones. Allen Dodworth, one of the most influential proponents of brass bands, wrote of trombones scathingly in describing the middle voices of a band. His recommended instrumentation did not include trombones. Dodworth's objection is the familiar one: they were too often played coarsely and spoiled the effect of the rest of the ensemble.[78]

In the late 1860s, the New York firm of Slater and Martin published catalogs that suggested instrumentation for brass bands of six to 17 members, consisting entirely of various combinations of cornets and saxhorns. Pictures of brass bands present a wide variety of instrumentation. Some show the cornet/saxhorn bands preferred by Dodworth and the Slater and Martin catalog. Some show one or more slide trombones. Some show one or more valve trombones. Some show both valve and slide trombones. Tenor trombones predominate, but altos and basses appear occasionally. The membership of bands varied as widely as their instrumentation. There were various professional bands, including many of the militia bands, bands attached to naval or cavalry units, circus bands, and dance bands. Some consisted entirely of members of a single family. Amateur bands vastly outnumbered professional bands, although there was no sharp distinction. Amateur musicians often played for money and professionals often worked at non-musical jobs to supplement their income.[79]

Eventually, nearly every town had its own band, including many towns of fewer than 500 residents. As in England, many factories and other employers sponsored bands, as well as organizations devoted to some aspect of social change. There were bands in fraternal organizations, bands whose members were all part of a particular ethnic group, women's bands, and bands in prisons. They played on a variety of occasions, usually outdoors, and often as an adjunct to some larger activity. How can anyone have a parade without bands?

Some important professional bands began to reintroduce woodwind instruments in the mid-1850s, notably the Seventh Regiment Band of New York, but the most important turning point in the development of American bands came in 1859, when Patrick Sarsfield Gilmore became leader of the Boston Brigade Band on the condi-

Fig. 8.7. Parade for the Six Counties Firemen Convention, ca. 1910. Hazen Collection, Archives Center, National Museum of American History, Smithsonian Institution.

tion that it become known as Gilmore's Band and that he have complete control of the finances and bookings. The Civil War interrupted his plans, but after the war, Gilmore's Band became the first of the major professional touring bands that served as the model for nearly all other large bands for almost a hundred years.

While solo numbers had been prominently featured on band concerts for most of the century, Gilmore's soloists, including trombonist Frederick Neil Innes, became nationally famous. Gilmore's success paved the way for the most famous of all American bands, that of John Philip Sousa. Innes and Sousa's first great trombone soloist, Arthur Pryor, along with many other well-known soloists, eventually formed their own bands. These bands consisted mostly of woodwinds, but there were always three trombone parts. The larger bands had more than one player per part.

Two major world's fairs have become well-known for their importance in the history of American bands. Gilmore's Band was supposed to be the featured band at the World's Columbian Exposition (Chicago, 1893), but he died before it opened. Sousa's new civilian band was offered a contract to be in residence for the entire fair, but had already accepted other engagements. Its six weeks in Chicago were among the most popular musical events of the summer and the beginning of Pryor's fame as a soloist. The remnants of Gilmore's band, conducted by D. W. Reeves, and Innes's band both had brief but successful engagements. Many other bands played either on the fairgrounds or the Midway, including at least three that performed the entire duration of the fair.[80]

The success of bands and the financial failure of orchestral concerts in Chicago were not lost on the organizers of the Louisiana Purchase Exposition (St. Louis, 1904). More than 30 well-known bands (including Sousa, Innes, the Marine Band, and two Philippine bands), along with more than 50 lesser-known bands played there. Cornetists played the overwhelming majority of solos, but the trombone was also frequently featured either as a solo instrument or part of an ensemble accompanied by a band. The fair had no resident orchestra, but organizers insisted that the bands include excellent music on their programs. Wagner's music was heard on nearly 600 concerts.[81]

For more than 40 years, large professional wind bands dominated American popular music. The Great Depression and changing popular taste put an end to their ascendancy. The Goldman Band, founded in 1918 by Edwin Franko Goldman, continued to perform regularly through the twentieth century. It did not tour, but made its reputation through radio broadcasts from New York.

After the Depression, professional bands were few. Most bands were either community bands or school bands (from elementary school through university).

Another important turning point in the history of bands came in 1952 when Frederick Fennell founded the Eastman Wind Ensemble. He believed that the concept of a band with a fixed, standard instrumentation could never attract serious composers to write artistic music for it. Instead, he established a group of wind instruments from which composers could choose the combinations that best met their needs for a particular piece, much as composers had never been compelled to use the entire orchestra. While the natural home of the traditional band had been outdoors, wind ensembles play strictly in concert halls. They attempt to reach an audience that wants to listen to serious music. In other words, Fennell and his followers wanted to take music for large ensembles of wind instruments from the realm of vernacular music into the realm of art music. He did not establish a group of professionals, but rather a group of conservatory students playing at a professional level.[82]

A vogue for British-style brass bands began to develop in the 1970s. The North American Brass Band Association sponsors annual contests. The American Championship Section is probably comparable to the British First Section. Even the best American bands cannot bear comparison with the best British bands.

Jazz

Jazz began in New Orleans around 1900 with a largely improvisatory style that has come to be known as Dixieland. By 1920, it was known all over the United States. Besides New Orleans, other important centers of jazz included Chicago, New York, Kansas City, and eventually Los Angeles. The swing style, with its larger ensembles and written arrangements, dominated the American popular music scene in the 1930s and '40s. Jazz and popular music began to part ways in the late 1940s with the development of bebop, a style that returned to improvisation by small groups, but with a much greater level of harmonic and rhythmic sophistication and mastery of instrumental technique than Dixieland bands ever aspired to. The three basic styles overlapped in time. Many of the people who embodied the Dixieland style remained professionally active into the bebop era. To this day, there are still Dixieland bands and swing bands. Bebop did not supersede the earlier styles.[83]

The creators of early jazz were descended from African slaves. There are rhythmic, melodic, and structural elements of jazz that can be traced to African roots. Other elements came from European roots, and these explain the role of the trombone. New Orleans was a very cosmopolitan city throughout the nineteenth century. The most prominent instrumental soloists in the 1830s were Alessandro Gambati (trumpet), James Kendall (clarinet), and Felippe Cioffi (trombone). Because of their popularity, amateurs took up these instruments with enthusiasm, and they remained popular throughout the century. It seems no coincidence that these three instruments formed the backbone of the Dixieland jazz band. Therefore their three early exponents ought to be regarded among the great-grandparents of New Orleans jazz.

New Orleans loved parades. Marching bands made up entirely of black musicians predate the Civil War and became much more numerous in the closing decades of the nineteenth century. The Excelsior Brass Band, which had a nationwide reputation as an excellent black band as early as 1885, trained in the same manner and played the same repertoire as bands everywhere else in America. On the other hand, many more or less ad hoc bands formed in the countryside. People who played in these bands had no training at all. They acquired instruments, figured out how to play the notes, and picked up tunes and harmonies by ear. Their repertoire was largely spirituals and other locally familiar music—music with strong remnants of an African heritage—and their performance practice was improvisatory.

Some country bandsmen eventually moved to the city and joined bands there, resulting in bands with a mixture of people trained to read music and people used to improvising harmonies and polyphony. Once these two groups of musicians learned from each other, the resulting bands could draw on both sets of skills and both kinds of repertoire.[84]

By the 1890s, two other styles of black origin, ragtime and blues, joined the mixture out of which jazz developed. Commercial aspects of the music industry likewise played a role in the dissemination of jazz. Blues legend W. C. Handy moved from Memphis to New York to establish a publishing business. Ragtime pioneer Scott Joplin, less successful in business, became well-known mostly through the sale of sheet music.

The Sousa Band, among many others, performed "ragtime" arrangements of Tin Pan Alley standards, however little they may have resembled "classic" piano rags. Arthur Pryor was one of the leading arrangers. The Original Dixieland Jazz Band, a white band in New Orleans, made the first jazz recording in 1917, the honor having been turned down by the black Creole Band.[85] Business imperatives of the publishing and recording industries, not to mention the development of recording and broadcasting technology, shaped the development of jazz as surely as the musical innovations of its practitioners.

The typical Dixieland ensemble consisted of trumpet or cornet on the melody, with the clarinet commenting and embellishing in a higher register and the trombone in a lower register. In addition, the trombone provided the link between the melody instruments and the rhythm instruments. The glissando was elevated from a technical error to stylistic feature. The bands usually played outdoors, often in a wagon. Because the trombonist sat in the back of the wagon in order to have full use of the slide, the glissando-laden style of playing became known as "tailgate." Jim Robinson, George Brunis, and especially Kid Ory developed this style.

As jazz became more sophisticated and professional in the 1920s, the tailgate style too easily became a cliché. The first trombonist to avoid its mannerisms, Miff Mole, had studied with Charles Randall, a respected trombone soloist and former member of the Sousa Band. Mole's polished technique and full command of both the upper and lower registers made him the envy of other jazz trombonists, yet he was quickly eclipsed by the even more amazing virtuosity of Jack Teagarden. Solo playing was not yet well developed. The reputations of individuals came from the fact that there was only one of each instrument, but the Dixieland style depended on improvisation as an ensemble.

At about the same time, a vogue for ballroom dancing swept the country. The typical dance band of the early 1920s had ten players: three saxophones (who doubled on other instruments), two trumpets, a trombone, and four rhythm players (guitar or banjo, piano, string bass or tuba, and drums). These bands played from written arrangements and were expected to provide all kinds of dance music. Although they were not necessarily founded as jazz bands, they began to add jazz to their repertoire. Fletcher Henderson, for example, frequently used jazz improvisations he heard as the basis of his arrangements. In 1924, Paul Whiteman decided to present a jazz concert, on which Gershwin's *Rhapsody in Blue* was introduced.

The invention of the microphone and the electric recording process had a tremendous impact on popular music. Radio, recordings, and motion pictures with sound tracks provided new job opportunities for musicians. As dance orchestras began to use sound systems in the ballrooms, they were able to experiment with sounds that would have otherwise been inaudible. Under the influence of singers like Bing Crosby, who crooned softly into a microphone and did not need a technique of vocal production capable of filling a large hall unaided, instrumentalists began to experiment with more intimate sounds. These include the singing style of trombone playing exemplified especially by Tommy Dorsey.[86]

At some time in the 1930s the swing style emerged. Even though the country was in the midst of the Great Depression, the size of the typical band had grown. The most prominent swing bands had three trombones. As in Dixieland, each instrument had its own role, but in the swing bands the roles included both section work and formal solos, whether written out or improvised. Some bands were primarily dance bands, while others were more successful in concert.

The growth of Duke Ellington's band is representative. When Ellington first formed a band early in 1923, it had no trombone. His first trombonist, John Anderson, joined that fall, but did not stay long. Charlie Irvis took his place the following year and used the plunger and other mutes, although not in the few recordings he made with the band. He was replaced in 1926 by Joe "Tricky Sam" Nanton, who became well-known for his growls and plunger technique. Nanton remained the only trombonist until 1929, when Ellington hired Puerto Rican valve trombonist Juan Tizol. The addition of a second trombonist forced Ellington to change his approach in scoring for brass. Lawrence Brown joined in 1932. Each

had a very individual style in solos, but as a section they achieved an excellent blend and balance. Although more than three dozen trombonists played with Ellington at one time or another, these three men made up the most renowned jazz trombone section in history.[87]

Stan Kenton achieved an equally remarkable, but very different trombone section. He formed his first band in 1940 with only one trombone. He did not have three trombones until 1942. In 1943, Bart Varsalona bought a bass trombone. No one had ever played one in a dance band before, but Kenton liked the sound. By 1946, he had five trombones and a tuba. The Kenton sound was brassier than most bands. Most trombone sections played with a fast slide vibrato, but under the leadership of Kai Winding, Kenton's used jaw vibrato or none at all.

Although Kenton did not have a section that stayed together as long as Nanton, Tizol, and Brown played with Ellington, many great trombonists played with him. Bauer lists 100 trombonists heard on the various Kenton recordings. Those on 20 or more of them are Jim Amlotte (bass trombone), Milt Bernhart, Harry Betts, Bob Fitzpatrick, Kent Larson, George Roberts (bass trombone), Bill Russo, Dick Shearer, and Bart Varsalona (bass trombone). Frank Rosolino and Carl Fontana also played with Kenton. By 1948, Kenton considered switching all

Fig. 8.8. Duke Ellington's great trombone section: Lawrence Brown, Juan Tizol, and Joe "Tricky Sam" Nanton. Collection of Duncan Schiedt.

of the trombones to valve trombone, believing that six-teenth-notes could not be played cleanly at a fast tempo on slide trombones.[88] Swing music traditionally did not require that of anyone, but by the late 1940s, bebop was making its influence felt.

Bebop grew out of the habit of swing musicians seeking somewhere to gather after gigs to continue playing in a more informal setting. These jam sessions, far from being a relaxing way to wind down after a job, became highly competitive as musicians attempted tunes with chromatic chord progressions and modulations of unprecedented complexity at breakneck speed. For a variety of reasons, including music union politics, postwar economics, and the racial climate of the country, it was both necessary and possible for the rising generation of black musicians to find some professional alternative to the big bands. Both the recording industry and small clubs provided suitable ways to make money playing the same kinds of music pioneered at the jam sessions.

Early bop leaders included saxophonists like Lester Young and Charlie Parker, trumpeters like Dizzie Gillespie, and piano players like Thelonious Monk, not to mention drummers, guitarists, bassists, in short, everyone but trombonists. It appeared that the slide trombone was, in Kenton's words, "a jazz has-been." Yet there were a number of excellent trombonists in the same generation. Some, including Bill Harris, tried to match the other instruments, but it was J. J. Johnson who first demonstrated that the slide trombone could be successful in bebop.

Bebop is based on small combinations of instruments, often one soloist with rhythm. The most appropriate place to mention most bop trombonists is in the section on soloists. Among bop highlights using more than one trombone, J. J. Johnson and Kai Winding teamed up for some very successful duet performances and recordings. Urbie Green and Slide Hampton have both played with the backing of larger trombone ensembles. Even so, the trombone is less important in bebop than in the earlier styles. Many, if not most, bebop combos do not use trombone at all.

Jazz rather quickly became a worldwide phenomenon. African American musicians found themselves welcome in Europe after World War I. A vogue for jazz began in earnest in Japan after World War II. Latin American and Caribbean countries, some with long-standing cultural ties to New Orleans, not only proved hospitable to jazz, but directly influenced its sound. Hardly any swing band gig is complete without some Latin numbers. Besides Latin and Caribbean performers, the German Albert Mangelsdorf was the most influential non-American jazz trombonist. One of the pioneers of the free jazz movement in the 1960s and 1970s, he developed the use of multiphonics and other avant-garde techniques.

Latin American and Caribbean Music

Although the use of the trombone has in many ways diminished in jazz since the end of the swing era and has had little presence in rock bands, it remains an important part of the sound of the popular music of Latin America, commonly labeled "salsa." Where jazz originated in New Orleans and spread from there, salsa includes styles that originated in a multitude of countries. As early as the late eighteenth century, Cuban dance orchestras known as *orquestras típicas* included trombones. The popularity of jazz beginning in the 1920s eventually put an end to these groups, but Cuban jazz bands incorporated their own traditional rhythms.[89]

Somewhat different varieties of salsa have developed in other Latin American countries. Common elements include their Spanish or Portuguese heritage, the cultures of pre-Hispanic peoples, the descendants of African slaves, and jazz. Among the Latin styles are bossa nova and choro from Brazil, mariachi from Mexico, criolla from Cuba, and merengue from the Dominican Republic. In part because there are so many national variations, it is difficult to generalize about the trombone in Latin American music. The slide trombone is preferred in some places, the valve trombone in others. Not every band includes a trombone at all. Salsa bands are of various sizes, some all reeds, some all brass, along with many varieties of mixed ensembles. Some make extensive use of improvisation, others hardly at all. Trombones may be featured in long solos, short solos, or used only as ensemble instruments. Like jazz, salsa has had an international impact. Besides numerous bands in the United States, there are successful salsa bands in Britain, Germany, and Japan. Jamaica, Haiti, and other non-Hispanic Caribbean nations have also developed popular genres that make conspicuous use of trombones, including ska, reggae, and zouk.

The Trombone in Non-Western Music

Just as African and Latin American elements have influenced North American and European music through jazz and salsa, European and American practices have affected music in other cultures. That fact long predates the worldwide impact of rock music and Hollywood movies. Like generations of rulers before them, colonial powers in Asia and Africa found wind band music an effective means of projecting their power and authority. British bands were stationed in West Africa as early as 1750. In 1866, someone writing about military life in an unnamed tropical country advised any readers who might have to play in an army band in a hot climate, "let them, unless they wish to make life a purgatory, avoid the trombone as they would grim death." After all, it gets painfully hot to the touch for both the player's hands and lips. Wherever the unfortunate trombonist in this account was stationed, the indigenous population frequently heard the band.[90]

The Salvation Army likewise used its bands as effectively on the foreign mission fields as it did in English-speaking countries. Other denominations also used brass instruments. Typically, after a colonial or missionary presence was firmly established, many bands were formed that consisted mostly or entirely of native people. The effect on local culture varied. In some places it was minimal. In others, trombones and other Western instruments were assimilated into new native musical styles.[91]

In a lengthy report from Kabul, Afghanistan, the *Times* reported that bands constantly performed in an open space outside the emir's new palace. Besides British regimental bands, the emir had his own 80-piece band, "who, with bagpipes, trombones, triangles, and drums, play a curious mixture of English, Scotch, Indian, and Afghan airs, the constant repetition in which of the same jingling and almost sorrowful cadence has a pleasing, though somewhat monotonous effect."[92] It appears that, in addition to playing music familiar to the writer, this band also used British instruments to play traditional Afghan music, which he did not understand.

At least some of these indigenous bands traveled. The Philippine Constabulary Band was among the most active bands at the St. Louis World's Fair of 1904. A band of Philippine boy scouts also played frequently. The United States had recently become an imperial power after the Spanish-American War, and many of the band members had served in similar bands under Spanish rule.[93]

British-style military bands and European symphonic music can still be heard in Ghana, but there is also a style of joint European and African parentage called "highlife," which uses the instrumentation of a British brass band. It borrows something resembling European harmonies, but not European tuning or melodic structures. Unlike other African music, it features a regular 4/4 meter, but otherwise its rhythmic practices are purely African. The inner voices (saxhorns and trombones) often play rhythmic patterns on a single note, functioning more like a tuned drum than as melodic or harmonic voices.[94]

The Trombone in Church Music

Some larger churches, both Catholic and Protestant, maintained their own bands or orchestras well into the twentieth century. Leipzig continued to sponsor a *Stadtpfeifer* until the kingdom of Saxony abolished such organizations by statute in 1862. Church music remained one of its primary responsibilities. In Bologna, San Petronio maintained its orchestra until 1920. Throughout most of the nineteenth century, it had between 20 and 30 members. From the 1860s through most of the 1880s it was even larger, but there was never more than one trombone. By 1887, however, it had been reduced to 28 members and thereafter shrank rapidly. By the time it was abolished in 1920, there were only two paid musicians. If any other Italian churches had trombonists in their orchestras, the practice stopped on the accession of Pope Pius X, who announced his attention to oversee a major reform of church music; among the "irreligious abuses" he specified was the use of instruments, including trombones, that were unsuited to the sacredness of a church.[95]

Novello heard several pieces at the cathedral in Antwerp in 1829. He made favorable comments about the trombone in Eybler's *Missa de Sancto Leopoldo* and a cryptic reference to a military mass. At Vespers, he noted that a symphony by Haydn was performed for the processional, but the effect was spoiled by the trombone's faulty intonation; the practice of adding trombone parts to older music was not limited to the concert hall. He did not list the instrumentation of the Antwerp orchestra, but it was apparently larger than the one he heard in Salzburg: two first violins, one second violin, one viola, one double bass (no violoncello), three trombones (alto, tenor, and bass), and organ; the three trombonists were the best players. That of St. Stephens in Vienna was about six violins; apparently one each of viola, violoncello, and double bass; and trombones.[96]

Novello did not write how many trombones he heard in Vienna, but the previous year, Holmes noted four of them accompanying Gregorian chant after a Requiem mass. The largest church orchestra I have identified was at the Catholic church of the royal court in Dresden: 10 first violins, 10 second violins, 6 violas, 5–6 violoncellos, and as many double basses, 4 bassoons, 2 oboes, 2 flutes, 2 clarinets, 2 horns, 2 trumpets, and drums; trombones were added to this group as necessary.[97]

After the French Revolution and its Napoleonic aftermath, there were far fewer royal chapels than before. These chapels had been the patrons of nearly all church music by composers of wide reputation, so church music was no longer a career path for composers who hoped to become well-known. With few exceptions, large-scale religious works by major composers were isolated compositions. While Berlioz and Verdi wrote their requiems for liturgical performance and Liszt wrote a mass for the coronation of Franz Josef as King of Hungary, they must have realized and calculated that most performances of these works would be in the concert hall.

Therefore, beginning in the nineteenth century, most church music was written by unknown composers, although many of them conscientiously carried on the traditions they had inherited and can therefore be considered composers of art music for the church. Gregorio Curto composed a mass with a trombone solo played by Cioffi for St. Cecelia's Day (November 22, 1837) at the St. Louis Cathedral in New Orleans.[98]

The early career of Anton Bruckner shows how good some of that music could be. From 1845 to 1855, he was assistant teacher and provisional organist at the monastery of St. Floran—an unknown, provincial composer. During this time, he wrote numerous works with trombone parts. These include a setting of Psalm 114 for five-part mixed chorus and three trombones; *Libera me* for mixed chorus, organ, three trombones, cello, and double bass; *Vor Artheths Grab* for male chorus and three trombones; *Laßt Jubeltöne laut erklingen* for male chorus, two trumpets, two horns, two tenor trombones, and two bass trombones; and *Auf, Bruder! Auf, und die Saiten zur Hand* for mixed chorus, male chorus, male quartet, two oboes, two bassoons, three horns, two trumpets, and two trombones. His two *Aequali* for three trombones were written during this time for the funeral of his godmother.[99]

While these works show flashes of the harmonic imagination that characterized his later career, they probably do not otherwise rise above the kind of traditional church music written in many other monasteries. In particular, the use of trombones was not an innovation, but continued a tradition described in the last chapter.

In 1856, Bruckner moved to Linz to take the position of cathedral organist and to study theory, counterpoint, form, and orchestration. One of his first works after completing his studies, *Afferentur regi* for mixed chorus and three trombones, differs from his earlier works only by displaying his new skills in polyphony. The most important smaller work with trombones of his time in Linz, *Inveni David* for male chorus and four trombones, was written in 1868 for the anniversary of a male chorus of which he had recently become conductor.

While in Linz, Bruckner wrote three large-scale masses for the cathedral. The *Mass in D Minor* (1864) and the *Mass in F Minor* (1867–68) are works of symphonic scale for chorus and large orchestra. The *Mass in E Minor* (1866), on the other hand, is a work of deliberately archaic style, accompanied by a wind ensemble of two oboes, two clarinets, two bassoons, two trumpets, four horns, and three trombones. He may have been aware of the ancient tradition of accompanying church music with a wind band. In any case, it is a more suitable ensemble for the style of the piece than a full orchestra would have been. At this time Bruckner was still a relatively unknown provincial composer.

In 1868, he moved to Vienna to teach harmony and counterpoint at the Conservatory. It was there that he became a world-famous symphonist. He only wrote one more liturgical piece with wind accompaniment the rest of his life, an incomparable masterpiece. *Ecce sacerdos magnus*, for eight-part chorus, organ, and three trombones, was commissioned in 1885 for the centennial of the founding of the diocese of Linz.

Nearly all of the church music examined so far in this book was composed for fairly large churches, either at courts, monasteries, or important urban centers, which could afford to hire professional musicians. It was very much a kind of art music. If rural churches ever had other music besides Gregorian chant (or in the case of Protestant churches, simple chorales or Psalm tunes), it had to be provided by amateur musicians and was closer in spirit to vernacular music. The music of the Moravian church, discussed in chapter 7, is probably the first body of religious music performed by amateur trombonists. Their traditions survive in some form to the present day. Three other musical movements deserve mention in this section.

Moravian brass playing (particularly at Herrnhut) is one of the antecedents of a later movement called *Posaunenchor*. It started modestly enough in about 1842 when a pastor in the village of Jöllenbeck founded a brass-playing group for a Christian youth society. Other nearby churches started similar groups, but it is not until Eduard Kuhlo became involved that such ensembles became a nationwide movement. Under Kuhlo's leadership, members were expected first of all to be committed, mission-minded Christian young men of impeccable character. Real musical talent was welcome, but secondary.[100]

Although the name literally means "trombone choir," it is in fact a mixed brass group that would be more properly called a flugelhorn choir if it were named for its most conspicuous instrument. The name comes from the fact that, wherever the English Bible uses the word *trumpet*, the German Bible uses *posaune* (trombone) for the instrument played in the Hebrew temple or by archangels. Trombones are among the instruments used to play the tenor and bass parts. Kuhlo published his first collection of *Posaunenchor* music in 1881. It looks like a hymnal, with four parts printed in close score. He decided that "military" notation, with its transposition, was too difficult. In *Posaunenchor*, everyone reads at concert pitch. Kuhlo's collection includes traditional chorales, newer sacred songs, and some secular music, including folk songs.[101]

The movement remains strong to this day. When Germany was divided, *Posaunenchor* groups flourished in both sectors. The groups are still likely to include members with a wide range of musical aptitude (and also by this time a wide range of ages). Everyone is welcome. The music exists for the sake of service to the church and community. In 1981, there were 15,000 participants in Württemberg alone.[102]

William Booth, founder of the Salvation Army, wanted the poorest of the poor to hear the gospel. It was difficult to get people living in slums to come to church, so he began to minister on street corners. For indoor meeting places, he rented music halls. Music therefore functioned not only as an aid to worship, but also as a means of attracting a congregation. Because not everyone welcomed the gospel message, music soon took on another function as well. One of Booth's associates ministering in Salisbury in 1878, faced with menacing crowds, asked a friend and his sons for help. Being amateur brass players (two cornets, valve trombone, and euphonium), they decided to play music to help with crowd control. That it was greatly helpful soon came to Booth's attention. In March 1880 he issued an order to his officers and soldiers to learn to play instruments.[103]

At first, the choice of instruments did not matter, but eventually the Salvation Army began to favor brass instruments. A Salvation Army band can have anywhere

Fig. 8.9.   Salvation Army Girl Guard Band, Hazelton, Pennsylvania (1918). Reproduced with permission of The Salvation Army National Archives.

from four to 50 players. The larger bands have standard-ized instrumentation that is very much like that of the contesting brass bands described earlier. Besides this coincidence, there is no connection between the Salva-tion Army and the brass band movement. The Salvation Army began to publish music for its own use in 1881. By 1885, its bands were forbidden to play any music not published by the Salvation Army, and until 1992, it did not sell any of its music to outside bands. Salvation Army bands, more than the other groups mentioned in this section, strive to balance an emphasis on service to God with musical excellence. The Salvation Army oper-ates in more than 100 countries.

In contrast to the worldwide reach of the Salva-tion Army, the United House of Prayer is a fairly small movement. Trombones are the major component of its most outstanding musical practice, the shout band. The predominantly African American denomination was founded near New Bedford, Massachusetts, in 1919 by Charles Manuel "Sweet Daddy" Grace, an immigrant from Cape Verde. In 1926 he moved to Charlotte, North Carolina, where his movement was more successful than it had been in Massachusetts. By 1940, shout bands were well established, and there were congregations from Georgia to New York. Cape Verde, a group of islands off the coast of Cameroon, West Africa, was claimed by Portugal in 1460. In 1466, the Roman Catholic Church began to evangelize there, but in the same year, Portugal granted settlers there the right to engage in the slave trade. Grace grew up listening to the various musical genres that developed over the centuries from the amal-gam of Portuguese and African culture.[104]

The American roots are in part also vestiges of Afri-can singing and dancing. With the notable exception of Louisiana, American slave owners attempted to suppress any expression of African culture, but the survival of the ring-shout tradition is well documented. It began as a pagan practice, but eventually found a home among Christians, especially those of the Wesleyan-Holiness tradition. As whites and blacks attended the same re-vival meetings and experienced the same spontaneous manifestations of spiritual enthusiasm, both groups be-gan to adopt the ring-shout, although black and white versions were significantly different.

The black variety became one of the elements that formed New Orleans jazz. In addition to what has already been described about the development of jazz, many country churches in Louisiana organized brass bands that played in a jazz style. When Grace emigrated to the United States, he held a succession of different jobs, including a stint as cook on the Southern Railway. He

may have encountered black church bands in Louisiana at that time.

Shout bands are typically led by a trombonist, sur-rounded by a semicircle of other trombonists, and typically a baritone horn, a sousaphone, and a drum set. The leader dances and sways as he plays. The other brass players stand very close to each other, often with shoulders touching. This formation allows a very intense concentration. A typical shout is divided into sections, each with its own chordal ostinato figure. These figures are worked out by ear in rehearsal, but not improvised. The leader, who does improvise, may signal a move to the next section by a movement of his trombone, or per-haps only with a subtle melodic cue that the rest of the ensemble follows.[105]

The Trombone as a Solo Instrument and in Chamber Music

Notable Trombone Soloists

The modern era of the trombone as a solo instrument began on April 6, 1815, when Friedrich August Belcke performed a potpourri with obbligato trombone by Carl Heinrich Meyer with the Gewandhaus orchestra in Leipzig.[106] In other words, it began before the distinc-tion between high culture and vernacular music around which this chapter is organized became apparent some time in the 1830s. It is impossible to place Belcke with any confidence in either of the two camps. He is hardly alone in occupying what now seem to be two worlds. The distinction between the two kinds of music was never as clear to working musicians in his lifetime as it is to later scholars or some of the more rabid polemicists among his contemporaries.

Belcke began his career in Leipzig, but soon moved to Berlin, where he served as royal chamber musician. He appears to have aspired to be a virtuoso on the travel circuit like Thalberg or Paganini, playing both trombone and tenor horn. His tours took him to various German cities, and also Copenhagen, Stockholm, and Paris to generally but not invariably good reviews.[107] (See Docu-ment 6, in the appendix.)

One sign of his tendencies toward "high status popular music" is his constantly changing repertoire. He did not play any one piece very long, because the audience for popular music expected novelty. Much popular music, in this sense, took place in private salons. Although one might not expect the trombone to be welcome in what were essentially large private parties, Belcke was very well received in the salons of Paris. Yet the same article that mentions that also refers to his performance with one of the leads of David's *Concertino*, which, as will be explained later, is the one German trombone solo that most clearly aspired to the status of high culture. Belcke played it at least in Berlin, Paris (with the Société des Concerts du Conservatoire) and Dresden.[108]

The incomparable Carl Traugott Queisser of Leipzig was almost the only renowned virtuoso of his generation who did not undertake any extended tours, yet by 1840 a review of a Gewandhaus concert said that he had played more than 100 solos. By the end of his life, he had played at least 26 solos with the Gewandhaus Orchestra, some with the Euterpe, several in various festivals in Germany, and probably many at a pleasure garden

that he owned and operated. Other important German soloists included Moritz Nabich and M. Schmidt, who got excellent reviews even if none of the critics gave his first name.[109]

As mentioned earlier, "classical" music and "high-status popular music" essentially merged about the middle of the century. Popular virtuosos began to play Mozart, Beethoven, and other more serious literature. Besides Ferdinand David's *Concertino*, the trombone had no serious literature to fall back on. After Robert Müller performed it for David's memorial concert in 1876, the solo trombone disappeared from Gewandhaus concerts. German soloists were excluded only from artistic concerts; they

Fig. 8.10. Carl Traugott Queisser, *Brass Bulletin* **117 (2002): 69. © by Editions Bim /The Brass Press, www.editions-bim.com.**

continued to perform in other venues. In the first decades of the twentieth century, Serafin Alschausky played numerous solos, but more often at a spa than in a concert hall. He emigrated to the United States after World War I and performed the David with the Cincinnati Symphony in 1923. In all, he played trombone solos on four continents.[110]

Félix Vobaron appears to have been the first to play a trombone solo in Paris, a year before the establishment of the Société des Concerts. The Parisian press did not chronicle trombone solos as eagerly as Leipzig's papers, but Dieppo and Dantonnet both appeared frequently with Musard's or Jullien's orchestras. Both men also visited London, where Dantonnet caused a sensation by collapsing on stage. He recovered and performed his solo later.[111]

Someone named Bean apparently played the first trombone solo in London, but the most active soloists were William Winterbottom, Felippe Cioffi, Henry Russell, and J. Harvey. Between 1889 and 1891, Alfred Phasey presented three series of springtime concerts at the Crystal Palace, in collaboration with an organist, which were occasionally billed as bass trombone recitals. Each apparently consisted of three short pieces. Trombone solos were advertised in the *Times* with some regularity through 1902.

In Italy, Enrico Marini, Gioacchino Bimbioni, and Attilio Romiti were all active trombone soloists. Their repertoire consisted almost entirely of operatic arias, or perhaps an occasional fantasia on operatic themes. Bimboni played at least one concert in Vienna. They probably all played valve trombone, although that fact is not explicitly mentioned. The Belgian trombonist Hollebecke, on the other hand, was employed by Adolphe Sax to demonstrate the independent valve design.[112]

Many of the soloists mentioned so far performed with concert orchestras. Critics, most of whom were high-culture partisans, frequently questioned the suitability of the trombone as a solo instrument. Fétis noted that Vobaron was a formidable artist who sang with the sweetness of a horn, but then added, "All of his skill is needed to make it forgivable to take his formidable instrument from the place it must occupy in the orchestra."[113] Similar comments frequently appeared in reviews of many trombone soloists. Until the premiere of David's *Concertino*, the repertoire drew uniformly negative remarks if it was mentioned at all. Musard, Jullien, Rivière, and leaders of other popular orchestras (low-status music according to Weber) frequently featured trombone soloists, including many of the ones already mentioned. No critic questioned the suitability of the trombone as a solo instrument in a piece like Jullien's *British Quadrille*.

Trombone solos appeared in classified ads for venues completely beneath critical mention. Trombonist Henry Russell and other musicians shared the bill with an acrobat, a tight-rope walker, and a contortionist during Cattle Show Week (Fig. 8.11). A card player named Toole promised a "sensational transition from cards to music" to play a trombone solo. At Proctor's Fifth Avenue Theatre in New York, trombone soloist Josephine Harvey appeared among some comedians, a magician, a family of whistlers, cakewalk exponents, and a coon singer. A study of classified advertisements in other countries would probably yield similar entertainments.[114]

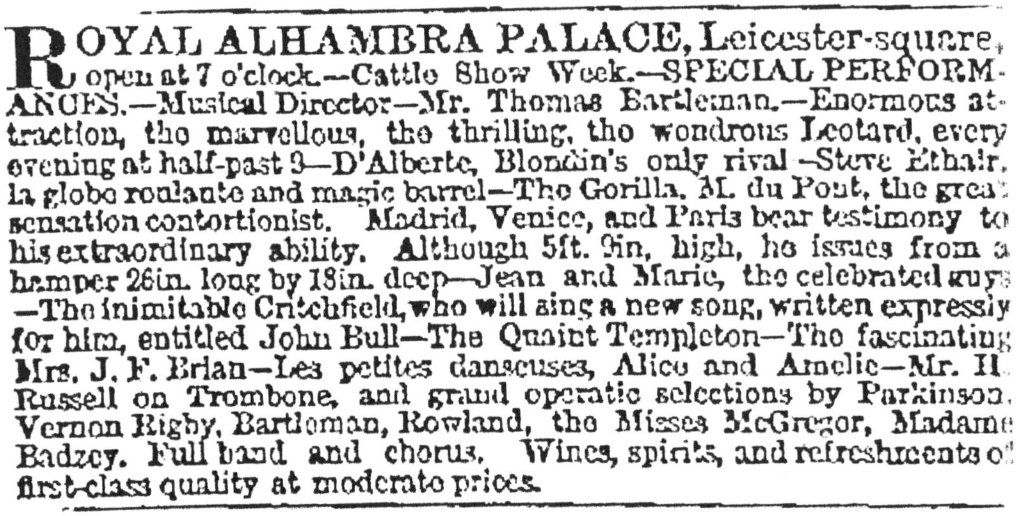
ROYAL ALHAMBRA PALACE, Leicester-square, open at 7 o'clock.—Cattle Show Week.—SPECIAL PERFORMANCES.—Musical Director—Mr. Thomas Bartleman.—Enormous attraction, the marvellous, the thrilling, the wondrous Leotard, every evening at half-past 9—D'Alberte, Blondin's only rival—Steve Ethair, la globe roulante and magic barrel—The Gorilla, M. du Pont, the great sensation contortionist. Madrid, Venice, and Paris bear testimony to his extraordinary ability. Although 5ft. 9in. high, he issues from a hamper 26in. long by 18in. deep—Jean and Marie, the celebrated —The inimitable Critchfield, who will sing a new song, written expressly for him, entitled John Bull—The Quaint Templeton—The fascinating Mrs. J. F. Brian—Les petites danseuses, Alice and Amelie—Mr. H. Russell on Trombone, and grand operatic selections by Parkinson, Vernon Rigby, Bartleman, Rowland, the Misses McGregor, Madame Badzey. Full band and chorus. Wines, spirits, and refreshments of first-class quality at moderate prices.

Fig. 8.11. An advertisement from the *Times*, December 9, 1861, for Cattle Show Week, with trombonist H. Russell.

In the United States, a distinction between high culture and vernacular music emerged at about the same time it did in Europe. Cioffi was a renowned soloist in New York and New Orleans from about 1830 until he moved to London in 1846. Most of his solo performances were at benefit concerts, between the acts of plays or operas, or in pleasure gardens. Frederick Letsch played 184 trombone solos with the Theodore Thomas Orchestra between 1866 and 1871. It was Thomas's intention to raise the taste of the American public, and he did so partly by programming more popular music than he especially liked; 84 of Letsch's performances were of *The Tear* by Giorgio Stigelli, and most others were lighter fare. He played David's *Concertino* twice. He continued to perform solos until 1887, including at least twice with Gilmore's band, at least once with Leipoldt's band, and several more times with the Thomas Orchestra in 1878.[115]

Trombone as a solo instrument with orchestra lasted longer in the United States than in Europe. In England, concerts that included operatic excerpts often replaced the singers with wind instrumental solos. In 1893, one critic complained,

> For the rest, the programme consisted almost entirely of transcriptions, or pieces perverted from their original intention. The orchestral accompaniment of various scraps of *Tristan und Isolde*, with the voice parts of the famous duet played now on cornet-à-pistons and trombone, now on oboe and clarinet, a piece for which a Herr Arthur Seidel is responsible, approaches dangerously near the *pot-pourris* which have hitherto been excluded from the Saturday programmes.

No such programs were described or advertised in the *Times* after this date, but the New York Symphony Orchestra devoted the second half of a concert to Wagner's music in 1896 with instrumental solos, including a Mr. Pfeiffenschneider playing the "Song to the Evening Star" on trombone. Samuel Tilken performed the same piece with the orchestra in 1903 and 1905.[116]

Most American trombone soloists well into the twentieth century clearly fit into the vernacular camp. They appeared with and often conducted wind bands. Frederick Neil Innes first made his reputation playing Jules Levy's cornet solos on trombone, right after Levy had finished playing. He especially created a stir among the young ladies of Louisville:

> The story that Innes, the trombone-player of Gilmore's band, has been breaking the hearts of the Louisville ladies seems incredible. But the public rebuke administered by the *Courier-Journal* has given such notoriety to the affair that the philosopher of society is warranted in taking notice of the mater. Innes is a good-looking young fellow, and yet he is not so very good looking, nor so very young, regarded from a man's point of view, that any group of sane women should run after him. But it is set down in the telegraphic reports that young women actually fought—"fought" is the word—for front seats from which they could gaze upon the face and form of their adored as he tooted his trombone at the Louisville concerts. To such an extent did this feminine rivalry go that the young men of Louisville, deeply incensed by the astonishing success of the stranger, refused to attend his performances, to the sorrow of Patrick Sarsfield Gilmore, and that stern moralist, the *Courier-Journal*, came out with a stinging rebuke of the handsome trombone-player. This last was too much. Public opinion, I am happy to say, immediately turned in favor of Innes. Surely, it is not the trombonist's fault that he is handsome. Possibly he would deny that he is as good looking as the Louisville girls declare him to be. And certainly he is not to be blamed if foolish young women admire him and advertise their admiration by "fighting for front seats."[117]

More than just a pretty face, he was widely regarded as the best trombonist of his generation. His contemporary Carlos Antonio Cappa was also a highly regarded trombone soloist and bandsman.[118]

Arthur Pryor dominated the next generation of soloists. He grew up in St. Joseph, Missouri, where his father, the local bandmaster, taught him to play all the usual instruments. The slide trombone was not among them. His father accepted one as payment for a debt, and Pryor learned to play it on his own. That is part of the secret of his success. No one taught him to believe that certain things were impossible on slide trombone. He used more alternate positions than anyone else of his time and developed amazing facility, yet his true love was playing simple melodies beautifully. He achieved world fame with Sousa's band, and then formed his own band in 1903. By the end of his career, he estimated that he had played 10,000 solos.[119]

Bridges traces the careers of several other notable soloists, including Charles Randall and Gardell Simons. All of these men finished their careers by the end of the 1930s. The Great Depression nearly put an end to the large wind bands with which they made their reputation. Roger Smith played a solo with the Goldman band in 1942.[120] Robert Isele and Larry Wiehe were among the outstanding soloists with American service bands (Isele with the Marine Band and Wiehe with the Air Force Band). In the closing decades of the twentieth century, a number of trombone soloists came to prominence with British brass bands, notably including Don Lusher, Nick Hudson, and Brett Baker.

Economics provides only one reason for the demise of large concert bands. At about the same time, the popular imagination turned to jazz. Jack Teagarden, the earliest of the great jazz soloists, developed a free and easy upper register. His slide technique and flexible embouchure enabled him to play rapid ornaments and lip trills, yet he rarely used his virtuosity merely to dazzle. His style was very lyrical, restrained, and emotionally expressive.[121]

If there was ever a jazz trombonist with an even more vocal, singing style than Teagarden, it was Tommy Dorsey. While Dorsey was quite capable of playing hot jazz, he specialized in ballads. Unlike Teagarden, he had the business acumen to run one of the most financially successful bands of his generation. Another consummate ballad player, Lawrence Brown, often considered the most versatile of jazz trombonists, used both the upper and lower register in his solos, unlike Teagarden and Dorsey.[122] In England, Lusher was a respected jazz soloist first with Ted Heath's band and later his own.

The soloistic nature of bebop ensured that, once trombonists were capable of playing it, there were a greater number of outstanding soloists in bop than in any previous style. J. J. Johnson was the first and foremost. He was able to play the most difficult changes cleanly and with blinding speed. Many listeners initially assumed that he played valve trombone. Once he had established his reputation, however, he began to concentrate more on expressive melody. His influence on other trombonists is enormous.[123] Other outstanding bop soloists include Carl Fontana, Curtis Fuller, Slide Hampton, and Frank Rosolino. Not all trombonists of this generation played bop, however. Jimmy Knepper's virtuosity owed little to Johnson's example. Urbie Green and Buddy Morrow specialized in lyrical ballad playing.

The 1960s saw the advent of free jazz, often characterized by abandonment of tonality and traditional jazz structures. It was closer to the avant-garde of art music than to traditional jazz. Leading trombonists of this movement, including Roswell Rudd, the English Paul Rutherford, and the German Albert Mangelsdorf, frequently introduced multiphonics into their improvisations. Free jazz was critically acclaimed, but not commercially viable. A number of highly successful jazz soloists cannot be easily labeled, including Robin Eubanks, Wycliffe Gordon, Steve Turre, Bill Watrous, and Jiggs Whigham. Bill Pearce was a leading recording artist of explicitly Christian music. His lyrical trombone playing

Fig. 8.12. Arthur Pryor, from *Pioneers in Brass* by Glenn D. Bridges, 4th CD-ROM edition. Permission granted by Paul T. Jackson, copyright owner/nephew, www.trescottresearch.com.

was most widely heard through his syndicated radio program "Nightsounds."[124]

Latin trombonists are less well-known (at least in the United States), but certainly important. According to Sloan, salsa trombonist Willie Colón, born in the United States of Puerto Rican parents, "has done more than anyone since Tommy Dorsey to keep [the] trombone before the public eye."[125] Other important soloists include Edson Maciel and Raul de Souza (Brazil), Juan Pablo Torres (a Cuban expatriate), César Monge (Venezuela), and William Cepeda and Jimmy Bosch (of Puerto Rican ancestry). Steve Turre, of Mexican ancestry, is active in salsa as well as jazz. The leading ska trombonist was Don Drummond.

A new era in solo trombone began in 1947 when Davis Shuman, professor of trombone at the Juilliard School of Music, presented a full-length trombone recital at Town Hall in New York. Where Phasey's "recitals" were only three brief selections, Shuman's consisted of Hindemith's *Sonata for Trombone*; Beethoven's *Sonata in F* for horn; Brahms's *Trio in E-Flat* for horn, violin, and piano (the horn part played on trombone); and three new American works that had been composed for the occasion: *Divertimento for Trombone and String Ensemble* by John Duncan, *Sonata for Trombone and Piano* by Sam Raphling, and *Meditation* for trombone and piano by Frederick Jacobi.[126]

Shuman clearly intended for the trombone to be taken every bit as seriously a concert instrument as the piano or violin. His recitals were received very favorably, with no snide comments about the unsuitability of the trombone as a solo instrument. He opened the door for other trombonists to participate in formal recitals. Meckna includes chapters on the following recitalists or concerto performers: Miles Anderson, Stuart Demptser, Vinko Globokar, Christian Lindberg, Armin Rosin, Ralph Sauer, Branimir Slokar, and Carsten Svanberg. Other prominent soloists who have toured and/or recorded extensively include Joseph Alessi, Ronald Baron, Abbie Conant, Kiril Ribarski, Henry Charles Smith,

M. Dee Stewart, Alain Trudel, Dennis Wick, and bass trombonist Douglas Yeo.

Most of these people have been either members of major symphony orchestras or university professors. The primary exception is Lindberg, so far the only trombonist in history to devote himself exclusively to solo performance. Anderson, Demptster, and Globokar (among others) specialized in music of the postwar avant-garde and developed a number of extended techniques. Much of this music requires costumes and theatrical ability as well as a high degree of musicianship and technical mastery. Although Lindberg can hardly be said to specialize in this style, he has commissioned, performed, and recorded a considerable amount of it.

Repertoire

Of the numerous trombone solo pieces composed in the nineteenth century, only a few survive in the repertoire. Ferdinand David's *Concertino* is the most successful of nineteenth-century German solos. Concertmaster of Leipzig's Gewandhaus Orchestra, David was a highly respected figure in high culture. By contrast, Leipzig's most prolific composer of trombone solos, Carl Hein-

Fig. 8.13. J. J. Johnson at Birdland. Collection of Duncan Schiedt.

Fig. 8.14.   Davis Shuman with a trombone of his own design, from the cover of his album of music by Martin, Hindemith, and Goeb on the Golden Crest Recital Series, RE 7011.

rich Meyer, was beloved as a composer of dance music. Where most solos appear to have attempted to astonish the audience with dazzling virtuosity, David wrote an emotionally dramatic work that was described after its premiere as "appropriate to the dignity of the instrument."[127] Its central movement is modeled after the funeral march from Beethoven's *Eroica* Symphony. Alone among its contemporaries, it clearly aspired to the status of high culture.

Ernst Sachse's *Concertino* is a distant second in the number of nineteenth-century performances I have found. It cannot match the David for its seriousness of purpose. It is a work of empty virtuosity that ends with a set of variations on an operatic aria. In the twentieth century, Friedebald Gräfe's *Grand Concerto*, another piece of apparently serious aspirations composed around 1895, has surpassed Sachse's in frequency of performance. The second movement of Berlioz's symphony for band, Rimsky-Korsakov's *Concerto*, Liszt's "Hosannah" for trombone and organ, the "Preludium, Chorale, Variations, and Fugue" by J. I. Müller, and the Concerto no. 2 of Eugen Reiche complete the list of nineteenth-century European pieces that are performed with any frequency.[128] A "Romanza appassionata" attributed to Carl Maria von Weber has lately become commonplace on trombone recitals. I have been unable to find any evidence either that it was written originally for trombone solo or that Weber actually composed it.

In the United States, the popular band soloists wrote many of the pieces that they played. Of these, Arthur Pryor's (especially "Thoughts of Love" and "Bluebells of Scotland") have had the greatest staying power. Some of the pieces in Henry Fillmore's set of novelty numbers called *The Trombone Family* (especially "Lassus Trombone") likewise remain popular.

Contest solos written for the Paris Conservatory provide the bulk of the solo literature from the earliest decades of the twentieth century. The best of them (Camille Saint-Saëns's "Cavatine" and Alexandre Guilmant's "Morceau symphonique") and several others are frequently performed. Frank Martin's "Ballade," composed for a contest at the Geneva Conservatory in 1940, is one of the first two solos for trombone that partake of the stylistic innovations of twentieth-century art music. Martin wrote it for trombone and piano and orchestrated it later. The other, Paul Hindemith's *Sonata* composed in the same year, is not the first sonata ever composed for trombone (one by B. Schroen was published in 1900)[129] but it marks a turning point. These two pieces led to an explosion of modern concert works for trombone and piano. It also probably accounts for a renewed seriousness in works for trombone and orchestra such as Paul Creston's *Fantasy*.

Many of these more modern pieces are vastly more difficult to play than earlier music. They demand a wider range and present tremendous rhythmic difficulties. When Christopher Rouse's *Concerto* won the Pulitzer Prize in music in 1993, it greatly boosted the credibility of the trombone as a serious solo instrument, but it remains to be seen whether any but world-class professionals will ever be able to perform it. The fascination of the postwar avant-garde for electronically generated sound led to the development of extended techniques for trombone, including singing through the instrument while playing it. The enduring masterpiece among pieces based on these techniques, Luciano Berio's *Sequenza V*, was jointly commissioned by Stuart Dempster and Vinko Globokar.[130]

Composers have not stopped providing lighter, more accessible music for trombone solo, including Jan Koetsier's tongue-in-cheek *Sonatina*. Gordon Langford's *Rhapsody* is but one of a large number of trombone solos written for British brass bands. When a Mr. Dando gave a benefit in 1834, the *Times* noted,

> A striking novelty of the evening was a trio for three trombones, played by Mr. Smithers, his son, and Albrecht, in which powers were displayed which that instrument is not known to possess. Some of the effects, from their very novelty, were a little startling to the ear, but the whole proved that the trombone is capable of being turned to better account in the symphonies and other compositions on the grand scale.

This concert took place five years before the first trombone solo mentioned in the *Times*. In a way, it was part of a long tradition of trombone ensembles, albeit after a long interruption in England, but it was not repeated in London until Henry Russell's Trombone Union, an octet, performed at a couple of Alfred Mellon's promenade concerts in 1861. In Paris, Rivière presented a triple quartet of trombones, conducted by Dieppo, in 1856. The first edition of Grove mentions an all-trombone band associated with Wombwell's show of wild beasts.[131]

London audiences became reconnected with the earlier tradition of trombone ensembles in 1890, when the Wind Instrument Chamber Music Society performed what the review said was the first performance of Beethoven's *Equali* and of Schütz's "Lamentation Davidi" (better known today as "Fili mi Absalon").[132]

Advertisements for a Concert Trombone Quartet began to appear in 1894, and the group continued to perform at least through 1896. Most of the advertisements do not mention what they performed, but at a Queen's Hall promenade concert, they played "The Little Church" by V. E. Becker and "Robin Adair (harmonized)." That, as it turns out, was their only performance mentioned in a review in the *Times*: "and a tiresome quartet of trombonists played some very poor compositions in a mediocre manner." They only appeared in one subsequent *Times* advertisement. A concert by a French sextet called La Saquebute, sponsored by Courtois, got more favorable mention.[133]

Most twentieth-century trombone quartets have likewise received little critical notice. Conspicuous exceptions to this rule include the Paris Trombone Quartet and the Slokar Quartet. Both of these ensembles achieved international acclaim over a period of more than 25 years. Works composed or arranged for the Slokar Quartet form the nucleus around which the firm Editions Marc Reift was built.[134] The trombone quartet's repertoire consists almost entirely of transcriptions or original compositions by little-known composers.

A different kind of trombone ensemble developed in Los Angeles. Just as jazz musicians played informal jam sessions after hours, studio trombonists began to meet under the leadership of Hoyt Bohannon in 1946. Even after his death in 1990, the group continued to meet every week in the room next to his garage. More than 100 different trombonists have taken part in these gatherings, rehearsals of very difficult music for anywhere from two to 16 trombones. Bohannon, Tommy Pederson, and others wrote or arranged more than 500 pieces. Pederson's music in particular occupies a conspicuous place in the repertoire of trombone ensembles everywhere.[135]

The notion that the trombone was an instrument suitable for chamber music at all barely existed before the twentieth century. Beethoven's *Equali* are not chamber music; they were intended for outdoor performance, as were the numerous five-part pieces for small British and American brass bands. The same is true of Bruckner's *Aequali* later in the century. Felicien David composed two *Nonets* (only one of which is still extant) for two cornets, four valved horns, two trombones, and ophicleide in 1839. One of them was apparently performed on several of Musard's promenade concerts, the other on a rival series, Concerts Valentino.[136] It is therefore a bit of a stretch to consider them chamber music. That audiences for these concerts demanded a steady stream of novelty adequately explains why the nonets were not heard for more than a season or two.

In 1846 a French pharmacist and sometime military trombonist, Auguste Léonard de la Tuilerie, published at his own expense two funeral marches by Beethoven and Rossini arranged for piano, violin, cello, and trombone, and four songs of Schubert arranged for three trombones.

Later that year, he addressed the Académie des Beaux Arts to explain the excellence of the trombone, that it belonged in the drawing room, not just playing chords in the orchestra. His proposal was met with indifference and ridicule.[137]

In 1851, Jean Bellon published 12 substantial quintets (mostly in four movements and averaging 14 minutes in length) for flugelhorn (or trumpet), cornet, horn, trombone, and ophicleide, possibly the first real chamber music for brass instruments. They appear to have been performed numerous times on various concert series, and possibly by Musard and/or Valentino as well, but the novelty eventually wore off and they were forgotten. Most other French works for trombone ensemble or brass ensemble written before the end of the nineteenth century were more likely intended for pedagogical use than for public performance. Others were intended for outdoor performance. Some works appeared for mixed ensembles including trombone with strings or woodwinds, but seem not to have been widely performed.[138]

Early in the twentieth century, Debussy, Dukas, and several other respected composers wrote fanfares for large brass ensembles. Edward Elgar, who played trombone, wrote a *Duett* for trombone and string bass in 1877, but it was not published in his lifetime. Victor Ewald and other composers working in Russia began to write pieces for five conical brass instruments (cornets, saxhorns, and tuba). Frequently performed to this day arranged for modern brass quintet, they are genuine chamber music in their texture. In 1922, Francis Poulenc composed a trio for trumpet, horn, and trombone.

The most important brass chamber ensemble is a quintet of two trumpets, horn, trombone, and tuba (or in some cases, a bass trombone). In 1947, English trumpeter Philip Jones heard members of the Concertgebouw Orchestra playing brass chamber music on the radio. Not satisfied with a career as an orchestral trumpeter, he founded the Philip Jones Brass Ensemble, which made its first radio broadcast in 1951.[139] From then until Jones disbanded it in 1986, it set a high standard of technique and musicianship and actively commissioned new repertoire. It was not, strictly speaking, a brass quintet, however. It was a group of 10 players from which any number of smaller ensembles could be formed.

The New York Brass Quintet was founded in 1954, although it had antecedents in a more informal brass group that started playing in 1947. The American Brass Quintet, founded in 1960, uses bass trombone instead of tuba. By the middle of the 1960s, nearly every important music department at American universities had a resident faculty brass quintet. Other important professional quintets include the Annapolis Brass Quintet, the Canadian Brass, the Empire Brass Quintet, and the Montreal Brass Quintet.

The brass quintet repertoire boasts important original works by such composers as Malcolm Arnold, Leonard Bernstein, William Bolcom, Morley Calvert, Elliott Carter, Ingolf Dahl, Peter Maxwell Davies, Lukas Foss, Vincent Persichetti, Ned Rorem, and Gunther Schuller. The style of these compositions varies from very conservative to avant-garde. The bulk of the repertoire, however, consists of transcriptions and arrangements of all kinds, from medieval and Renaissance music to modern popular music and jazz.

The acceptance of the trombone as an orchestral instrument, the early twentieth-century reaction against large Romantic orchestras, and the difficult economic times during and after the First World War worked together to make a place for the trombone in mixed chamber ensembles. When Stravinsky was forced to mount a theatrical spectacle with minimal resources, the trombone was one of only seven instruments used in *L'histoire du soldat*. His *Octet* includes two trombones. Late in his career, he composed *In Memoriam Dylan Thomas* for tenor, string quartet, and four trombones.

Few other major twentieth-century composers followed Stravinsky's example, but lesser-known composers produced an impressive array of chamber music with trombone. Among pieces for trombone and string quartet are *Five* by John Cage (1991), *Quintet* (or *Concertino*) by Roger Goeb (1950), *Sonata* by Patrick McCarty (1961), *The Brass Larynx* by Byron McCulloh (1982), and *Archangel* (for bass trombone and strings) by Charles Wuorinen (1977).[140]

Miscellaneous ensembles with trombone include *Four All* for clarinet, trombone, cello, and percussion by William Bergsma (1982); *Divertimento* for trumpet, trombone, and piano by Boris Blacher (1946); *Commedie* for trombone and percussion by Roger Campo (1971); *Myzycka IV* for trombone, clarinet, cello, and piano by Henryk Gorecki (1976); *Sonata da Camera* for oboe, two clarinets, bassoon, and trombone by Walter Hartley (1950); *Suite for Five Winds* for flute, oboe, clarinet, saxophone, and trombone by Walter Hartley (1951); *Esque* for trombone and double bass by Roger Kellaway (1971); *Caramel mou* for clarinet, trumpet, trombone, tenor saxophone, piano, percussion (and voice ad lib.) by Darius Milhaud (1921); *Serenade no. 6* for viola, cello, and trombone by Vincent Persichetti (1964); *Concertino* for flute, oboe, clarinet, bassoon, and trombone by Raymond Premru (1962); and *Sonata da Chiesa* for E♭

clarinet, viola, trumpet, horn, and trombone by Virgil Thomson (1943).

The Education of Trombonists

Traditionally, trombonists learned their craft through the various guilds and town bands. Seasoned professionals would accept apprentices, who became unpaid assistants once they were proficient enough. In Italy the various orphanages functioned as schools for musicians. A new era in music education began with the foundation of the Paris Conservatory. Its first trombone teacher was probably Philippe Widerkehr, who remained on the faculty until 1815. Pierre Marciliac joined him in 1793 and apparently became the sole trombone teacher some time later. After Marciliac's departure in 1802, there was probably no trombonist until 1833, when Felix Vobaron started a provisional class. Antoine Dieppo ushered in a new era of trombone education in France in 1836 when he was named the permanent professor. Students have always been taught in classes, not given private lessons as is the practice in American universities.

In addition to his class at the Conservatory, beginning in 1866 Dieppo was also required to teach the Sax-system valve trombone for the benefit of military musicians. When the military school was closed in 1871, Dieppo's successor Paul Delisse successfully resisted incorporation of any kind of valve trombone into the curriculum of the Conservatory, which helped contribute to the demise of the Sax system. Delisse also began to require his students to practice on transcriptions of classical masterpieces.[141] A professorship at the Conservatory has always been a position of great influence, but not a full-time job. Each of the professors has simultaneously served as an orchestral musician or otherwise remained professionally active in performance.

During the nineteenth century, conservatories were established in numerous other cities. Not all of them offered trombone from the beginning. It appears that most nineteenth-century trombonists got their training the old-fashioned way. Queisser accepted students in his capacity as leader of the Leipzig *Stadtpfeifer*. A conservatory was founded in Leipzig in 1843, but its first trombone professor, Robert Müller, did not join the faculty until around 1882.

Schoengen was listed as the trombone professor of the Royal Academy of Music in London beginning in 1825. John Smithies held that title from 1826 to 1853. It appears that neither of them actually had any students. As late as 1893, an administrator of the Royal College of Music could note that there was finally a student for

Charles Geard, nominally trombone professor at both the Royal Academy and the Royal College.[142] As an institution specializing in wind instruments, the Royal Military School of Music (Kneller Hall) probably had students for its trombone professors right from the start. From its founding in 1857 through the end of the nineteenth century, the trombone professors were Thomas Sullivan, Mr. Hanks, Signor Cioffi, and Albert Cousins. Other works that mention these four teachers are mistaken about at least one detail: Cioffi cannot have taught there from 1860–1866. He died in 1860 after a long illness.[143]

Trombone instruction began earlier at the Prague Conservatory, where there had been a long tradition of trombone playing. In 1826, however, the Conservatory dismissed František Weiss, its professor of slide trombone, and hired valve trombonist Josef Kail in his place. Kail remained until 1867, but his successor Auguste Bolze played and taught slide trombone.[144]

Clubs devoted to performing instrumental music were conspicuous on American college and university campuses at least as early as Harvard's Pierian Sodality, founded in 1808, but music did not become part of the curriculum anywhere until much later in the nineteenth century. The numerous college bands that played at the Louisiana Purchase Exposition (St. Louis, 1904) were probably all clubs, not ensembles offered for credit. The earliest music departments offered degrees for composers and musicologists. Northwestern University appears to have been the first to grant a bachelor's degree in applied music (in 1917).[145]

Emory Remington, who joined the faculty of the Eastman School of Music of the University of Rochester in 1922, was probably the first trombone teacher at an American university. In any case, there cannot have been many before him. The most influential American trombone teacher of all time, he emphasized a singing style of playing as opposed to the military marcato of so many earlier method books. He appears to have invented the concept of a formal warm-up and to have been the first to emphasize the importance of relaxation, two hallmarks of American pedagogy. Although American teaching is based on private lessons, ensemble rehearsal was important to Remington. Like Delisse in Paris, he insisted that his students play transcriptions of the classics. Alumni of Remington's studio went on to occupy many of the most prestigious chairs in major American orchestras and universities.

Fig. 8.15. Christian Lindberg, from his album _Mandrake in the Corner_, BIS CD-1128. Photograph by Henrik Svanberg. Used by permission.

The normal career path for anyone desiring a position in an orchestra is through a college or university music department. Many of the trombonists in America's leading professional orchestras teach at institutions of higher learning. Many accept private students. Beyond the bachelors degree, students can earn a masters or, if they desire to teach at a university, a doctoral degree designed especially for performers: the Doctor of Musical Arts.

University music majors have usually already studied music for years before enrolling. American wind players typically start out in their elementary school music program somewhere between the age of 10 and 12. They have played in bands in junior high school (or middle school, depending on the practice in each school district) and then high school band. High school orchestras are less common than bands. Although some high schools had bands as early as the last quarter of the nineteenth century, school bands became a national movement only in the 1920s.[146] Typically, one band director is responsible for teaching all of the instruments, so unless a student pays for outside private lessons, it is entirely possible for a young trombonist not to study with another trombonist until beginning college.

While pianists and string players typically start playing in early childhood, trombonists usually wait until they have developed permanent teeth and grown big enough to reach the outer positions, but under the influence of the Suzuki method of teaching violin to very young children, a Norwegian teacher began to teach preschoolers, children as young as four, to play alto trombone in 1995.[147]

At the Turn of the Century

At the beginning of the twenty-first century, trombonists are better technically than at any time in history. They pay more sophisticated attention to breathing, tonguing, and slide technique. They command a wider tonal range, from low pedals to the altissimo register, and a wider dynamic range. They are trained more rigorously in ensemble playing. Under the influence of jazz and the avant-garde, they have developed extended techniques never before conceived. Even without those techniques, twentieth-century orchestral parts routinely demand greater virtuosity than earlier parts. The average player today probably plays better than the very best trombonists of 200 years ago.

Trombonists are also more versatile. Nineteenth-century professionals had to be equally at home in operatic orchestras, symphony orchestras, dance orchestras, military bands, and perhaps even as soloists. Conditions

in the twentieth century enabled some trombonists to specialize, but most of today's trombonists do much of what nineteenth-century trombonists did plus play some combination of jazz and other new vernacular styles, chamber music, early music, and studio music.

At the same time trombonists are technically more proficient and more versatile, they are less in the public eye than at any other time over most of the last two centuries. Trombones are little used in most styles of popular music. The most innovative uses of the trombone in popular culture occur in commercials, sound tracks to television shows and films, or other similarly anonymous settings where music is in the background.

The distinction between high culture and vernacular music that appeared in the 1830s has become a yawning chasm. To modern ears, the classical and vernacular music of the nineteenth century sounds similar, while most modern "art music" does not sound much like modern "popular music" at all. Until the 1970s, there was a general cultural consensus that "classical" music was somehow better than other music, even among people who did not like it very much, but that consensus no longer exists. There even seems to be little point in talking about two broad kinds of music any more. The audiences for both art music and popular music have fragmented.

Every month or so, it seems, a magazine article appears claiming that orchestras are dying—or that they are thriving; that classical music is irrelevant to modern society—or that it is still vitally important. The death and life of jazz is also hotly debated. Some of the same kinds of arguments have been raging since the very beginning of music journalism. Part of the problem in the middle decades of the twentieth century is that composers of art music grew away from their audience. The proportion of new music performed in opera houses or symphony concerts had declined since Mendelssohn's day, but audiences especially resisted much post-Wagnerian music. Some composers, like Stravinsky, Hindemith, and Copland, attempted to reconnect with audiences. Others, like Schoenberg and Webern, attempted to "educate" them to learn to accept their music. The effort failed, but an entire generation of composers after the Second World War chose to use Webern's music as a point of departure. Not only did the public thoroughly reject this new music, but composers began to return their active contempt. The avant-garde appealed only to a niche audience. A number of very successful trombone soloists have specialized in this style, however, and composers provided a large and varied repertoire.

It is no coincidence that the early music movement came into prominence at about the same time. It

Fig. 8.16. A lesson with Emory Remington. Courtesy of the Sibley Music Library, Eastman School of Music, University of Rochester.

provided a fresh sound without the jarring unattractive-ness of the avant-garde. For trombonists, that meant the rediscovery of the repertoire described in earlier chap-ters, and also the rediscovery of earlier approaches to technique, historically informed performance practices, and the manufacture of Baroque-model trombones, preferably built with the old-fashioned hand techniques. This juxtaposition of avant-garde and early music un-derscores the importance of versatility. It is not unusual for the same trombonist to play both early music on a "sackbut" and avant-garde music on a modern trombone, sometimes on the same program.

Technology, as always, is both a promise of new things and a threat. The invention of the microphone enabled a new, more intimate style of trombone playing. Films, recordings, and broadcast media created new ways of making money and new audiences. They also threaten traditional sources of income. Musicians have made good money from weddings and other private parties for cen-turies, but more and more people now hire disc jockeys instead. Musicians' unions must also fight to preserve

jobs for live musicians when producers would prefer less expensive synthesizers.

The recording industry in particular has had unfore-seen consequences. Once individuals could own record-ing equipment, it became possible to use it as an adjunct to practicing and to send recordings to audition for jobs. Commercial recordings have made a vast repertoire ac-cessible that is not often performed live. In live perfor-mance a mistake can easily pass, but on a recording the hearer must listen to the same mistake over and over. Recordings therefore attempt to be mistake-free, which sets the unrealistic expectation that live performances will also attain the same standard. It is a matter of some controversy whether the increase in technical polish makes up for the increase in caution and a decrease in spontaneity.

Now that commercial recordings have been available for a century, it is possible to track changes in perfor-mance practice. A recording of a British brass band made in the 1930s, for example, will use the old high pitch and narrow-bore instruments. The same piece recorded in the 1970s or later will sound half a step lower and be played on large-bore instruments. Early in the twentieth century, recordings demonstrated a variety of national styles. French, English, Russian, German, and American musicians all sounded different in terms of the equipment used, ideals of tone quality, articulation, phrasing, and so on. These differences are apparent in recordings of orchestras, bands, and soloists. As the century progressed, national differences began to diminish, partly as a consequence of everyone listening to the same recordings.[148]

Even early in the twentieth century, there were few really excellent trombonists and fewer still available as teachers. The primary influences on the best trombonists were as likely to be singers or players of other instruments as other trombonists. Nowadays, it is possible, although certainly not desirable, for trombonists to occupy something of a trombone ghetto. Organizations of and for trombonists present annual conventions and publish magazines. Any number of well-known trombonists offer regular master classes. There are online forums and e-mail lists that cater especially to trombonists. It might actually take more effort now than ever before for trombonists to pay careful attention to what they can learn from other musicians.

Therefore as we look at the current situation, there are reasons for hope and reasons for concern. There are opportunities and threats. Something has been gained and something lost in recent changes. It is an unsettling time. In that, it is not much different from any other.

Notes

1. William Weber, *Music in the Middle Class: The Social Structure of Concert Life in London, Paris and Vienna* (New York: Holmes & Meier, 1975), 16–29; H. Wiley Hitchcock, *Music in the United States: A Historical Introduction*, 4th ed. (Upper Saddle River, N.J.: Prentice Hall, 2000), 55–65. I use Weber's term "high culture" in preference to Hitchcock's "cultivated tradition" and Hitchcock's "vernacular" in preference to Weber's "high status popular music" and "low status" music.

2. Gute Posaunen gehören zu den frommen Wünschen. Die Wichtigkeit und Schönheit dieses Instruments ist noch nicht allgemein genug anerkannt. Ein Posaunen-Ton kann von der herrlichsten Wirkung seyn, aber auch Ein Posaunenton Alles verderben. In Opern, wie Don Juan, Jacob und seine Söhne, und Fidelio, wird die Noth recht fühlbar, und der Zuhörer ist froh, wenn am Posaunenpult die Lichter wieder gelöscht werden. *Allgemeine musikalische Zeitung* (hereafter AMZ) 19 (1817): col. 375.

3. AMZ 32 (1830): col. 425–28; *Times* (August 28, 1846): 6; (July 23, 1847): 5; (September 2, 1858): 6; (July 27, 1869): 6; AMZ 3, Folge 10 (June 30, 1875): col. 411–12.

4. Diese Aufführung zeichnete sich auch vor frühern dadurch aus, dass man die Posaunen nicht weggelassen hatte, durch welche mehrere Stellen, z. B. Et lux perpetua, und die dieser Stelle ähnliche im Benedictus, Dies irae, Oro supplex—erst in ihrer ganzen Fülle und Kraft hervortraten. Man hatte aber früher diese Instrumente nicht zu besetzen wagen können, weil sie von Mozart sehr schwer (zuweilen über die Gebühr) geschrieben worden sind, wir aber keine Posaunisten besassen, die das alles sicher und gut hätten ausführen können. Jetzt aber hat sich unter den jungen Männern, die nach der verbesserten Einrichtung mit den Stadtmusikern, hier Instrumentalmusik studiren, ein Chor Posaunen gebildet, das schon jetzt vorzüglich genannt werden darf, und sich bey dieser, so wie bey andern Produktionen des Konzerts, und das Theaters, sehr vortheilhaft zeigte. AMZ 7 (1805): col. 484–85.

5. "das vollkommen nach der Vorschrift des Komponisten, nur mit ausnahme der durch Klarinetten vertretenen Bassethörner,—wurde, mit der nicht üblen Posaune, von Hrn. Gern ganz vorzüglich schön und ausdrucksvoll vorgetragen;—Die Posaunen machten hier einen pompösen Effekt . . . ." AMZ 7 (1805): col. 430, 431.

6. Augustin Sundelin, *Die Instrumentirung für das Orchester* (Berlin: Wagenführ, 1828), 38.

7. Clive Brown, "The Orchestra in Beethoven's Vienna," *Early Music* 16 (1988): 10–12; Howard Weiner, "Andreas Nemetz's *Neueste Posaun-Schule*: An Early Viennese Trombone Method," *Historic Brass Society Journal* 7 (1995): 12.

8. Adam Carse, *The Orchestra from Beethoven to Berlioz* (Cambridge: W. Heffer, 1948), 263–64.

9. Gerhard Zechmeister, "Die Stellung der (Contra) Bassposaune im Wiener Klangstil, 1. Teil," *Brass Bulletin* 102 (1998): 21–23; Gunther Joppig, "Vaclav Frantisek Červený: Leading European Inventor and Manufacturer," trans. Veronica von der Lancken, *Historic Brass Society Journal* 4 (1992): 214; Ken Shifrin, "The Valve Trombone, Part 2," *Brass Bulletin* 112 (2000): 119–24.

10. François-Auguste Gevaert, *Nouveau traité d'instrumentation* (Paris: Lemoine, 1885), 256.

11. D. Kern Holomon, *The Société des Concerts du Conservatoire, 1828–1967* (Berkeley: University of California Press, 2004), 161–62.

12. Marcello Conati and Marcello Pavarani, eds., *Orchestre in Emilia-Romagna nell'ottocento e novecento* (Parma: Orchestra Sinfonica dell'Emilia-Romagna "Arturo Toscanini," 1982), 34–35.

13. "Posaunen sind hier so lang nicht mehr im Gebrauch, dass sie ganz unbekannt geworden, und einige halten sie sogar für eine neue französische Erfindung." AMZ 8 (1806): col. 767; *Harmonicon* 8 (1830): 229; Lawrence T. Sisk, "Giovanni Simone Mayr (1763–1845): His Writings on Music" (Ph.D. diss.: Northwestern University, 1986), 251.

14. *Il teatro illustrato* 1 (July 1881): 7; Lucio Pardi, "Trombonate," *Paganini* 3 (July 15, 1889): 79; R. M. Longyear, "The 'Banda sul Palco': Wind Bands in Nineteenth-Century Opera," *Journal of Band Research* 13 (Spring 1978): 26–27.

15. John Humphries, "John Smithies: Trombonist and Enigma," *Brass Bulletin* 101 (1998): 62–64; *Times* (Feb. 17, 1847): 5.

16. Carse, *Orchestra*, 205–6.

17. *Times* (Oct. 28, 1853): 6.

18. *Harmonicon* 1 (1823): 153.

19. *Harmonicon* 4 (1826): 217; *Musical World* 20 (1845): 422.

20. George Maxted, *Talking about the Trombone* (London: John Baker, 1970), 38; Denis Wick, *Trombone Technique*, 2nd ed. (Oxford: Oxford University Press, 1984), 79.

21. *Harmonicon* 9 (1831): 284; Igor Krivokapic, "La musique de cuivres en Slovénie: Compte-rendu historique, 1ère partie," *Brass Bulletin* 105 (1999): 56.

22. Michael Broyles, *Music of the Highest Class: Elitism and Populism in Antebellum Boston* (New Haven, Conn.: Yale University Press, 1992), 325; Louis C. Maderia, *Annals of Music in Philadelphia and History of the Musical Fund Society from Its Organization in 1820 to the Year 1858* (Philadelphia: Lippincott, 1896; repr., New York: Da Capo, 1973), 84–85.

23. *New-York Evening Post* (May 28, 1816): 2; David M. Guion, "Felippe Cioffi: A Trombonist in Antebellum America," *American Music* 14 (1996): 3.

24. Virginia Larkin Redway, *Music Directory of Early New York City* (New York: New York Public Library, 1941), 4, 6, 14, 19.

25. Henry A. Kmen, *Music in New Orleans: The Formative Years, 1791–1841* (Baton Rouge: Louisiana State University Press, 1966), passim.

26. Broyles, *Music of the Highest Class*, 176, 336.

27. Vera Brodsky Lawrence, *Strong on Music: The New York Music Scene in the Days of George Templeton Strong, 1836–1875*, vol. 1, *Resonances, 1836–1850* (New York: Oxford University Press, 1988), xxx, xl–xlv; Howard Shanet, *Philharmonic: A History of New York's Orchestra* (Garden City, N.Y.: Doubleday, 1975), 491; Oscar Coon, *Harmony and Instrumentation* (New York: Carl Fischer, 1883), 72.

28. Frances Anne Wister, *Twenty-five Years of the Philadelphia Orchestra: 1900–1925* (Philadelphia: Women's Committees for the Philadelphia Orchestra, 1925), 230–31.

29. Steve Dillon, contributions to the thread "Large Bore Trombones in American Orchestras," *The Trombone Forum*, especially October 20, 2005, 5:12 a.m., and December 22, 2005, 6:11 a.m., tromboneforum.org/index.php/topic,19093.0.html; Maxted, *Talking about the Trombone*, 12.

30. *Encyclopedia of Music in Canada*, 2nd ed. (Toronto: University of Toronto Press, 1992), s.v. "Opera performance," "Orchestras."

31. Daniel Mendoza de Arce, *Music in Ibero-America to 1850: A Historical Survey* (Lanham, Md.: Scarecrow, 2001), 411–412.

32. Sources: Robert R. Craven, ed., *Symphony Orchestras of the World: Selected Profiles* (New York: Greenwood Press, 1987); *Grove Music Online*; www.nso-ghana.com/, viewed November 6, 2007; *Wikipedia*, s.v. "Iraqi National Symphony Orchestra," en.wikipedia.org/wiki/Iraqi_National_Orchestra, viewed November 6, 2007.

33. William Weber, "The Rise of the Classical Repertoire in Nineteenth-Century Orchestra Concerts," in *The Orchestra: Origins and Transformations*, ed. Joan Peyser (New York: Scribner, 1986), 371; Richard Mount Edgcumbe, *Musical Reminiscences of the Earl of Mount Edgcumbe: Containing an Account of the Italian Opera in England from 1773 to 1834*, 4th ed. (London: John Andrews and F. H. Wall, 1834; repr., New York: Da Capo, 1973), 124–25, 127.

34. Quoted in Hugh MacDonald, *Berlioz's Orchestration Treatise: A Translation and Commentary* (Cambridge: Cambridge University Press, 2002), 226.

35. François-Joseph Fétis, "On the Revolutions of the Orchestra," *Harmonicon* 6 (1828): 196.

36. See Hugh MacDonald, "Berlioz's Orchestration: Human or Divine?" *Musical Times* 110 (1969): 256.

37. *Le temps* (December 26, 1830), quoted in Michael Rose, *Berlioz Remembered* (London: Faber and Faber, 2001), 40–41.

38. *Times* (September 1, 1849): 8; (April 23, 1850): 8.

39. Weber, *Music and the Middle Class*, 60–61.

40. *Times* (December 3, 1878): 6; (March 31, 1879): 6.

41. Daniel J. Koury, *Orchestral Performance Practices in the Nineteenth Century: Size, Proportion, and Seating* (Ann Arbor, Mich.: UMI Research Press, 1986), 117, 132, 138.

42. Hector Berlioz, *Instrumentenslehre*, revised and enlarged by Richard Strauss (Leipzig: C. F. Peters, 1904), iii; English translation by Theodore Front, *Treatise on Instruments* (New York: Kalmus, 1948), ii.

43. Douglas Yeo, via e-mail, December 19, 2007.

44. Julian Horton, "Bruckner and the Symphony Orchestra," in *The Cambridge Companion to Bruckner*, ed. John Williamson (Cambridge: Cambridge University Press, 2004): 141, 155–69.

45. See for example, Tibor Kozma, "Heroes of Wood and Brass: The Trombone in *Aida*," *Opera News* 16 (March 3, 1952): 30–31.

46. Gardner Read, *Thesaurus of Orchestral Devices* (New York: Pitman, 1953), 104–11, 131–32, 138–39, 146–48.

47. See Edward Kleinhammer and Douglas Yeo, *Mastering the Trombone* (Hannover, Germany: Edition Piccolo, 1997), 40, for various approaches to the passage in *Concerto for Orchestra*. Any of these solutions would be more difficult for the multiple repetitions of the glissando in *The Miraculous Mandarin*.

48. Peter Kemp, *The Strauss Family: Portrait of a Musical Dynasty* (Tunbridge Wells, England: Baton Press, 1985), 50.

49. Kemp, *The Strauss Family*, 25–26; Philipp Fahrbach, "Geschichte der Tanzmusik seit 25 Jahren" (Part 2), *Wiener allgemeine Musik-Zeitung* 7 (1847): 141.

50. Jim Samson, ed., *The Cambridge History of Nineteenth-Century Music* (Cambridge: Cambridge University Press, 2001), 665.

51. Jules Rivière, *My Musical Life and Recollections* (London: Sampson, Low, Marston, 1893), 36, 38; Arthur Pougin,

Supplément et complément to *Biographie universelle des musiciens et bibliographie générale de la musique* by François-Joseph Fétis (Paris: Culture et Civilisation, 1880), s.v. "Musard."

52. *Times* (March 19, 1839): 1.

53. *Times* (Jan. 24, 1855): 10.

54. *Times* (June 19, 1845): 1; *Musical World* 20 (1845): 336.

55. Rivière, *My Musical Life*, 77, 81–82.

56. Thomas S. Hischak, *Stage It with Music: An Encyclopedic Guide to the American Musical Theatre* (Westport, Conn.: Greenwood Press, 1993), 191–92.

57. Roy Newsome, *Brass Roots: A Hundred Years of Brass Bands and Their Music (1836–1936)* (Aldershot, England: Ashgate, 1998), 78.

58. Jon C. Mitchell, "The Kneller Hall Archives: The British Military Band Tradition in Manuscript," in *Kongressbericht Mainz 1996*, ed. Eugen Brixel (Tutzing: Schneider, 1998), 18; Gabriel Parès, *Traité d'instrumentation et d'orchestration à l'usage des musiques militaires d'harmonie et de fanfare* (Paris: Lemoine, 1898), 5–6.

59. David Whitwell, *The History and Literature of the Wind Band and Wind Ensemble*, vol. 5, *The Nineteenth Century Wind Band and Wind Ensemble in Eastern Europe* (Northridge, Calif.: Winds, 1982–84), 143–44; Antonio Carlini, "Le bande musicali nell'Italia dell'Ottocento: Il modello militare, i rapporti con il teatro e la cultura dell'orchestra negli organici strumentali," *Rivista italiana di musicologia* 30 (1995): 85.

60. Augustin Sundelin, *Die Instrumentirung für sämmtliche Militär-Musik-Chöre* (Berlin: Wagenführ, 1828); Whitwell, *Nineteenth Century Wind Band*, 15–17; Edward Holmes, *A Ramble among the Musicians of Germany* (London: Hunt and Clarke, 1828; repr., New York: Da Capo, 1969), 234.

61. Lowell Mason, *Musical Letters from Abroad* (New York: Mason Bros., 1854; repr., New York: Da Capo, 1967), 128, 146.

62. *AMZ* 48 (1846): col. 460; Whitwell, *Nineteenth Century Wind Band*, 155–57; Lowell Mason, *A Yankee Musician in Europe: The 1837 Journals of Lowell Mason*, ed. Michael Broyles (Ann Arbor, Mich.: UMI Research Press, 1990), 59.

63. Weiner, "Andreas Nemetz," 13.

64. Giuseppe Fahrbach, "Organizzazione della musica militare austriaca" (pt. 5), *Gazzetta musicale di Milano* 5 (December 13, 1846): 397.

65. Georges Kastner, *Manuel général de musique militaire a l'usage des armées françaises* (Paris: F. Didot, 1848; repr., Geneva: Minkoff, 1973), 262–69; Rivière, *My Musical Life*, 49–56.

66. Whitwell, *Nineteenth Century Wind Band*, 171–74.

67. Unless otherwise noted, information about Italian bands comes from James Wesley Herbert, "The Wind Band of Nineteenth-Century Italy: Its Origins and Transformation from the Late 1700's to Mid-Century" (D.E. diss.: Columbia University, 1986).

68. "Lettre sur la musique à Naples," *Revue musicale* 7 (1830): 174.

69. Carlini, "Le bande musicali nell'Italia dell'Ottocento," 110–14.

70. Adam Carse, "The Prince Regent's Band," *Music & Letters* 27 (1946): 150.

71. Gordon Turner and Alwyn W. Turner, *The Trumpets Will Sound: The Story of the Royal Military School of Music, Kneller Hall* (Tunbridge Wells, Kent: Parapress Limited, 1996), 14–15, 18.

72. James C. Moss, "British Military Journals from 1845 through 1900: A Study of Instrumentation and Content with an Emphasis on *Boosé's Military Journal*" (D.M.A. thesis: University of Cincinnati, 2001), passim.

73. Trevor Herbert, "Nineteenth-Century Bands: Making a Movement," in *The British Brass Band: A Musical and Social History*, ed. Trevor Herbert (Oxford: Oxford University Press: 2000), 15, 22; Newsome, *Brass Roots*, 3–5.

74. Newsome, *Brass Roots*, 82.

75. Raoul Camus, "The Military Band in the United States Army prior to 1834" (Ph.D. diss.: New York University, 1969), 452, 457, 459.

76. Clyde S. Shive, "The First Music for Brass Published in America," *Historic Brass Society Journal* 5 (1993): 204.

77. For example, [Elizabethtown] *New Jersey Journal* (May 5, 1812): 4 (presumably Hoffman's ad, but no name is in it); [Goshen, New York] *Orange County Patriot* (April 13, 1813): 3; [Virginia] *Alexandria Gazette* (February 3, 1814): 4; [Charlestown, West Virginia] *Farmer's Repository* (December 29, 1814): 3; [Chambersburg, Pennsylvania] *Democratic Republican* (September 30, 1816): 3; [Norfolk, Virginia] *American Beacon* (April 28, 1818): 3; [Washington, D.C.] *Daily National Intelligence* (January 26, 1819): 3, and undoubtedly more.

78. (Boston: G. Graupner, 1835), described in Shive, "The First Music for Brass Published in America," 204ff; Allen Dodworth, "Brass Instruments," *The Message Bird* 1 (November 1, 1849): 116.

79. Margaret Hindle Hazen and Robert M. Hazen, *The Music Men: An Illustrated History of Brass Bands in America, 1800–1920* (Washington, D.C.: Smithsonian Institution Press, 1987). The recommendations from the catalog are on 106.

80. David M. Guion, "From Yankee Doodle Thro' to Handel's Largo: Music at the World's Columbian Exposition," *College Music Symposium* 24 (1984): 88–89, 92–94; Sandy R. Mazola, "Bands and Orchestras at the World's Columbian Exposition," *American Music* 4 (1986): 415–420.

81. Richard I. Schwartz and Iris J. Schwartz, *Bands at the St. Louis World's Fair of 1904: Information, Photographs, and Database* (n.p.: Self-Published, 2003), I:7–25; II:iv. The database in pt. II lists every piece performed at the fair and identifies soloists as given in the programs.

82. Frank L. Battisti, *The Winds of Change: The Evolution of the Contemporary American Wind Band/Ensemble and Its Conductor* (Galesville, Md.: Meredith Music Publications, 2002), 53–60.

83. The basic sources of information for this section are various essays in *The Oxford Companion to Jazz*, ed. Bill Kirchner

(New York: Oxford University Press, 2000), especially "The Trombone in Jazz," by Gunther Schuller, 628–41.

84. William J. Schafer, *Brass Bands and New Orleans Jazz* (Baton Rouge: Louisiana State University Press, 1977), 7–15.

85. Lawrence Gushee, *Pioneers of Jazz: The Story of the Creole Band* (Oxford: Oxford University Press, 2005), 169–73.

86. Robert Lindsay, "Professional Music in the 1920s and the Rise of the Singing Trombone," *Online Trombone Journal* (2006): trombone.org/articles/library/viewarticles. asp?ArtID=275, par. 37–46.

87. See Kurt Dietrich, *Duke's 'Bones: Ellington's Great Trombonists* (Rottenburg, Germany: Advance Music, 1995).

88. Paul Bauer, "The Trombone in the Orchestras of Stan Kenton" (part 1), *ITA Journal* 10 (July 1982): 25–26; (part 2), *ITA Journal* 10 (October 1982): 21–22.

89. Luis Tamargo, "A Brief History of the Latin Trombone," *Latin Beat Magazine* 8 (March 1998): 8–21; Gerald Sloan, "Los Huesos: A Closer Look at Latin Trombonists," *ITA Journal* 31 (January 2003): 30–47.

90. *Musical Standard* 5 (July 28, 1866): 51.

91. Trevor Herbert and Margaret Sarkissian, "Victorian Bands and Their Dissemination in the Colonies," *Popular Music* 16 (1997): passim.

92. *Times* (January 8, 1895): 13.

93. Schwartz, *Bands at the St. Louis World's Fair*, 1:49.

94. James T. Koetting, "Africa/Ghana" in *Worlds of Music: An Introduction to the Music of the World's Peoples*, 2nd ed., ed. Jeff Todd Titon (New York: Schirmer Books, 1992), 99–103.

95. David M. Guion, "Wind Bands in Towns, Courts, and Churches: Middle Ages to Baroque," *Journal of Band Research* 42 (Spring 2007): 49; Osvaldo Gambassi, *La capella musicale de S. Petronia: Maestri, organisti, cantori e strumentisti dal 1436 al 1920* (Florence: Olschki, 1987), passim; *Times* (August 13, 1903): 4.

96. Vincent and Mary Novello, *A Mozart Pilgrimage: Being the Travel Diaries of Vincent & Mary Novello in the Year 1829*, transcribed and compiled by Nerina Medici di Marignano, ed. Rosemary Hughes (London: Eulenburg Books, 1975), 288, 290 303–4, 310.

97. Holmes, *Ramble*, 140; AMZ 37 (1835): col. 69–70.

98. Guion, "Felippe Cioffi," 16.

99. Information about Bruckner's music comes from Keith William Kinder, *The Wind and Wind-Chorus Music of Anton Bruckner* (Westport, Conn.: Greenwood Press, 2000). Kinder calls *Psalm 114* Bruckner's "first indisputable masterpiece for chorus and winds," 10.

100. Volker Kalisch, "Posaunenchöre: Mission und Funktion," in *Kongressbericht: Mainz 1996*, ed. Eugen Brixel (Tutzing: Schneider, 1998), 263–64.

101. Wilhelm Ehmann, "100 Jahre Kuhlo-Posaunenbuch," *Brass Bulletin* 38 (1982): 39.

102. Max Sommerhalder, "Posaunen-Arbeit," *Brass Bulletin* 34 (1981): 56.

103. Arthur R. Taylor, *Brass Bands* (London: Granada, 1979), 335.

104. Sherri Marcia Damon, "The Trombone in the Shout Band of the United House of Prayer for All People," (D.M.A. thesis: University of North Carolina, Greensboro, 1999), 5–17.

105. Matthew A. Hafar, "The Shout Band Tradition in the Southeastern United States," *Historic Brass Society Journal* 15 (2003): 171.

106. Alfred Dörffel, *Geschichte der Gewandhausconcerte zu Leipzig vom 25. November 1781 bis 25. November 1881* (Leipzig, 1884), 2:41, 88; AMZ 17 (1815): col. 324.

107. See AMZ 37 (1835): col. 869; 40 (1838): col. 216; 44 (1842): col. 146, 176; *Revue et gazette musicale de Paris* (hereafter *RGMP*) 11 (1843): 433; 12 (1844): 22; *Allgemeine Wiener Musik-Zeitung* 4 (1844): 84.

108. AMZ 42 (1840): col. 1069–70; *RGMP* 12 (1844): 22; *Neue Zeitschrift für Musik* (hereafter *NZfM*) 20 (1844): 42–43, 191–92.

109. *NZfM* 13 (1840): 144; Holmes, *Ramble*, 254; Sebastian Krause, "Der Posaunengott," *Brass Bulletin* 117 (2002): 73, 78.

110. Robert Reifsnyder, "The Romantic Trombone and Its Place in the German Solo Tradition: Part II," *ITA Journal* 15 (Summer 1987): 32.

111. *Revue musicale* 1 (1827): 262–63; *Times* (Feb. 15, 1842): 7.

112. *Gazzetta musicale di Firenze* 1 (1853): 8. *Gazzetta musicale di Milano* 4 (1845): 63; 6 (1847): 204; 8 (1850): 90; *Italia musicale* 2 (1850): 322; *Allgemeine Wiener Musik-Zeitung* (1845): 279 ; *RGMP* 26 (1859): 306; 29 (1862): 262; 30 (1863): 220, 237; 32 (1865): 68.

113. "Il faut toute son habileté pour se faire pardonner de tirer son formidable instrument de la place qu'il doit occuper dans l'orchestre." *Revue musicale* 1 (1827): 263.

114. *Times* (Dec. 9, 1861): 1; (March 11, 1862): 1; *Times* (Dec. 8, 1883): 8; *New York Times* (Aug. 5, 1900): 15.

115. Guion, "Felippe Cioffi," 8–20; David M. Guion, "Four American Trombone Soloists before Arthur Pryor: Some Preliminary Findings," *ITA Journal* 20 (Fall 1992): 34; Hugh Anthony Callison, "Nineteenth-Century Orchestral Trombone Playing in the United States" (D.A. diss.: Ball State University, 1986), 115–121.

116. *Times* (Oct. 16, 1893): 10; *New York Times* (Nov. 22, 1896): 11; (Nov. 8, 1903): 22; (May 21, 1905): X5.

117. "The Philosopher in Society," *New York Times* (Nov. 11, 1883): 14 (5th par.).

118. Guion, "Four American Trombone Soloists," 36–37.

119. Michael Meckna, *Twentieth-Century Brass Soloists* (Westport, Conn.: Greenwood Press, 1994), 190–93; *New York Times* (Feb. 7, 1932): X14.

120. Glenn Bridges, *Pioneers in Brass*, CD-ROM (Trescott Research, 2001); *New York Times* (Aug. 2, 1942): X6.

121. Meckna, *Twentieth-Century Brass Soloists*, 228–29; Schuller, "Trombone in Jazz," 631–32; Robert Bruns, "Jack

Teagarden: His Career and Music," *ITA Journal* 35 (January 2007): 22–26.

122. Meckna, *Twentieth-Century Brass Soloists*, 73–74; Dietrich, *Duke's 'Bones*, 69–101.

123. Meckna, *Twentieth-Century Brass Soloists*, 146–150; Tom Everett, "J. J. Johnson: The Architect of the Modern Jazz Trombone," *ITA Journal* 16 (Spring 1988): 31–35; Tom Everett, "J. J. Johnson: On the Road Again," *ITA Journal* 16 (Summer 1988): 22–29.

124. Douglas Yeo, "An Interview with Bill Pearce," *Online Trombone Journal* (1998, updated August 2007): www.trombone.org/articles/library/pearce-int.asp

125. Sloan, "Los Huesos," 30.

126. *New York Times* (Apr. 14, 1947): 24.

127. AMZ 22 (1820): 259; 39; "der Würde des Instruments angemessen." (1837): col. 836.

128. David M. Guion, "Recital Repertoire of the Trombone as Shown by Programs Published by the International Trombone Association," *Online Trombone Journal* (1999): www.trombone.org/articles/library/recitalrep.asp; David M. Guion, "25 Years of Trombone Recitals: An Examination of Programs Published by the International Trombone Association," *ITA Journal* 27 (Winter 1999): 22–29.

129. Percy Scholes, *The Oxford Companion to Music* (London: Oxford University Press, 1938), 956.

130. See Eileen Massinon, "Joseph Alessi's Premiere of a Pulitzer Prize Winner," *ITA Journal* 24 (Spring 1996): 27, for Alessi's description of his difficulties in learning the second movement; Buddy Baker, "Why? How about Who, Where, What, When? The Development of Berio's *Sequenza V*," *ITA Journal* 22 (Spring 1994): 30–33.

131. *Times* (Apr. 4, 1834): 2; (Sept. 28, 1861): 8; (Oct. 11, 1861): 6; Rivière, *My Musical Life*, 81; George Grove, *A Dictionary of Music and Musicians* (London: Macmillan, 1883), s. v. "Trombone," by William H. Stone, 178.

132. *Times* (Mar. 24, 1890): 7. The society presented these two pieces two more times that year. These three performances were included in a review of the most significant musical events of 1890. See *Times* (Apr. 23, 1890): 1; (Oct. 16, 1890): 5; and (Jan. 12, 1891): 13; *Revue musicale* 9 (Mar. 15, 1909): 157.

133. *Times* (Apr. 2, 1894): 1 (the earliest advertisement); (Nov. 14, 1896): 1; (Nov. 16, 1896): 10 (advertisement and review).

134. Jean-Pierre Mathez, "Le quatuor Slokar," *Brass Bulletin* 106 (1999): 44–51.

135. Jim Boltinghouse, "Hoyt's Garage," *ITA Journal* 24 (Spring 1996): 32–35. See also Michelle Poland Devlin, "The Contributions of Tommy Pederson (1920–1988) to Trombone Performance and Literature in the Twentieth Century" (D.M.A. essay: University of North Carolina at Greensboro, 2007), libres.uncg.edu/edocs/etd/1303/umi-uncg-1303.pdf

136. Chris Larkin, "Felicien David's *Nonetto en Ut Majeur*: A New Discovery and New Light on the Early Use of Valved Instruments in France," *Historic Brass Society Journal* 5 (1993): 194–97.

137. Benny Sluchin, "Un martyr du trombone," *Brass Bulletin* 31 (1980): 57–66; Henri Blanchard, "Le trombone!" *RGMP* 15 (July 16, 1848): 215–17; Henri Blanchard, "Flanerie de la pensée artistique," *RGMP* 17 (Aug. 18, 1850): 276–77; Henri Blanchard, "M. C. Basler et M. A.-F.-M. Léonard de la Tuilerie," *RGMP* 17 (Oct. 27, 1850): 355–56.

138. Raymond Lapie, "Une découverte sensationnelle: 12 grands quintettes de cuivres français originaux datant de 1848–1850!" (pt. 1) *Brass Bulletin* 109 (2000): 32–38; Raymond Lapie, "French Chamber Music with Trombone (1795–1924): Bibliographic Notes," *ITA Journal* (October 2002): 32–45.

139. Meckna, *Twentieth-Century Brass Soloists*, 152.

140. Selected from William Stanley, "Annotated Bibliography of Compositions for Trombone and String Quartet," *ITA Journal* 24 (Summer 1996): 26–31.

141. G. Flandrin, "Le Trombone," in *Encyclopédie de la musique et dictionnaire du conservatoire*, part II, *Technique, esthétique, pédagogie: 3. Technique instrumentale*. (Paris: Librarie Delagrave, 1927), 1657–58; Lapie, "French Chamber Music," 39.

142. John Humphries, "The Royal Academy of Music and Its Tradition," *Brass Bulletin* 101 (1998): 46–47.

143. Turner, *The Trumpets Will Sound*, 153; *Musical World* (Aug. 11, 1860), 508.

144. Shifrin, "Valve Trombone," 119–20.

145. Rodney E. Miller, *Institutionalizing Music: The Administration of Music Programs in Higher Education* (Springfield, Ill.: Charles C. Thomas, 1993), 42.

146. James A. Keane, *A History of Music Education in the United States* (Hanover, N.H.: University Press of New England, 1982), 285.

147. Lee Hill Kavanaugh, "Babes in Slideland," *ITA Journal* 24 (Fall 1996): 38.

148. For the details and nuances of the influence of recordings, see Trevor Herbert, *The Trombone* (New Haven, Conn.: Yale University Press, 2006), 243–62.

APPENDIX

~

Selected Documents

When I began work on this book, I intended to include an extensive selection of primary source material. Following that plan would have required a second volume, which no publisher would have accepted. It was an easy decision to omit anything protected by copyright. That leaves an abundance of little-known, yet interesting and instructive material. What follows are selected documents for which there is no English translation in the public domain and that are too long to incorporate into the text.

I was also unable to use all of the illustrations I wanted to, partly for reasons of space and partly because some especially useful ones were unavailable except at an exorbitant price. Therefore, several pictures described in the text could not be illustrated.

Document 1

Johann Pezel. Preface to *Hora Decima Musicorum Lipsiensium*. Leipzig: Johann Köhler, 1670. Reprinted in *Denkmäler deutscher Tonkuste* 1. folge, bd. 63, *Johann Pezel Turmmusiken und Suiten*, ed. Arnold Schering. Leipzig: Breitkopf & Härtel, 1928.

Magnificent, most noble, best, most learned, most wise, most honorable burgomasters, proconsuls, master builders, and all of the council, highly honored patrons and great supporters of a highly praiseworthy city government: Just as the city of Thebes was enclosed within walls set in place by Amphion's harmonious harp with which Mercury had honored him (with which their poets referred to the harmonious laws of that city), so must everyone confess of your highly commendable and wonderfully flourishing government that it fits together like a musical harmony and is provided and preserved with the most salutary of laws.

And although all your regulations are very commendable and glorious, what above all else deserves immortal fame is that your republic is based on the genuine saving religion and in Christian zeal leaves nothing undone that can advance the honor of God the Almighty, which

Magnifici, Wohl-Edle, Beste, Hoch- und Wohlgelahrte, Hoch- und Wohlweise Eines Hochlöbl.Stadt-Regiments Hochansehnliche Bürgermeistere, Proconsules, Baumeistere, und sämptliche des Raths, Hochgeehrte Patroni und Grosse Fördere, GLeich wie die Stade Thebä durch die lieblich-klingende Harffe des Amphions, so ihm Mercurius verehret, mit volgeseßten Mauern umbschlossen worden, (womit aber die innerl. Poeten hätten auff die wohlzusammen stimmenden Gesetze derselben Stadt gezielet) also muß iederman von Dero Hochlöblichen und herrlich-florierenden Regiment gestehen, daß es gleich einer Musicalischen Harmonie ineinander geschrencket, und mit allerheilsamsten Gesetzen versehen und verwahrt sey.

Und wie nun all dero Anordnungen sehr löblich und preißbar sind, so verdienet doch dieses vor andern unsterblichen Ruhm, daß Ihre Republic auff die rechte seelig-machende Religion sich stützet, und nichts aus Christlichem Eyfer unterläst, was Gottes des Allerhöch-

should be the ultimate aim in everything. This end without doubt is the purpose of the regulation that from [the tower of] your city hall at 10 o'clock an *Abblasen* [i.e., a musical sounding of the hours] must be performed by the town musicians with trombones and cornetts. Truly a most Christian work, which above all others is able to ignite the Christian heart to God's praise and honor!

And if the minds are otherwise stimulated to all kinds of activity by the sound of music (for which reason Pythagoras caused the lyre to be played every morning for his students), and still today soldiers are instilled with the lion's courage by the sound of the trumpets, why should the Christian mind not let itself be inflamed to God's fame and honor by the sound of the cornett and trombone? In this connection I recall, however, the custom of the Persians and Turks. These [peoples], when in former times they thought it best to sacrifice to Jupiter, went to a tower or an otherwise raised place, and through this became aware of his infinity, called and proclaimed him a circle of the heavens, as Barnabé Brisson recorded in his book *De regio Persarum*.

These [peoples] continue still to this day to shout to each other every morning from high towers, "La alle elle alla," which the Jesuit [Athanasius] Kircher reports in *Oedipus Aegyptiacus*, or as Bartolomey Georgijevic puts it in *De Turcarum moribus epitome*, "Allach hechber," that is, "the one true God." How much more should we Christians be entitled to reflect all day, indeed every hour upon God's honor? And certainly the *Abblasen*, which is done by the tower watchmen of this city at certain hours, and by the city musicians at 10 o'clock from the city hall, has no small similarity and equal purpose.

Your humble servant, who was most graciously admitted by your most magnificent and honored [council] into the number of the town musicians, and composed up to now pieces appropriate for the *Abblasen*, seeks first and foremost nothing more than God's honor. And because I perceived that also at other places the same is required, I have submitted some of them for printing and will help spread God's honor in this way, too. Moreover, I have wanted to demonstrate my grateful soul for your most gracious patronage, and therefore do not hesitate to offer these published pieces in deepest humility to the most noble and honorable council of this city, humbly beseeching you to continue to include me in your high protection and favor.

sten Ehre, die doch in allen der Endzweck seyn soll, befördern kan; Wohin denn sonder Zweifel auch diese Verordnung ihr Absehen hat, daß von Ihren Rathhaus herunter um 10. Ur von denen Raths-Musicis ein Abblasen mit Posaunen und Zincken muß verrichtet werden. Traun ein recht Christliches Werck, und welches vor andern die Christlichen Hertzen zu Gottes Preiß und Ehre zu entzünden vermag!

Und werden sonsten die Gemüther durch den Musicalischen Thon zu allem Thun gleichsam angespornet, (deswegen Pythagoras auch alle morgen die Leyer vor seyne Schüler erklingen lassen) und wird noch heutiges Tages den Soldaten durch den Schall und Hall der Trompeten ein Löwenmuth eingejaget, worum solte nicht ein Christlich-gesintes Gemüth durch den Zinken- und Posaunen-klang zu Gottes Ruhm und Ehre sich anfeyren lassen? Ich erinnere mich aber hierbey der Perser und Türcken Gewonheit. Jene, wenn sie dem Jupiter vor Alters am besten zu opffern vermeynt, haben auf einen Thurm oder sonst erhabenen Ort sich begeben, und ihn einen Circkel des Himmels, seine Unendlichkeit dadurch bemerckende, genennt und ausgeruffen, wie Barn. Brissonius im Buch *de regno Persarum* auffgezeichnet.

Diese pflegen noch heutiges Tages alle Morgen auff hohen Thürmen einander zuzuruffen: La alle elle alla, wie der Jesuit Kircherus in *Oedip. Aegypt.* berichtet, Oder wie Barthol. Georgewiz *de Moribus Turcorum* besaget, Allach hechber, das ist, der einige warhafftige Gott. Wievielmehr will uns Christen zustehen, alle Tage ja alle Stunden auff Gottes Ehre zu dencken? Und hat gewißlich das Abblasen, welches von den Thürmern in dieser Stadt zu gewissen stunden, und von denen Raths-Musicis umb 10. Uhr von dem Rathhause geschieht, nicht eine geringe Verwandnüß, und ebenmässiges Absehen.

Meine Wenigkeit, so von Ihr. Magnif. und Hochachtb. in die Zahl derer Raths-Musicor. hochgünstig auffgenommen worden, und bißhero zum Abblasen dienliche Stücke componiret, suche zuförderst keine andere als Gottes Ehre; Und weil ich denn verspüret, daß auch an ander Orten dergleichen verlanget werden, als habe ich derer etliche dem Druck untergeben, und auch hiermit Gottes Ehre ausbreiten helffen wollen. Ich habe aber auch benebenst mein dankbares Gemüth vor Dero Hochgeneigte Beförderung erweisen wollen, und deswegen auch kein Bedencken getragen, diese herausgegebene Abblasungs-Stücke E.Hoch Edl. und Hochw. Rath dieser Stadt in tieffster Demuth zu offeriren, inständigst und unterdienstlichst bittend, mich ferner in Dero Hohen Schutz v. Gunst einzuschliessen.

In all other respects, just as one reads in Albert Krantz in *Metropolis* that Louis the Pious released Theodolphus of Orleans from prison upon hearing him sing the hymn that he had written, "Gloria, laus & honor Tibi sit Rex Christe Redemptor," etc., it is thus my heartfelt wish that the gracious God save your most magnificent and honorable [council], as spreader and promoter of his glory, from all danger to body and soul, and will bless your blossoming state with continuing prosperity and growth, with which I close, remaining your magnificent and honored [council's] most humble servant and musician, Johann Pezel, Leipzig, this eighth day of February, 1670.

Im übrigen, gleich wie man beym Alb. Cranzio in Metrop. lieset, daß Ludov. Pius dem Theodulpho der Gesängnüs befreyet, weil er den vom ihm gemachten Hymnum singen hören, Gloria, laus & honor Tibi sit Rex Christe Redemptor &c. Also ist mien hertzliches Wünschen, daß der fromme Gott Ihr. Magnif. und Hochw. als Ausbreiter und Beförderer seiner Ehre, aus aller Leibes und Seelengefahr erretten, und Dero wolblühenden Staat mit fernern Flor und Wachsthumb beseeligen wolle, Womit ich schliesse verharrende

Ihrer Magnig. und Hochw. unterdienstlichster Diener und Musicus Johann Bezeld.

Leipzig, den 8. Febr. Anno 1670.

Document 2

Gottfried Weber. From "Ueber Instrumentalbässe bey vollstimmigen Tonstücken," *Allgemeine musikalische Zeitung* no. 41 (1816): col. 701-02; no. 44 (1816): col. 749-53.

Bass Trombone
§8

The bass trombone provides magnificent, strongly penetrating bass notes and plays simple figures appropriate to its nature with great energy and firmness; playing it, however, is fatiguing, because for nearly every note it is necessary to push or pull the slide at least three inches and often as much as two feet. That is to say, if the notes B♭ and A are played one after the other, after I play the B♭ and before I can play the A, I must move the slide out about three inches. If I next want to play F, I must go 12–14 inches farther out, and in order to play the following figure:

Bassposaune
§8

Herrliche, kräftig durchschneidende Basstöne gewährt die Bassposaune, und giebt einfache, der Natur des Instruments angemessne Figuren mit grossem Nachdruck und aller Bestimmtheit: allein das Tonspiel auf derselben ist sehr beschwerlich, weil man nicht nur fast bei jedem Ton die Schiebröhre heraus- oder hineinziehen muss, sondern weil dies Heraus- oder Hineinziehen immer allerwenigstens 3 Zoll, oft aber auch bis an zwey Schuh betragt. Sollen z. B. die Töne B und A nacheinander angegeben werden, so muss ich, nachdem ich B geblasen, und eh' ich A angeben kann, die Röhre ungefähr 3 Zoll herausziehen. Will ich demnächst F blasen, so muss ich noch 12 bis 14 Zoll weiter ausziehen, und um z. B. folgende Figur zu spielen

I must push out about a foot and a half before I play the second note and then pull in 12–14 inches before I can play the following A, etc.

So it is easy to see why one cannot demand more from this instrument than strong simple notes or moderately fast passages that the trombonist, by the way, can only play detached and not slurred. He can never play them with roundness, flexibility and easy agility, much less with velocity—and in rapid figures almost never with strength and clarity. All of this is even worse with bass

muss ich, eh' ich die zweyte Note blase, erst anderthalb Schuh herausziehen, und eben so, bevor ich das folgende A blasen kann, wieder 12 bis 14 Zoll hineinschieben, u. s. f.

Man Sieht nun leicht, dass und warum von diesem Instrumente mehr nicht zu fordern ist, als blos kräftig einfache Noten, oder mässig geschwinde Gänge, die übrigens der Posaunist fast immer nur abgestossen und nicht gebunden herausbringen kann: nie aber Rundung, Geschwindigkeit und leichte Beweglichkeit noch Geschwindigkeit, und in geschwinden Figuren fast nie

trombones of a lower pitch than the one just mentioned. There are some that do not just go down to *E*, but even to low *C* or possibly even lower, which therefore must be built even much larger than already described. The positions are even farther apart, so that a man's arm cannot reach the end. For this reason an iron rod must be attached to the slide in order to push it out far enough and pull it in again – making all of the clumsiness of the instrument even worse.

Kraft und Deutlichkeit. Dies alles wird noch weit ärger bey Bassposaunen, welche noch tiefer sind, als die eben angeführten. Man hat deren nämlich nicht blos bis E, sondern bis gross C, oder auch wol noch tiefer gehend, welche also durchaus weit grösser gebaut seyn müssen, als die oben angegebene, wobey also auch die Züge noch viel weiter, als bey dieser auseinander liegen, ja sogar weiter, als ein Mannsarm zu reichten vermag, weshalb denn an der Schiebröhre eine eiserne Stange angebracht werden muss, vermittelst welcher man dieselbe bis zur erforderlichen Entfernung hinausstösst, und die man beym Wiederhereinziehen wieder fahren lässt--durch welches alles die Unbeholfenheit des Instruments noch immer ärger wird.

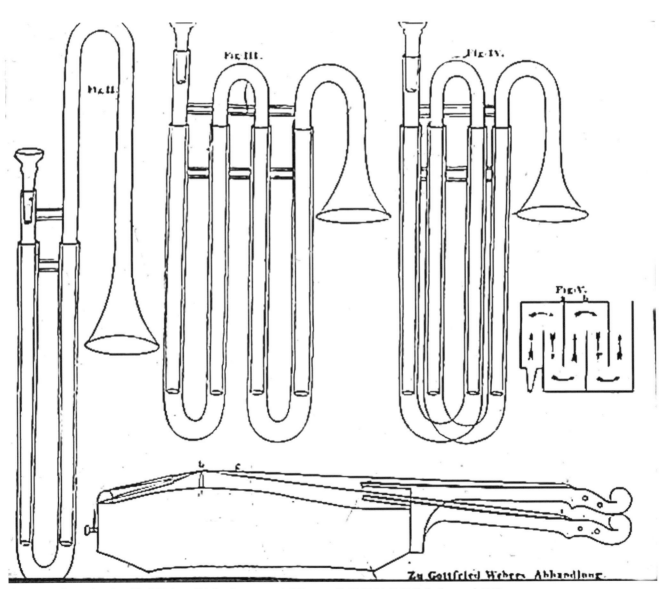

Fig. A.1.   Figure for Gottfried Weber, "Ueber Instrumentalbässe . . ." *AMZ* **44 (1816): before col. 749.**

Bass Trombone
§19

We have also already become acquainted with the weak side of the bass trombone in §8.

Should there not be a means of at least reducing the toil that results from excessively dragging the slide in and out, and thereby provide easier mobility and thus a greater sphere of activity to this very sonorous and powerful instrument?

Actually, there is such a means; yes, and it does not even have to be invented. It was invented long ago and even already applied to all of our trombones. We need not do anything but expand its application.

If I push the slide out about an inch on an ordinary trombone, then I make *each of the two* legs of the slide, which are parallel to each other, longer by an inch, and the whole slide thereby becomes *two* inches longer; the means through which one inch of movement results in two inches of length, as we see, was found long ago and has been in use for a long time. We must only want to go farther to get farther: let there be *four* legs run parallel to one another instead of *two* parallel legs. Instead of *one* double slide, make *two* of them, and join them together so that they slide together; in this way then, we suddenly have achieved the advantage of having to push only half an inch in order to lengthen the whole tube two inches.

A comparison of figures II, III, and IV of the illustration will make my idea even clearer. Figure II illustrates the current setup of the trombone with one slide. Figure III represents the doubling of the same; to make it easier to visualize, the instrument is shown here unfolded. Figure IV shows what it will look like when it is put together for actual use.

This device suddenly reduces by half the entire clumsiness of the instrument, which, as we have seen, results only from the wide distance between the positions, because now all of the notes lie half as close together as they did before.

§20

I already know the objections that will be raised against me. First, it will be said that by doubling the legs the friction will also double; second, it will be said that

Bassposaune
§19

Die schwache Seite der Bassposaune haben wir ebenfalls schon §. 8. kennen gelernt.

Sollte es nun kein Mittel geben, die Beschwerlichkeit, die aus dem weitschichtigen Hin- und Herziehen entspringt, wo nicht zu heben, doch sehr zu vermindern, und dadurch dem so tonreichen und kräftigen Instrumente leichtere Beweglichkeit, und also einen erweiterten Wirkungskreis zu verschaffen?

Allerdings giebt es ein solches Mittel; ja, es braucht nicht einmal erst erfunden zu werden: es ist schon längst erfunden, sogar an all unsern Posaunen schon wirklich angewendet, und wir haben nichts zu thun, als nur seine Anwendung zu erweitern.

Wenn ich an einer gewöhnlichen Posaune die Schiebröhre um einen Zoll heraus ziehe, so mache ich dadurch *jeden der zwey* parallel nebeneinander herlaufenden Schenkel der Röhre um einen Zoll länger, und die Röhre ist also dadurch im Ganzen um *zwey* Zoll länger geworden: das Mittel, durch einen Zoll Zug zwey Zoll Verlängerung zu wirken, ist also, wie wir sehen, schon längst gefunden, schon längst angewendet. Wir dürfen nur wollen, dürfen nur weiter gehn, um weiter zu gelangen; dürfen nur, statt *zwey* neben einander liegender Schenkel, deren *viere* parallel neben einander hinlaufen lassen, statt *einer* doppelten Schiebröhre, deren *zwey* machen, und sie so miteinander verbinden, dass sie sich zugleich mit einander verschieben, so haben wir plötzlich den Vortheil errungen, dass wir, um die Röhre im Ganzen um zwey Zoll zu verlängern, nur einen halben Zoll zu schieben brauchen.

Die Vergleichung der Figuren, II, III, und IV, der Kupfertafel, der vorigen No. wird meine Idee noch anschaulicher machen. Fig. II, vergegenwärtigt die bisherige Einrichtung der Posaune mit Einer Schiebröhre: Fig. III, versinnlicht der Verdoppelung derselben; der leichtern Anschauung halber ist hier das Instrument auseinander gebogen dargestellt. Fig. IV, stellt dasselbe in der Stellung vor, wie es zum wirklichen Gebrauch zusammengesetzt aussehen wird.

Die ganze Unbeholfenheit des Instruments, insofern sie aus der Weitschichtigkeit der Züge entsteht, (und diese ist ja, wie wir gesehen haben, die einzige Ursache derselben,) ist durch diese Einrichtung plötzlich auf die Hälfte vermindert, indem nun alle Töne gerade noch einmal so nahe beysammen liegen, als bisher.

§20

Ich weis schon die Einwendungen, die man mir entgegensetzen wird. Ersten wird man sagen: durch Verdoppelung der Schenkel wird sich auch die Reibung verdop-

through the increase in the number of bends in the slide the instrument's tone will also become weaker, or less round and penetrating. However, the *first* apprehension is as matters stand *thoroughly* groundless, erroneous, and false, for I contend and can easily prove, as paradoxical as it might appear at first glance, that the friction of this doubly wound trombone *will inevitably be far less* than the already negligible friction of today's simple trombone.

First of all, to move four legs half an inch, no more friction has to be overcome than to move two legs a whole inch; (a half of four is certainly not more than one times two!) and therefore the doubly wound trombone at least offers *no more* friction than the usual trombone.

But that calculation would be true even if each of the four legs were the same length as those of a simple trombone. Now, however, each leg of a four-legged trombone would naturally be half as long as on the ordinary trombone with only two legs. Therefore, the friction of the former will also be on the whole *not only not greater, but rather much less*, approximately only half as much as on the ordinary trombone, because 1/2 times 4/2 = (1 x 2)/2. (I say approximately because the proportional laws of friction have not yet been identified and determined with mathematical reliability and precision.)

§21

I will concede the *second objection*, that the tone of the doubly wound trombone will lose some strength compared to the single-wound; it will come out perhaps less round, strident, and brassy; except that the first, best, so-called Inventionstrompete [hand-trumpet with slide crooks], a metal instrument with multiple windings, can sound round and brassy enough. In the most extreme case, on the other hand, it [the new trombone] could be helped by enlarging the bell, and also, instead of bending the bell downward again in the usual unnecessary manner, allowing it to extend in a straight line beyond the player's shoulder, which eliminates an extra bend. In no case, by the way, would the small loss of volume of sound (which in the most extreme cases can be remedied perfectly by means of somewhat more numerous players) be noticeable compared to the gain in agility and clearer performance of otherwise impossible passages, which is possible to supply at any time with no more numerous, subjective distribution of the parts.

peln; zweytens, wird man mir entgegensetzen, wird durch Vermehrung der Windungen der Röhre der Ton des Instruments auch schwächer, oder doch weniger prall und durchschneidend werden. Allein die *erste* Besorgniss ist einmal *durchaus* ungegründet, irrig und falsch; denn ich behaupte und beweise leicht, so paradoxes im ersten Augenblick auch scheinen mag, dass an dieser doppelt gewundnen Posaune die Reibung *nothwendig weit geringer seyn wird,* als die ohne--dies schon geringe Reibung der jetzt gewöhnlichen, einfach gewundnen.

Denn für's Erste wird, um vier Schenkel einen halben Zoll zu verscheiben, wenigstens nicht mehr Reibung zu überwinden seyn, als, um zwey Schenkel einen ganzen Zoll zu verschieben; (ein halbmal vier ist ja doch nicht mehr, als einmal zwey!) und folglich bietet die doppelt gewundne Posaune wenigstens *nicht mehr* Reibung dar, als die gewöhnliche.

Allein die eben erwähnte Berechnung würde ja selbst dann wahr seyn, wenn jeder der vier Schenkel so lang wäre bey der vierschenklichen Posaune jeder Schenkel natürlicher Weise nur etwa halb so lang, als ein Schenkel der einfach gewunden: nun aber wird bey der vier schenklichen Posaune jeder Schenkel natürlicher Weise nur etwa halb so lang, als an der gewöhlichen Posaune von nur zwey Schenkeln: folglich wird auch die Reibung bey jener in Ganzen *nicht nur nicht grosser, sondern viel geringer,* ungefähr nur halb so gross seyn, als an der gewöhnlichen: denn 1/2 . 4/2 = 1.2/2. (Ich sage *ungefähr,* weil die Proportinalgesetze der Reibung eigentlich noch nicht mit mathematischer Zuverlässigkeit und Schärfe erkannt und bestimmt sind.)

§21

Den *zweyten Einwurf,* dass der Ton der doppelt gewundnen Posaune gegen den, der einfach gewundnen, etwas an Stärke verlieren werde, will ich zugeben; er wird vielleicht etwas weniger prall, grell und schmetternd ausfallen: allein die erste, beste, sogenannte Inventionstrompete beweist uns, dass ein auch mehrfach gewundnes Metallinstrument noch immer prall und schmetternd genug tönen kann. Aeussersten Falles liesse sich auch auf einer andern Seite wieder nachhelfen, durch Vergrösserung des Schallbechers, und etwa auch dadurch, dass man denselben, statt seinen Hals, wie gewöhnlich, unnöthiger Weise noch ein Mal abwärts zu biegen, in gerader Linie hinterwärts über die Schulter des Spielers hinausstehen lässt, wodurch eine Krümmung wieder gespart wird. In keinem Fall möchte übrigens der geringe etwaige Verlust an Tonstärke (welcher sich äussersten Falls durch etwas zahlreichere Besetzung vollkommen vergüten liesse) in Anschlag und Vergleichung kommen dürfen, gegen den Gewinn an Beweglich-

§22

In addition to this main advantage, the only one intended so far, a trombone so adapted would offer some other not insignificant incidental advantages.

Since, first of all, the legs need be only half as long as until now, and its positions again closer together, one could easily give such a trombone a new position or two by making the legs somewhat more than half the length of the old long-positioned, long-legged trombone. That would make playing it extraordinarily easier in another way. Let us suppose, for example, that the four legs are given two inches more than half of the usual length. This extension would not only add the note E♭ to the previous compass of the trombone, which only reaches down to low E, but would add in this E♭ position, the notes B♭, e♭, g, b♭, etc. And so now the tone B♭ would be available twice (once all the way in and once all the way out) instead of just once as it is now, the notes e♭ and g likewise twice instead of once, the note b♭ three times instead of twice (in the BB♭ position, the G♭/F♯ position, and in the new E♭ position). See §24 and following in my article on acoustics in the sixth issue of this journal, from which the important advantages that the use of this device would afford the other kinds of trombones can be easily deduced.

§23

A second incidental advantage of the doubly wound trombone lies in the fact that such an instrument is much shorter (more compact) when assembled than is the present one—a circumstance that is not unimportant, particularly in *military bands*, where handling a long bass trombone is indeed a sour piece of work for the one condemned to this business, who is, not unreasonably, in the habit of making his compulsory labor easier by frequent pauses, that is, omissions.

This is precisely why I decided to give doubly wound bass trombones to the bands of all the middle-Rhine district militia battalions, whose organization I had undertaken the previous year (1814). The capable and intelligent instrument-maker Haltenhof in Hanau, whom I commissioned, agreed to the idea with evident pleasure and eagerness; I can cite the most definite approval of a practical expert for the idea. The provisional administra-

keit und an deutlicher Ausführbarkeit sonst unmöglicher Passagen, welche durch keine zahlreichere, subjective Besetzung der Partie jemals zu ersetzen möglich ist.

§22

Nebst diesem letztern, bisher einzig beabsichtigten Hauptvortheil würde eine so eingerichtete Posaune auch noch einige nicht unbedeutende Nebenvortheile darbieten.

Da erstens die Schenkel daran nur halb so lang seyn müssen, als die bisherigen, und die Züge daran noch einmal so kurz beysammen liegen: so könnte man dadurch, dass man den Schenkeln nur ein Geringes mehr, als die Hälfte der bisherigen Länge gäbe, einer solchen Posaune leicht auch noch eine oder ein Paar Züge mehr geben, als an der bisherigen, langzügigen und langschenkligen Posaune möglich war; wodurch das Spiel auch wieder von einer andern Seite ausserordentlich erleichtert würde. Denn, nehmen wir z. B. an, man gäbe der vier Schenkeln nur etwa zwey Zoll mehr, als die halbe bisherige Länge: so würde man dadurch nicht nur zu dem bisherigen Umfang der nur bis gross E hinabreichenden Posaune auch noch den Ton Es gewinnen, sondern auf diesem neuen Es-Zug würden auch noch die Töne B, es, g, b etc. herauszubringen seyn, und man hätte nun den Ton B, statt bisher nur einmal, nun zweymal, (einmal ganz herein und einmal ganz hinaus,) die Töne es und g ebenfals zwey-, statt einmal, den Ton b, statt bisher zweymal, jetzt dreyfach; im B-Zug, im Ges- oder Fis-Zug, und im neuen Es-Zug. Man sehe §. 24. folgg. meiner *Akustik* in no. 6. folgg. dieser Blätter, woraus sich auch leicht abnehmen lässt, wie wichtige Vortheile die Anwendung dieser Einrichtung auch den übrigen Gattungen von Posaunen gewähren müsste.

§23

Ein zweyter Nebenvortheil der doppelt gewundnen Posaune liegt darin, dass ein solches Instrument ungleich kürzer beysammen (compendiöser) ist, als die bisherige; ein Umstand, welcher, zumal bey *Feldmusiken*, nicht unwichtig ist, wo das Handhaben einer langen Bassposaune ein wahrlich saures Stück Arbeit für den, zu diesem Geschäft Verdammten ist, welcher sich denn auch seiner Frohnarbeit nicht unbillig durch häufiges Pausiren, d. h. Auslassen, zu erleichtern pflegt.

Eben dies hatte mich bestimmt, den Musikgesellschaften der sämmtlichen mittelrheinischen Landwehrbataillons, deren Organisation ich mich im vorigen Jahre (1814) unterzogen hatte, solche doppelt gewundne Bassposaunen zu geben. Der geschickte und verständige Instrumentmacher, Haltenhof, in Hanau, dem ich die Bestellung aufgab, ging mit sichtbarem Wohlgefallen und Eifer in die Idee ein, und in so fern kann ich denn

tive commission that followed the general government dissolved the still barely organized middle-Rhein militia, which has meanwhile brought the production of the doubly wound trombone to a halt.

auch den entschiedensten Beyfall eines praktischen Sachkenners für dieselbe Idee anführen. Die Auflösung der noch kaum in Entstehn begriffnen mittelrheinischen Landwehr durch die dem Generalgouvernement nachgefolgte provisorische Regierungscommission brachte indessen auch die Ausführung der doppelt gewundnen Posaunen ins Stocken.

§24

I hardly need to remind that the designs appended above are intended *only* to describe my idea and make it understandable, not for an instrument-maker to work from them. They are too incomplete for the latter purpose, and once any intelligent instrument maker has gotten a hold of the idea, he will not require a drawing to carry it out.

§24

Ich brauche übrigens wol kaum zu erinnern, dass die oben beygefügten Zeichnungen *nur dazu* bestimmt sind, meine Idee verständlich und anschaulich zu machen, nicht aber, dass ein Instrumentenmacher darnach arbeiten solle, indem sie zu letztern Behufe theils überhaupt viel zu unvollkommen sind, theils auch ein irgend verständiger Instrumentenmacher, so wie er die Idee einmal gefasst hat, zu Ausführung derselben keiner Zeichnung mehr bedürfen wird.

Document 3

Giacomo Gotifredo Ferrari. *Aneddoti piacevoli e interessanti occorsi nella vita di Giacomo Gotifredo Ferrari* (London: Self-Published, 1830): 1:139–40; English translation: *Harmonicon* 8 (1830): 372.

Ferdinand IV of Naples was an enthusiastic lover of music, and himself no mean performer on the *ghironda*. No sooner was the arrival of any distinguished professor in his capital known, than he signified his wish to hear him, and was sure to reward him liberally. Mariotti, a native of Bologna, and a celebrated performer on the trombone, had arrived in this city [Naples] shortly before me. He had recently come from Rome, where he had witnessed the imposing ceremonies of Holy Week, and had seen the public benedictions given by the Pontiff at the Vatican. The latter ceremony, in particular, had made so deep an impression on his mind, that he could not banish thence the idea of his Holiness. The King of Naples, hearing of the arrival of a professor with so new and powerful an instrument, signified his pleasure to hear him at the *Palazzo di Caserta*. Mariotti's first performance, in a quartet, was timid, but it pleased the king. Encouraged by this, the artist exerted all the powers of his instrument in a thundering overture, which quite delighted his majesty. When it was finished, he approached the artist and, placing his hand upon his shoulder, said, "You are the trombone of my chapel, and of the theatre San Carlo." Poor Mariotti was all confusion, and the image of the pope and the grand benediction being still uppermost in his mind, he replied, "Most Holy Father, I am grateful for your kindness." His majesty burst into a laugh, and turning to the queen, exclaimed, "Nenna, Nenna, come here, come here; this blockhead of a Bolognese calls me Holy Father, as if I were the pope!"

Ferdinando IV. sonava la ghironda, ed era veramente trasportato per ogni sorta di musica. Se arrivava un professore distinto nella sua metropoli, lo volea sentire, e lo incorraggiava liberalmente. Giunse colà poco primo di me un certo Antonio Mariotti, Bolognese, celebre suonator di trombone, e forse l'unico a quel tempo che sonasse tale istromento in Italia. Passando egli per Roma, vide le funzioni di Pasqua, e la benedizione che suol dare in tal giorno il Papa del Vaticano. Ciò gli fece tanta impressione che per diverse settimane non potea levarsi dalla mente Sua Santità. Udendo il Rè di Napoli che vi era arrivato un professore con un nuovo e potente istromento, lo chiamò subito al suo palazzo di Caserta per sentirlo. Suona timidamente Mariotti il basso in un quartetto, pur piace a Sua Maestà: suona poscia con coraggio e forza il basso in un'overtura strepitosa, e vi fischia certe trombonate, che fanno alzare il Rè dalla sua sedia e avvinciarsi al suonatore. Finita l'overtura, gli mette una mano sulle spalle, dicendo; tu sei lo trombone della mia Cappella e dello teatro di San Carlo. Il povero Mariotti, felice, confuso, e col suo Papa nella mente, gli risponde; "Santo padre benedetto, vi ringrazio della vostra bontà." Sua Maestà schiattando dalle risa si volta verso la Regina e la chiama. "Nenna, Nenna, vieni cà, vieni ca! Senti chisto pazzo di Bolognese che mi chiamo Santo padre come s'io fosse lo Papa!"

Document 4

Félix Vobaron. *Grande méthode de trombone*. Paris: Gambaro, 1834, p. 2.

NOTICE

The trombone is a very ancient instrument. Its origin occurred centuries ago. It was used only for basso continuo. Its dimension was disproportionate, like that of the trumpet and other warlike instruments of olden times.

About 40 years ago, German makers sought to improve this instrument, but they did not succeed completely. Ours, encouraged by several artists, finally obtained the degree of perfection one could hope for, more or less.

Some army trombonists in 1815 played their parts rather well, but they were extremely simple, and a passage like this one

was admired at the time. It was then that I resolved to devote myself entirely to the study of the trombone. I took great pains to learn the seven positions, which no one could show me; I searched for the complete mechanism and all its effects. At every moment, disheartened by the great difficulties that I had to overcome, I was ready to give up, when, finally, encouraged by many amateurs, I redoubled my efforts and managed to carry out some airs with variations, which I was obliged to make for myself.

Satisfied with the flattering reception given to me by a number of artists and amateurs in France and Belgium, like what I received from the Royal Society of Fine Arts in Ghent, of which I am honored to be a part, I went to Paris to offer the homage of my work to the Royal Academy of Music, which condescended to honor me with its approval. I have also not forgotten the interest with which the company of the Art School of Bordeaux agreed to admit me into its membership.

Having been asked for several years, I believe it is my duty to answer the desires of artists and amateurs by presenting this method. I took all my care and all my experience so that all the elements necessary for rapid advancement of the students and what it is necessary to know were joined together. The instrument is developed here in all its resources, and one can draw a very profitable advantage from it if one follows exactly the principles I indicate. The position of the body, the head, the left arm, and right arm must be observed carefully, but in working

AVERTISSEMENT

Le Trombonne est un instrument très ancien; son origine remonte à des siècles. On ne s'en servait que comme basse-continue. Sa dimension était aussi démesurée que celle des trompettes et autres instruments de musique guerrière des époques reculées.

Il y a quarante ans environ que les facteurs Allemands ont cherché à perfectionner cet instrument; mais ils n'ont pas réussi complettement. Les nôtres, encouragés par plusieurs artistes, ont enfin obtenu le degré de perfection que l'on pouvait désirer, à peu de choses près.

Quelques Trombonnistes de l'armée, en 1815, faisaient assez bien leurs parties, mais elles étaient fort simples et des passages comme celui-ci:

était admirés à cette époque. C'est alors que je résolus de me livrer entièrement à l'étude du Trombonne. J'eus beaucoup de peine à m'en créer les sept positions, que personne ne pouvait me procurer; et j'en cherchai le mécanisme complet avec tous ses effets. A chaque instant, rebuté par les grandes difficultés que j'avais à vaincre, j'étais prèl [près?] à renoncer, lorsqu'enfin, encouragé par de nombreux amateurs, je redoublai d'efforts et parvins à exécuter quelques airs variés que je fus obligé de me faire.

Satisfait de l'accueil flatteur que me firent nombre d'artistes et d'amateurs en France et en Belgique, comme de celui que je reçus à la société royale des Beaux-Arts de Gand, dont j'ai l'honneur de faire partie, je vins à Paris offrir l'hommage de mes travaux à l'Académie-Royale-de-Musique qui daigna m'honorer de son approbation. Je n'oublié pas non plus avec quel intérêt la société des Beaux-Arts de Bordeaux a bien voulu m'admettre au nombre de ses membres.

Sollicité depuis quelques années, j'ai cru de mon devoir de répondre au désir des artistes et des amateurs, en présentant cette Méthode. J'ai apporté tous mes soins et toute mon expérience pour que tous les éléments nécessaires à l'avancement rapide des élèves, et qu'il est indispensable de connaître, y fussent réunis. L'instrument y est développé dans toutes ses ressources, et l'on peut en tirer un parti très avantageux si l'on suit exactement les principes que j'ai indiqués. La pose du corps, de la tête, du bras gauche, du bras droit, doit être observée avec

on posture, one should not neglect the quality of sound. When one overcomes the difficulty of the mechanism in the first two octaves,

soin; mais en travaillant les positions il ne faut pas négliger la qualité des sons. Quand on aura vaincu la difficulté du mécanisme des deux premières octaves

one will imperceptibly arrive at the difficulty presented by the whole range. At that time, one will be able to deliver oneself to the charm of the *adagio*, which, constant with slowness and solemnity, produces on the instrument the most touching sounds, and in which the thought represents in forms both sweet and religious; in the *forte*, on the other hand, the instrument raises itself with fierceness and subjugates the ear of the least attentive listener.

on arrivera insensiblement à la difficulté que présente la portée entière. C'est alors que l'on pourra se livrer au charme de l'ADAGIO, qui, soutenu avec lenteur et solennité, produit sur cet instrument les sons les plus touchants, et dans lequel la pensée se représente sous des formes aussi suaves que religieuses; dans le FORTE au contraire l'instrument s'élève avec fierté et subjugue l'oreille de l'auditeur le moins attentif.

Document 5

G. W. Fink. "Wichtige Verbesserung der Posaune." *Allgemeine musikalische Zeitung* 41 (1839): col. 257–58.

After repeated experimentation, the long famous, well-known brass instrument maker, Sattler of Leipzig, has succeeded in giving the powerful trombone the ultimate, most desirable perfection. *Christian Friedr. Sattler*, the son of the woodwind instrument maker Sattler in Leipzig, was born here on 20 January 1778, came in 1794 to the local brass instrument maker Sattler for instruction, and established his own business in 1809. For a long time, his brass instruments were the most sought after. Now, to the advantage of both players and composers, he has attached a device to the tenor-bass trombone that will completely replace the quart- and quint-trombones [bass trombones in F and E♭] used until now in orchestras and bands. With this device, both simple and reliable, the notes,

Durch mehrfache Versuche ist es dem längst rühmlich bekannten Herrn Messinginstrumentenmacher Sattler in Leipzig gelungen, der wirksamen Posaune die letzte, höchst erwünschte Vollendung zu geben. *Christian Friedr. Sattler*, Sohn des Holzinstrumentenmachers S. in Leipzig, wurde hier am 20. Januar 1778 geb., kam 1794 bei dem hiesigen Messinginstrumentenmacher Sattler auf die Lehre und etablirte sich 1809. Seit lange waren seine Messinginstrumente die gesuchtesten. Jetzt hat er nun sowohl zum Vortheil der Bläser als der Komponisten an der Tenor-Bass-Posaune eine Vorrichtung angebracht, wodurch die bisher in Orchestern und Musikchören gebrauchte Quart- und Quintposaune völlig ersetzt wird. durch diese even so einfache als sichere Vorrichtung sind die bis jetzt auf der Tenor-Bassposaune fehlenden Töne

missing up to now on the tenor-bass trombone, are strongly and beautifully obtained, and indeed in such a way that they can be obtained by every player with complete security, without changing the slide position, by pressing the thumb of the left hand. Mr. Karl Queisser of Leipzig, the trombone virtuoso known by everyone, has done the favor of carefully testing the new instrument. He has found it in every regard worthy of highest consideration. We have heard him play it; all of the notes from the highest to the lowest sound magnificent, and the contrabass notes E♭, D, D♭, C, C♭, and BB came out

kräftig und schön gewonnen worden und zwar dergestalt, dass sie von jedem Bläser, ohne die Züge zu verändern, durch einen Druck des Daumens der linken Hand mit aller Sicherheit hervorgebracht werden können.—Herr Karl Queisser in Leipzig, der allgekannte Posaunenvirtuos, hat die Gefälligkeit gehabt, das neue Instrument sorgfältig zu probiren. Er hat es in jeder Hinsicht höchst empfehlenswerth gefunden. Wir hörten es von ihm blasen; alle Töne von der Höhe bis zur Tiefe klangen überaus herrlich, und die Kontratöne *Es, D, Des, C, Ces, B* kamen in grösster Rundung, Fülle und Schönheit

with the greatest roundness, fullness, and beauty. This much-improved instrument must therefore be highly recommended to all orchestra and solo players as very practical. It needs only a short introduction; everyone can see the advantages for himself.

heraus. Das so verbesserte Instrument muss also allen Orchester- und Solobläsern als sehr zweckmässig bestens empfohlen werden. Es braucht nur der kurzen Anzeige; die Vortheile sieht jeder selbst.

Document 6

Henri Blanchard. "Le premier trombone du roi de Prusse." *Revue et gazette musicale de Paris* 11 (24 December 1843): 433.

We beg our readers to excuse us if we speak to them about old mythology. It is almost to suppose them in their studies, and in the fifth grade; but all forms are good to make a truth felt. The fable presents us with Orpheus attracting the wildest animals to him by the charm of his voice and lyre. There is in this fiction the entire history of civilization by means of the musical art. Now, said Orpheus, managing to make an attentive and benevolent audience of hyenas and jackals, showing us the lion and the tiger ready to mix their raucous accents with his, can give an idea rather right of Mr. Belcke taming the terrible trombone and making it sigh a love song or dialogue in brilliant variations with the flute. But first, is it right to ask us who is this Mr. Belcke? Mr. Belcke is the first trombone, trombone solo, of the King of Prussia, now directed, as far as music is concerned, by the famous maestro Giacomo Meyerbeer.

Just as the drummer of the emperor of Morocco is famous in the instrumental army for his silver drums, Mr. Belcke is remarkable among the European instrumentalists by his tenor trombone of the same metal. But it is especially by the soft and suave sounds that he draws from this ungrateful instrument, howling and blasting, that Mr. Belcke is distinguished. We heard this exceptional artist in a musical benefit given expressly for him, attended by his patron, Mr. Meyerbeer, and several other qualified artists of the capital; and we were astonished, like all the audience, by the ease of sound, by the melody, but especially by the brilliant and sustained trill that Mr. Belcke can obtain from the proud and not very tamable trombone. If this artist leaves something to be desired as far as the distinction of his style and the equality of his sounds, he sings with much softness on his terrible instrument, and the sound of the *fortissimo*, which he attacks with vigor, goes *perdendosi* with an astonishing degradation of tone that points to the vaporous Claude Lorain or the remote sounds of the Ranz des Vaches of Switzerland.

Nous prions nos lecteurs de nous excuser si nous leur parlons de la vieille mythologie. C'est presque les supposer dans leurs études, et en cinquième encore; mais toutes les formes sont bonnes pour faire sentir un vérité. La fable nous présente M. Orphée attirant à lui les bêtes les plus féroces par le charme de sa voix et de sa lyre. Il y a dans cette fiction tout l'histoire de la civilisation au moyen de l'art musical. Or, le dit Orphée, parvenant à se faire un auditoire attentif et bienbeillant d'hyènes et de chacals, nous montrant le lion et le tigre prêts à mêler leurs rauques accents aux siens, peut donner un idée assez juste de M. Belcké apprivoisant le terrible trombone et lui faisant soupirer la romance ou dialoguer de brillantes variations avec la flûte. Mais d'abord, est-on en droit de nous demander, qu'est-ce que M. Belcké? M. Belcké est le premier trombone, tombone [sic] solo de la musique du roi de Prusse, que dirige maintenant—la musique bien entendu—l'illustre maestro Giacomo Meyerbeer.

De même que le timbalier de l'empereur de Maroc est célèbre dans l'armée instrumentale par ses timbales d'argent, M. Belcké se fait remarquer aussi parmi les instrumentistes européens par son magnifique trombone ténor de même métal. Mais c'est surtout par les sons doux et suaves qu'il tire de cet instrument ingrat, hurlant et foudroyant, que se distingue M. Belcké. Nous avons entendu cet artiste exceptionnel dans une matiné musicale donné exprès pour lui, et à laquelle assistait son patron, M. Meyerbeer, et plusieurs autres artistes compétents de la capitale; et nous avons été étonné, comme tout l'auditoire, de l'assouplissement des sons, de la mélodie, mais surtout du trille brillant et soutenu que M. Belcké sait obtenir du fier et peu domptable trombone. Si cet artiste laisse quelque chose à désirer du côté de la distinction du style et de l'égalité des sons, il chante avec beaucoup de douceur sur son terrible instrument, et le son *fortissimo* qu'il attaque avec vigueur va *perdendosi* avec une étonnante dégradation de ton qui rappelle les horizons vaporeux de Claude Lorain, ou les sons lointains d'un Ranz des Vaches dans les montagnes de la Suisse.

Although in fact among the instruments suitable to play the solo in a concert, the trombone is somewhat in the category of the double bass, guitar, ophicleide, serpent, accordion, and other *poïkilorgues*, Mr. Belcke promises not to be heard any the less at the Academy, where he will undoubtedly obtain astonishing success. It will be an artistic exchange of hospitality of which Mr. Berlioz felt the effects in Germany. Reciprocal honors thus between these interpreters of the trombone, between him who makes it speak poetically by his pen and him who animates its pathetic or graceful breath. Mr. Belcke was accompanied by his brother, an able flutist, with whom he executed some duets, as we have already said, duets that represent for us the dialogues that could take place between the eagle and the dove, the wolf and the lamb, the lion and the nightingale. For the rest, it results from these contrasted sonorities, pleasant and often curious effects.

Bien qu'en fait d'instruments propres à jouer le solo dans un concert, le trombone soit un peu dans la catégorie de la contrebasse, de la guitare, de l'ophicleide, du serpent, de l'accordéon et autres poïkilorgues, M. Belcké ne s'en promet pas moins de se faire entendre au Conservatoire, où il obtiendra sans doute un succès d'étonnement. Ce sera un échange d'hospitalité artistique dont M. Berlioz a éprouvé les effets en Allemagne. Honneurs réciproques donc entre ces interprètes du trombone, entre celui qui le fait parler poétiquement par sa plume et celui qui l'anime de son souffle pathétique ou gracieux. M. Belcké est accompagné de son frère, flûtiste hablie, avec lequel il exécute des duos, ainsi que nous l'avons déjà dit, duos qui nous représentent les dialogues qui pourraient avoir lieu entre l'aigle et la colombe, le loup et l'agneau, le lion et le rossignol. Au reste, il résulte de ces sonorités contrastées des effets agréables et souvent curieux.

Document 7

François-Auguste Gevaert. *Nouveau traité d'instrumentation.* Paris: Lemoine & Fils, 1885; English translation by E. F. E. Suddard as *A New Treatise on Instrumentation.* Paris: Henry Lemoine, 1906, 239–41 in both publications. All footnotes are omitted.

§173. Except in the grave register, where tone-production is always heavy, the Trombone is capable of about as much execution as the Horn. It experiences no difficulty in sounding the various harmonics of one and the same fundamental in quick succession, although figures of this description are not met with in orchestral music.

§173. En dehors du registre grave, ou se produit toujours pesamment, le trombone est susceptible d'une vivacité d'émission à peu près égal à celle du cor. Il n'a aucune difficulté a parcourir avec vitesse les harmoniques procédant de la même fondamentale bien que des traits ainsi conçus ne se rencontrent pas dans la musique d'orchestre.

However, the rudimentary mechanism of the slide does not allow of the easy execution of florid figures that involve frequent changes of position. In the acute and medium registers, it is always possible to obtain the same note in two or three different ways (see the preceding figure, p. 237), the performer can easily avoid wide

Mais le mécanisme rudimentaire de la coulisse ne lui permet pas de rendre avec aisance des traits rapides tant soit peu prolongés, dès qu'ils entraînent de fréquents changements de position. A l'aigu et dans le medium de l'échelle, la même intonation pouvant se prendre toujours de deux ou trois manières (voir le tableau pré-

skips, and the composer must not think himself bound to eschew diatonic or chromatic scales (the latter being easier), or even pretty quick melodic figures, provided they are short. In the grave register, the case is different. Some successive notes require great and sudden changes of position, and are therefore incompatible with a rapid rate of slide movement.

cédant) l'exécutant évite facilement les grands écarts et le compositeur ne doit pas s'interdire les gammes diatoniques ou chromatiques (celles-ci sont les plus faciles), même les dessins mélodique assez vifs, pourvu qu'ils soient courts. Dans le registre grave il n'en est pas de même. Certaines successions de sons exigent le passage subit à une position très élongée et sont par là incompatibles avec un mouvement précipité.

At a time when dramatic composers did not give so much thought to minute details as they usually do nowadays, many of them did not scruple to require Trombones to double all kinds of bass passages, constantly running the risk of tasking the performer beyond his strength. In this connection it will suffice to recall too [sic] well-known passages.

À une époque où l'instrumentation de la musique de théâtre était moins détaillée qu'elle ne l'est généralement aujourd'hui, les compositeurs ne se faisaient pas scrupule de renforcer par le trombone des traits de basse de toute sorte, au risque d'imposer à l'exécutant une tâche audessus de ses forces. Je me contenterai de rappeler à ces propos deux pages bien connues.

Rossini, Orage de l'ouverture de Guillaume Tell.

Meyerbeer, LES HUGUENOTS. 1ʳ acte, Chœur: "Des beaux jours de la jeunesse" (p. 24 de la gr. partit.).

A valve-instrument is alone able to play so many notes distinctly. Those among modern composers who continue to pin their faith to the Slide-Trombone will do well to abstain from writing similar passages, if they are in the least concerned with hearing what they write. Each instrument has its qualities and its defects: the main point is to write for each the kind of music which suits it.

Several sounds in succession cannot be played strictly *legato* on the Slide-Trombone, when they belong to different fundamental tones, on account of the intermediate intervals which the moving slide would inevitably produce. True *legato* playing can therefore be practised on the Trombone in a very limited number of cases only: in actual performance, passages marked *legato* are merely played *sostenuto*, unless the composer has taken into account the special technique of the instrument. This, however, is rare. As most of the melodic passages for Trombones are doubled by other grave instruments, the composer does not scruple to put delusive slurs, depending upon the mass of instruments to cover individual weaknesses. In the following example the passage marked N. B. is impracticable on the Slide-Trombone.

Un instrument à postions est seul capable de jouer distinctement tant de notes. Ceux de nos contemporains qui continuent à donner la préférence aux trombones à coulisse feront donc bien de s'abstenir de pareils passages, s'ils tiennent à entendre ce qu'ils ont écrit. Tous les instruments ont leurs qualité et leurs défauts: l'essentiel est d'écrire la musique qui leur convient.

La réunion de plusieurs sons dans une seule articulation ne peut s'effectuer d'une manière irréprochable, lorsque les intonations liées proviennent de positions différentes, à cause des intervalles intermédiaires que le glissement de la coulisse produit inévitablement. Le vrai *legato* n'a donc qu'une application très restreinte sur le trombone à coulisse: à l'exécution il se convertit en un simple *sostenuto*, à moins que le compositeur n'ait eu égard au mécanisme de l'instrument. Mais ce cas est assez rare. Comme la plupart des traits chantants des trombones sont doublés par d'autres instruments graves, le compositeur n'a scrupule de mettre des liaisons illusoires, comptant sur l'effet de la masse pour couvrir les défaillances individuelles. Dans le passage suivant la mesure désigné par N. B. est inexécutable sur le trombone à coulisse.

R. *Wagner,* LOHENGRIN, IIIe acte,
Marche nuptiale (p. 264 et suiv.
de la gr. partit. autographiée).

[One paragraph omitted]

Although in former times, concertos and airs with variations were written for Tenor Trombone, this instrument, as will be seen, afforded but little technical resources to individual *virtuosi*. Mozart, inspired by the words of the celebrated Hymn for the Dead, has written a true solo for the Trombone in his posthumous *Requiem*.

[One paragraph omitted]

Bien qu'on ne se soit pas fait faute autrefois de composer pour le trombone-ténor à coulisse des concertos et des airs variés, cet instrument, on le voit, offrait d'assez maigres ressources techniques à la virtuosité individuelle. Mozart, s'inspirant des paroles de la célèbre Prose des Morts, a confié au trombone-ténor un véritable solo dans sa messe posthume.

Tu - ba mi - rum spar-gens so - - -

- - - - - num Tu - ba mi - rum spar - gens

so - num. Per se - pul - chra re - gi - o - num Co - get om - nes an - te

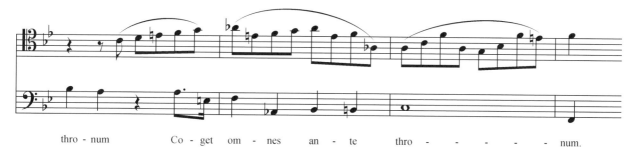

thro - num Co - get om - nes an - te thro - - - - num.

Édition des œuvres complètes (Leipzig, Breitkopf et Härtel),
Série XXIV, Supplément N°. 1.)

However, this is a mere isolated exception, and we may be allowed to add, without being guilty of disrespect towards the immortal author of *Don Giovanni*, that the innovation is not one of those that mark a new era in the history of musical art. Generally speaking, the great German masters have treated the Slide-Trombone in the manner of a choral voice, only assigning to it long notes or short phrases with vigorous rhythms, and never separating the Tenor Trombone from its two companions.

Mais c'est là une exception tout à fait isolée, et il nous sera permis d'ajouter, sans manquer de respect envers l'immortel auteur de *Don Giovanni*, que l'innovation n'est pas une de celles qui ont fait époque dans l'histoire de l'art. En général les maîtres allemands ont traité le trombone à coulisse à la manière d'une voix chorale, ne lui donnant que de grosses notes ou de courtes phrases d'un vigoureux dessin rythmique, et ne séparant jamais le ténor de ses deux compagnons.

~

Bibliography

Periodicals

Allgemeine musikalische Zeitung
Allgemeine musikalische Zeitung. 3. Folge
Allgemeine Wiener Musik-Zeitung
Art musical
Athenaeum
Berlin musikalische Zeitung
Berliner allgemeine muskalische Zeitung
British Musician
Dwight's Journal of Music
Early American Newspapers. infoweb.newsbank.com/. Proprietary database, available by subscription only.
Gazette musicale de Paris
Gazzetta musicale di Firenze
Gazzetta musicale di Milano
Harmonicon
Illustrated London News
Italia musicale
Message Bird
Musical Standard
Musical Times and Singing-Class Circular
Musical World
Neue Zeitschrift für Musik
New York Times
Paganini
Revue et gazette musicale de Paris
Revue musicale (1827)
Revue musicale (1902)
Teatri
Teatro illustrato
Times (London)

Books, Articles, Dissertations, and Other Printed Sources

Adler, Samuel. *The Study of Orchestration*. New York: Norton, 1982; 3rd ed., 2002.

Agazzari, Agostino. "Of Playing upon a Bass with All Instruments and of Their Use in a Consort." In *Source Readings in Music History*, edited by Oliver Strunk, rev. ed., 622–28. New York: Norton, 1998.

Agricola, Martin. *Musica instrumentalis deudsch*. Witternberg: Georg Rhau, 1529. Facsimile edition by Robert Eitner. Leipzig: Breitkopf & Härtel, 1896. Translated by William E. Hettrick as *The 'Musia instrumentalis deudsch' of Martin Agricola: A Treatise on Musical Instruments, 1529 and 1545*. Cambridge: Cambridge University Press, 1994.

Albrecht, Theodore. "Beethoven's Brass Players: New Discoveries in Composer-Performer Relations." *Historic Brass Society Journal* 18 (2006): 47–72.

Anderson, Stephen C. "Selected Works from the 17th-Century Music Collection of Prince-Bishop Karl Liechtenstein-Kastelkorn: A Study of the Soloistic Use of the Trombone." *ITA Journal* 11 (Jan. 1983): 17–20; 11 (Apr. 1983): 35–38; 11 (July 1983): 29–32; 11 (Oct. 1983): 20–22; 12 (Jan. 1984): 33–37; 12 (Apr. 1984): 32–38.

Anderson, Thomas Jerome. "The Collegium Musicum Salem, 1780–1790: Origins and Repertoire." Ph.D. diss., Florida State University, 1976.

Anglès, Higinio. "Alfonso V d'Aragona mecenate della musica ed il suo ménestral Jean Boisard." In *Hygini Anglés: Scripta musicologica*, edited by Joseph Lopéz-Calo, 3 vols., 765–78. Rome: Edizione de Storia e Letteratura, 1975–76 (=HASM).

——. "Die Instrumentalmusik bis zum 16. Jahrhundert in Spanien." In *HASM*, 1415–42.

——. *La música en la corte de Carlos V*. Vol. 1. Barcelona: Consejo Superior de Investigaciones Científicas, 1965.

——. "La música en la corte del Rey Don Alfonso V de Aragon, el Magnánimo (años 1413–1420)." In *HASM*, 913–62.

——. "La música en la corte real de Aragón y de Nápoles durante el reinado de Alfonso en Magnànimo." In *HASM*, 963–1028.

——. "Spanien in der Musikgeschichte des 15. Jahrhunderts." In *HASM*, 869–911.

Anthon, Carl Gustav. "Music and Musicians in Northern Italy during the Sixteenth Century." Ph.D. diss., Harvard University, 1943.

Arnold, Denis. *Giovanni Gabrieli and the Music of the Venetian High Renaissance*. London: Oxford University Press, 1979.

———. "Orchestras in Eighteenth-Century Venice." *Galpin Society Journal* 19 (1966): 3–19.

Artusi, Giovanni Maria. *L'Artusi, ouero Delle imperfettioni della moderna musica*. Venice: Giacomo Vincenti, 1600.

Ashbee, Andrew. "Groomed for Service: Musicians in the Privy Chamber at the English Court, c. 1495–1558." *Early Music* 25 (1997): 185–97.

———. *Records of English Court Music*. Hants, England: Scolar Press, 1986–95.

Ashbee, Andrew, and David Lasocki. *A Biographical Dictionary of English Court Musicians 1485–1714*. Aldershot, England: Ashgate, 1998.

Atlas, Allan W. *Music at the Aragonese Court of Naples*. Cambridge: Cambridge University Press, 1985.

Baines, Anthony. *Brass Instruments: Their History and Development*. New York: Scribner, 1978.

———. "Fifteenth-Century Instruments in Tinctoris's *De Inventione et Usu Musicae*." *Galpin Society Journal* 3 (1950): 19–26.

———. "James Talbot's Manuscript (Christ Church Library Music MS 1187). I. Wind Instruments." *Galpin Society Journal* 1 (1948): 9–26.

———. "Two Cassel Inventories." *Galpin Society Journal* 4 (1951): 30–38.

Baker, Buddy. "Why? How about Who, Where, What, When? The Development of Berio's *Sequenza V*." *ITA Journal* 22 (Spring 1994): 30–33.

Baker, David N. *Contemporary Techniques for the Trombone*. New York: Charles Colin, 1974.

Baker, Geoffrey. "Music at Corpus Christi in Colonial Cuzco." *Early Music* 32 (2004): 355–67.

Banks, Jon. "Performing Instrumental Music in the Segovia Codex." *Early Music* 27 (1999): 295–309.

Barblan, Guglielmo. "Vita musicale alla corte sforzesca." In *Storia di Milano*, edited by Giovanni Treccani degli Alfieri, 16 vols., 9:787–852. Milan: Fondazione Treccani degli Alfieri, 1961.

Barclay, Robert. *The Art of the Trumpet-Maker: The Materials, Tools, and Techniques of the Seventeenth and Eighteenth Centuries in Nuremberg*. Oxford: Clarendon Press, 1992.

Baroncini, Rodolfo. "Zorzi Trombetta and the Band of *Piffari* and Trombones of the *Serenissima*: New Documentary Evidence." Translated by Hugh Ward-Perkins. *Historic Brass Society Journal* 14 (2002): 59–82.

———. "Zorzi Trombetta da Modon and the Founding of the Band of *Piffari* and *Tromboni* of the *Serenissima*." *Historic Brass Society Journal* 16 (2004): 1–17.

Battisti, Frank L. *The Winds of Change: The Evolution of the Contemporary American Wind Band/Ensemble and Its Conductor*. Galesville, Md.: Meredith Music Publications, 2002.

Bauer, Paul. "The Trombones in the Orchestras of Stan Kenton." *ITA Journal* 10 (July 1982): 23–26; 10 (Oct. 1982): 16–24.

Beaujoyeulx, Balthazar de. *Le balet comique*. Facsimile edition with introduction by Margaret M. McGowan. Binghamton, N.Y.: Center for Medieval & Early Renaissance Studies, 1982.

Benton, Rita. *Ignace Pleyel: A Thematic Catalogue of His Compositions*. New York: Pendragon, 1977.

Berardi, Angelo. *Miscellanea musicale*. Bologna: Giacomo Monti, 1689.

Berlioz, Hector. *Grand traité d'instrumentation et d'orchestration modernes* (1843, 1855). Edited by Peter Bloom. Kassel: Bärenreiter, 2003. English translation by Hugh MacDonald as *Berlioz's Orchestration Treatise: A Translation and Commentary*. Cambridge: Cambridge University Press, 2002.

———. *Instrumentenslehre*. Revised and enlarged by Richard Strauss. Leipzig: C. F. Peters, 1904. Translated by Theodore Front as *Treatise on Instruments*. New York: Kalmus, 1948.

Bermúdez, Egberto. "The *Ministriles* Tradition in Latin America: Part One: South America 1. The Cases of Santafe (Colombia) and La Plata (Bolivia) in the Seventeenth Century." *Historic Brass Society Journal* 11 (1999): 149–62.

———. "Urban Musical Life in the European Colonies: Spanish America, 1530–1650." In *Music and Musicians in Renaissance Cities and Towns*, edited by Fiona Kisby, 167–80. Cambridge: Cambridge University Press, 2001.

Bessaraboff, Nicholas. *Ancient European Musical Instruments*. Cambridge, Mass.: Harvard University Press, 1941.

Besseler, Heinrich. "Die Entstehung der Posaune." *Acta musicologica* 22 (1950): 8–35.

Blackburn, Bonnie J. "Music and Festivities at the Court of Leo X: A Venetian View." *Early Music History* 11 (1992): 1–37.

Bloom, Peter. "The Public for Orchestral Music in the Nineteenth Century." In *The Orchestra: Origins and Transformations*, edited by Joan Peyser, 251–81. New York: Scribner, 1986.

Boltinghouse, Jim. "Hoyt's Garage." *ITA Journal* 24 (Spring 1996): 32–35.

Bonime, Stephen. "The Musicians of the Royal Stable under Charles VIII and Louis XII (1484–1514)." *Current Musicology* 25 (1978): 7–21.

Bonta, Stephen. "The Use of Instruments in Sacred Music in Italy, 1560–1700." *Early Music* 18 (1990): 519–35.

———. "The Uses of Sonata da Chiesa." *Journal of the American Musicological Society* 22 (1969): 54–84.

Borch, Gaston. *Practical Manual of Instrumentation*. Boston: Boston Music Co., 1918.

Bosch, Ben van den. *The Origin and Development of the Trombone-Work of the Moravian Churches in Germany and All the World*. Translated by C. Daniel Crews. Winston-Salem, N.C.: Moravian Music Foundation, 1990.

Bottrigari, Ercole. *Il desiderio overo De' concerti di varii strumenti musicali* (Venice, 1594, 2nd ed. 1599). Facs ed. of 1599 ed. Edited by Kathi Meyer-Baer. Berlin: Martin Breslauer, 1924.

Translation by Carol MacClintock. n.p.: American Institute of Musicology, 1962.

Bouckaert, Bruno, and Eugeen Schreurs. "Hans Nagel, Performer and Spy in England and Flanders (ca. 1490–1531)." In *Tielman Susato and the Music of His Time: Print Culture, Compositional Technique, and Instrumental Music in the Renaissance*, edited by Keith Polk, 101–15. Hillsdale, N.Y.: Pendragon, 2005.

Bowles, Edmund A. *Musical Ensembles in Festival Books, 1500–1800: An Iconographical & Documentary Survey*. Ann Arbor, Mich.: UMI Research Press, 1989.

———. "The Role of Musical Instruments in the Medieval Sacred Drama." *Musical Quarterly* 45 (1959): 67–84.

———. "Were Musical Instruments Used in the Liturgical Services during the Middle Ages?" *Galpin Society Journal* 10 (1957): 40–56.

Braun, André. See Weiner, Howard, "André Braun's *Gamme et méthod . . .*"

Bridges, Glenn. *Pioneers in Brass*. Published on CD-ROM, Trescott Research, 2001.

Brown, Clive. "The Orchestra in Beethoven's Vienna." *Early Music* 16 (1988): 4–20.

Brown, Howard Mayer. "A Cook's Tour of Ferrara in 1529." *Rivista italiana di musicologia* 16 (1975): 216–41.

———. "Instruments and Voices in the Fifteenth-Century Chanson." In *Current Thought in Musicology*, edited by John W. Grubbs, 89–138. Austin: University of Texas Press, 1976.

———. "Minstrels and Their Repertory in Fifteenth-Century France: Music in an Urban Environment." In *Urban Life in the Renaissance*, edited by Susan Zimmerman and Ronald F. E. Weissman, 142–64. Newark: University of Delaware Press, 1989.

———. *Music in the French Secular Theater, 1400–1550*. Cambridge, Mass.: Harvard University Press, 1963.

———. *Sixteenth Century Instrumentation: The Music for the Florentine Intermedii*. n.p.: American Institute of Musicology, 1973.

Brown, Maurice J. E. *Schubert: A Critical Biography*. London: Macmillan, 1958.

Broyles, Michael. *Music of the Highest Class: Elitism and Populism in Antebellum Boston*. New Haven, Conn.: Yale University Press, 1992.

Bruns, Robert. "Jack Teagarden: His Career and Music." *ITA Journal* 35 (Jan. 2007): 22–26.

Buonanni, Filippo. *Gabinetto armonico*. Rome: Giorgio Placho, 1722. Facsimile reprint of the plates with new captions by Frank Ll. Harrison and Joan Rimmer. *The Showcase of Musical Instruments*. New York: Dover, 1964.

Burney, Charles. *An Account of the Musical Performances in Westminster-Abbey, and the Pantheon, May 26th, 27th, 29th; and June the 3d, and 5th, 1784: In Commemoration of Handel*. London: T. Payne, 1785.

Burrows, Donald. "Handel, the Dead March, and a Newly Identified Trombone Movement." *Early Music* 18 (1990): 408–16.

Burton, Johathan. "Orchestration." In *The Wagner Compendium*, edited by Barry Millington, 334–49. New York: Schirmer Books, 1992.

Butler, Bartlett Russell. "Liturgical Music in Sixteenth-Century Nürnberg: A Socio-Musical Study." Ph.D. diss., University of Illinois, 1970.

Butler, Charles. *The Principles of Musick, in Singing and Setting: With the Two-Fold Use Thereof (Ecclesiastical and Civil)*. London: John Haviland, 1636.

Callison, Hugh Anthony. "Nineteenth-Century Orchestral Trombone Playing in the United States." D.A. diss., Ball State University, 1986.

Camus, Raoul. "The Military Band in the United States Army prior to 1834." Ph.D. diss., New York University, 1969.

Carlini, Antonio. "Le bande musicali nell'Italia dell'Ottocento: Il modello militare, i rapporti con il teatro e la cultura dell'orchestra negli organici strumentali." *Rivista italiana di musicologia* 30 (1995): 85–133.

Carse, Adam. *The History of Orchestration*. London: Kegan Paul, 1925. Reprinted, New York: Dover, 1964.

———. *Musical Wind Instruments: A History of the Wind Instruments Used in European Orchestras and Wind-Bands from the Later Middle Ages up to the Present Time*. London: Macmillan, 1939. Reprinted, New York: Da Capo, 1965.

———. *The Orchestra from Beethoven to Berlioz*. Cambridge: W. Heffer, 1948.

———. "The Prince Regent's Band." *Music & Letters* 27 (1946): 147–55.

Carter, Stewart. "Early Trombones in America's Shrine to Music Museum." *Historic Brass Society Journal* 10 (1998): 92–115.

———. "Georges Kastner on Brass Instruments: The Influence of Technology on the Theory of Orchestration." In *Perspectives on Brass Scholarship*, edited by Stewart Carter, 171–92. Stuyvesant, N.Y.: Pendragon, 1997.

———. "The String Tremolo in the 17th Century." *Early Music* 19 (1990): 43–59.

———. "Trombone Obbligatos in Viennese Oratorios of the Baroque." *Historic Brass Society Journal* 2 (1990): 52–77.

———. "Trombone Pitch in the Eighteenth Century: An Overview." In *Posaunen und Trompeten: Geschichte, Akustik, Spieltechnik*, edited by Monika Lustig and Howard Weiner, 53–66. Blankenburg: Stiftung Kloster Michaelstein, 2000.

Carter, Tim. "A Florentine Wedding of 1608." *Acta musicologica* 55 (1983): 89–107.

Castellani, Marcello. "A 1593 Veronese Inventory." *Galpin Society Journal* 26 (1973): 15–24.

Cerone, Pietro. *El Melopeo y Maestro*. Naples: I.G. Gargano and L. Nucci, 1613.

Chafe, Eric Thomas. *The Church Music of Heinrich Biber*. Ann Arbor, Mich.: UMI Research Press, 1987.

Cipolla, Carlo M. *Fighting the Plague in Seventeenth-Century Italy*. Madison: University of Wisconsin Press, 1981.

Clarke, Hamilton. *A Manual of Orchestration*. London: J. Curwen, [1888].

Conati, Marcello, and Marcello Pavarani, eds. *Orchestre in Emilia-Romagna nell'ottocento e novecento.* Parma: Orchestra Sinfonica dell'Emilia-Romagna "Arturo Toscanini," 1982.

Coon, Oscar. *Harmony and Instrumentation.* New York: Carl Fischer, 1883.

Cornette, Victor. *Méthode de trombone.* Paris: Richaut, 1831; German/French edition, Mainz: Schott, [between 1832 and 1835].

Cox, H. Bertram, and C. L. E. Cox. *Leaves from the Journals of Sir George Smart.* New York: Longmans, Green, 1907. Reprinted, New York: Da Capo Press, 1971.

Crabtree, Philip. "The Vocal Works of Gioseffo (ca. 1540–1611) and Francesco Guami (ca. 1544–1602)." Ph.D. diss., University of Cincinnati, 1971.

Craven, Robert R., ed. *Symphony Orchestras of the United States: Selected Profiles.* New York: Greenwood Press, 1986.

———. *Symphony Orchestras of the World: Selected Profiles.* New York: Greenwood Press, 1987.

Crookes, David Z. *See* Praetorius, Michael, *Syntagma musicum: Tomus secundus; De organographia.*

Cucuel, Georges. *Études sur un orchestre au 18me siècle.* Paris: Fischbacher, 1913.

Cummings, Anthony M. *The Politicized Muse: Music for the Medici Festivals, 1512–1537.* Princeton, N.J.: Princeton University Press, 1992.

Cuyler, Louise. "Music in Biographies of Emperor Maximilian." In *Aspects of Medieval and Renaissance Music,* edited by Jan LaRue, 111–21. New York: Norton, 1966.

D'Accone, Frank. "Music at the Siennese Cathedral in the Later 16th Century." In *Report of the 14th Congress of the International Musicological Society (Bologna 1987),* 3:729–31. Turin: Edizioni di Torino, 1990.

———. "The Performance of Sacred Music in Italy during Josquin's Time, c. 1475–1525." In *Josquin des Prez,* edited by Edward E. Lowinsky, 601–18. London: Oxford University Press, 1976.

Dalmonte, Rossana. *Camillo Cortellini: Madrigalista Bolognese.* Florence: Oschki, 1980.

Damon, Sherri Marcia. "The Trombone in the Shout Band of the United House of Prayer for All People." D.M.A. essay, University of North Carolina at Greensboro, 1999.

Dart, Thurston. "The Repertory of the Royal Wind Music." *Galpin Society Journal* 11 (1958): 70–77.

De Keyser, Ignace. "The Paradigm of Industrial Thinking in Brass Instrument Making during the Nineteenth Century." *Historic Brass Society Journal* 15 (2003): 233–58.

Dean, Winton. *Handel's Dramatic Oratorios and Masques.* London: Oxford University Press, 1959.

DelDonna, Anthony. "Behind the Scenes: The Musical Life and Organizational Structure of the San Carlo Opera Orchestra in Late-18th Century Naples." In *Fonti d'archivio per la storia della musica e dello spettacolo a Napoli tra XVI e XVIII secolo,* edited by Paologiovanni Maione, 427–48. Naples: Editorial Scientifica, 2001.

———. "Production Practices at the Teatro di San Carlo, Naples, in the Late 18th Century." *Early Music* 30 (2002): 429–45.

Dempster, Stuart. *The Modern Trombone: A Definition of Its Idiom.* Berkeley: University of California Press, 1979.

Deutsch, Otto Erich. *Franz Schubert Thematisches Verzeichnis seiner Werke in chronologischer Folge.* New edition by Werner Aderhold. Kassel: Bärenreiter, 1978.

Devlin, Michelle Poland. "The Contributions of Tommy Pederson (1920–1988) to Trombone Performance and Literature in the Twentieth Century." D.M.A. essay, University of North Carolina at Greensboro, 2007. libres.uncg.edu/edocs/etd/1303/umi-uncg-1303.pdf

Dieppo, Antoine. *Méthode complète pour le trombonnne: Adoptée pour l'enseignement de cet instrument dans les classes du Conservatoire de Musique.* Paris: Troupenas, 1837.

Dietrich, Kurt. *Duke's 'Bones: Ellington's Great Trombonists.* Rottenburg, Germany: Advance Music, 1995.

———. *Jazz 'Bones: The World of Jazz Trombone.* Rottenburg, Germany: Advance Music, 2005.

Dobbins, Frank. *Music in Renaissance Lyons.* Oxford: Clarendon Press, 1992.

Dodworth, Allen. *Dodworth's Brass Band School.* New York: H. B. Dodworth, 1853. Facsimile reprint, Mendocino, Calif.: Lark in the Morning, 1980.

Doorslaer, Georges van. "La chapelle musicale de Philippe le Beau." *Revue belge d'archéologie et d'histoire de l'art* 4 (1934): 21–57, 139–65.

Doppelmayr, Johann Gabriel. *Historische Nachricht von der Nürnbergischen Mathematicis und Künstlern.* Nuremberg: P. C. Monath, 1730. Fascimile reprint, Hildesheim: G. Olds, 1972.

Dörffel, Alfred. *Geschichte der Gewandhausconcerte zu Leipzig vom 25. November 1781 bis 25. November 1881.* Leipzig, 1884.

Downey, Peter. "Adam Drese's 1648 Funeral Music and the Invention of the Slide Trumpet." In *Musicology in Ireland,* edited by Gerard Gillen and Harry White, 200–217. Dublin: Irish Academic Press, 1990.

———. "From the Rim to the Hub: Fortuna's Wheel and Instrumental Music at the German-Speaking Renaissance Courts." In *Perspectives in Brass Scholarship,* edited by Stewart Carter, 1–18. Stuyvesant, N.Y.: Pendragon, 1997.

———. "'In tubis ductilibus et voce tubae': Trumpets, Slides, and Performance Practices in Late Medieval and Renaissance Europe." In *Music and the Church,* edited by Gerard Gillen and Harry White, 302–32. Dublin: Irish Academic Press, 1993.

———. "The Renaissance Slide Trumpet: Fact or Fiction?" *Early Music* 12 (1984): 26–33.

Duffin, Ross. "Backward Bells and Barrel Bells: Some Notes on the Early History of Loud Instruments." *Historic Brass Society Journal* 9 (1997): 113–29.

Dundas, Richard J. *Twentieth Century Brass Musical Instruments in the United States,* rev. ed. Norwood, Mass.: Bryant Altman, 1998.

"Early Orchestras: Some Contemporary Accounts." *Galpin Society Journal* 1 (1948): 27.

Edge, Dexter. "Mozart's Viennese Orchestras." *Early Music* 20 (1992): 64–88.

Egan, Geoff. "A Late Medieval Trumpet from Billingsgate." *London Archaeologist* 5, no. 6 (1986): 168.

Ehmann, Willhelm. "100 Jahre Kuhlo-Posaunenbuch." *Brass Bulletin* 38 (1982): 33–53.

Elders, Willem. "The Performance of Cantus Firmi in Josquin's Masses Based on Secular Monophonic Song." *Early Music* 17 (1989): 330–41.

Encyclopedia of Music in Canada, 2nd ed. Toronto: University of Toronto Press, 1992, s.v. "Opera performance," "Orchestras."

États de la France (1644–1789): La musique. Recherches sur la musique française classique 30: *La vie musicale en France sous les rois Bourbons*. Paris: Picard, 2003.

Everett, Tom. "J. J. Johnson: On the Road Again." *ITA Journal* 16 (Summer 1988): 22–29.

———. "J. J. Johnson: The Architect of the Modern Jazz Trombone." *ITA Journal* 16 (Spring 1988): 31–35.

Farkas, Philip. *The Art of Brass Playing*. Bloomington, Ind.: Brass Publications, 1962.

Federhofer, Hellmut. "Biographische Beiträge zu Erasmus Lapicida und Stephan Mahu." *Die Musikforschung* 5 (1952): 37–46.

Fenlon, Iain. *Music and Patronage in Sixteenth-Century Mantua*. 2 vols. Cambridge: Cambridge University Press, 1980.

Ferrari, Giacomo Gotifredo. *Aneddoti piacevoli e interessanti occorsi nella vita di Giacomo Gotifredo Ferrari*. 2 vols. London: Self-Published, 1830.

Fetis, François-Joseph. *Manuel des compositeurs, directeurs de musique, chef d'orchestre & de musique militaire, or Traité méthodique de l'harmonie, des instrumens, des voix et de tout ce qui est relatif à la composition, à la direction et à l'execution de la musique*. Paris: Schlesinger, [1837].

———. "Notice sur Ignace Pleyel." *La revue musicale* 5, no. 43 (Dec. 3, 1831): 344–47.

———. "On the Revolutions of the Orchestra." *Harmonicon* 6 (1828): 194–97.

Fiedler, Eric F. "Zingen, Pumart, Pusaun: The Manuscript Regensburg, Bischöfliche Zentralbibliothek, MS A.R. 775–777 as a Source of Information about Wind-Band Performing Practice in Late Sixteenth-Century Southern Germany." In *Festschrift für Winfried Kirsch zum 65. Geburtstag*, edited by Peter Ackermann, Ulrike Kienzle, and Adolf Nowak, 34–48. Tutzing: Schneider, 1996.

Fink, Reginald H. *The Trombonist's Handbook*. Athens, Ohio: Accura Music, 1977.

Fischer, Henry George. *The Renaissance Sackbut and Its Use Today*. New York: Metropolitan Museum of Art, 1984.

———. "The Tenor Sackbut of Anton Schnitzer the Elder at Nice." *Historic Brass Society Journal* 1 (1989): 65–74.

Flandrin, M. G. "Le Trombone." In *Encyclopédie de la musique et dictionnaire du conservatoire*. Part II, *Technique, esthétique, pédagogie: 3. Technique instrumentale*, 1649–59. Paris: Librarie Delagrave, 1927.

Forney, Kristine K. "Music, Ritual and Patronage at the Church of Our Lady, Antwerp." *Early Music History* 7 (1987): 1–57.

———. "New Documents of the Life of Tielman Susato, Sixteenth-Century Music Printer and Musician." *Revue belge de musicologie* 36–38 (1982–1984): 18–52.

———. "New Insights into the Career and Musical Contributions of Tielman Susato." In *Tielman Susato and the Music of His Time: Print Culture, Compositional Technique, and Instrumental Music in the Renaissance*, edited by Keith Polk, 1–44. Hillsdale, N.Y.: Pendragon, 2005.

Forsyth, Cecil. *Orchestration*. 2nd ed. London: Macmillan, 1935.

Francoeur, Louis Joseph. *Traité général des voix et des instruments d'orchestre: Nouvelle édition revue et augmentée des insntruments modernes*. Edited by Alexandre Choron. Paris: Aux adresses ordinaires de musique, [1813].

Freeman, Robert N. *Franz Schneider (1737–1812): A Thematic Catalogue of His Works*. New York: Pendragon, 1979.

———. "The Fux Tradition and the Mystery of the Music Archive at Melk Abbey." In *Johann Joseph Fux and the Music of the Austro-Italian Baroque*, edited by Harry White, 18–39. Aldershot, England: Scolar Press, 1992.

———. *The Practice of Music at Melk Abbey, Based upon the Documents, 1681–1826*. Vienna: Österreichischen Akademie der Wissenschaften, 1989.

Fröhlich, Joseph. *Vollständige theoretisch- pracktisch Musikschule*. Vol. 3. Bonn: Simrock, 1811.

Galilei, Vincenzo. *Dialogo di Vincentio Galilei nobile fiorentino della musica antica, et della moderna*. Florence: G. Marescotti, 1581. Translated by Claude V. Palisca as *Dialog on Ancient and Modern Music*. New Haven, Conn.: Yale University Press, 2003.

Gallo, Stanislao. *The Modern Band*. Boston: Birchard, 1935.

Galpin, Francis W. "The Sackbut, Its Evolution and History." *Proceedings of the Musical Association* 33 (1906): 1–25.

Gambassi, Osvaldo. *L'Accademia Filarmonico di Bologna: Fonddazione, statuti e aggregazioni*. Florence: Olschki, 1992.

———. *La capella musicale de S. Petronia: Maestri, organisti, cantori e strumentisti dal 1436 al 1920*. Florence: Olschki, 1987.

———. *Il Concerto Palatino della signoria di Bologna: Cinque secoli di vita musical a corte (1250–1797)*. Florence: Olschki, 1989.

Gevaert, François-Auguste. *Nouveau traité d'instrumentation*. Paris: Lemoine & Fils, 1885. English translation by E. F. E. Suddard as *A New Treatise on Instrumentation*. Paris: Henry Lemoine, 1906.

Ghisi, Federico. "La tradition musicale des fêtes et les origines de l'opera." In *Les fêtes du mariage de Ferdinand de Médicis et de Christine de Lorraine, Florence 1589: I. Musique des intermèdes de "La Pellegrina*, edited by D. P. Walker, xi–xxii. Paris: Centre National de la Recherche Scientifique, 1963.

Glixon, Jonathan. "Music at the Venetian 'Scuole Grandi,' 1440–1540." Ph.D. diss., Princeton University, 1979.

Gomez, Maricarmen. "Minstrel Schools in the Late Middle Ages." *Early Music* 18 (1990): 213–15.

Gossec, François-Joseph. "Notice sur l'introduction des cors, des clarinettes et des trombones dans les orchestres français, extraite des manuscrits autographes de Gossec." *Revue musicale* 5 (1829): 217–23.

Gould, Ronald L. "The Latin Lutheran Mass at Wittenberg, 1523–1545: A Survey of the Early Reformation Mass and the Lutheran Theology of Music. . . ." D.S.M. diss., Union Theological Seminary, 1970.

[Grove's] A *Dictionary of Music and Musicians*. Edited by George Grove, 4 vols. London: Macmillan, 1879–89, s.v. "Sackbut" by William H. Stone and "Trombone" by William H. Stone.

Grove's Dictionary of Music and Musicians. 2nd. ed. Edited by J. A. Fuller Maitland, 5 vols. Philadelphia: Theodore Presser, 1914, s.v. "Sackbut" by Francis W. Galpin and "Trombone" by William H. Stone and David J. Blaikley.

———. 3rd ed. Edited by H. C. Colles, 5 vols. London: Macmillan, 1927–28, s.v. "Trombone" by Nicholas Comyn Gatty.

———. 4th ed. Edited by H. C. Colles, 6 vols. London: Macmillan, 1940, s.v. "Trombone" by Nicholas Comyn Gatty.

———. 5th ed. Edited by Eric Blom, 20 vols. London: Macmillan, 1954, s.v. "Trombone" by Anthony Baines.

Grove Music Online. www.oxfordmusiconline.com/. Proprietary database, available by subscription only.

Guion, David M. "25 Years of Trombone Recitals: An Examination of Programs Published by the International Trombone Association." *ITA Journal* 27 (Winter 1999): 22–29.

———. "Felippe Cioffi: A Trombonist in Antebellum America." *American Music* 14 (1996): 1–41.

———. "Four American Trombone Soloists before Arthur Pryor: Some Preliminary Findings." *ITA Journal* 20 (Fall 1997): 32–37.

———. "From Yankee Doodle Thro' to Handel's Largo: Music at the World's Columbian Exposition." *College Music Symposium* 24 (1984): 81–96.

———. "Great but Forgotten Trombonists: Some Biographical Sketches." *Brass Bulletin* 97 (1997): 62–73.

———. "The Instrumentation of Operas Published in France in the 18th Century." *Journal of Musicological Research* 4 (1982): 115–43.

———. "The Missing Link: The Trombone in Italy in the 17th and 18th centuries." *Early Music* 34 (2006): 227–30.

———. "On the Trail of the Medieval Slide Trumpet." *Brass Bulletin* 109 (2000): 90–97; 110 (2000): 46–54

———. "Recital Repertoire of the Trombone as Shown by Programs Published by the International Trombone Association." *Online Trombone Journal* (1999). www.trombone.org/articles/library/recitalrep.asp

———. "Theories of Tuning and Ensemble Practice in Italian Dramatic Music of the Early Baroque, or, Oh Where, Oh Where Have the Wind Instruments Gone?" *Historic Brass Society Journal* 12 (2000): 230–43.

———. *The Trombone: Its History and Music, 1697–1811*. New York: Gordon and Breach, 1988.

———. "What Handel Taught the Viennese about the Trombone." *Historic Brass Society Journal* 15 (2003): 291–321.

———. "Wind Bands in Towns, Courts, and Churches: Middle Ages to Baroque." *Journal of Band Research* 42 (Spring 2007): 19–56.

Gushee, Lawrence. *Pioneers of Jazz: The Story of the Creole Band*. Oxford: Oxford University Press, 2003.

Hachenberg, Karl. "Brass in Central European Instrument-Making from the 16th through the 18th Centuries." Translated by Jutta Backes von Machui. *Historic Brass Society Journal* 4 (1992): 229–52.

———. "The Complaint of the Markneukirchen Brass-Instrument Makers about the Poor Quality of Brass from the Rodewich Foundry, 1787–1795." Translated by Howard Weiner. *Historic Brass Society Journal* 10 (1998): 116–45.

Hafar, Matthew A. "The Shout Band Tradition in the Southeastern United States." *Historic Brass Society Journal* 15 (2003): 163–71.

Hall, Harry H. "Early Sounds of Moravian Brass Music in America: A Cultural Note from Colonial Georgia." *Brass Quarterly* 7 (1964): 115–23.

———. "The Moravian Wind Ensemble: Distinctive Chapter in America's Music." Ph.D. diss., George Peabody College for Teachers, 1967.

Hannas, Ruth. "Cerone, Philosopher and Teacher." *Musical Quarterly* 21 (1935): 408–22.

Hazen, Margaret Hindle, and Robert M. Hazen, *The Music Men: An Illustrated History of Brass Bands in America, 1800–1920*. Washington, D.C.: Smithsonian Institution Press, 1987.

Heartz, Daniel. "The Basse Dance: Its Evolution circa 1450–1550." *Annales musicologiques* 6 (1958–63): 287–340.

———. "Hoftanz and Basse Dance." *Journal of the American Musicological Society* 19 (1966): 13–36.

Heide, Geert Jan van der. "Brass Instrument Metalworking Techniques: The Bronze Age to the Industrial Revolution." *Historic Brass Society Journal* 3 (1991): 121–50.

Herbert, James Wesley. "The Wind Band of Nineteenth-Century Italy: Its Origins and Transformation from the Late 1700's to Mid-Century." D.E. diss., Teachers College, Columbia University, 1986.

Herbert, Trevor. "Nineteenth-Century Bands: Making a Movement." In *The British Brass Band: A Musical and Social History*, edited by Trevor Herbert, 10–67. Oxford: Oxford University Press: 2000

———. "The Trombone in Britain before 1800." Ph.D. diss., Open University, 1984.

———. *The Trombone*. New Haven, Conn.: Yale University Press, 2006.

Herbert, Trevor, and Margaret Sarkissian. "Victorian Bands and Their Dissemination in the Colonies." *Popular Music* 16 (1997): 165–79.

Heuchemer, Dane. "Italian Musicians in Dresden in the Second Half of the Sixteenth Century, with an Emphasis on the Lives and Works of Antonio Scandello and Giovanni Battista Pinello di Ghirardi." Ph.D. diss., University of Cincinnati, 1997.

Heyde, Herbert. "The Brass Instrument Makers of Schmied of Pfaffendorf." In *Perspectives in Brass Scholarship*, edited by Stewart Carter, 91–113. Stuyvesant, N.Y.: Pendragon, 1997.

———. "Brass Instrument Making in Berlin from the 17th to the 20th Century: A Survey." *Historic Brass Society Journal* 3 (1991): 43–47.

———. *Trompeten, Posaunen, Tuben*. Leipzig: Deutscher Verlag für Musik, 1980.

Highfill, Philip, Jr., Kalman A. Burnim, and Edward A. Langhans. *A Biographical Dictionary of Actors, Actresses, Musicians, Dancers, Managers & Other Stage Personnel in London, 1660–1800*. 16 vols. Carbondale and Edwardsville: Southern Illinois University Press, 1973–93.

Hischack, Thomas S. *Stage It with Music: An Encyclopedic Guide to the American Musical Theatre*. Westport, Conn.: Greenwood Press, 1993.

Hitchcock, H. Wiley. *Music in the United States: A Historical Introduction*. 4th ed. Upper Saddle River, N.J.: Prentice-Hall, 2000.

Höfler, Janez. "Der 'Trompette de Menestrels' und sein Instrument." *Tijdschrift van de Vereniging voor Nederlandse Muziekgeschiedenis* 29 (1979): 92–132.

Holmes, Edward. *A Ramble among the Musicians of Germany*. London: Hunt and Clarke, 1828. Reprinted, New York: Da Capo, 1969.

Holomon, D. Kern. *The Société des Concerts du Conservatoire, 1828–1967*. Berkeley: University of California Press, 2004.

Hornbostel, Erich M., and Curt Sachs. "Classification of Musical Instruments: Translated from the Original German by Anthony Baines and Klaus P. Wachsmann." *Galpin Society Journal* 14 (1961): 3–29.

Horton, Julian. "Bruckner and the Symphony Orchestra." In *The Cambridge Companion to Bruckner*, edited by John Williamson, 138–69. Cambridge: Cambridge University Press, 2004.

Howey, Henry. "The Lives of *Hoftrompeter* and *Stadtpfeiffer* as Portrayed in Three Novels of Daniel Speer." *Historic Brass Society Journal* 3 (1991): 65–78.

Hulsen, Esaias van. *Repraesentatio der furstlichen Aufzug und Ritterspil*. 1616. Facsimile reprint of the plates with transcription of the original captions: *Stuttgarter Hoffeste*, edited by Ludwig Krapf and Christian Wagenknecht. Tübingen: Max Niemeyer, 1979.

Humphries, John. "John Smithies: Trombonist and Enigma." *Brass Bulletin* 101 (1998): 62–64.

———. "The Royal Academy of Music and Its Tradition." *Brass Bulletin* 101 (1998): 42–52.

"Hydraulic Forming Techniques Applied to the Manufacture of Musical Instruments: Interesting Methods Developed by Boosey & Hawkes, Ltd. Edgeware, Middx." *Machinery* (London) 82 (1953): 1089–99, 1194–96.

Isherwood, Robert M. *Music in the Service of the King: France in the Seventeenth Century*. Ithaca, N.Y.: Cornell University Press, 1973.

Jensen, Niels Martin. "The Instrumental Music for Small Ensemble of Antonio Bertali: The Sources." *Dansk aarbog for musikforskning* 20 (1992): 25–43.

Joppig, Gunther. "Vaclav Frantisek Červený: Leading European Inventor and Manufacturer." Translated by Veronica von der Lancken. *Historic Brass Society Journal* 4 (1992): 210–28.

Kalisch, Volker. "Posaunenchöre: Mission und Funktion." In *Kongressbericht: Mainz 1996*, edited by Eugen Brixel, 263–74. Tutzing: Schneider, 1998.

Kallai, Avishai. "Joachim Eggert: Authenticating the Premiere Performance of His E-Flat Symphony." *STM Online* 4 (2001). www.musik.uu.se/ssm/stmonline/vol_4/kallai/index.html

Kappey, J. A. *Military Music*. London: Boosey, [1894].

Kastner, Georges. *Manuel général de musique militaire a l'usage des armées françaises*. Paris: F. Didot, 1848; Reprinted, Geneva: Minkoff, 1973.

———. *Traité général d'instrumentation*. Paris: Prilipp, 1837; 2nd ed. with supplement, Paris: Prilipp, 1844.

Kavanaugh, Lee Hill. "Babes in Slideland." *ITA Journal* 24 (Fall 1996): 38–45.

Keane, James A. *A History of Music Education in the United States*. Hanover, N.H.: University Press of New England, 1982.

Kemp, Peter. *The Strauss Family: Portrait of a Musical Dynasty*. Tunbridge Wells, England: Baton Press, 1985.

Kennan, Kent. *The Technique of Orchestration*. New York: Prentice-Hall, 1952. 6th ed., with Donald Grantham, Upper Saddle River, N.J.: Prentice Hall, 2002.

Kenton, Egon. *Life and Works of Giovanni Gabrieli*. n.p.: American Institute of Musicology, 1967.

Kenyon de Pascal, Beryl. "Brass Instruments and Instrumentalists in the Spanish Royal Chapel from the Late Seventeenth to Mid-Eighteenth Centuries." In *Brass Music at the Cross Roads of Europe*, edited by Keith Polk, 69–83. Utrecht: Foundation for Historical Performance Practice, 2005.

———. "A Brief Survey of the Late Spanish Bajón." *Galpin Society Journal* 37 (1984): 72–79.

———. "The Wind Instrument Maker, Bartolomé de Selma (†1616), His Family and Workshop." *Galpin Society Journal* 39 (1986): 21–34.

Kinder, Keith William. *The Wind and Wind-Chorus Music of Anton Bruckner*. Westport, Conn.: Greenwood Press, 2000.

Kircher, Athanasius. *Musurgia universalis*. Rome: F. Corbeletti, 1650. Translated by Frederick Baron Crane as "Athanasius Kircher, *Musurgia universalis* (Rome, 1650): The Section on Musical Instruments." M.A. thesis: University of Iowa, 1956.

Kirchner, Bill, ed. *The Oxford Companion to Jazz*. New York: Oxford University Press, 2000.

Kirk, Douglas. "Churching the Shawms in Renaissance Spain: 'Lerma, Archivo de San Pedro Ms. Mus.1.'" Ph.D. diss., McGill University, 1993.

———. "Instrumental Music in Lerma, c.1608." *Early Music* 23 (1995): 393–408.

Kirkendale, Warren. *The Court Musicians in Florence during the Principate of the Medici, with a Reconstruction of the Artistic Establishment.* Florence: Olschki, 1993.

Kirnbauer, Martin. "Die Nürnberger Trompeten- und Posaunenmacher vor 1500 im Spiegel Nürnberger Quellen." In *Musik und Tanz zur Zeit Kaiser Maximilian I,* edited by Walter Salmen, 131–42. Innsbruck: Helbling, 1992.

Kisby, Fiona. "Royal Minstrels in the City and Suburbs of Early Tudor London: Professional Activities and Private Interests." *Early Music* 25 (1997): 212–23.

Kleinhammer, Edward. *The Art of Trombone Playing.* Evanston, Ill.: Summy-Birchard, 1963.

Kleinhammer, Edward, and Douglas Yeo. *Mastering the Trombone.* Hannover, Germany: Edition Piccolo, 1997.

Kmen, Henry A. *Music in New Orleans: The Formative Years, 1791–1841.* Baton Rouge: Louisiana State University Press, 1966.

Knighton, Tess. "Music and Musicians at the Court of Fernando of Aragon, 1474–1516." Ph.D. diss., University of Cambridge, 1983.

Köchel, Ludwig von. *Die kaiserliche Hof-musikkappelle in Wien von 1543 bis 1867.* Vienna: Beck'sche Universitätsbuchhandlung, 1869.

Koetting, James T. "Africa/Ghana." In *Worlds of Music: An Introduction to the Music of the World's Peoples,* 2nd ed., edited by Jeff Todd Titon, 67–105. New York: Schirmer Books, 1992.

Korrick, Leslie. "Instrumental Music in the Early 16th-Century Mass: New Evidence." *Early Music* 18 (1990): 359–70.

Koury, Daniel J. *Orchestral Performance Practices in the Nineteenth Century: Size, Proportion, and Seating.* Ann Arbor, Mich.: UMI Research Press, 1986.

Kozma, Tibor. "Heros of Wood and Brass: The Trombone in Aida." *Opera News* 16 (Mar. 3, 1952): 30–31.

Krause, Sebastian. "Der Posaunengott." *Brass Bulletin* 117 (2002): 68–80.

Kreitner, Kenneth. "Minstrels in Spanish Churches, 1400–1600." *Early Music* 20 (1992): 532–46.

———. "Music and Civic Ceremony in Late Fifteenth-Century Barcelona." Ph.D. diss., Duke University, 1990.

Krivokapic, Igor. "La musique de cuivres en Slovénie: Compterendu historique, 1ère partie." *Brass Bulletin* 105 (1999): 50–58.

Lafosse, André. *Méthode complète de trombone à coulisse.* Nouvelle édition, 3 vols. Paris: Alphonse Leduc, 1946.

Lajarte, Théodore de. "Introduction du trombone dans l'orchestre de l'Opéra." *La chronique musicale* 6 (Oct.-Dec. 1874): 75–79.

Lampl, Hans. *See* Praetorius, Michael, *Syntagma musicum: Tomus tertuis; Termini musici.*

Landmann, Ortrun. "The Dresden Hofkapelle during the Lifetime of Johann Sebastian Bach." *Early Music* 17 (1989): 17–30.

Langwill, Lyndesay G. "Two Rare Eighteenth-Century London Directories." *Music & Letters* 30 (1949): 37–43.

———. "The Waites: A Short Historical Study." *Hinrichsen's Musical Yearbook* 7 (1953): 170–83.

Lapie, Raymond. "Une découverte sensationnelle: 12 grands quintettes de cuivres français originaux datant de 1848–1850!" *Brass Bulletin* 109 (2000): 32–43; 110 (2000): 58–71.

———. "French Chamber Music with Trombone (1795–1924): Bibliographic Notes." *ITA Journal* (Oct. 2002): 32–45.

———. "Le trombone d'après les traités d'orchestration (France, 1700–1914)." *Brass Bulletin* 105 (1999): 122–30; 107 (1999): 84–93.

Larkin, Chris. "Felicien David's *Nonetto en Ut Majeur:* A New Discovery and New Light on the Early Use of Valved Instruments in France." *Historic Brass Society Journal* 5 (1993): 192–202.

LaRue, Jan, and Howard Brofsky. "Parisian Brass Players, 1751–1793." *Brass Quarterly* 3 (1960): 133–40.

Lasocki, David. *The Bassanos: Venetian Musicians and Instrument Makers in England, 1531–1665.* Hants, England: Scolar Press, 1995.

Laurencie, L. de la. "La musique à la cour des ducs de Bretagne auz XIVe e XVe siècles." *Revue de musicologie* 14 (1935): 1–15.

Lawson, Grame. "Medieval Trumpet from the City of London, II." *Galpin Society Journal* 44 (1991): 150–56.

Lawson, Grame, and Geoff Egan. "Medieval Trumpet from the City of London." *Galpin Society Journal* 41 (1988): 63–66.

Lee, William R. "Wind Music of the Baroque: J. G. C. Stoerl and His Tower Sonatas." *Journal of Band Research* 20 (Fall 1984): 2–8.

Leonard, Charlotte A. "The Role of the Trombone and Its *Affekt* in the Lutheran Church Music of Seventeenth-Century Saxony and Thuringia: The Early Seventeenth-Century." *Historic Brass Society Journal* 10 (1998): 57–91.

———. "The Role of the Trombone and Its Affekt in the Lutheran Church Music of Seventeenth-Century Saxony and Thuringia: The Mid- and Late-Seventeenth Century." *Historic Brass Society Journal* 12 (2000): 161–209.

Lesure, François. *Musique et musiciens français du XVIe siecle.* Geneva: Minkoff, 1976.

Liessem, Franz. "Phileno Agostino Cornazzani, oberster Instrumentalist der herzoglichen Hofkapelle zu München under Orlando di Lasso." *Die Musikforschung* 24 (1970): 368–85.

Lindsay, Robert. "Professional Music in the 1920s and the Rise of the Singing Trombone." *Online Trombone Journal* (2006). trombone.org/articles/library/viewarticles.asp?ArtID=275

Litchfield, Malcolm. "Giovanni Maria Artusi's L'Artusi, overo Delle imperfettioni della moderna musica." M.A. thesis, Brigham Young University, 1987.

Litterick, Louise. "Performing Franco-Netherlandish Secular Music of the Late Fifteenth Century." *Early Music* 8 (1980): 474–85.

Lockwood, Lewis. *Music in Renaissance Ferrara, 1400–1505: The Creation of a Musical Center in the Fifteenth Century.* Cambridge, Mass.: Harvard University Press, 1984.

Longyear, R. M. "The 'Banda sul Palco': Wind Bands in Nineteenth-Century Opera." *Journal of Band Research* 13 (Spring 1978): 25–40.

Luscinius, Ottmar. *Musurgia seu praxis Musicae.* Strasbourg: Joan Schott, 1536.

MacDonald, Hugh. "Berlioz's Orchestration: Human or Divine?" *Musical Times* 110 (1969): 255–58.

MacIntyre, Bruce C. *The Viennese Concerted Mass of the Early Classic Period.* Ann Arbor, Mich.: UMI Research Press, 1986.

Madeira, Louis C. *Annals of Music in Philadelphia and History of the Musical Fund Society from Its Organization in 1820 to the Year 1858.* Philadelphia: Lippincott, 1896; Reprinted, New York: Da Capo, 1973.

Mahillon, Victor. *Catalogue descriptif et analytique du Musée instrumental du Conservatoire royal de musique de Bruxelle: Avec un essai de classification méthodique de tous les instruments anciens et modernes.* 2nd ed., 5 vols. Ghent: Ad. Hoste, 1893–1912; vol. 5, Brussels: Th. Lombaerts, 1922; Reprinted, Brussels: Les Amis de la Musique, 1978.

———. *Le trombone: Son histoire, sa théorie, sa construction.* Brussels: Mahillon, 1906.

Marix, Jeanne. *Histoire de la musique et des musiciens de la cour de Bourgogne sous le règne de Philippe le Bon (1420–1467).* Strasbourg: Heitz, 1939.

Marpurg, Friedrich Wilhelm. *Historisch-Kritische Beyträge zur Aufnahme der Musik.* 5 vols. Berlin: Gottlieb August Lange, 1757.

Marsh, John. *Hints to Young Composers of Instrumental Music.* London: Clementi, Banger, Hyde, Collard & Davis, ca. 1807. Reprinted with an introduction by Charles Cudworth in *Galpin Society Journal* 18 (1965): 57–71.

———. *The John Marsh Journals: The Life and Times of a Gentleman Composer (1752–1828).* Edited by Brian Robins. Stuyvesant, N.Y.: Pendragon Press, 1998.

Marx, Adolf Bernhard. *Die Lehre von der musikalischen Komposition: Praktisch theoretisch.* Vierter Theil. Leipzig: Breitkopf & Härtel, 1847.

Marx, Hans Joachim. Introduction to *Arcangelo Corelli: Historisch-kritische Gesamtausgabe der musikalischen Werke.* Vol. 5: *Werke ohne Opuszahl,* 17–24. Edited by Hans Joachim Marx. Cologne: Arno Volk, 1976.

Mason, Lowell. *Musical Letters from Abroad.* New York: Mason Bros., 1854. Reprinted, New York: Da Capo, 1967.

———. *A Yankee Musician in Europe: The 1837 Journals of Lowell Mason.* Edited by Michael Broyles. Ann Arbor, Mich.: UMI Research Press, 1990.

Massinon, Eileen. "Joseph Alessi's Premiere of a Pulitzer Prize Winner." *ITA Journal* 24 (Spring 1996): 26–31.

Mathez, Jean-Pierre. "Antoine Courtois, Paris." *Brass Bulletin* 97 (1997): 76–85.

———. "Le quatuor Slokar." *Brass Bulletin* 106 (1999): 44–51.

Mattheson, Johann. *Der vollkommene Capellmeister.* Hamburg: Christian Herold, 1739. Translated by Ernest C. Harriss as *Johann Mattheson's "Der vollkommene Capellmeister": A Revised Translation with Critical Commentary.* Ann Arbor, Mich.: UMI Research Press, 1981.

Maxted, George. *Talking about the Trombone.* London: John Baker, 1970.

Mazola, Sandy R. "Bands and Orchestras at the World's Columbian Exposition." *American Music* 4 (1986): 404–24.

McGee, Timothy J. "Misleading Iconography: The Case of the 'Adimari Wedding Cassone.'" *Imago musicae* 9–12 (1992–1995): 39–157.

McGowan, Keith. "A Chance Encounter with a Unicorn? A Possible Sighting of the Renaissance Slide Trumpet." *Historic Brass Society Journal* 8 (1996): 90–101.

———. "The Prince and the Piper: *Haut, bas* and the Whole Body in Early Modern Europe." *Early Music* 27 (1999): 211–32.

———. "The World of the Early Sackbut Player: Flat or Round?" *Early Music* 22 (Aug. 1994): 441–66.

McKinnon, James. "The Meaning of the Patristic Polemic against Musical Instruments." *Current Musicology* 1 (1965): 69–82.

McVeigh, Simon. "The Professional Concert and Rival Subscription Series in London, 1783–1793." *R. M. A. Research Chronicle* 22 (1989): 1–135.

Meckna, Michael. *Twentieth-Century Brass Soloists.* Westport, Conn.: Greenwood Press, 1994.

Meer, John Henry van der. *Musikinstrumente von der Antike bis zur Gegenwart.* Munich: Prestel, 1983.

Mendoza de Arce, Daniel. *Music in Ibero-America to 1850: A Historical Survey.* Lanham, Md.: Scarecrow, 2001.

Mersenne, Marin. *Harmonie universelle, contenant la theorie et la practique de la musique.* Paris: Sebastian Cramoisy, 1636. Facsimile edition, Paris: Centre National de la Recherche Scientifique, 1963. Translated by Roger E. Chapman as *Harmonie universelle: The Books on Instruments.* The Hague: Martinus Nijhoff, 1957.

Meucci, Renato. "The Cimbasso and Related Instruments in 19th-Century Italy." Translated by William Waterhouse. *Galpin Society Journal* 49 (1996): 143–79.

———. "The Pelitti Firm: Makers of Brass Instruments in Nineteenth-Century Milan." Translated by Enrico Pelitti. *Historic Brass Society Journal* 6 (1994): 304–33.

Mezières, Philippe de. *Le songe du vieil pelerin (1389).* Edited by G. W. Coopland. Cambridge: Cambridge University Press, 1969.

Miller, Frederick Staten. "A Comprehensive Performance Project in Trombone Literature with an Essay on the Use of Trombone in the Music of Heinrich Schütz." D.M.A. essay, University of Iowa, 1974.

Miller, Robert. "The Miller Valve." *ITA Journal* 28 (Summer 2000): 43.

Miller, Rodney E. *Institutionalizing Music: The Administration of Music Programs in Higher Education.* Springfield, Ill.: Charles C. Thomas, 1993.

Minor, Andrew C., and Bonner Mitchell. *A Renaissance Entertainment: Festivities for the Marriage of Cosimo I, Duke of Florence, in 1539.* Columbia: University of Missouri Press, 1968.

Mitchell, Jon C. "The Kneller Hall Archives: The British Military Band Tradition in Manuscript." In *Kongressbericht Mainz 1996,* edited by Eugen Brixel, 11–30. Tutzing: Schneider, 1998.

Monson, Craig A. "Disembodied Voices: Music in the Nunneries of Bologna in the Midst of the Counter-Reformation." In *The Crannied Wall: Women, Religion, and the Arts in Early Modern Europe,* edited by Craig A. Monson, 191–209. Ann Arbor: University of Michigan Press, 1992.

Monteverdi, Claudio. *The Letters of Claudio Monteverdi.* Translated by Denis Stevens. London: Faber and Faber, 1980.

Moss, James C. "British Military Journals from 1845 through 1900: A Study of Instrumentation and Content with an Emphasis on Boosé's Military Journal." D.M.A. essay, University of Cincinnati, 2001.

Mount Edgcumbe, Richard. *Musical Reminiscences of the Earl of Mount Edgcumbe: Containing and Account of the Italian Opera in England from 1773 to 1834.* 4th ed. London: John Andrews and F. H. Wall, 1834. Reprinted, New York: Da Capo, 1973.

Myers, Arnold. "Brasswind Innovation and Output of Boosey & Co. in the Blaikley Era." *Historic Brass Society Journal* 14 (2002): 391–423.

———. "Brasswind Manufacturing at Boosey & Hawkes, 1930–1959." *Historic Brass Society Journal* 15 (2003): 55–72.

———. "Design, Technology and Manufacture since 1800." In *The Cambridge Companion to Brass Instruments,* edited by Trevor Herbert and John Wallace, 115–30. Cambridge: Cambridge University Press, 1997.

———, ed. *Historic Musical Instruments in the Edinburgh University Collection.* 2nd ed., vol. 2, part H, fasc. iii: *Trumpets and Trombones.* Edinburgh: Edinburgh University Collection of Historic Musical Instruments, 1998.

Myers, Arnold, and Niles Eldridge. "The Brasswind Production of Marthe Besson's London Factory." *Galpin Society Journal* 59 (2006): 43–75.

Myers, Herbert W. "Evidence of the Emerging Trombone in the Late Fifteenth Century: What Iconography May Be Trying to Tell Us." *Historic Brass Society Journal* 17 (2005): 7–35.

Nagler, A. M. *Theatre Festivals of the Medici, 1539–1637.* New Haven, Conn.: Yale University Press, 1964.

Naylor, Tom L. *The Trumpet and Trombone in Graphic Arts, 1500–1800,* Nashville, Tenn.: Brass Press, 1979.

Nerici, Luigi. *Storia della musica in Lucca.* Lucca: Tipografia Giusti, 1879. Reprinted, Bologna: Forni, 1969.

Nemetz, Andreas. *See* Weiner, Howard, "Andreas Nemetz's Neuste Posaun-Schule . . ."

Neuschel, Jorg. "Briefen von Jorg Neuschel in Nürnberg, nebst einigen anderen (Im Besitze des kg. geh. Archivs in Königsbert i/Pr.)." *Monatshefte für Musikgeschichte* 9 (1877): 149–59.

New Grove Dictionary of Music and Musicians. Edited by Stanley Sadie, 20 vols. New York: Macmillan, Grove's Dictionaries, 1980, s.v. "Trombone" by Anthony Baines.

Newcomb, Anthony. *The Madrigal at Ferrara, 1579–1597.* Princeton, N.J.: Princeton University Press, 1980.

Newman, William S. *The Sonata in the Baroque Era.* 3rd ed. New York: Norton, 1972.

Newsome, Roy. *Brass Roots: A Hundred Years of Brass Bands and Their Music (1836–1936).* Aldershot, England: Ashgate, 1998.

Nicolai, Friedrich. *Beschreibung einer Reise durch Deutchland und die Schweitz, im Jahre 1781.* 12 vols. Berlin and Stettin, 1784.

Novello, Vincent, and Mary Novello. *A Mozart Pilgrimage: Being the Travel Diaries of Vincent & Mary Novello in the year 1829.* Transcribed and compiled by Nerina Medici di Marignano. Edited by Rosemary Hughes. London: Eulenburg Books, 1975.

Page, Christopher. "German Musicians and Their Instruments: A 14th-Century Account by Konrad of Megenberg." *Early Music* 10 (1982): 192–200.

Palisca, Claude V. "Scientific Empiricism in Musical Thought." In *Seventeenth Century Science and the Arts,* edited by Hedley Howell Rhys, 91–137. Princeton, N.J.: Princeton University Press, 1961.

Parès, Gabriel. *Traité d'instrumentation et d'orchestration à l'usage des musiques militaires d'harmonie et de fanfare.* Paris: Lemoine, 1898.

Parisi, Susan. "Ducal Patronage of Music in Mantua, 1587–1627: An Archival Study." Ph.D. diss., University of Illinois, 1989.

Perkins, Leeman. "Musical Patronage at the Royal Court of France under Charles VII and Louis XI (1422–83)." *Journal of the American Musicological Society* 37 (1984): 507–66.

Peters, Gretchen. "Civic Subsidy and Musicians in Southern France during the Fourteenth and Fifteenth Centuries: A Comparison of Montpellier, Toulouse and Avignon." In *Music and Musicians in Renaissance Cities and Towns,* edited by Fiona Kisby, 57–69. Cambridge: Cambridge University Press, 2001.

———. "Urban Minstrels in Late Medieval Southern France: Opportunities, Status, and Professional Relationships." *Early Music History* 19 (2000): 201–35.

Peucker, Paul. "The Role and Development of Brass Music in the Moravian Church." In *The Music of the Moravian Church in America,* edited by Nola Reed Knouse, 169–88. Rochester, N.Y.: University of Rochester Press, 2008.

Peverada, Enrico. "Vita musicale nella cattedrale di Ferrara nel quattrocento: Note e documenti." *Rivista italiana di musicologia* 15 (1980): 3–30.

Piccolomini, Alessandro. *De la institutione de tutta la vita de l'homo nato nobile e in città libera*. Venice: Hieronymum Scotum, 1542.

Pierre, Constant. *Le Conservatoire National de Musique et de Déclamation*. Paris: Imprimerie National, 1900.

———. *Les facteurs d'instruments de musique: Les luthiers et la facture instrumentale; Précis historique*. Paris: Sagot, 1893. Reprinted, Geneva: Minkoff, 1971.

Pirro, André. "Leo X and Music." *Musical Quarterly* 21 (1935): 1–16.

Piston, Walter. *Orchestration*. New York: Norton, 1955.

Polk, Keith. "Augustein Schubinger and the Zinck: Innovation in Performance Practice." *Historic Brass Society Journal* 1 (1989): 83–92.

———. "Civic Patronage and Instrumental Ensembles in Renaissance Florence." *Augsburger Jahrbuch für Musikwissenschaft* 3 (1986): 51–68.

———. "Ensemble Music in Flanders: 1450–1550." *Journal of Band Research* 11 (Spring 1975): 12–27.

———. *German Instrumental Music of the Late Middle Ages: Players, Patrons, and Performance Practice*. Cambridge: Cambridge University Press, 1992.

———. "Instrumental Music in the Urban Centers of Renaissance Germany." *Early Music History* 7 (1987): 159–86.

———. "The Invention of the Slide Principle and the Earliest Trombone, or, the Birth of a Notion." In *Perspectives in Brass Scholarship*, edited by Stewart Carter, 19–27. Stuyvesant, N.Y.: Pendragon, 1997.

———. "Patronage and Innovation in Instrumental Music in the 15th Century." *Historic Brass Society Journal* 3 (1991): 151–78.

———. "Patronage, Imperial Image, and the Emperor's Musical Retinue: On the Road with Maximilian I." In *Musik und Tanz zur Zeit Kaiser Macimilian I*, edited by Walter Salmen, 79–88. Innsbruck: Edition Helbling, 1992.

———. "The Schubingers of Augsburg: Innovation in Renaissance Instrumental Music." In *Quaestiones in musica: Festschrift für Franz Krautworst zum 65. Geburtstag*, edited by Friedhelm Brusniak and Horst Leuchtmann, 495–503. Tutzing: Schneider, 1989.

———. "Susato and Instrumental Music in Flanders in the 16th Century." In *Tielman Susato and the Music of His Time: Print Culture, Compositional Technique, and Instrumental Music in the Renaissance*, edited by Keith Polk, 61–100. Hillsdale, N.Y.: Pendragon, 2005.

———. "The Trombone in Archival Documents, 1350–1500." *ITA Journal* 15 (Summer 1987): 24–31.

———. "The Trombone, the Slide Trumpet, and the Ensemble Tradition of the Early Renaissance." *Early Music* 17 (1989): 389–97.

Pougin, Arthur. *Supplément et complément* to *Biographie universelle des musiciens et bibliographie générale de la musique* by François-Joseph Fétis. 2 vols. Paris: Culture et Civilisation, 1880. s.v. "Musard."

Praetorius, Michael. *Syntagma musicum: Tomus secundus; De organographia*. Wolffenbuttel: Holwein, 1619. Facsimile reprint, Berlin: Trautwein, 1884. English translation by David Z. Crookes as *Syntagma musicum II: De organographia, Parts I and II*. Oxford: Oxford University Press, 1986.

———. *Syntagma musicum: Tomus tertuis; Termini musici*. Wolffenbuttel: Holwein, 1619. Facsimile reprint, Berlin: Trautwein, 1884. Translated by Hans Lampl as *The Syntagma musicum of Michael Praetorius, Volume Three: An Annotated Translation*. n.p.: American Choral Directors Association, 2001.

Prizer, William F. "Bernardino Piffaro e i pifferi e tromboni di Montova: Strumenti a fiato in una corte italiana." *Rivista italiana de musicologia* 16 (1981): 151–84.

Prout, Ebenezer. *The Orchestra*. Vol. 1: *Technique of the Instruments*. London: Augener, 1897.

Prunières, Henri. "La musique de la chambre et de l'écurie." *L'année musicale* 1 (1912): 215–51.

Pulis, Gordon M. "On Trombone Technique." *Symphony* (New York) 2 (1948): 5.

Ramalingam, Vivian S[afowitz]. "The Trumpetum in Strasbourg M222 C2." In *Le musique et le rite sacré et profane: Transactions of the 13th Congress of the International Musicological Society, 1982*, edited by Marc Honneger, Christian Meyer, and Paul Prévost, 2 vols., 2:143–60. Strasbourg: Association des Publications près les Unversités de Strasbourg, 1986.

[Ramalingam], Vivian Safowitz. "Trumpet Music and Trumpet Style in the Early Renaissance." M.M. thesis, University of Illinois, 1965.

Raquet, Markus, and Klaus Martius. "The Schnitzer Family of Nuremberg and a Newly Rediscovered Trombone." *Historic Brass Society Journal* 19 (2007): 11–24.

Rasmussen, Mary. "Gottfried Reiche and His *Vier und zwanzig Neue Quatricinia* (Leipzig 1696)." *Brass Quarterly* 4 (1960): 3–17.

———. "Two Early Nineteenth-Century Trombone Virtuosi: Carl Traugott Queisser and Freidrich August Belcke." *Brass Quarterly* 5 (1961): 3–17.

Rastall, Richard. "The Minstrels of the English Royal Households, 25 Edward I–1 Henry VIII: An Inventory." *R. M. A. Research Chronicle* 4 (1964): 1–41.

Raum, J. Richard. "Extending the Solo and Chamber Repertoire for the Alto Trombone." *ITA Journal* 16 (Spring 1988): 11–23.

———. "An Historic Perspective of an 18th-Century Trombonist." *Brass Bulletin* 87 (1994): 10–29; 88 (1994): 18–35; 89 (1995): 31–49.

Raynor, Henry. *Music and Society since 1815*. New York: Schocken, 1976.

Read, Gardner. *Thesaurus of Orchestral Devices*. New York: Pitman, 1953.

Redway, Virginia Larkin. *Music Directory of Early New York City*. New York: New York Public Library, 1941.

Reifsnyder, Robert. "The Romantic Trombone and Its Place in the German Solo Tradition." *ITA Journal* 15 (Spring 1987): 20–23; 15 (Summer 1987): 32–37.

Reinhardt, Donald S. *The Encyclopedia of the Pivot System for All Cupped Mouthpiece Brass Instruments*, Augmented Version. New York: Charles Colin, 1973.

Rice, John A. *Antonio Salieri and Viennese Opera*. Chicago: University of Chicago Press, 1998.

Rimsky-Korsakov, Nikolay. *Principles of Orchestration*. Edited by Maximilian Steinberg. English translation by Edward Agate. Berlin: Éditions russe de musique, 1922. Reprinted, New York: Dover, 1964.

Rivière, Jules. *My Musical Life and Recollections*. London: Sampson, Low, Marston, 1893.

Robinson, Michael F. *Giovanni Paisiello: A Thematic Catalogue of His Works*. Vol. 1: *Dramatic Works*. Stuyvesant, N.Y.: Pendragon, 1991.

Robledo, Luis. "Questions of Performance Practice in Philip III's Chapel." *Early Music* 22 (1994): 198–220.

Rogers, Bernard. *The Art of Orchestration: Principles of Tone Color in Modern Scoring*. New York: Appleton Century-Crofts, 1951.

Rose, Michael. *Berlioz Remembered*. London: Faber and Faber, 2001.

Rostirolla, Giancarlo. "Strumentisti e costruttori di strumenti nella Roma dei papi: Materiali per una storia della musical strumentale a Roma durante i secoli XV–XVII." In *Restauro conservazione e recupero di antichi strumenti musicali*, 171–226. Florence: Olschki, 1986.

Sachs, Curt. "Chromatic Trumpets in the Renaissance." *Musical Quarterly* 36 (1950): 62–65.

———. *Handbuch der Musikinstrumentenkunde*. 2nd ed. Leipzig: Breitkopf & Härtel, 1930.

———. *The History of Musical Instruments*. New York: Norton, 1940.

———. *Real-Lexikon der Musikinsntrumente zugleich ein Polyglossar für das gesamte Instrumentengebiet* (1913). Revised and enlarged reprint. New York: Dover, 1964.

Safowitz, Vivian. See Ramalingam, Vivian Safowitz.

Salmen, Walter. "The Social Status of Professional Musicians in the Middle Ages." In *The Social Status of the Professional Musician from the Middle Ages to the 19th Century*, edited by Walter Salmen, 3–29. New York: Pendragon, 1983.

Samson, Jim, ed. *The Cambridge History of Nineteenth-Century Music*. Cambridge: Cambridge University Press, 2001.

Sartori, Claudio. *Bibliografia della musica strumentale italiana stampata in Italia fino al 1700*. 2 vols. Florence: Olschki, 1952, 1968.

Saunders, Steven. *Cross, Sword, and Lyre: Sacred Music at the Imperial Court of Ferdinand II Habsburg (1619–1637)*. Oxford: Clarendon Press, 1995.

Searle, Arthur. "Pleyel's 'London' Symphonies." *Early Music* 36 (2008): 231–44.

Schafer, William J. *Brass Bands and New Orleans Jazz*. Baton Rouge: Louisiana State University Press, 1977.

Schmidt, Carl B. "Antonio Cesti's *Il pomo d'oro*: A Reexamination of a Famous Hapsburg Court Spectacle." *Journal of the American Musicological Society* 29 (1976): 381–412.

Schnoebelen, Anne. "The Concerted Mass at San Petronio in Bologna ca. 1660–1730: A Documentary and Analytical Study." Ph.D. diss., University of Illinois, 1960.

Scholes, Percy. *The Oxford Companion to Music*. London: Oxford University Press, 1938.

Schramm, Robert. "Not Musicians Merely." *Woodwind World Brass & Percussion* 17 (May-June 1978): 6–7.

Schreiber, Otthmar. *Orchester und Orchesterpraxis in Deutschland zwischen 1780 und 1850*. Berlin: Junker und Dünnhaupt, 1938.

Schuler, Manfred. "Die Musik in Konstanz während des Konzils 1414–1418." *Acta musicologica* 38 (1966): 150–68.

Schuller, Gunther. "The Trombone in Jazz." In *The Oxford Companion to Jazz*, edited by Bill Kirchner, 628–41. New York: Oxford University Press, 2000.

Schwartz, Richard I., and Iris J. Schwartz. *Bands at the St. Louis World's Fair of 1904: Information, Photographs, and Database*. n.p.: Self-Published, 2003.

Sehnal, Jiři. "Das Musikinventar des Olmützer Bischofs Leopold Egk aus dem Jahre 1760 als Quelle vorklassischer Instrumentalmusik." *Archiv für Musikwissenschaft* 29 (1972): 285–317.

Selfridge-Field, Eleanor. "Instrumentation and Genre in Italian Music, 1600–1670." *Early Music* 19 (1991): 61–67.

———. *Venetian Instrumental Music from Gabrieli to Vivaldi*. 3rd rev. ed. New York: Dover, 1994.

———. "The Viennese Court Orchestra in the Time of Caldara." In *Antonio Caldara: Essays on His Life and Times*, edited by Brian Pritchard, 117–51. Aldershot, England: Scolar Press, 1987.

Senn, Walter. *Musik und Theater am Hof Innsbruck: Geschichte der Hofkapelle vom 15. Jahrhundert bis zu deren Auflösung im Jahre 1748*. Innsbruck: Österreichische Verlagsanstalt, 1954.

Shanet, Howard. *Philharmonic: A History of New York's Orchestra*. Garden City, N.Y.: Doubleday, 1975.

Shifrin, Ken. "The Alto Trombone in the Orchestra: 1800–2000." www.trombone-society.org.uk/resources/articles/shifrin/shifrin01.php

———. "The Moravian Brotherhood Trombone Choirs: Neither Moravian nor Choirs." *Brass Bulletin* 121 (2003): 56–64.

———. "The Solo Trombone of the Bohemian Baroque." *Brass Bulletin* 119 (2002): 58–67; 120 (2002): 48–54.

———. "The Valve Trombone." *Brass Bulletin* 111 (2000): 118–26 and 112 (2000): 126–44.

Shive, Clyde S. "The First Music for Brass Published in America." *Historic Brass Society Journal* 5 (1993): 203–12.

Siegmund-Schultze, Walther. "Georg Friedrich Händel als ein Wegbereiter der Wiener Klassik." *Händel-Jahrbuch* 27 (1981): 23–36.

Singer, Gerhard. See Zacconi, Lodovico.

Sisk, Lawrence T. "Giovanni Simone Mayr (1763–1845): His Writings on Music." Ph.D. diss., Northwestern University, 1986.

Sloan, Gerald. "Los Huesos: A Closer Look at Latin Trombonists." *ITA Journal* 31 (Jan. 2003): 30–47.

Sluchin, Benny. "Les instruments 'duplex'—hier et aujourd'hui." *Brass Bulletin* 115 (2001): 112–15.

———. "Un martyr du trombone." *Brass Bulletin* 31 (1980): 57–66.

Sluchin, Benny, and Raymond Lapie. "Slide Trombone Teaching and Method Books in France (1794–1960)." *Historic Brass Society Journal* 9 (1997): 4–27.

Smithers, Don L. *The Music and History of the Baroque Trumpet before 1721.* 2nd ed. Carbondale and Edwardsville: Southern Illinois University Press, 1988.

———. "A New Look at the Historical, Linguistic and Taxonomic Bases for the Evolution of Lip-Blown Instruments from Classical Antiquity until the End of the Middle Ages." *Historic Brass Society Journal* 1 (1989): 3–64.

Somerset, H. V. F. "The Habsburg Emperors as Musicians." *Music & Letters* 30 (1949): 204–15.

Sommerhalder, Max. "Posaunen-Arbeit." *Brass Bulletin* 34 (1981): 55–59.

Spagnoli, Gina. *Letters and Documents of Heinrich Schütz, 1656–1672: An Annotated Translation.* Ann Arbor, Mich.: UMI Research Press, 1990.

Speer, Daniel. *Grundrichtiger kurtz- leicht- unt nöthiger Unterricht der musikalischen Kunst.* Ulm: Kühnen, 1687. Revised and enlarged as *Grundrichtiger kurtz-leicht- unt nothiger jetzt wolvermehrter Unterricht der musikalischen Kunst oder vierfaches musikalisches Kleeblatt.* Ulm: Kühnen, 1697. English translation by Henry Howey as "A Comprehensive Performance Project in Trombone Literature with an Essay Consisting of a Translation of Daniel Speer's *Vierfaches musikalisches Kleeblatt.*" D.M.A. essay, University of Iowa, 1971.

Spitzer, John. "The Birth of the Orchestra in Rome: An Iconographic Study." *Early Music* 19 (1991): 9–28.

Stanley, William. "Annotated Bibliography of Compositions for Trombone and String Quartet." *ITA Journal* 24 (Summer 1996): 26–31.

Stevenson, Robert. *Music in Mexico: A Historical Survey.* New York: Crowell, 1952.

———. *Spanish Cathedral Music in the Golden Age.* Berkeley and Los Angeles: University of California Press, 1961.

Stiller, Andrew. *Handbook of Instrumentation.* Berkeley: University of California Press, 1985.

Strohm, Reinhard. *Music in Late Medieval Bruges.* Oxford: Oxford University Press, 1985.

Sundelin, Augustin. *Die Instrumentirung für das Orchester.* Berlin: Wagenführ, 1828.

———. *Die Instrumentirung für sämmtliche Militär-Musik-Chöre.* Berlin: Wagenführ, 1828.

Tamargo, Luis. "A Brief History of the Latin Trombone." *Latin Beat Magazine* 8 (Mar. 1998): 18–21.

Tarr, Edward. *The Trumpet.* Translated by S. E. Plank and Edward Tarr. London: Batsford, 1988.

Taylor, Arthur R. *Brass Bands.* London: Granada, 1979.

Thayer, Orla Edward. "The Axial Flow Valve Update." *ITA Journal* 10 (Apr. 1982): 34–35.

Thein, Max, and Heinrich Thein. "Neues über Alt-Posaune." *Brass Bulletin* 40 (1982): 33.

Thomas, T. Donley. "Michael Haydn's Trombone Symphony." *Brass Quarterly* 6 (1962): 3–8.

Todd, R. Larry. "Orchestral Texture and the Art of Orchestration." In *The Orchestra: Origins and Transformations*, edited by Joan Peyser, 191–226. New York: Scribner, 1986.

Towne, Gary. "Gaspar de Albertis and Music at Santa Maria Maggiore in Bergamo in the Sixteenth Century." Ph.D. diss., University of California, Santa Barbara, 1985.

———. "Tubatori e Piffari: Civic Wind Players in Medieval and Renaissance Bergamo." *Historic Brass Society Journal* 9 (1997): 175–95.

Trichet, Pierre. "De la saqueboute ou trompette harmonique (vers 1640)." *Brass Bulletin* 45 (1984): 10–12.

The Triumph of Maximilian I: 137 Woodcuts by Hans Burgkmair and Others, with a translation of descriptive text, introduction and notes by Stanley Appelbaum. New York: Dover, 1964.

Troiano, Massimo. *Dialoghi di Massimo Troiano.* Venice, 1569. Facsimile edition by Horst Leuchtmann, *Die Münchner Fürstenhochzeit von 1568: Massimo Troiano; Dialoge.* Munich: Katzbichler, 1980.

Tröster, Patrick. "More about Renaissance Slide Trumpets: Fact or Fiction?" *Early Music* 23 (2004): 252–68.

Turner, Gordon, and Alwyn W. Turner. *The Trumpets Will Sound: The Story of the Royal Military School of Music, Kneller Hall.* Tunbridge Wells, England: Parapress Limited, 1996.

Vaillancourt, Michael Grant. "Instrumental Ensemble Music at the Court of Leopold I (1658–1705)." Ph.D. diss., University of Illinois, Urbana-Champaign, 1991.

Velimirovi, Miloš. "Warsaw, Moscow and St Petersburg." In *The Late Baroque Era: From the 1680s to 1740*, edited by George J. Buelow, 435–65. Englewood Cliffs, N. J.: Prentice Hall, 1994.

Virdung, Sebastian. *Musica getutscht.* Basel, 1511. Facsimile edition by Robert Eitner. Berlin: Trautwein, 1882. English translation by Beth Bullard as *Musica getutscht: A Treatise on Musical Instruments (1511) by Sebastian Virdung.* Cambridge: Cambridge University Press, 1993.

Virgiliano, Aurelio. "Il dolcimielo" (Ms.). Facsimile edition. Florence: Studio per Edizione Scelte, 1979.

Vobaron, Felix. *Grand méthode de trombonne.* Paris: Gambaro, 1834.

Wallis, John. "Of the Trembling of Consonant Strings." *Philosophical Transactions* 134 (Apr. 23, 1677), 839–44.

Waterhouse, William. *The New Langwill Index: A Dictionary of Musical Wind-Instrument Makers and Inventors.* London: Tony Bingham, 1993.

Webb, John. "The Billingsgate Trumpet." *Galpin Society Journal* 41 (1988): 59–62.

Weber, Gottfried. "Ueber Instrumentalbässe bey vollstimmigen Tonstücken." *Allgemeine musikalische Zeitung* 18, no. 41 (1816): col. 694–702; no. 42: col. 709–14; no. 43: col. 725–29; no. 44: col. 749–53; no. 45: col. 765–69.

———. "Versuch einer praktischen Akustik" [pt. 2]. *Allgemeine musikalische Zeitung* 18, no. 3 (1816): col. 33–44; no. 4: col. 50–60; no. 5: col. 65–74; no. 6: col. 87–90.

Weber, William. *Music and the Middle Class: The Social Structure of Concert Life in London, Paris and Vienna.* New York: Holmes and Meier, 1975.

———. "The Rise of the Classical Repertoire in Nineteenth-Century Orchestra Concerts." In *The Orchestra: Origins and Transformations*, edited by Joan Peyser, 301–86. New York: Scribner, 1986.

Wegman, Rob C. "The Minstrel School in the Late Middle Ages." *Historic Brass Society Journal* 14 (2002): 11–30.

Weiner, Howard. "André Braun's *Gamme et méthod pour les trombones*: The Earliest Modern Trombone Method Rediscovered." *Historic Brass Society Journal* 5 (1993): 288–308.

———. "Andreas Nemetz's *Neust Posaun-Schule*: An Early Viennese Trombone Method." *Historic Brass Society Journal* 7 (1995): 12–35.

———. "Beethoven's *Equali* (WoO 30): A New Perspective." *Historic Brass Society Journal* 14 (2002): 215–77.

———. "The Soprano Trombone Hoax." *Historic Brass Society Journal* 13 (2001), 138–60.

———. "When Is an Alto Trombone an Alto Trombone? When Is a Bass Trombone a Bass Trombone?—The Makeup of the Trombone Section in Eighteenth- and Early Nineteenth-Century Orchestras." *Historic Brass Society Journal* 17 (2005): 37–79.

Welker, Lorenz. "'Alta Capella' zur Ensemblepraxis der Blasinstrumente im 15. Jahrhundert." *Basler Jahrbuch für historische Musikpraxis* 7 (1983): 119–65.

Wheat, James Raymond. "The Tuba/Trompetta Repertoire of the Fifteenth Century." D.M.A. essay, University of Wisconsin-Madison, 1994.

Whitwell, David. *Band Music of the French Revolution.* Tutzing: Hans Schneider, 1979.

———. *The History and Literature of the Wind Band and Wind Ensemble.* Vol. 3: *The Baroque Wind Band and Wind Ensemble.* Northridge, Calif.: Winds, 1983.

———. *The History and Literature of the Wind Band and Wind Ensemble.* Vol. 5: *The Nineteenth Century Wind Band and Wind Ensemble in Western Europe.* Northridge, Calif.: Winds, 1982.

Wick, Denis. *Trombone Technique.* 2nd ed. Oxford: Oxford University Press, 1984.

Widor, Charles-Marie. *Technique de l'orchestre moderne.* 5th ed. Paris: Henry Lemoine, 1925. English translation of the 1st

(1904) edition by Edward Suddard as *The Technique of the Modern Orchestra.* London: Joseph Williams, 1906.

Wienandt, Elwyn A. *Johann Pezel (1639–1694): A Thematic Catalogue of His Instrumental Works.* New York: Pendragon, 1983.

Wigness, C. Robert. *The Soloistic Use of the Trombone in Eighteenth-Century Vienna.* Nashville, Tenn.: Brass Press, 1978.

Wister, Frances Anne. *Twenty-five Years of the Philadelphia Orchestra: 1900–1925.* Philadelphia: Women's Committees for the Philadelphia Orchestra, 1925.

Woodfill, Walter L. *Musicians in English Society from Elizabeth to Charles I.* Princeton, N.J.: Princeton University Press, 1953.

Wright, Craig. *Music and Ceremony at Notre Dame de Paris, 500–1550.* Cambridge: Cambridge University Press, 1989.

———. *Music at the Court of Burgundy, 1364–1419: A Documentary History.* Henryville, Penn.: Institute of Medieval Music, 1979.

Wright, Denis. *Scoring for Brass Band.* 5th ed. London: Studio Music, 1986.

Yates, Frances A. "Dramatic Religious Processions in Paris in the Late Sixteenth Century." *Annales musicologiques* 2 (1954): 215–70.

Yeo, Douglas. "An Interview with Bill Pearce." *Online Trombone Journal* (1998, updated Aug. 2007). www.trombone.org/articles/library/pearce-int.asp

———. "A Pictorial History of Low Brass Players in the Boston Symphony Orchestra, 1887–1986." *ITA Journal* 14 (Fall 1986): 12–21.

Zacconi, Lodovico. *Prattica di musica.* Venice: Bartolomeo Carampello, 1596. English translation by Gerhard Singer as "Lodovico Zacconi's Treatment of the 'Suitability and Classification of All Musical Instruments' in the *Prattica de musica* of 1592." Ph.D. diss., University of Southern California, 1968.

Zarlino, Gioseffo. *Dimonstrationi harmoniche.* Venice: Senese, 1571.

———. *Istitutioni harmoniche.* Venice: Senese, 1558.

———. *Sopplimenti musicali.* Venice: Senese, 1588.

Zaslaw, Neal. "When Is an Orchestra Not an Orchestra?" *Early Music* 16 (1988): 483–95.

Zechmeister, Gerhard. "Die Stellung der (Contra) Bass-Posaune im Wiener Klangstil," pt. 1. *Brass Bulletin* 102 (1998): 19–28.

Index

Note: In the first section in this index (trombonists listed by century), entries with three or more pages and/or page ranges and those with *see* references to a main entry have their own entry in the index.

~

About the Author

David M. Guion is a trombonist, musicologist, librarian, and freelance writer. He has studied trombone with David Glasmire, John Hill, Audrey Morrison, and Frank Crisafulli. He earned his Ph.D. in musicology from the University of Iowa and M.L.I.S. from Rosary College (now Dominican University) in River Forest, Illinois. He is author of *The Trombone: Its History and Music, 1697–1811* (1988) and articles in numerous journals, including *American Music, Brass Bulletin, Early Music, College Music Symposium, Historic Brass Society Journal, ITA Journal, Journal of American Culture, Journal of Band Research, Journal of Musicological Research, Online Trombone Journal,* and *Welsh Music.*